Be Opened!

Be Opened!

THE CATHOLIC CHURCH
& DEAF CULTURE

Lana Portolano

The Catholic University of America Press
Washington, D.C.

The paper used in this publication meets the requirements of American
National Standards for Information Science—Permanence of Paper
for Printed Library Materials, ANSI z39.48-1992.
∞

Companion website: https://www.icfdeafservice.org/beopened

Cataloging-in-Publication Data available
from the Library of Congress
ISBN 978-0-8132-3339-0

CONTENTS

Part I. Deaf Catholic Heritage

Part II. New Deaf Evangelization

A Hearing Author on a Deaf Pilgrimage

This book provides an overview of the history and heritage of deaf culture and sign language in the Catholic Church. It is the first attempt at a connected narrative about Deaf Catholics from the monastic origins of deaf ministry in Europe to twentieth-century advances in civil and religious rights to today's deaf missions in Asia, Africa, and Latin America. For this reason, I wish to be clear about my relationship to the deaf community: I am a hearing person. My world is full of sound, and I never met a deaf person who used sign language until well into adulthood. I have, however, always had a passion for the study of language in religious contexts. I grew up the child and grandchild of well-spoken Protestant preachers, converted to Catholicism in graduate school, and completed a PhD in the history and theory of rhetoric. The challenges of deafness in religious communication became a primary interest to me only later, when my husband and I adopted a four-year-old deaf child. Little did I know, in my early studies of rhetoric and oratory, how deeply entwined my life would become with a group of people who could not hear speech at all. Researching and writing this book has been my pilgrimage into that world.

Hearing people often come to deaf culture through a loved one who is deaf. In my case, this person is my daughter Lena, who happens to be a good example of the kind of people served by deaf ministries. For this reason, I will recount her story as a way of introducing some of the main issues in this book. Born in a poor region of eastern Ukraine, Lena was abandoned in an orphanage where the caretakers had no experience with early intervention for deaf preschoolers. As a result, she suffered major developmental delays. This was alarming in terms of her prospects for language development, but it was not much different from delays many deaf children face when raised at home, especially in underdeveloped countries or among immigrant populations where technological assistance and social acceptance for deaf people are lacking. Although most children born deaf in economically developed countries today receive early intervention, these services did not exist for much of the history described in this book. Even today, most congenitally deaf children are born to hearing parents who have no prior experience with deafness or sign language.[1] As a result, many congenitally deaf adults, now as in the past, came late to sign language after they entered school. They may have acquired English (or whatever language their family spoke) even later as an incomplete second language through lipreading and text. Because of these language differences, reading comprehension levels for those born deaf or those deafened in early childhood are typically lower than the average reading levels for hearing children the same age.[2]

Lena's story is a good example of the effects a lack of visual access to language can have on a deaf child's learning and development. Most four-year-olds have a vocabulary of over a thousand words and are constantly pestering their parents with questions in a natural drive to increase language and knowledge. Lena had not a single word at that age, not even her name. When doctors and audiologists tested Lena for the first time, they found she had no hearing at all, at least none measurable by audiological equipment. She had been deaf from birth because her mother contracted rubella during pregnancy—still a common cause of deafness worldwide, although vaccination nearly eliminated rubella in Western Europe and North America by the end of the twentieth century. Armed only with a diagnosis of profound deafness, with no background in deaf education, my husband and I faced crucial decisions about how Lena would acquire language as a preschooler. I threw myself into research on the subject.

Contemporary approaches to deaf education in the United States resemble those available in most other first world countries and therefore reflect the different modes of language found among deaf adults in

1. Ten percent is the most-cited statistic for deaf children with deaf parents, but scholars have contested this number in the past fifteen years. See, for example, Ross E. Mitchell and Michael A. Karchmer, "Chasing the Mythical Ten Percent: Parental Hearing Status of Deaf and Hard of Hearing Students in the United States," *Sign Language Studies* 4, no. 2 (2004): 138–63.

2. See, for example, Sen Qi and Ross E. Mitchell, "Large-Scale Academic Achievement Testing of Deaf and Hard-of-Hearing Students: Past, Present, and Future," *Journal of Deaf Studies and Deaf Education* 17, no. 1 (2012): 1–18.

those countries today. Our school district offered three main choices. First, there were oral-aural approaches that use residual hearing with spoken language and lipreading. Second, there was Total Communication, which in our school district meant the simultaneous use of spoken language and manual signs to approximate English syntax visually. And finally, there was American Sign Language (ASL, the "national" sign language unique to the deaf community in the United States and much of Canada). We found ourselves faced with choosing one of these methods for a child whose developmental window for rapid language-learning (typically considered birth to five or six years) would soon close.

Lena's doctors found that she had no residual hearing and therefore could not benefit from hearing aids. This ruled out oral-aural methods: Lena could not make use of sound, so her language had to come entirely through a visual channel. When I investigated Total Communication, I found that this educational philosophy did not have a good track record for producing strong reading skills in profoundly deaf children. Therefore, I took classes in sign language. Surely, I thought, I could study sign language for several years, help my deaf child acquire strong native ASL, and then use those language skills to teach her to read English. It did not take long, however, to discover my naivety. Soon I learned there is no correspondence between ASL and English. They are not even in the same family of languages: they have different vocabularies, different word orders, and entirely different modes of expression—space and movement for ASL versus sound for English. If I had been a culturally deaf, ASL-using mother, I would have naturally raised my child with grammatically correct ASL in the home, after which she would have acquired English as a second language through print. Historically, deaf children of deaf adults have much higher reading levels than the 90 percent who have hearing parents, because the former begin kindergarten with a complete first language (such as ASL). However, like most hearing parents, I could not become competent in sign language quickly enough to be a good ASL language model. Becoming fluent in ASL would require extended periods of immersion in that language community. When I did learn ASL a decade later, it took years of exposure to the ASL community— the same commitment it takes to become fluent in any foreign language, if not more, because of the profound cognitive shift required to communicate solely in a spatial and visual mode.

Ultimately, our family decided on a fourth, less popular route to first language acquisition. I met some deaf people who had grown up using a method called Cued Speech, a visual system using eight hand shapes to code the mouth movements of speech so they look different for each syllable. Orin Cornett developed Cued Speech at Gallaudet University in 1966. I was especially impressed with the written English skills and broad knowledge base of these congenitally deaf adults. Advocates told me that profoundly deaf children raised with this mode of communication typically have reading and writing skills equal to their hearing peers, and they learn to read with the same phonetic strategies I already knew how to teach. In addition, it would not take years to master as ASL would. We decided to begin with Cued Speech for Lena, augmented with some signs for convenience, then have her learn grammatically correct ASL as a second language from native signers a few years down the road. This worked for our family, but it would not have worked for everyone. Every method has its strengths and weaknesses, and there have always been bitter divisions in deaf education over methodology. Those who are born deaf have different levels of residual hearing, different family situations and cultural backgrounds, and varying access to educational, technological, and financial resources. Deafness is not a one-size-fits-all condition.

Lena's first year in her new home was intense. Although I did not use sign language yet, my method of communicating resembled sign in that it was entirely visual. Lena's severe delays meant I had to cram language into her at desperate speed, so family life became a constant, deliberate language lab. Using Cued Speech, I named her clothing as I dressed her, her food and dishes as I served her lunch, her toys before she could play, and her body parts as I bathed her. I structured all our daily routines as lessons in basic English phrases and vocabulary and added a longer, more formal lesson each day. I kept meticulous records of every word she understood and noted gaps in her grammar so I could focus on those areas. Many deaf children do not have the advantage of this kind of undivided attention. Most deaf children with hearing parents cannot acquire a complete language from a single language model (a parent or caregiver). I have met many deaf adults who lived at home as children and went to mainstream or oral/aural schools before hearing aid technology was as effective as it is today. Most of them say they were not very close to their families and felt isolated until introduced to a sign language community through church, school, or a social organization. These adults value sign language all the more because, socially and academically, their lives began when they entered the company of others with whom they could communicate.

Since the late twentieth century, the deaf experience has changed rapidly because of technology, making it radically different from much of the history described in this book. Technology also entered Lena's young life when we adopted her. Our next choice involved permanently altering her anatomy with cochlear implant surgery. At the time, this was a controversial decision that people at one extreme considered barbaric and, at the other extreme, a miracle that could turn a deaf child into a hearing one. The cochlear implant is the first sensory prosthetic in the history of science. An array of electrodes is implanted in the inner ear and wired to a computerized speech and sound processor that is worn behind the ear like a conventional hearing aid. A separate, silver-dollar-sized headpiece is wired to the processor and held on the head by a small magnet. Under a full head of hair, the whole device may be invisible, like a small conventional hearing aid. Opponents of the device say it turns a child into a cyborg without her consent and removes her from secure membership in the deaf community while never making her a hearing person. She is not hearing, and she does not fit in with signing deaf people. Proponents of the implant point to examples of profoundly deaf children, who otherwise could never have perceived speech, being able to mainstream in school without any support but weekly speech therapy. I have met dozens of congenitally deaf children who can use a telephone adequately and whose speech after years of cochlear implant use (from infancy or toddlerhood) is nearly indistinguishable from a hearing person's. Many of these deaf people use speech rather than sign, consider themselves hard of hearing rather than deaf, and do not identify with the sign language community. I have also met children and teens who rejected their implants and decided not to wear them as adults, especially if surgery occurred after the language-developing preschool and elementary years.

Some people in the deaf community fear that cochlear implants and other advances in medical technology (such as gene therapy) will eliminate sign language and instigate a cultural genocide. Others believe this technology cannot, by itself, eliminate deaf culture—including Deaf Catholic culture and deaf ministries. Without a doubt, these communities are undergoing dramatic changes. Yet today's deaf students, even those with cochlear implants, continue to need visual language, and many naturally prefer deaf peer groups and communication in sign language to speech and lipreading with hearing friends. Many still have gaps in their knowledge of spoken language because they lacked early access to visual language or to consistent, high quality deaf education. Because of her late adoption, my daughter falls into this common category.

Medically, Lena's implant was a success, especially considering the lateness of her surgery (infants now regularly receive an implant as early as six to nine months). Since she had a visually accessible mode of English for everyday communication, she quickly came to associate it with the basic sounds of spoken language. However, it took a long time—six years of daily speech-language therapy in elementary school—for Lena to train her brain to use speech sounds with optimal results. Lena had to work hard to achieve even limited access to spoken language, because learning to decode it demanded constant concentration from a tender age when most children learn language without trying. By the time she was in middle school, Lena made very good use of her implant. She was learning new English (and even some Russian) through both vision and hearing, and she even enjoyed limited phone conversations with family and friends. From friends and teachers who were native users of ASL, she learned basic sign language, which she continued to develop during her high school years.

Today, like many in the younger generation of Deaf Americans, Lena is fully bilingual (English/ASL) and reads as well as most high school graduates, but it was not an easy road. Basic communication in any situation with hearing people beyond one-on-one in a quiet setting usually causes Lena some degree of painful anxiety. A cochlear implant or hearing aid coupled with good speech does not make someone like Lena a hearing person. In fact, good speech can be a cause of misunderstanding and stress for a deaf person—for example, when someone assumes that a well-spoken person can understand without seeing the mouth of the speaker. In scenarios like this, deaf people routinely encounter impatience, anger, and rejection from others in everyday exchanges that hearing people take for granted.

Establishing communication is important in every area of a child's life. For faith-centered families, it is especially important for church to be a place where children are welcomed and included. Sadly, a lack of inclusion for deaf people is still the norm in many places of worship. Our Catholic parish would not hire an interpreter for just one child because of the cost. This is not an uncommon experience for families with

deaf children. For years I solved this problem of religious access by interpreting Masses and catechism classes for Lena every Sunday using Cued
Speech. With my back turned to the altar, I mediated exclusively for my
child. Onlookers were impressed, and Lena obediently followed along,
but the inherent separation meant she never connected with the other
people at church. She always received the language of Mass and religious
instruction through me, never from a priest or catechist directly. In effect, my role as an intermediary was a barrier that kept her from understanding the communication as a message meant for her. Finally, when
Lena entered her teens and began to prepare for confirmation, she needed independence from me and direct access to a church community as
she matured in faith. At this time, we discovered a model parish for the
deaf community in our archdiocese, Washington, D.C. To include Lena
in sacramental preparation with other deaf teens, our family of eight left
our home parish and became a part of the community at St. Francis of
Assisi Deaf Catholic Church in Landover, Maryland.

At this Deaf Catholic parish, a deaf Jesuit, Father Joseph Bruce,
signed the Masses. For the first time in her life, Lena could receive the
Mass and homily as direct communication, from the priest's hands and
face to her eyes. Because she understood ASL, she could engage in religious education with a deaf catechist and a group of peers. Ease of
communication, inclusion she could take for granted, and a feeling of
normalcy replaced the isolation and alienation she had experienced at
our mainstream hearing church (and, truly, in the world at large). She
began to offer prayers before the congregation and volunteered to proclaim Scripture readings in sign language. We were delighted to watch
her open up and gladly participate in parish life with a group of Deaf
Catholics of all ages, from newborns to a grandmotherly eighty-six-year-
old who had been a religious sister in an all-deaf community. It was clear
to me and my family that this is the way the church community should
receive every individual.

As Lena grew to adulthood, our family remained part of the St. Francis Deaf Catholic community, and my knowledge of sign language grew.
Preaching in a gestural language, especially in the hands of deaf priests,
had a flavor and appeal that was strikingly different from preaching at
our large home parish. One Sunday, during a homily on the pearl of great
price (Mt 13:45–46), I found myself carried away with admiration of the
priest's connection to the assembly during his homily. After months of

exhausting concentration while learning a new language, I had finally gained enough sign to appreciate the priest's rhetorical skill. He could share the assembly's experience as people with a common history of struggle and isolation in the world and turn that into an experience of unity in belief through his signed explanation of the parable. The assembly of fifty people hung on everything he signed, reacting in unison first with delight, then thoughtfulness. I experienced my own understanding as a pearl of great price, and I found myself thinking: this man is eloquent. He was eloquent in a way one seldom sees behind a pulpit or in any public speaking arena these days. Part of it was his understanding, not just of deafness, but of human nature. The fact that this assembly was deaf required an enhancement of communication skills, not a diminishment, as some might presume.

Often on Sundays this priest would draw churchgoers into an exchange of questions and answers or have a teenager stand up with him to play out a dialogue. Sometimes he would bring hymn lyrics to his aid or otherwise draw in a poetic sequence of elevated, even sublime, style in sign language. Father Joseph preached with his whole body rather than his voice alone, reminding me of many passages from my study of rhetoric, elocution, and semiotics. Liturgy and preaching in sign language had theological relevance as well, especially for Catholics interested in the doctrines of the church as the Body of Christ and the Incarnation, the very Word made flesh.

That moment of illumination was the seed that grew into this book. I spent the next six years studying and researching sacred eloquence in sign language, deafness in the priesthood, and the history of Deaf Catholics as an apostolate. I learned that deaf people pass down much of their cultural history in the form of sign language stories that do not have a written form. Because of this mode of collective memory in the Deaf Catholic community, narrative biography and its research methods greatly influenced the style and structure of the book. Interviews with priests, lay ministers, interpreters, and other members of the deaf community were invaluable. Video of events in sign language helped, but this was nonexistent during much of the history described.

I have attempted to write a people's history of Deaf Catholics, one that especially highlights the development of deaf shepherds emerging from a long-suffering deaf flock. This focus is admittedly limited, and other scholars could—and should—explore it fruitfully from other points of view. A devoted cadre of hearing and deaf pastoral workers, including laypeople, religious sisters, deacons, and priests in partnership with the deaf community, helped pave the way for deaf spiritual leadership in the church and are still essential members of the Deaf Catholic community today. Deaf lay leadership was also essential in the development of social justice and religious inclusion for the deaf community in many countries around the world. As many of the stories in this book illustrate, there could never have been deaf priests without self-sacrificing hearing religious and lay leaders who led the way and kept the faith in the deaf community. My emphasis on deafness in the priesthood is not meant to minimize these equally important contributions. Other readers, particularly sign language linguists, might hope for an even more limited focus on communities that use only linguistically complete sign languages such as American Sign Language (ASL) or British Sign Language (BSL). My scope, however, has tended toward inclusion. I have tried to tell stories not only about deaf individuals in isolation from the hearing mainstream but also about their families and larger communities, where cultures and modes of communication mix—sign language, spoken languages, and often both together.

In the course of collecting these stories of Deaf Catholic heritage, my research became a process of learning beyond the narration of historical events. Before my sign language epiphany, as I sat every Sunday unable to understand the sign language people were using, I got a taste of what it is like to be deaf in a hearing world. I could see people communicating all around me, but I could not understand them. My experience resembled that of any immigrant or visitor to another culture who does not yet understand the language, but there was one big difference. Those who are deaf may, in fact, walk around in the hearing world excluded from conversations like an outsider, but for a hearing person similarly immersed in a foreign-language environment, the bridge into a new culture is apparent: learn the spoken language, then participate in conversation. A deaf person, however, cannot learn to be a hearing person. Hearing aids and cochlear implants aside, prelingually deaf people continue to have the handicap of deafness with all its communication challenges in a hearing world, especially in group situations. Technology and speech and language therapy may help with one-on-one oral communication in close proximity, but, in the life of the church, the only way to include deaf people culturally is by entering into their chosen modes of communication.

Time and again, the history of Deaf Catholics bears witness to this need for inclusive communication.

Because deaf people have so often in their history looked to the Catholic Church as a spiritual home, Catholics are called to assist deaf people as they struggle for religious inclusion and social justice around the world. In Africa and Asia, the history of deaf ministry is just beginning. For deaf people in these areas, the church's evangelization must come through a region's native signed languages and local deaf culture. Deaf Catholic history in the West points to a continued need to reach out to deaf people around the world who remain tragically isolated from basic communication with others. Participation in the Eucharist, liturgy in sign languages, and accessible sacramental preparation foster real community connections that can lead to a full range of vocations for deaf laypeople. Today, in many countries in the West and increasingly in Asia, Deaf Catholic communities are striving to help deaf people answer their true callings in the church and in the world. No matter how difficult it is to quantify the needs of marginalized people statistically, the church's mission has always included those whose voices are silenced. With expanded inclusion, gifted servant-leaders from within the deaf community will continue to step up to the challenge of helping others like themselves integrate with the life of the church—and what's more, they will reach out to other abandoned, disabled, and excluded populations. May these future pastoral leaders be encouraged to answer their call to "live as good shepherds that know their sheep."[3]

---

3. Vatican Council II, *Presbyterorum Ordinis* (hereafter, *PO*), no. 3 (December 7, 1965), in *The Sixteen Documents of Vatican II*, trans. N.C.W.C. (Boston: Daughters of St. Paul, 1967).

A NOTE ON CAPITALIZATION

Anyone who writes about people who are deaf must decide whether or not to capitalize the word "deaf." Whatever the final decision, the results are bound to irritate someone. Those who are part of Deaf Culture in North America (and increasingly in Europe) may say that the word should always be capitalized when referring to individuals who have a hearing loss and use sign language. For historians, however, the issue is complicated by writing about different eras, nationalities, and subgroups in the same book. According to Gallaudet University's *Office of Publications Style Guide* (2016), the capitalization of "Deaf" originated as an American sociopolitical convention of certain groups of people—a convention that solidified only a few decades ago. Lowercased "deaf" is the most inclusive term; therefore, it is the default form in this book. I use capitalized "Deaf" only for naming self-identified cultural groups: Deaf Catholics, American Deaf Culture, Deaf-World. I apologize for any confusion this may cause the reader.

ACKNOWLEDGMENTS

This book brings together the life's work of countless individuals, deaf and hearing. Through their history and heritage in the church, deaf people have gained religious sign language and a full range of vocations, as well as great spiritual and philosophical traditions they now call their own. In return, Deaf Catholics have contributed to the church their own charismatic gifts. Their deafness has become part of the church's cultural and spiritual riches. In this sense, their deafness is not a handicap but a gift. Through the spiritual gift of deafness, the church has gained a new family of human languages; new art forms and liturgical practices; a deepened sensitivity to people who are isolated, disabled, or poor; and new opportunities to grow on our journey to Christ.

During my research for this book, I benefited from many spiritual gifts of deafness, but one had a profound effect on me. While attending several retreats with Deaf Catholics, I learned about the "deaf way" of practicing *lectio divina* (an ancient Benedictine practice of meditative scriptural reading). In spiritual retreats adapting *lectio divina* for deaf groups, Ignatian spiritual directors (Father Peter Monty, SJ, of Canada and Father Paul Fletcher, SJ, of England being excellent examples) employ a type of meditative prayer that encourages imaginative projection of a scene in Scripture into the participant's own sensory world. The deaf individual places himself or herself in the scene through embodied signs and the use of space, thereby experiencing the messages and actions of Jesus in a new, more present way. A hearing person praying *lectio divina* may focus on a word or a phrase, allowing it to resonate in the mind, but a deaf person moves from discursive words on the page to an image in space using sign language and the body. In sign language, Scripture is a mind-body experience. This "incarnated" mode of prayer is more tactile and visual than written or spoken words alone can facilitate, and it helps the deaf person move into a space of contemplation. This path also helped me, a hearing person, move from meditation to contemplation in prayer, and I am deeply grateful to the Deaf Catholic community for sharing this gift with me.

Ultimately, wherever I went looking for history and heritage, for the hearts and souls of Deaf Catholic people, the person I found was Christ. On my pilgrimage into the Deaf-World, so many generous people enriched my research and writing.

First, I want to thank my "research angel," Father Joseph Bruce, SJ. In addition to finding a steady stream of sources and reading my drafts for errors time and time again, he helped me to believe that even as a hearing person I could trust myself to enter into the Deaf Catholic community and write about it honestly. In 1974, when Father Joe entered the Jesuits and began to visit the elderly deaf and sick in their homes, a deaf widow named Mary Garland gave him a box of old Deaf Catholic newsletters. At that time, he had never met a deaf priest or seen a homily preached in sign language. The evidence of a nationwide community of Deaf Catholics in these old newsletters encouraged him to continue his vocation to the priesthood and his interest in Deaf Catholic heritage. Around 1975, pastoral workers who knew of his special interest began to send him materials about Deaf Catholics in their regions. After he became a priest in 1981, and still today, Father Joe continues to collect print materials and signed stories related to Deaf Catholic cultural history, often during visits to elderly deaf people to offer spiritual friendship and communion. In this way, the collection, which he gave to the College of the Holy Cross in Worcester, Massachusetts, in 1990 continues to grow. Father Joe, as an archivist, is responsible for much of the deaf-led primary research in this book. Seldom do lifelong collectors of primary material or archivists receive the recognition they deserve for their scholarship, and preserving deaf history from a deaf perspective is an even more hidden undertaking. As a Jesuit and a Deaf historian, Father Joe is an unsung hero.

Equally important to this writing was Father Anthony Shurgerer. He patiently read multiple drafts of chapters as I wrote them and offered solid advice on how to fill in essential topics, especially theological matters. Father Tony shepherded me as I became a Catholic writer. His patience never flagged, even when I confessed to removing what amounts to a second-class relic from holy ground during an early research trip to Auriesville, New York. As I stood by the rocky creek associated in Catholic and Mohawk tradition with René Goupil's martyrdom, I felt moved to lay hands on an ax-head-like stone that now sits in a place of honor on my desk. Father Tony suggested I return it eventually, but for now it reminds me to thank Saint René, Saint Francis de Sales, Charles Marie La Fonta, and many Christians I have not met, but of whose help I am sure.

For reading every chapter I sent and offering valuable editorial advice from a deaf perspective, I am grateful to Gina Donofrio and to others who offered important feedback on certain chapters: Sr. Judith Desmarais, Rose Folsom, Fr. Raymond Fleming, Rick Johnston, Jane Long, Sr. Maria McCready, Fr. Edward Moran, and Charlotte Baker Shenk. Trevor Lipscombe of the Catholic University Press of America offered steady encouragement and experienced editorial advice. Abigail Murphy deserves special mention: she copyedited an early version of the manuscript for love of the subject, and later, when she helped me standardize my notes and compile an index, I became the fortunate beneficiary of her quest for editorial excellence.

Many of the best parts of this book come from oral or signed histories, for which many Deaf Catholics set aside multiple days for long interviews and difficult questions. For their trust and openness, I owe special thanks to the following priests and deacons: Fr. Cyril Axelrod, CSsR; Fr. Shawn Carey; Fr. Thomas Coughlin, OP Miss; Fr. Michael Depcik, OSFS; Fr. Charles Dittmeier; Fr. Paul Fletcher, SJ; Fr. Carmelo Giuffre; Deacon Patrick Graybill; Fr. Matthew Hysell; Archbishop Patrick Kelly; Fr. Christopher Klusman; Fr. Richard Luberti, CSsR; Fr. Peter Monty, SJ; Fr. Joseph Mulcrone; Fr. Anthony Russo, CSsR; Fr. Gerard Trancone; Fr. Rowland Yeo, OSF; and Fr. Paul Zirimenya.

Certain lifelong pastoral workers in the Deaf Catholic community are essential both to this history and my telling of it: Terry and Mary O'Meara, Peter McDonough, the Sisters of Evron, Sister Dorothy Stefanik, Sister Dolores Beere, and Arvila Rank. Many archivists were a big help, but two were essential both for finding sources and for supporting my commitment to write this book: Mark Savolis of Holy Cross College and Patrick Hayes of the Redemptorists' Philadelphia Archives. I also thank Towson University for support and leave to research and write.

Thank you, beloved members of St. Francis of Assisi Deaf Catholic Church, for teaching me to sign and for welcoming me as one of your own. For sharing my love of history from a Deaf Catholic perspective, thank you Antônio Abreu and Joseph Thermadom. Sr. Patricia Francis, OP, thank you for listening to me when I was clueless; and Audrey Seah, thank you for being a great colleague and friend during so much of this research, especially important parts to which you contributed liturgical expertise and archival research during trips abroad. Finally, to my daughters and especially my husband, Joe, thank you, my loves, for putting up with my quirky research and writing habits. ILY.

Be Opened!

Introduction

> They brought to Jesus a man who was deaf who had an impedi-
> ment in his speech.... He took him aside in private, away from
> the crowd, and put his fingers into his ears, and he spat and
> touched his tongue. Then looking up to heaven, he sighed, and
> said to him, "*Ephphatha*," that is, "Be opened."—Mark 7:31–34

The sacrament of baptism, every Christian's rite of initiation, includes
several signs and symbols evoking family, belonging, and inclusion. In
the Catholic Church, infant baptism ordinarily occurs as a parent or
godparent holds the child over a baptismal font, while a priest or deacon pours holy water over the child's head in the name of the Father,
the Son, and the Holy Spirit. He anoints the child with chrism, and the
parents light a candle and clothe the child in a new, white garment. In
a traditional part of the baptismal rite, optional since post-Vatican II re-
form but still common today, the priest also touches the child's ears and
mouth, saying, "The Lord Jesus made the deaf hear and the dumb speak.
May he soon touch your ears to receive his word, and your mouth to
proclaim his faith."[1]

Now imagine that this child and one or both parents are profoundly deaf. They live and work in a community where many of the people
they encounter daily are also deaf, and they happily communicate in sign

All scriptural quotes, including the epigraph to this chapter, are from the New Revised Standard
Version (NRSV).

1. International Commission on English in the Liturgy, *Rite of Baptism for Children* (Totowa,
N.J.: Catholic Book Publishing, 2004).

language to learn in school, do business, form relationships, and teach their children. They are excluded only when people they encounter in the world presume they can—or should—speak and hear. How might this family interpret those words, an allusion to the passage above in the gospel of Mark where Jesus encounters a deaf man? Would this baptismal rite convey its intended message of welcome to people who have lived most of their lives within deaf culture?

It may at first seem odd to compare Deaf Catholics to a broad cultural category or ethnicity, similar, for example, to Hispanic Catholics, Catholics of African descent, or any other cultural group with a strong Catholic heritage. The presumption of much of mainstream society is that deafness is a disability and, like many other kinds of disability, should be handled primarily with medical and therapeutic intervention. It is true that advances in medical knowledge and hearing aid technology have enriched the lives of many deaf people, but there is another way of thinking about deafness that treats the language and history of deaf people as shared cultural traits. This perspective is especially important in the religious history of people who are deaf.

The gradual adaptation of Christian ministry in different cultures—enculturation—has been a part of evangelization since the early church. Though it may come as a surprise to those who have encountered deafness only as a disability, this cultural approach has been important to the church's ministry in deaf communities for hundreds of years. From the perspective of culturally deaf people in the Catholic Church today, the history of deaf ministry tells a story that has all the attributes of missionary transformation for a people who—quite literally—never encountered the gospel before it was communicated in their own language. In ancient Greece, congenitally deaf people were not considered fully human, and in extreme cases they were put to death so as not to be a burden to society. Today, due in large part to Christian missionary promotion of human rights and social justice in communities of deaf people around the world, it is possible for a deaf person to become a leader, not only in the sign language community but also in mainstream culture at large. Today, a deaf man may even become a Catholic priest. This did not occur without struggle.

This book explores the participation of deaf people and the use of sign language in the Catholic Church from their beginnings on the fringe of society to a flourishing New Evangelization that began in the mid-twentieth century. It traces a progression of historical stages, from the earliest encounters between deaf people and the church to the flowering of an established Deaf Catholic culture that is self-consciously international in scope. From this perspective, the narrative is about the development of Deaf Catholics as a language-based group with certain cultural and liturgical conventions reflected in pastoral leadership over time. A pivotal point in this history is the shift from missionaries in deaf communities before the mid-twentieth century to the modern establishment of chaplains for the deaf apostolate, especially those who use sign language and are part of deaf culture themselves. In order to tell the story of Deaf Catholics from a cultural (as opposed to medical) perspective, the narrative illustrates how both the understanding of deafness and the church's pastoral care for deaf people have "opened" over time in response to Jesus' command to the deaf man with the Aramaic word *ephphatha,* or "Be opened!" (Mk 7:34).

The protagonists of this story, Deaf Catholics themselves, have faced endangerment of their culture more than once, and today deaf people are still struggling to protect their heritage in many regions. Beginning in Europe and the Americas and then expanding to Asia and Africa, a strikingly similar historical pattern recurred in many nations. In the most fruitful communities, the stages moved from educating deaf people and evangelizing them as charitable work, to evangelizing side-by-side in partnership, to finally turning the tables and listening to what deaf people can teach the rest of the church. This story of transformation bears witness to a maturation of the church's understanding of the mission of evangelization, and, at the same time, sheds light on how Catholics of the twenty-first century may understand and interact with others who are culturally different from themselves.

Deafness as a Culture

Much of this book concerns the gradual development of deafness as a cultural identity during the twentieth century. To be clear, not all people who are medically classified as deaf identify culturally as deaf, and there are also culturally deaf people who are hearing, such as children of deaf adults. The current editorial convention in many Western nations is to capitalize the word "Deaf" to indicate a shared language, history, and other attributes of a definable identity and culture. In this sense of the word, deafness resembles an ethnicity because it concerns a group of people who have shared cultural and linguistic traits. The use of this convention varies in this narrative to reflect the shifting historical understanding of deafness, first as a disability, and later also as a cultural group. The difference of deafness in comparison to other disabilities is that it cannot be accommodated by simply improving physical access (as, for example, impaired vision can be accommodated by providing braille and audio description). Adding printed or projected text to an otherwise unchanged religious service is not enough to include people who use sign language. Cultural deafness requires translation and different modalities of communication in religious services because it is, in fact, a language difference.

Documents and records from the late Middle Ages to the mid-twentieth century illustrate common misconceptions and prejudices that so often separated deaf people from meaningful discourse with others in their communities. For example, the terms "deaf-mute" and "deaf and dumb" were commonly used well into the twentieth century to refer to all deaf people whether or not they could speak. Deafness has commonly been described as an "infirmity," as if being born deaf means being permanently sick. However, to otherwise healthy individuals who are born and raised in a deaf family or who have become acculturated to it through schools or other deaf gathering places, deafness is not something "missing" or "broken" in their being. Since deaf people first began to gather together, there have been distinctly deaf behavioral norms, values, and performing arts, all springing from the visual and tactile mode of signed language. Deafness, from this perspective, is simply a way of being fully human and something to celebrate for that reason. This is not to say that hearing aid technology or medical treatments for deafness are unimportant. The point is only that deaf culture is not, to the deaf individual, a broken way of life. It is, rather, the context through which faith can develop in real relationships and events. The lives and language of deaf people are the raw material of their faith.[2] For this reason, the evangelization of the culture of deaf people itself, their enculturation in the fullest sense of the word, has rightly been a primary concern of Deaf Catholic history and heritage.

---

2. For a particularly strong statement about deaf peoples' lives as the raw material of deaf faith, see Marcel Broesterhuizen, "Faith in Deaf Culture," *Theological Studies* 66 (2005): 325–28.

For hundreds of years, deaf people were largely excluded from education for reading because their lack of access to speech restricted their ability to make use of print texts. Consequently, the knowledge base that comes from constant exposure to the spoken and written word was for much of history out of reach for people who were deaf from childhood. Because sign language is gestural, it has no spoken—and, therefore, no written—mode. In this sense, deaf culture is much like oral traditions before literacy became widespread. Its histories are "signed histories" that have been passed on in person through stories about deaf people and events. Or, more frequently until the late twentieth century, scant history was preserved from a deaf perspective at all, but rather stories were written down by privileged hearing people who educated, shepherded, and studied them. This book could easily be classed as one more of this kind, but I have made an earnest effort to privilege the stories of deaf people, and even to de-emphasize the supporting stories of important hearing educators and missionaries to illustrate more clearly the contributions of deaf people themselves to Catholic heritage.

Deaf people and their signed languages were marginalized through much of history precisely because sign language cannot be expressed in the dominant print and spoken modes. Even with today's visually rich online media, we live in a world where the spoken and written word determines the transmission of knowledge. This is expected, based on the overwhelming majority of human beings born with five senses for whom spoken language is a given. Yet the "hearing majority," as people in today's deaf minority sometimes say, cannot make deaf people in their image by turning them all into medically or culturally hearing people. Like the poor, deaf people have always—and very likely will always—be with us. According to the World Health Organization's 2018 fact sheet on deafness and hearing loss, four hundred sixty-six million people worldwide have a hearing loss that is considered disabling by medical standards; thirty-four million of these are children. Taking population growth into account, by the year 2050 up to nine hundred million people of all ages will have a disabling hearing loss. Yet the current production of hearing aids meets a mere 10 percent of this global need.[3] For many of these

3. Disabling hearing loss refers to hearing loss greater than 40dB in the better hearing ear in adults and a hearing loss greater than 30dB in the better hearing ear in children. Fact Sheet on Deafness and Hearing Loss, World Health Organization, accessed March 2018, https://www.who.int/en/news-room/fact-sheets/detail/deafness-and-hearing-loss.

people, their native language for communication and transmission of knowledge is a signed language. Even allowing for abundant distribution of hearing aid technology in the future, successful deaf education and advancements in human rights necessarily start at the level of cultural dialogue and transformation, as it did in the United States with the acceptance of American Sign Language in 1965 for instruction in schools. Similarly, in countries where Deaf Catholic communities have been successful, the church has been their champion, advocating for and embracing deaf people, with their language and their culture, as full members of the Body of Christ.

Deaf People Are Not Defective People

Sadly, society has often labeled deaf people defective as human beings because of their inability to access spoken language. In the field of Deaf Studies, histories of the deaf are replete with glossed references to Aristotle's devastating mention in *History of Animals*, often translated "Those born deaf all become senseless and incapable of reason."[4] Equally problematic are Paul's insistence that "Faith comes by hearing" (Rom 10:17) and the oft-repeated but completely erroneous assertion that St. Augustine declared deaf people could have no faith because, as the Apostle said, faith comes by hearing.[5] The lack of context in the way these sources are sometimes quoted does not erase the stark reality that deaf people were, and often still are, generally excluded from religious communication. In parts of the world today where deaf education, health care, and social acceptance of disabilities remain undeveloped, things have not much changed.

4. K. W. Hodgson, *The Deaf and Their Problems* (New York: Philosophical Library, 1954), 62. A slightly more nuanced translation into twentieth-century English is A. L. Peck's translation of Aristotle: "All persons who are deaf from birth are dumb as well: they can utter a sort of voice, they cannot talk" (*History of Animals Books IV–VI* [Cambridge, Mass.: Harvard University Press, 1970], 81).

5. The seventh through eleventh editions of the *Encyclopedia Britannica* (1827–1919) stated that St. Augustine had declared "the deaf could have no faith since 'faith comes by hearing only.'" This gross misrepresentation appeared in influential texts on deafness for many decades, most notably the "Historical Sketch" by W. H. Addison in James Kerr Love's *Deaf Mutism: A Clinical and Pathological Study* (Glasgow: James MacLehose, 1896), 244.

Father Michael MacCarthy, SJ, an early chaplain of the Deaf Catholic community in New York City, dispelled this myth in the November 18, 1911, edition of *America* magazine. After finding no such statements in all seven volumes of Augustine, he wrote to Rev. Arnold Paine, author of the Britannica article, to ask his source. Paine promptly admitted that he had merely repeated what was said in an earlier edition. See Edward Allen Fay, "What Did Augustine Say?" *American Annals of the Deaf* 57, no. 1 (1912), 108–20; and Michael MacCarthy, *America* 6, no 4 (1911), 144. Father MacCarthy's contributions to Deaf Catholic culture are covered in chapter 8.

This line of thought in the church and in society at large portrays deaf people as unhappy victims—or worse, as a sign of unredeemed or degenerate existence. Such thinking has its roots in an ancient understanding of sin and its consequences. The disciples asked Jesus about a man who was blind from birth, "Who sinned, this man or his parents?" Of course, it was neither who caused the blindness. The man in this example was not possessed by demons, nor was he being punished for the sins of his ancestors, but instead "he was born blind that the works of God might be revealed in him" (Jn 9:1–3). Likewise, in Christian teaching from the earliest times, the person who is born deaf is created—not as a defective human being but for a divine purpose. Nor are deaf people objects of pity by default in Catholic theology, although historically deaf missions have often presumed they are.

The iconic passage from the gospel of Mark that heads this introduction presents a special challenge—but also hope—for deaf Christians. It is the only passage in Scripture in which communication occurs with a deaf person. Significantly, that person is Jesus. He puts his fingers in the man's ears, spits and touches his tongue, and tells him in Aramaic, "*Ephphatha*," be opened. The man receives miraculous healing and can then hear and speak. When today's more fortunate deaf users of sign language first encounter this passage, some find it offensive. For deaf people who grew up connected to resources in sign language in a visual culture of their own, the passage may indeed seem to be about healing—but in a way that turns healing into an outright rejection of sign language and conformity to a dominant speaking culture. On top of this, the conformity required appears to be impossible without miraculous, benevolent intervention from a person in authority representing that dominant culture. Many of today's deaf readers may wonder: Why do these stories emphasize the importance of speech above all other modes of communication? A formerly deaf man who went forth and proclaimed his faith by speech would still be excluding deaf people who use sign language. Historically, whenever deaf people have come together, they form sign language communities. The visual culture of the deaf is the normal context of their human lives, and that visual world is the lived experience through which the Word of God must reach them.

They may require contemplation over the course of a lifetime, but deaf Christians do not shy away from the challenges of these stories. In spiritual maturity, many embrace the complexities and mysteries of such passages as an opportunity to reflect on their relationship with God. Among Deaf Catholics, the passage in Mark 7 in which Jesus encounters the deaf man has become a cornerstone of religious identity, and holy pictures and stained-glass windows depict the scene in many a chapel designed for deaf worship today. It is a commonplace in Deaf Catholic culture that Jesus was speaking directly to deaf people for all times in this passage. In this sense, *Ephphatha!* was a command to open more than the ears and mouths of deaf people. Reaching far beyond the material body, the command refers to opening the whole person in his current situation—mind, heart, and community belonging. It is not an exaggeration to say that, today, most culturally Deaf Catholics emphasize that Jesus gestured or even used sign language when he took the deaf man aside from other people. After all, touching the ear and then touching the tongue is a gesture that resembles the sign for "deaf" in most of the world's sign languages. Regardless of whether Jesus himself spent much time preaching to deaf people, the Mark 7 story demonstrates that effective evangelization works within the language and cultural worldview of the people it seeks to reach.

The encounter between Jesus and the deaf man in Mark 7 illustrates a basic tenant of Christianity from its beginning: the belief that God is the creator of all, not just certain groups or those with able bodies and minds, and therefore through Christ all can have access to salvation. The earliest pastoral epistles of the church express this: "God our Savior desires all men to be saved and to come to the knowledge of the truth" (1 Tm 2:3–4). For most of history, however, the linguistic inaccessibility of "knowledge of truth" for deaf people is further complicated by a misunderstanding of the doctrine of original sin.

The Catholic Church's theology on the universality of original sin was articulated most precisely in the fifth century by St. Augustine of Hippo in his reflections against Pelagianism. Histories of the deaf often misrepresent Augustine, saying he purportedly taught that deaf people have no access to salvation. Consistent with his theology of the human person, Augustine explains in his treatise *Against Julian* that deafness, as a bodily defect, is a result of original sin.[6] However, secular deaf histories often fail to see that the doctrine of original sin is not unique to deaf people. As the *Catechism of the Catholic Church* clearly lays out, the doctrine

---

6. Augustine, *Against Julian*, trans. Matthew A. Schumacher, The Fathers of the Church: A New Translation 35 (Washington, D.C.: The Catholic University of America Press, 1957), 115.

of original sin establishes that *all* human beings are in need of salvation. The effect of original sin is a deprivation of holiness and justice requiring the grace of salvation for everyone. In salvation history, the universality of sin and death is matched and overcome by the universality of salvation in Christ. This salvation is fulfilled by the church through the visible sign of baptism.[7]

Miscommunication occurs when we focus too much on the medium through which the message of salvation is delivered. In deaf history, the most common error is equating speech, one faculty of humanity, with human reason or even humanity itself. Augustine accurately observed that deafness can preclude the acquisition of faith when the gospel is delivered only in the spoken word. Neither Paul nor Augustine proclaimed that faith comes by hearing alone, and in fact, Augustine showed interest in signs for the deaf as a form of human communication. In his treatise on *The Greatness of the Soul*, Augustine relates firsthand experience of a man who used sign language to communicate: "Did you not see at Milan a young man of most distinguished appearance and most charming manners, yet so mute and deaf that he could not understand others except by gestures and could not signify what he wished to communicate in any other way?"[8] Augustine knew that human deafness can preclude access to the spoken word and, as a result, to written literacy. However, the church's deaf heritage shows that deafness creates an opportunity to convey the message of salvation in a new way—through the natural medium that deaf people use to communicate with one another, sign language.

Once we move beyond misconceptions about Augustine's opinion of deaf people's access to salvation, we can gain useful insight from his other writings on signs. In *De Doctrina Christiana* (AD 426), he divides signs into "natural" and "made" or conventional signs. Natural signs, apart from any intention to use them as signs, lead us to the knowledge of something else. Conventional signs, on the other hand, are signs that show feelings, interpretations, or thoughts. Sign language is unique among languages in that it consists of both natural and conventional signs at one and the same time. This immediacy of sign language gives

7. Catholic Church, *Catechism of the Catholic Church in accordance with the Official Latin Text Promulgated by Pope John Paul II* (Vatican City: Libreria Editrice Vaticana, 1997), no. 97–101.

8. Augustine, *The Greatness of the Soul; The Teacher*, trans. Joseph M. Colleran, Ancient Christian Writers: The Works of the Fathers in Translation 9 (Westminster, Md.: Newman Press, 1950), 49.

rise to another commonplace in Deaf Catholic culture: proclaiming the gospel in sign language is, quite literally, the Word made flesh. Of course, Catholics think of all proclamations of the gospel this way, but worship and prayer in sign language is a particularly visible illustration of what Catholics believe. The church, full of speaking and hearing people, naturally takes for granted the spoken and written word. Yet the literal way the Word is made flesh in every signed proclamation of the gospel tangibly reminds us of the mystery of Incarnation. Sign language will not let us forget that the Word, as Christians speak of it, is not human speech. The Word is a person.

Missionary Transformation of Deaf Culture

From the time of the apostles, the mission of the church has been evangelization, but the understanding of this mission has developed over time. Recent scholars in Catholic missiology have suggested that there are elements of this mission that have been constant from the church's beginnings. Evangelization has always been preoccupied with the meaning of salvation, the role of the church, the nature of human beings, and an abiding dialogue with human cultures. However, missionaries have approached these common elements of evangelization in different ways. While every Christian era contains traces of all three approaches, certain times and places have called for an emphasis on one or another. In the early church through the colonial era, mission was defined as an imperative to expand the church by saving souls—as many as possible. Later on, especially as the Enlightenment took hold in Western philosophy, missionaries began to think of their work as the discovery and sharing of truth through both reason and revelation. Finally, in the modern era, a third approach developed in response to certain political and cultural constraints: mission could be a commitment to cultural transformation or even liberation from oppressive conditions.[9] Deaf missions participated robustly in each of these approaches to evangelization during their development. For this reason, another kind of *ephphatha*, an opening-up

9. For a comprehensive Catholic treatment of the history and development of mission and evangelization, see Stephen Bevans and Roger Schroeder, *Constants in Context: A Theology of Mission for Today*, American Society of Missiology Series 30 (Ossining, N.Y.: Orbis Books, 2004). Their framework (and therefore my definitions of mission here) are indebted to the work of Justo Gonzáles and Dorothe Sölle.

of the very meaning of evangelization, has been central to the story of Deaf Catholics as a cultural group.

Catholics often overlook missionary work in the deaf community as an example of evangelization and see it instead as an act of mercy or charity. However, the pattern of change in Deaf Catholic culture during the past two hundred years bears a striking resemblance to the transformation of other marginalized cultures that embraced the church through missionary activity. It is comparable, for example, to the changes that occurred in Native American communities during the eighteenth and nineteenth centuries. Just as Catholic education for deaf children has often been blamed for oralism and the suppression of sign languages, the Catholic Church is often attacked for crimes against Native Americans dating back to the sixteenth century. Historians have written much about the severe oppression of indigenous peoples in the Americas by European conquerors and settlers, as well as disease and displacement forced upon these people. Yet the plight of Native Americans was a tremendous concern to the church, and countless missionaries laid down their lives defending and serving native peoples. Of course, no historian would claim these missionaries were faultless. When Native Americans were ghettoized in reservations and their languages and cultures were left to waste away, missionaries routinely spoke of Native Americans as being "barely out of a savage condition and only recently encountering the habits of civilization."[10] In retrospect, it is easy to see that nineteenth-century missionaries to Native Americans sometimes lacked the deeper respect for indigenous languages and cultures that twentieth-century church teachings would require. Still, like early Catholic educators of the deaf, missionaries in the Americas did a great deal of good at a time when no one else dared to help, and some proved heroic.

Motivated by charity and evangelical zeal, missionaries brought education, health care, and the teachings of Christ to Native Americans. Through this contact between the church and native tribes, new evangelized forms of Native American culture developed in North America. Tribes such as the Crow and the Chippewa embraced Catholicism and found ways to make it their own, expressing the essence of native cultural values in a new way through the church's rituals, ceremonies, and traditions of spirituality. It may even be argued that this intersection of

10. This illustrative phrase is borrowed from Charles Warren Currier, "Our Indian Schools," *The Catholic Educational Association Bulletin* 4, no. 1 (1907): 54.

Catholic and native cultures helped preserve spiritual aspects of indigenous culture in ways that secular interventions were ill equipped to do.
Certainly, the church provided a needed bridge from isolated native cultures to the more powerful mainstream culture. At an advanced stage of
development, religious vocations began to develop within these tribes,
and priests were ordained who identified as native tribesmen rather than
missionaries from a strange outside world. Vernacular religious vocabulary and liturgy began to develop, and finally, in 1996, Laguna became
the first Native American language accepted by the National Conference
of Catholic Bishops in the United States for use in celebrating the Mass.
It is no coincidence that the United States bishops approved a request
to the Holy See for American Sign Language—also a native language of
North America—to be used for celebrating the Mass in the very same
petition.[11] While Pope Paul VI had approved the use of sign language
in general for all parts of the Mass that were said in the vernacular in
1965,[12] the specific request made clear that ASL is not just an adjunct
to the spoken Eucharistic prayer but potentially a language for valid
vernacular translation. As missionary activity has demonstrated around
the world, only when the Word of God is expressed through a people's
language and culture can a full expression of Catholic faith become
possible.

The first steps the church took to reach out to deaf people, as with
Native Americans and other unchurched groups, were education and
traveling mission work. The missionaries whose stories appear in Part
I of this book helped to establish deaf schools, social clubs, and civic
organizations in countries around the world. It is hard to ignore the col-
onizing connotations that some historians detect in the development
of these early ministries for the deaf. Secular histories often compared
Christian missions for the deaf to colonialism in underdeveloped nations. Whether intended or not, this comparison can take on the connotations of cultural imperialism. This assumption contains a seed of
truth from a deaf perspective. Yet these missions—including monastic
centers, early schools for the deaf, and residences for deaf people—creat-

11. See Helen Hull Hitchcock and Susan Bendofy, "Translation without Words: Should
American Sign Language Become an Official Liturgical Language?" *Adoremus Bulletin* 3, no. 4
(June 1997).

12. An English translation of the original 1965 Latin reply can be found in *The Jurist* 26 (1966):
388–89; International Commission on English in the Liturgy, *Documents on the Liturgy 1963–1979:
Conciliar, Papal, and Curial Texts* (Collegeville: Liturgical Press, 1982), no. 2119, 274.

ed unprecedented opportunities for the advancement and development of sign languages and culture. They also left a lasting impression on those languages and cultures. By the twentieth century, these types of organizations, first motivated by charity for the "poor deaf," began to contribute to a new stage of Deaf Catholic culture that emphasized mature church membership, service of Deaf Christians to the church, and participation in civic life.

In 1965, at the Second Vatican Council, the Catholic Church issued a Decree on Missionary Activity, *Ad Gentes* (*To the Nations*). With this document and with the translation of the Mass into the people's vernaculars, the church began to reframe the teaching on its mission for an approaching new millennium. *Ad Gentes* begins with the theological idea that the church's participation in missionary activity is identical with the church's participation in the life of the Trinity: "The pilgrim Church is missionary by her very nature, since it is from the mission of the Son and the mission of the Holy Spirit that she draws her origin, in accordance with the decree of God the Father."[13] A second implication of *Ad Gentes* is that missionary activity could no longer be defined simply as a territorial concept as it was during colonial expansion. Since *Ad Gentes*, mission is about serving people, whether across the ocean in a culture that had never been exposed to the Gospel or within one's own family. People with disabilities were not excused from this injunction.

The church's teaching on mission in the twentieth century reached its fullest expression in Pope John Paul II's 1990 encyclical *Redemptoris Missio* (Decree on the Mission Activity of the Church). In it the pope insisted that the reign of God is not an abstract concept or program; it is a person, Jesus of Nazareth. He laid out an expanded idea of mission that deeply influenced Deaf Catholics as they clung to their heritage amid a decline in religious practice and faith in the West. In addition to a continued need for direct witnessing to non-Christians, this document described a "new evangelization … where entire groups of the baptized have lost a living sense of the faith."[14] In defining what would come to be known as the New Evangelization, Pope John Paul II singles out modern areas of human life such as the world of communication, the culture of science, and situations in need of liberation from oppression. Deafness

13. Vatican Council II, *Ad Gentes*, (hereafter, *AG*), no. 2 (December 7, 1965), in *The Sixteen Documents of Vatican II*, trans. N.C.W.C. (Boston: Daughters of St. Paul, 1967).

14. John Paul II, *Redemptoris Missio* (hereafter, *RM*), Encyclical Letter (December 7, 1990), 18, 33.

and communication in sign language fit squarely into each of these categories then as they do today.

In each period of missionary activity with deaf people, the changing definitions of evangelization play an important part. It is only recently that Christians have reached a point of being able to describe the "missionary transformation" of any culture in the fullest of terms. Sadly, for some, it is possible that sign languages may, in fact, dwindle in the West where medical technology is diffuse and advanced. Already in most Western countries more than half of all infants born deaf receive cochlear implants. Many of these children may never feel the need to seek out sign language communities. In Denmark, where there has been entirely government funded, universal health care since 1998, the number of congenitally deaf infants receiving cochlear implants recently reached 100 percent. From the perspective of an overwhelmingly larger and more powerful hearing society, this is a blessing for these individuals and their families. From the perspective of deaf people who use a signed language, this could lead to the destruction of their language and culture—and a future when there would no longer be native users of sign language. Signed history and storytelling would be lost in the way that much of Native American language and culture has been lost.

The gifts that Deaf Catholics have given the world in the form of signed languages and literature, liturgical celebrations, and knowledge of deaf history should not be devalued or forgotten simply because there have been advancements in hearing aid technology and the prevention of deafness through disease control. After all, deaf people remain indigenous to every human civilization. Deaf individuals will continue to be with us in one form or another, and sign language culture will persist in densely populated nations where technology and civil rights are at different stages of advancement from the West. In other words, the stories of Deaf Catholic culture contained in this book are not isolated or insular anecdotes. They are more than mere tribalism or local deaf ideology. The stories of Deaf Catholic history are valuable for anyone who values heroic action for the sake of human life in its fullness and diversity.

As we look at ministry with deaf people in the chapters ahead, all these teachings, which continue to open up our understanding of evangelization, will inform—and, one hopes, inspire—the historical narrative as it unfolds. Even in the twenty-first century, Pope Francis has begun to add to our understanding of evangelization with his emphases on marginalized people and the family in today's changing society. He is the first pope in history to address deaf people using sign language in a video broadcast internationally (his Italian Sign Language Christmas greeting in 2016). Through the work of the Holy Spirit, we can properly expect a fuller and more dynamic modern concept of mission to develop in the years to come. Because Deaf Catholics have contributed to this expanding understanding of evangelization, their story needs to be told. Deaf Catholics deserve to be recognized as a long-suffering people in the church, and their Catholic heritage should be preserved as a treasure for the church as a whole.

A Road Map for Our Journey

The chapters of this book offer a narrative of deaf missionary transformation and the resulting development of the Deaf Catholic community, often through stories of deaf priests and pastoral leaders. Wherever possible, I rely heavily on personal interviews and storytelling of Deaf Catholics themselves, allowing their own historical narrative to emerge rather than imposing the interpretative lens of any one academic discipline. The book is divided into parts: part I, "Deaf Catholic Heritage," and part II, "New Deaf Evangelization." At the end of each part, there is a recommended reading list of seminal works in deaf history and Deaf Studies. Readers are also invited to consult the companion website to this book at http://icfdeafservice.org/beopened.

Part I focuses on the pioneering, apostolic stage of Deaf Catholic history, during which individuals from many regions of the globe, independently of each other, answered the call to bring the gospel to deaf people in their own countries. Chapter 1 briefly reviews the background of late medieval monastic education for deaf children and adults and some well-known Enlightenment-era developments, including the earliest ideological battles between educators using sign language and educators using oral/aural techniques. The rest of part I provides biographical histories of early twentieth-century priests, lay ministers, and religious sisters. All are forerunners who nurtured and developed communities that were deaf and Catholic, bearing traits with a remarkable resemblance across geographic boundaries. Separate chapters highlight "Deaf Apostles" who founded the earliest missions and fostered the development of religious sign language specific to Catholic sacraments, traditions, and communities in France, England, Ireland, Brazil, and the United States, as well as other European and Latin American countries. Wherever possible, the narrative highlights and privileges the contributions of deaf people called to evangelization and sign language ministry as it developed over time.

Part II of the book describes the worldwide flowering of Deaf Catholic culture after the Second Vatican Council, including several important advances in civil and religious rights for deaf people. Each of the six chapters in part II illustrates recent issues and developments in Deaf Catholic life, often through biographical portraits describing challenges that Deaf Catholics still face in the twenty-first century. It is difficult—perhaps impossible—to boil down the current attitudes and changing conditions of deaf people's lives into meaningful data. Instead, the portraits of deaf church leaders in part II draw upon journalistic research, ethnographic observations, and the techniques of biographical narrative, all with the aim of presenting real lives for better understanding and as endangered cultural treasures. Where there are controversies in liturgical practice or in theological and philosophical approaches to deafness, I avoid advocating strongly for one side or the other; instead, as a firsthand observer and participant, I attempt to present a balanced introduction to multiple perspectives.

Historically speaking, the chapters of part II introduce readers to the flowering of Deaf Catholic culture, including developments in sign language for the Mass. The stories in chapters 9 through 12 illustrate a contemporary spirit of hope and reconciliation, deep listening, and acceptance of difference embodied by Deaf Catholics around the world. These developments include several culturally deaf priests, a trend that increasingly garnered attention from mainstream media in the final decades of the twentieth century. The internet and easy access to video communication, combined with heightened global awareness, continue to transform Deaf Catholic culture and expand its influence. The story of Deaf Catholic history shifts to Asia and Africa in chapter 13, where many nations are still at the educational or missionary stages of deaf ministry. Only in the book's conclusion do I look ahead and venture important considerations for the church's continued inclusion of culturally deaf people.

As the church begins to embrace deaf ministry on an international scale, it seems likely that Deaf Catholic culture is not, after all, on the brink of extinction—but it is changing rapidly. By identifying with and helping poor and isolated deaf people around the world, the privileged populations of today's Deaf Catholic community in the West transcend their origins in poverty and isolation. From the transcendent perspective of salvation history, what we have in Deaf Catholic culture is the kind of leadership the church has always promised: "the first will be last, and the last will be first" (Mt 19:30). And if we are ready, perhaps the deaf will teach us to listen.

Part I

Deaf Catholic Heritage

CHAPTER 1

Catholic Education as Deaf
Cultural History

In a speaking, hearing world, deaf people are no strangers to painful experiences with education. Consider the story of Laura McDill Bates, a physician's daughter born in 1885. After experiencing friendlessness, ridicule, and academic struggle in her mainstream school in Illinois, Laura put all her efforts into lipreading and using a large ear trumpet in school. When she graduated with honors, she set off to Gallaudet College in Washington, D.C., determined to become a teacher of deaf children so that she might make life better for others like herself. Eight hundred miles from home, she went to her first church service for deaf people. The Episcopal minister, Dr. Edward Miner Gallaudet, opened with the Lord's Prayer in American Sign Language, a mode of communication completely unknown to her. In her long-anticipated encounter with the deaf community, she came face to face with the shortcomings of her education. Her ear trumpet was useless, and she still faced a language barrier. But this time, Laura could learn to understand. In her words,

As I stood there in unutterable loneliness, the grace and beauty of the sign language began to fascinate and to hold me. I raised my eyes to the motto above the platform, "Ephphatha!" The word seemed to speak to me directly as it must have appealed to that deaf man when it came from Christ's lips. "Ephphatha!" spoke this new language, and ever since I have cherished the word and sought to master the language of signs. I came to realize the power, the beauty, the majesty of that sign language as it is used in prayer, in lecture, in Shakespeare readings, in story, and in song. When all else fails to hold the interest of the deaf, when all other avenues fail to reach their hearts, the sign language speaks their "Ephphtha."[1]

In this moment of isolation, Laura experienced a penetrating longing for oneness with a body of believers and saw that, as a deaf person, the way to that oneness—her Word made flesh—was sign language.

Many of the first Catholic educators of deaf people in Europe and America came to this same realization. From their earliest attempts to overcome the social isolation of deaf people and, in the process, save their souls, missionaries developed deaf education using signed languages. While it would be wrong to attribute the cultural achievements of deaf people solely to hearing patrons, undoubtedly these early educators enabled deaf people to come together and form sign language communities that would eventually embody deaf culture. In turn, sign languages drew character and regional flavor from the dominant hearing cultures in which they originated.

This chapter provides a review of early deaf education from a Catholic perspective. It lays the foundations for the stories of deaf heritage in part I of this book by introducing key Catholic patrons and educators of this population before the twentieth century. We begin with examples of sixteenth-century monastic schools in Spain, founded primarily to teach deaf people to speak and read, then proceed to French mission schools in the eighteenth century, especially those that began to use sign language for classroom instruction in religion and other subjects. The overview concludes with a discussion of momentous battles in the nineteenth century between educators who used sign language and educators who preferred oral methods. In many historical sources, the depiction of hearing educators as heroes and saviors is a recurring theme, but for our purposes, the often-unsung contributions of deaf people themselves take precedence.[2]

1. Laura McDill Bates, "Ephphatha," *American Annals of the Deaf* 59, no. 2 (Washington, D.C.: American Schools for the Deaf, 1914), 153–54. Note that in this book, several different spellings— Ephpheta/Ephphatha/Efeta—have been retained for historical accuracy.

2. Those interested in a more encyclopedic account of the early history of deaf education and the Church's role in it would do well to read Ferdinand Moeller's 1912 *Catholic Encyclopedia* article on "Education of the Deaf and Dumb," which compiles an excellent list of early forays into oral education and manual alphabets, especially by those in religious orders but also by secular and Protestant educators (in *The Catholic Encyclopedia: An International Reference on the Constitution, Doctrine, Discipline, and History of the Catholic Church*, vol. 5, ed. Charles Herdermann et al. [New York: Encyclopedia Press, 1913] http://www.newadvent.org/cathen/05315a.htm).

Fuller treatments of Catholic deaf education in specific eras may be found in Susan Plann, *A Silent Minority: Deaf Education in Spain, 1550–1835* (Berkeley: University of California Press, 1997);

Sixteenth-Century Monastic Beginnings

The earliest record of education using sign language is from sixteenth-century Spanish monasteries.[3] At the San Salvador Monastery in Oña, a Benedictine monk named Pedro Ponce de León (1520–1584) established a small school for deaf children, almost all of whom belonged to wealthy families who could afford private tutoring. The primary goal of his monastic school was to teach these children to speak audibly and clearly, but he also instructed them in writing and some gestural communication. There is some indication from the writings of Juan Pablo Bonet (1573–1633), a seventeenth-century Spanish priest and tutor of wealthy deaf students, that Pedro Ponce de León used at least a manual alphabet for instruction in writing and speech, and perhaps even some of the native signs of his deaf students.[4] Among his most successful pupils were two brothers, Pedro and Francisco, sons of Juan Fernández de Velasco, the marquis of Berlanga and Astudillo.

Aristocratic families generally kept disabled children out of sight so as not to affect the family's public image, but it seems Juan Fernández had earnest hopes of educating his sons. The elder brother, Don Pedro, was linguistically skilled in the methods taught by de León, and some sources indicate that he may have had a priestly vocation. According to one source, a servant of the House of Velasco said that Don Pedro Velasco was "certainly a priest" who "celebrated Mass in the estate's chapel."[5] However, record of a request for his dispensation—either by Don Pe-

Marilyn Daniels, *Benedictine Roots in the Development of Deaf Education: Listening with the Heart* (Westport, Conn.: Bergin and Garvey, 1997); Joselyn Taylor, *Boston Spa: The Story of St. John's School for Deaf Children, 1875–1975* (Addlestone: British Deaf History Society, 2007); and R. A. R. Edwards, *Words Made Flesh: Nineteenth-Century Deaf Education and the Growth of Deaf Culture* (New York: New York University Press, 2012).

3. In my summary of early Benedictine educators of the deaf, I rely on the seminal work of historians in this area. Important primary documents relating to early Benedictine education of deaf students may be found in *Deaf History and Culture in Spain: A Reader of Primary Documents*, ed. Benjamin Fraser (Washington, D.C.: Gallaudet University Press, 2009).

4. Susan Plann, "Pedro Ponce de León: Myth and Reality," in *Deaf History Unveiled: Interpretations of the New Scholarship*, ed. John V. Van Cleve, (Washington, D.C.: Gallaudet University Press, 1996), 1–10; Plann, *A Silent Minority: Deaf Education in Spain, 1550–1835* (Berkeley: University of California Press, 1997), 1–27. See also A. Eguíluz Angoítia, *Pedro Ponce de León, la Nueva Personalidad del Sordomudo* (Madrid: Instituto Profesional de Sordomudos "Ponce de León," 1987); Teresa Labarta de Chaves and Jorge L. Soler, "Pedro Ponce de León, First Teacher of the Deaf," *Sign Language Studies* 5 (1974): 48–63.

5. See Labarta de Chaves and Soler, "*Pedro Ponce de León*," 52.

dro's local bishop or by authorities in Rome—remains to be discovered. What is certain is that, in his last will and testament, he transferred to his mother, the Marquesa de Berlanga, a pension of four hundred ducats per year that he received from the bishopric of the Canaries.[6] Undoubtedly, Don Pedro could speak Latin words, as religious education required it. Possibly this was enough for a cloistered community to accept him for priestly ordination. The classical and medieval philosophy taught at the time held that language and speech were not separate faculties and that speech was the defining characteristic of humans as reasoning beings. Teaching young "deaf-mutes" to speak (as opposed to late-deafened individuals who had already learned to speak) would have seemed almost miraculous. In practical terms, it opened the Velasco heirs to legal rights and civic powers routinely denied to those who had no speech, including the right to bear witness, make a will, or inherit a feudal estate.

In addition to their use of speech, the Velasco brothers used a sign language extensively as their first language. Moreover, the school, as the site of a deaf community, would naturally have fostered the development of sign language among those students who could not acquire speech. Primarily because the monks adhered to a rule of silence and used a gestural system to communicate basic needs inside the monastery, some historians have gone so far as to credit Benedictine monasteries like the one at Oña with the development of sign language for education. It does not take much speculation to assume that de León would have borrowed some of the hand signs meant to facilitate communication in areas of the monastery where monks were obliged to keep silence. Such gestural systems were little more than a practical way to indicate the necessities of daily life and the immediate environment: eating utensils, food, clothing, tools, important people in the church, including signs for certain religious terms such as God, the Virgin Mary, Saint Benedict, wine, and the Mass. However, these signs differed from monastery to monastery and were not consistent in Spain. Although they proved inviting for deaf people and may have provided some of the conditions necessary for deaf education, such systems were not complete visual languages for discussing serious matters. Most of the education in Ponce de León's school focused instead on spoken and written language, both Spanish and Latin. In one document, he wrote of his pupils:

6. Angoítia, *Pedro Ponce de León*, 174–76.

I have had disciples who were deaf and mute from birth, sons of great nobles and men of distinction, whom I taught to speak, and read, and write, and reckon, to pray, to assist at Mass and to know Christian doctrine and to confess by speech, and to some I taught Latin, and to others Latin and Greek, and to understand the Italian language, and one came to be ordained and to hold an office and benefice of the Church, and to pray the Canonical Hours; also this one and some others came to know and understand natural philosophy and astrology [cf. astronomy]; and another was heir to an estate and marquisate, and was to follow the career of arms. In addition to all that he knew, as has been said, he was instructed in the use of all kinds of arms, and was a very skillful equestrian. Besides all this they were great historians of Spanish and foreign history; and above all, they made use of the Doctrine, Policy and Discipline of which Aristotle had deprived them.[7]

It may be safe to assume that the deaf pupils whom de León describes were the Velasco brothers, but the absence of clear identification and the general nature of his comment leaves room for speculation.

Deaf Studies and historical scholarship on de León during the 1980s and 1990s focus on inferring the teacher's probable methods for educating the deaf. Unfortunately, modern historians have shown little interest in whether one of de León's pupils may have had a priestly vocation, fulfilled or not. This is astounding to overlook when the subject turns from methods of education to the accomplishments undertaken by deaf people themselves. Certainly, the educational methods are important, but just as important—and a great deal more surprising—would be any indication that a congenitally deaf man became a priest in the sixteenth century. Nineteenth- and twentieth-century biographies of Pedro Ponce de León, though based on questionable evidence, show more interest in the possible priestly calling of Don Pedro Velasco than most twentieth-century historians do. In his 1886 Spanish biography of Ponce de León, Father Antonio Eguíliuz Angoítia insists that Don Pedro Velasco was ordained a priest with pontifical dispensation, but much of his account seems to be based on nineteenth-century assumptions. "Indeed," he writes,

being deaf-mute constituted an impediment to priestly ordination, because, it was said, words pronounced orally form the main part of the sacraments. This was a point discussed in detail by jurists and moralists. It was not easy to obtain the Holy See's authorization for the first deaf-mute priest. No doubt he was helped by information given by his teacher and the mediation of some monks of Oña who were present in Rome as theologians of the Council [of Trent]. Father Ponce would have rebelled against anyone who denied the priesthood to his student. Without doubt the day of greatest joy and satisfaction in his career as a teacher of the deaf was the one on which he watched, marveling, as Pedro de Tovar went up to the altar to receive from the Bishop the anointing that made him a minister of the Lord. This fulfilled the proverb that says, "God can write straight on crooked lines." The intentions of the Marquesses of Belanga to consecrate their handicapped children to divine service were also fulfilled in this way, to the great and unexpected joy of the parents, thanks to the brilliant work of the monk Brother Ponce, truly a virtuous and wise man.[8]

Although Angoítia focuses at length on the difficulty of ordaining a deaf man, his praise is for de León as a great teacher of the deaf, not for Pedro de Velasco as a pioneering deaf priest. Angoítia's heroizing of de León is not, however, his own invention, as he is only reproducing the attitudes described in Spanish historical documents. One such document went so far as to proclaim, "Everything was taught him by Brother Ponce, monk of St. Benedict in Oña, from which he emerges as a perfect man skilled in all subjects."[9]

Unfortunately, we do not know what pastoral ministries Don Pedro Velasco may have performed, if any. Perhaps he only served in the confines of the monastery or at his estate; perhaps he assisted with teaching other deaf pupils in the school. However, Velasco's loyalty and gratitude to his "master and father" is undisputed. He named Ponce de León the executor of his will and reserved for him all mementos and objects that he used personally, with the suggestion that Ponce de León keep them for himself. He left his family's jewels and valuables to the monastery, where they were displayed for many years in the church and sacristy.[10] For the Deaf Catholic community today, Don Pedro Velasco is important in an almost mythical way. Since Angoítia's biography, he has appeared first on lists of ordained deaf men wherever there is an effort to reconstruct Deaf Catholic cultural history or to encourage deaf religious vocations.[11]

---

8. Angoítia, *Pedro Ponce de León*, translated for the author by Prof. John McLucas, 174–76.

9. Angoítia, *Pedro Ponce de León*, 174–76.

10. Angoítia, *Pedro Ponce de León*, 174–76.

11. For example, the archives of the International Catholic Deaf Association keep such a list, as does the Italian website of Franco Zatini, Storia dei Sordi, http://www.storiadeisordi.it.

The Catholic Roots of Early French and American Deaf Education

Education in sign language would not be what it is today were it not for Abbé Charles-Michel de l'Épée (1712–1789), a Catholic priest who worked with deaf people in France during the eighteenth century. While early twentieth-century historians mistakenly attributed the invention of sign language to l'Épée, he did not invent most of his signs but instead borrowed them from the deaf community, just as Pedro Ponce de León had done. After meeting two deaf sisters and working with them for some time, l'Épée observed that the deaf community in Paris already used a natural sign language, now referred to as Old French Sign. (In fact, wherever there are two or more deaf people, basic natural signs arise as a matter of human nature and the inherent need for humans to communicate in language.) A true inheritor of Cartesian philosophies and an Enlightenment sensibility, l'Épée understood that his students were fully rational and capable of learning languages, with or without speech. His primary motivation, however, was the spiritual welfare of deaf people. A missionary, l'Épée wanted to save souls. He aimed to teach his pupils enough French to participate in religious and moral education, lest they fall into sin. More generally, he wanted to ensure their full inclusion in the life of the church and society in general. With this urgent motive in mind, he founded a free shelter in Paris for poor deaf children and adults. There he adapted his students' vocabulary of natural signs for use in catechism. He also proceeded to create several new signs to teach verb tenses and other parts of speech that he assumed (wrongly, as it later became apparent) did not exist in the spatial grammar of Old French Sign Language.

Unlike educators before him, l'Épée believed that deaf people could learn through the eye everything that other people learned through the ear. This new educational philosophy, along with the system of sign-supported French he developed, was an advancement that would come to influence educators in countries around the world. In 1760, his charitable shelter became the world's first free school for the deaf—a Catholic Institute of Deaf-Mutes. That same year, l'Épée published a French Sign Language dictionary that Catholic and Protestant teachers alike translated into other languages to spread his system abroad. Eventually, he contributed to the training of foreign teachers of the deaf and helped to found twenty-one different schools in Europe. Educators in Spain, Germany, Holland, Russia, Ireland, and England begin to follow his methods. He urged teachers to learn the natural sign languages of deaf communities in their regions to facilitate communication with pupils outside of school but to use only sign-supported spoken language in the classroom. This consisted of lipreading, speech training, spoken language accompanied word for word by signed vocabulary, symbols for parts of speech like articles and prepositions, and a manual alphabet for spelling words for which there were no signs. Although critics were doubtful of his students' higher learning, many Deaf Catholics in France were finally able to participate in the life of the church because of his advocacy. Some were also able to have fuller self-determination in civic life—for example, defending themselves in court—for the first time. The school began to receive public funding in 1791 after l'Épée's death, and it still exists today as the National Institute of the Deaf in Paris. Before government funding secularized them, many of the first schools for the deaf began as religious schools like this one and can rightly be called a part of Deaf Catholic history. The lives of some of the National Institute's students are of great interest because of events that helped establish a more widespread Deaf Catholic culture.

From the Catholic point of view, there are points to highlight in the history of French sign language education that secular deaf histories do not recount. For example, few historians mention that l'Épée's most famous pupil, Louis Laurent Marie Clerc (1785–1869), was a confirmed Catholic. Born on December 26, 1785, Laurent was the son of Joseph Francois Clerc, a royal civil attorney. As an infant, he fell into a fireplace, damaging the right half of his face and contracting an infection that may have caused his deafness. Without the benefit of either early deaf education or deaf signing parents, Laurent developed no language at all as a child. He spent his boyhood in isolation, taking care of animals on his parents' estate and exploring his village in southern France. In 1798, at the age of twelve, his uncle enrolled him in the National Institute of Deaf-Mutes, by then under the direction of Abbé Roch-Ambroise Sicard.

The young Laurent Clerc excelled in his classes, and Sicard often included him in public lectures to demonstrate the effectiveness of the school's educational philosophy and methods. One such lecture circuit, in England in 1815, resulted in a book published in French and English on facing pages. Sicard clearly designed the question-and-answer dialogue in these lectures to prove deaf people capable of reason and language, and therefore worthy of the expense and trouble of educating them. L'Épée and Sicard freely made their methods available to anyone who wanted to use them, in hopes that deaf people everywhere might be able to exercise the higher moral faculties that Enlightenment philosophers believed universal to human nature.

The aim of Sicard's public exhibition of his pupils (which the dialogue resembles more than a lecture) was to show "to what degree of intelligence the deaf and dumb may arrive," when their instruction is founded on a systematic method that leads naturally to understanding purely intellectual ideas. In this purpose, the dialogue is oddly like another set of public lectures, that of former American slave Frederick Douglass, who had such eloquent language that many listeners did not believe he had been a slave. To demonstrate Clerc's intelligence and language ability, an English lady would test Clerc with questions and Clerc wrote his answers on a board; these were then copied to publish and disseminate. It is easy to infer, from a dialogue such as this, how the development of sign language functioned in tandem with missionary teaching of theological ideas and Catholic values:

> *English Lady*: Do you love the Abbé Sicard much?
>
> *Clerc*: Deprived, from infancy, of the faculty of hearing, and consequently of that of speaking, the deaf and dumb were condemned to the most wretched state of existence; the Abbé de l'Épée and the Abbé Sicard appeared, and the unfortunate creatures entrusted to their regenerating cares are passing from the class of brutes into that of men. You may easily imagine, therefore, how much I love the Abbé Sicard.

When asked about the "natural language" of signs, he gave an answer that suggested critical reflection on then-current philosophies of Descartes and Rousseau:

Natural language is the language of nature; a language which, by means of gestures, enables us to express the most usual wants and the most common necessaries of life. There are many sorts: physiognomy, or the language of the face, the language of the eyes, the language of signs. Artificial language is an imitated, borrowed, conventional language, used by men to express their thoughts, either by writing or speaking.

When asked about the advantages of a civilized life for deaf people, Clerc replied:

The advantages of a civilized life are those of being sensible that there is a God in the universe, consequently that we are to render him the worship he is due; of being polite and compliant toward our fellow-creatures, of making ourselves agreeable to everybody, of participating in arts and sciences: whereas, a solitary and savage life is the life of a being who shuns society, and wishes to have no kind of connection with the rest of mankind. Such is the life of silly and ignorant men, who are more beasts than the beasts themselves.[12]

With this method of reason and the ability to initiate communication in sign language, Abbé Sicard had equipped his students with the means to evangelize deaf people like themselves. In this mode of teaching through clear language and reason, Sicard regarded his mission work as nothing less than his pupils' discovery of truth, and the truth (in the Enlightenment mindset as well as the Catholic mission) was for all humankind.

Appended to the dialogue in this book is a letter from Sicard's colleague, a Monsieur Sievrac, who summarizes Sicard's method and begs him to publish more. Sievrac explains that Sicard's philosophy and findings may prove of interest—not only for the instruction of the deaf but for the study of language as a universal human attribute. Sicard's ideas, he hints, may even be useful for the adaptation of a natural language for use across national boundaries when different spoken languages pose a barrier to communication. Sievrac explains that this method begins with the principle that everything human beings learn by hearing can also be learned through the sense of sight. If a teacher presents ideas beginning with what is known and then progresses in a systematic way to what is unknown, then any person of normal mental faculties may advance to the most abstract concepts, including religious and philosophical concepts of human nature and God. According to Sicard's philosophy, signs worked the same way as words for this progression of reason. First, Sicard introduced concrete nouns, then action verbs, then more detached qualities, such as color and speed, or past and present. Finally, he introduced concepts of free will and the soul to his students. At this point Sievrac's description of abstract and theological ideas, influenced perhaps by his English audience's obligatory anti-Catholicism, veers from Sicard's traditional Catholic teachings to a more transcendentalist perspective: "After this, directing their thoughts toward all the physical existences submit-

12. Jean Massieu, Laurent Clerc, Roch A. Sicard, Andrés D. Laffon de Ladebat, and Jean H. Sievrac, *A Collection of the Most Remarkable Definitions and Answers of Massieu and Clerc, Deaf and Dumb, to the Various Questions Put to Them at Public Lectures of the Abbé Sicard* (London: Cox and Baylis, 1815), 2–21.

ted to their view through the immensity of space, or on the globe which we inhabit ... you made them feel that Nature also had a soul, of which the power, the action, and the immensity extends through every thing existing in the universe. Filled with these great ideas ... you have told them that this soul of Nature is that God whom all men are called upon to worship."[13] This method of teaching (but with an end in Catholic theology rather than the soul of nature) Sicard carried out through his "artificial language" of signs in the exact order and grammar of spoken or written French—which many an Enlightenment philosopher considered the best language for representing universal human logic.

Sievrac notes that Sicard had also used the oral method but found that speech was an artificial method for most congenitally deaf people: "You afterwards learned, by your own experience, that it was possible to make the deaf and dumb speak through imitation of the movement of the organs of speech.... You saw that they could thus express the accents of words which they did not understand; but this artificial speech, not being susceptible, with the deaf and dumb, of modification and regulation through the sense of hearing, is most often painful, harsh and un-tuned. It has neither the rapidity nor the expressiveness of signs, nor the precision of writing."[14] As Sievrac's critique illustrates, the deaf commu-nity's "natural language of signs" was a topic of heated debate in Parisian deaf culture and education. Some deaf intellectuals in France, including Pierre Desloges and deaf author and educator Ferdinand Berthier, pro-moted the use of the deaf community's own "natural signs" because of their native clarity and spatial imagery—without the artificial imposition of linear French grammar adapted from spoken and written modes. From the perspective of deaf culture, these deaf intellectuals, most of them Deaf Catholics educated at the National Institute of the Deaf in Par-is, opposed their teachers' methods by elevating "natural sign language" (now referred to as Old French Sign) as a clearer mode of language for deaf people. L'Épée's artificial sign system, they argued, was more accu-rately described as a visual mode for teaching French literacy rather than a language itself, whereas a true language was needed for free exchange of ideas in deaf people's discourse. The godson of Abbé Sicard, Auguste Bébian, became the first hearing man who was fluent in the natural sign

13. Massieu et al., *A Collection of the Most Remarkable Definitions and Answers of Massieu and Clerc*, 187.

14. Massieu et al., *A Collection of the Most Remarkable Definitions and Answers of Massieu and Clerc*, 167.

language of deaf Parisians. As he discerned the inadequacies of l'Épée's and Sicard's artificial sign system, Bébian grew eager to overhaul it completely, but he feared being accused of educational heresy if he defied the school's teachings.[15] Bébian wrote two important books on his preference for sign language in deaf education: *An Essay on Deaf-Mutes and Their Natural Language* (1817) and *Mimic Writing: A Method of Writing to Regularize the Language of Deaf-Mutes* (1825).[16]

By 1816, Laurent Clerc had advanced so far that he became Sicard's assistant at the school. However, in his own opinions about the best methods for educating deaf students, he had begun to align with his deaf colleagues in Paris. While Sicard encouraged the practical use of sign language, he also retained oral methods to facilitate pupils' acquisition of speech. It was his belief that they would need as much speech training as possible to work with others in factories or trades. Clerc had found it painful and humiliating when his teachers punished him for making mistakes that he could not hear. When he developed a reputation as a master teacher independent of Sicard, Clerc began to emphasize natural sign language as the primary means of communication with deaf pupils, even in the classroom.

While lecturing in England, Clerc and Sicard met Reverend Thomas Hopkins Gallaudet, a Protestant minister and graduate of Andover Theological Seminary who had taken an interest in education for the deaf. A close friend of his, the father of a deaf child, wished to establish a school for deaf children in Connecticut. Gallaudet had read Sicard's *Théorie des Signes*, and now he was meeting Sicard and his most successful pupil in person. After accepting an invitation to visit the Institute in Paris, Gallaudet took private lessons in sign language from Laurent Clerc himself. Gallaudet was so impressed with his teaching that he invited Clerc to America in 1817 to help establish the first nonreligious public school for the deaf, the Asylum for the Education and Instruction of the Deaf and Dumb in Hartford, Connecticut, later renamed the American School for the Deaf. In the contract created for the partnership between his student and Dr. Hopkins, Abbé Sicard was careful to specify

---

15. Ferdinand Berthier, *Forging Deaf Education in Nineteenth-Century France: Biographical Sketches of Bébian, Sicard, Massieu, and Clerc*, ed. and trans. Freeman G. Henry (Washington, D.C.: Gallaudet University Press, 2009), 1–5.

16. For a discussion of deaf intellectual discourse in sign language and the competing educational methods advanced by hearing people, see Paddy Ladd, *Understanding Deaf Culture: In Search of Deafhood* (Clevedon: Multilingual Matters, 2003).

the Catholic nature of Laurent Clerc's mission, saying, "He is not to be called upon to teach anything contrary to the Roman Catholic religion." In his letter to Bishop Jean-Louis Cheverus of Boston, he further emphasized this point:

The extreme desire to procure for the unfortunate deaf-mutes of the country in which you dwell and fulfill so well the mission of the Holy Apostles, the happiness of knowing our holy religion leads me to a sacrifice which would exceed human strength. I send to the United States the best taught of my pupils, a deaf-mute whom my art restored to society and religion. He goes fully resolved to live and be faithful to the principles of the Catholic religion which I have taught him.[17]

As Father Ferdinand Moeller explained it, the Catholic formation that Clerc had received from Abbé Sicard fell to the wayside as he made his way in America: "Like so many thousand deaf-mutes in this country deprived of constant religious instruction, in his non-Catholic surroundings [Clerc] weakened in the faith and apostatized. Little did the good Abbé Sicard think that his kindness only served to lay the foundation of a Protestant propaganda which has monopolized the education of the deaf ever since the opening of the Hartford School in 1817."[18]

True to Moeller's account, it was Anglicans and Methodists who pioneered much of the earliest deaf education in England, Germany, and America during the eighteenth and nineteenth centuries. There were signing deaf ministers for Deaf Protestant congregations well before the Catholic Church would achieve the same missionary development by allowing deaf religious vocations.[19] Whether Clerc "apostatized" from his Catholic faith, however, is a question for historical debate. His immigration to America took place during the Second Great Awakening, a time of evangelical revival of Protestant religious identity. During the first two years of the school's existence, there was a conspicuous lack of newspaper coverage about Clerc. When reporters do mention him, they discuss his Christian mission but seem ignorant of his Catholic faith. Because Clerc immigrated to America a decade before the first Catholic church

17. Quoted in Rev. Ferdinand A. Moeller, SJ, Chaplain of the Ephpheta School, Chicago, "The Appeal of the Deaf" (lecture, First American Catholic Missionary Congress, Chicago, Ill., 1908). Deaf Catholic Archives, Worchester, Mass.

18. Moeller, "The Appeal of the Deaf."

19. For a full account of Episcopal mission work with the deaf, see Otto Benjamin Berg, *A Missionary Chronicle: Being a History of the Ministry to the Deaf in the Episcopal Church (1850–1980)* (Silver Spring, Md.: National Association of the Deaf, 1984).

(St. Patrick-St. Anthony Church) was established in Hartford, it was impossible for him to attend Mass. In any case, Rev. Gallaudet would not have publicized the fact that he had engaged a committed French Catholic to educate deaf pupils as they became good Protestant Americans.[20]

At the age of twenty-eight, Clerc made the fifty-two-day sea voyage to Connecticut, and on April 15, 1817, the Connecticut Asylum for the Deaf opened its doors. Poor and uneducated students, ranging in age from ten to fifty-one years old, came to live at the school within the first year. In 1818, Clerc and Gallaudet presented their methods and philosophies of public education for the deaf in the Connecticut and United States legislatures, inspiring Representative Henry Clay to sponsor a successful bill granting the school twenty-three thousand acres of federal government land in Alabama. This land was promptly sold and the proceeds used to start an endowment and construct school buildings at the American Asylum for the Deaf in Hartford, Connecticut. Students could live and study in the school for five years at the state's expense. Many of the students and teachers Clerc trained, hearing and deaf, were successful, and some went on to start other schools in New York and Philadelphia. Over thirty residential schools for the deaf were founded in America during Clerc's lifetime.[21] These groundbreaking events would become an iconic example for sign language educators around the world. Like Clerc, many of the earliest deaf educators learned their methods in church schools or missions, Catholic and Protestant. Those individuals were then able to equip their own deaf students with the knowledge and communication necessary not only for religious participation but also for greater secular and civic participation.

During this time of expanding deaf education, the Sisters of St. Joseph founded St. Joseph's School in St. Louis—the first Catholic school for deaf children in America (1837). Other long-lived Catholic schools soon followed their example: St. Mary's School for the Deaf in Buffalo (1859), St. John's School for the Deaf in Milwaukee (1876), and Ephpheta School in Chicago (1884). By 1908 there were thirteen schools for deaf children under Catholic auspices in the United States, most of them

20. Sari Altschuler, "He That Hath an Ear to Hear: Deaf America and the Second Great Awakening," *Disabilities Studies Quarterly* 31, no. 1 (2011), accessed May 31, 2011, http://dsq-sds.org/article/view/1368/1498#card_1495914108834_7342.

21. See Harlan Lane, *When the Mind Hears: A History of the Deaf* (New York: Random House, 1984); Cathryn Carroll and Harlan Lane, *Laurent Clerc: The Story of His Early Years* (Washington, D.C.: Gallaudet University Press, 1991), 7.

founded by orders of religious sisters in major cities where centers and associations of Deaf Catholic adults were also beginning to develop.[22] Methods of instruction in these schools varied during this period, with some preferring oral methods, perhaps with the addition of finger spelling, and others championing sign language education.

American Catholic families typically feared widespread anti-Catholic sentiment in any level of public education, but many came to rely on public schools for deaf children because of the comparatively limited availability of Catholic schools for this population. As state-funded residential schools for the deaf began to appear all over the country, the effect was broader establishment of American Deaf Culture. College-level public education for the deaf was also developing. In 1864, the U.S. Congress passed a bill establishing the Columbia Institution for the Instruction of the Deaf-and-Dumb and the Blind, the first institution in the world founded specifically to grant college degrees to deaf graduates. Edward Miner Gallaudet, son of Thomas Hopkins Gallaudet, was the first president of the school, later renamed in his honor. Today, Gallaudet University is a bastion of international deaf culture. Deaf Americans who use American Sign Language and deaf international students from around the world consider Gallaudet University the premier site for both education and social mobility. Like many secular deaf leaders in the United States and abroad, several of the Deaf Catholic priests and pastoral workers introduced in Part II of this book engaged in academic and social pursuits there.

Oralism in the Nineteenth Century

Sign language, however important it was to deaf people and deaf schools in the nineteenth century, was not the only force at work in eighteenth and nineteenth-century deaf education. As French and American sign languages grew in popularity, a competing method of educating the deaf developed, one that aimed to perfect lipreading and the production of audible speech. Oralism, as it came to be known, had been in practice from the time of Pedro Ponce de León (and probably earlier, wherever hearing people attempted to teach a deaf child to speak). In the modern era, a German teacher, Samuel Heinicke (1727–1790), became known as

22. Moeller, "The Appeal of the Deaf." The contributions of religious sisters to deaf education are discussed in chapter 3. A more detailed account of U.S. Catholic Deaf associations is found in chapter 8.

the "father of oralism." In 1778 he founded the Electoral Saxon Institute for Mutes and Other Persons Afflicted with Speech Defects (known as the Samuel Heinicke School today) in Eppendorf, Germany. Heinicke believed that spoken language and the phonemic system of reading were indispensable to higher levels of literacy and that their absence impeded intellectual thought and social integration. Although there is evidence he used a manual alphabet, Heinicke bitterly opposed dependence on sign language. In 1780 he published a book attacking Abbé de l'Épée's Parisian school and its use of signs to facilitate French language acquisition. John Baptist Graser (1766–1841) and Frederick Maritz Hill (1805–1874) continued to promote Heinicke's method, and oralism spread across Europe and over the Atlantic through the teaching of speech therapy and "elocution," a method of speech-focused rhetorical education popular among class-conscious social climbers during the postcolonial era.

Alexander Graham Bell, famous for his invention of the telephone in America, was primarily an elocutionist and an oralist teacher of the deaf. In 1872, he used the funds from his famous invention to establish the Volta Bureau, an organization that advocated the suppression of sign language in schools and promoted the exclusive use of speech and lip-reading to teach deaf children. A supporter of nineteenth-century social Darwinism and eugenic improvement of society, Bell was alarmed by the tendency of deaf people to marry each other and form small communities that used sign language. Bell was well acquainted with the deaf community of his day, as both his mother and his wife were deaf. He feared, however, that deaf communities and marriages of deaf couples would increase the deaf population by heredity. In 1884, he published a paper "Upon the Formation of a Deaf Variety of the Human Race," warning of the "great calamity" of deaf communities and marriages. The creation of a "deaf race" would naturally follow, he insisted. "A special language adapted for the use of such a race" and "a language as different from English as French or German or Russian" already existed. He believed that, since sign language was the cause of deaf separatism and intermarriage, the solution was to establish day schools taught only by hearing teachers who would absolutely ban sign language.[23]

The peak of oralism's popularity in deaf education coincided with the first international conference for educators of deaf children. The Interna-

23. Alexander Graham Bell, "Memoir Upon the Formation of a Deaf Variety of the Human Race" (Washington, D.C.: National Academy of Sciences, 1884), 47.

tional Congress on Education for the Deaf took place in September 1880 in Milan, Italy. Proceedings from the Milan Conference declared oralism superior to manual modes of deaf education and proposed a ban on sign language in public schools.

From the perspective of deaf history, a dark age followed. Schools for the deaf systematically dismissed deaf staff members, including teachers. Well into the 1950s and 1960s in the United States and Europe, teachers frequently punished students for using sign language and forced them to sit on their hands in school. Contrary to the hopes and educational philosophy of the oralists, however, deaf children still did not gain English literacy at higher levels than they had with sign language in the classroom. Many supporters of sign language attributed low literacy to the ban on visual communication. This series of events resulted in vehement opposition to oralism in American Deaf Culture that continues today.

Early in the twentieth century, deaf community organizations and the National Association of the Deaf (NAD) in America took steps to preserve and protect deaf culture from the encroachment of oralism, which they often attributed to mainstream "hearing culture" in general. In 1910, the NAD raised $5,000 to produce eighteen films to preserve American Sign Language. In his own contribution to the film library, NAD president George Veditz made an impassioned call for the preservation of sign language and its protection against "false prophets":

We American deaf are now facing bad times for our schools. False prophets are now appearing, announcing to the public that our American means of teaching the deaf are all wrong. These men have tried to educate the public and make them believe that the oral method is really the one best means of educating the deaf. But we American deaf know, the French deaf know, the German deaf know that in truth, the oral method is the worst. A new race of pharaohs that knew not Joseph is taking over the land and many of our American schools. They do not understand signs for they cannot sign. They proclaim that signs are worthless and of no help to the deaf. Enemies of the sign language, they are enemies of the true welfare of the deaf. We must use our films to pass on the beauty of the signs we have now. As long as we have deaf people on earth, we will have signs. And as long as we have our films, we can preserve signs in their old purity. It is my hope that we will all love and guard our beautiful sign language as the noblest gift God has given to deaf people.[24]

24. George Veditz, *The Preservation of the Sign Language* (Washington, D.C.: Gallaudet University, 1913), film, translated from ASL by Carol Padden and Eric Malzkuhn for the PBS film *Through Deaf Eyes*, 2007.

These films are a treasure for the history of sign language as well as the history of rhetoric in American public life. Many contain prayers and other religious discourse used in deaf churches and social clubs at the turn of the century.

Supporters of sign language and supporters of oral education were bitterly at odds for decades. Proponents of American Deaf Culture, firmly on the side of sign language, struggled to preserve their deaf identity without many resources to help them until the 1960s, when the Civil Rights movement emerged as a model of activism, resistance, and protest. For Deaf Catholics, the Second Vatican Council's emphasis on social justice augmented these cultural advances with religious participation and vernacular languages in the Mass. Together, these developments led many Catholics engaged in deaf ministry to embrace sign language for education and evangelization.

The history of deaf education from the sixteenth through nineteenth centuries set the stage for a new breed of missionaries to the deaf community—those who encouraged and enriched deaf culture through liturgy and other religious practices in sign language. Subsequent chapters in part I tell the stories of several religious orders and dedicated individuals, deaf and hearing, who were among the first apostles to deaf communities to use sign language. Chapter 2 introduces spiritual traditions in the Deaf Catholic community, including the veneration of patron saints and traditions of service to deaf people in several religious orders. Chapter 3 addresses the important place of women in the history of Deaf Catholic ministry, and chapter 4 focuses on the contributions of two particularly fruitful men's religious orders, Redemptorists and Jesuits. The remaining chapters of part I profile Catholic communities in France, Brazil, England, Ireland, and the United States, bringing together for the first time in one volume the stories of these historic ministries that laid the foundations of Deaf Catholic heritage.

CHAPTER 2

Saints and Founding Fathers

The earliest stories of Catholic saints in deaf ministry are healing narratives. In one of the first, the Venerable Bede writes of a healing miracle attributed to an eighth-century English bishop, Saint John of Beverley. While walking in a village close to his home, the saint met a deaf youth begging for alms. This young man had never spoken a word, and his head was covered in oozing sores. Saint John of Beverley had a dwelling built for him next to his own home and began to treat the young man's head daily with ointment. Soon the scabs healed, and his hair grew back shiny and healthy. On the second Sunday of Lent, the saintly bishop visited this young man and made the sign of the cross over his tongue. Afterward, he successfully taught the young man to say his first word, "Yea," and in time he taught him to say the letters of the alphabet, syllables, more words, and finally full sentences.[1] Thus, it was a combination of prayer and hard work that led to the "miracle" of speech for this young man. This story held a place of honor in Catholic and Protestant deaf ministry for hundreds of years, especially in England during periods when oralist education was the dominant educational method for deaf children.[2]

Saint John of Beverley's example of deaf ministry is clearly a story of medical healing and speech training, but in the eighteenth and nineteenth centuries, Catholics involved in deaf ministry began to highlight

1. Venerable Bede, *Bede's Ecclesiastical History of England*, trans. A. M. Sellar (London: George Bell and Sons, 1907).

2. In 1925, pioneer Anglican deaf educator Selwyn Oxley named his charitable service for deaf people in London after Saint John of Beverley, and the Canterbury Anglican Diocesan Association for the Deaf is still called the Guild of Saint John of Beverley in the saint's honor. The Lutheran Church also honors Saint John of Beverley, and for many years the Lutheran Friends of the Deaf in New York published a series of religious education books for children called the John of Beverley Series.

stories illustrating the positive roles sign language could play, both as a means of communication and as a valuable gift which deaf people bring to the church. Deaf Catholics themselves, as well as those who served the deaf community, began to pass on a different kind of Catholic story to younger generations—stories that featured deaf people using sign language to express their Christian faith.

This chapter begins with a discussion of the most important saints traditionally venerated by deaf people, then turns to early modern-era religious orders inspired by Catholic traditions of service to deaf people, especially those orders that facilitated the development of sign language and the Catholic enculturation of deaf people. Among the first organized groups of Catholics to cultivate deaf ministries were orders of men and women who started schools and services for neglected children in their own European communities or who left their homelands to start schools overseas. It is no surprise that these orders took inspiration from saints who served deaf people, such as Saint John of Beverley and Saint Francis de Sales, as well as Catholic educators like Abbé Charles-Michel de l'Épée and Abbé Roch-Ambroise Sicard, as they continued to develop new teaching methods for both oral education and sign language. The history of these orders illustrates that, in matters of sacrifice and hard work in the service of deaf people, pastoral workers and educators have often surpassed their saintly role models.

Saint Frances de Sales and Martin

In his *Introduction to the Devout Life*, Saint Francis de Sales (1567–1622) taught that God's call to holiness is universal and that this call adapts to each individual according to that person's state in life. The church emphasized this teaching strongly during Vatican II, and it continues to be essential today. For the Deaf Catholic community, the unusual friendship between Saint Francis de Sales and Martin, a young man profoundly deaf from birth, is an enduring and iconic example of the universal call to holiness. Saint Francis first met Martin in 1605 during an extended retreat to La Roche, a small township he often praised in his letters for its simple and pious population. At the estate where de Sales resided, the servants enjoyed Martin's company and often employed him to help around the house. Knowing de Sales's love for the poor, they brought the deaf man to meet him one night at dinner. De Sales's biographer Peter

Gallitia writes that the saint found Martin "remarkably ready in understanding and in making himself understood by signs."[3] Although he faced objections, de Sales invited the young man into the house and kept him by his side during his stay, then brought him home to his episcopal residence in Annecy, where the young man became de Sales's gardener and a permanent member of his household. According to the Sisters of the Visitation of Holy Mary, founded in 1610 by Saint Francis de Sales and Saint Jane de Chantal, it was Martin who designed the order's habit.[4]

After sustained daily practice, de Sales learned to communicate fluently with Martin in signs. He is the only deaf person described in the saint's biographies, so it is unlikely anyone but Martin himself could have taught him. Most summaries of the story written for devotional purposes suggest that de Sales created the language he used for Martin, but this could only be a misinterpretation. Understandably, biographers emphasized de Sales's charity and teaching, but in their desire to praise the saint they have often overlooked Martin's gifts and minimized his contributions to this unusual friendship. Rather than teaching the young man sign language, it is far more likely that de Sales learned Martin's native sign language and then, in the process of communication, expanded it with new religious signs to teach him the mysteries of faith. Within a year, Martin had learned enough to receive his first Holy Communion, and after two years he was confirmed.

Some biographers describe how de Sales became Martin's regular confessor. Whenever Martin wished to make a confession, he entered the saint's room and closed the windows and doors for privacy. There, according to imaginative accounts, Martin would use sign language to accuse himself of his sins and secret thoughts, weeping bitterly and striking his breast. De Sales was often so moved that he, too, would emerge with tears on his cheeks.[5] The two became dear friends, and de Sales was known to

3. Peter Hyacinth Gallitia, *The Life of St. Francis de Sales, Bishop and Prince of Geneva, from the Italian book by Peter Hyacinth Gallitia*, trans. Pier Giacinto Gallizia, vol. 2 (London: Thomas Richardson, 1854), 78–79. Although many later biographies of Francis de Sales mention in passing that the saint acquired a deaf servant in La Roche, most do not mention Martin by name or go into detail about Saint Francis's teaching in sign language. Beyond Gallitia's book, perhaps the most complete source for the story is the French biography by André Jean-Marie Hamon, *Vie de Saint François de Sales, évêque et prince de Genève, par le Curé de Saint-Sulpice*, 2nd ed. (Paris: Jacques Lecoffre, 1862), 425–27. Cornelius J. Warren, CSsR, translated and published an English version of Hamon's work in America in 1910, cited below.

4. Fr. Joseph Bruce, a deaf Jesuit priest and historian of deaf culture, collected this detail of oral history while visiting the Sisters of the Visitation in Guatemala City in 2002–2004.

5. Gallitia, *The Life of St. Francis de Sales*, 78–79.

refer to Martin as an example of piety and virtue, on one occasion even asking him to "preach" to visitors in his drawing room using signs and vocal sounds that he no doubt added when communicating with hearing people who did not understand sign language. As nineteenth-century biographer Andre Hamon records, one contemporary of de Sales wrote of these occasions, "It was amusing to see him represent theft, murder, gluttony, vanity and the other vices. To express their gravity, he would raise his eyes to heaven and stretch out his hands; to show that vice led to hell, he would turn towards the fire and make gestures as though he wished to plunge the lovers of the world into it."[6] Perhaps hearing onlookers and early biographers found Martin's preaching amusing, but it is likely that Martin and de Sales took this preaching quite seriously as a fulfillment of the deaf man's mature Christian calling to evangelize others.

Undoubtedly, this unique friendship required as much learning from de Sales as it did from Martin, and the pair probably spent countless hours laboring to communicate until they could do so fluently—as do learners of any foreign language. A nobleman, Béné Favre, once asked de Sales if teaching the young man was worth all this effort and whether it would not be easier to pray for a miraculous cure that would enable him to hear and to speak. Francis replied with his characteristic gentleness, saying that he gained so much from Martin through the opportunity to practice charity and friendship every day that it had never occurred to him to ask God to make Martin a hearing person for his own convenience. Understandably, Martin became so attached to his confessor and friend that he reportedly died of grief a few days after the saint died.[7] Over two hundred and fifty years later, Pope Pius XII proclaimed Francis de Sales the patron saint of deaf people. As a result, iconic images of Saint Francis de Sales teaching Martin are now common internationally, not only in Salesian-influenced religious orders but everywhere there are churches with deaf populations.

Since Francis de Sales was a hearing person, one may wonder who Deaf Catholics regard as deaf role models in their Catholic identity and practice of faith. For a long time, deaf people looked primarily to hearing people who encouraged and educated them in religious matters. Few saints and martyrs are remembered for being deaf themselves, and those

6. Andre Jean-Marie Hamon, *The Spirit of St. Francis, by a Curé of Saint-Sulpice*, trans. Cornelius J. Warren, CSsR (Boston: Mission Church Press, 1910), 148.

7. Gallitia, *The Life of St. Francis de Sales*, 78–79.

who are have been members of religious orders that had the community resources and the influence to advance an official cause for sainthood. At present, there are no congenitally or culturally deaf saints recognized by the Catholic Church. One factor contributing to this may be the fact that sign language has no written form, and therefore few writings are left by deaf persons of faith. There are a few saints, like Bernadette Soubirous, who became deaf late in life and had to rely on basic signs for day-to-day communication with hearing sisters in her order, but this is hardly cultural deafness. There is one late-deafened martyr, however, who has inspired significant devotion in the Deaf Catholic community in North America today.

Saint René Goupil

René Goupil was a deaf man who became the first of eight Jesuit missionaries to be martyred in French Canada. In his mission diary, the French Jesuit priest Abbé Isaac Jogues relates the story of how Goupil, after training to be a surgeon, discerned a vocation to religious life. He had been in the Jesuit novitiate in Paris for several months when he contracted an illness that resulted in partial deafness. As Jogues writes, "His bodily ailments having deprived him of the happiness of consecrating himself in the holy state of religion as he had wished, he crossed over to New France to serve the Society there."[8] From 1640 to 1642, he served as a lay volunteer under the supervision of the Jesuit Superior of the mission in Sillery near Quebec. The purpose of the mission was to save the lives and souls of native Hurons, a people suffering brutal attacks and enslavement at the hands of their hereditary enemies, the Iroquois nation. Five hundred miles away, east of Lake Huron in what is now Ontario, there was another Huron mission desperately in need of health care because of ongoing raids. In 1642, the superior decided to send René Goupil there with Abbé Isaac Jogues and William Couture (another lay volunteer) to treat and minister to the Hurons.

Although Goupil understood the dangers awaiting him on the St. Lawrence River, he was filled with joy to serve as a Jesuit missionary. With a large party of forty Algonquin and Huron people, they began what they

8. Isaac Jogues, *Narrative of a Captivity among the Mohawk Indians, and a Description of New Netherland in 1642–3 with a Memoir of John Gilmary Shea* (New York: Press of the Historical Society, 1856), 61–67.

believed would be a month-long journey in canoes. However, as Jogues relates in his mission diary, an opportunity for Goupil to prove his devotion as a missionary would not be long in coming. Two weeks into their journey, Goupil, Couture, and Jogues were seized by Mohawk warriors (the Mohawk being one of six tribes comprising the Iroquois nation). Once in captivity, Goupil embraced these dangers, telling Abbé Jogues, "Father, may God be praised, He has allowed this, He has wished it. May His holy will be done!" As they were marched through Mohawk country, Goupil continued to be "caught up in God." According to Jogues, his conversation and demeanor reflected submission to divine providence and ready acceptance of the death God would send. After reaching the Mohawk village of Ossernenon near present-day Auriesville, New York, Mohawk warriors beat Goupil to unconsciousness with clubs and iron rods and carried him to a scaffold in the middle of a Huron slave camp. First seizing Jogues and sawing off his thumb and forefinger with a sharpened clam shell, the Mohawks then turned on Goupil and cut off his right thumb. During this torture, he kept his wits about him by continuously murmuring: "Jesus, Mary, and Joseph."[9] After Jogues and Goupil had recovered somewhat from this ordeal, they continued to serve both Mohawk and Huron patients in captured Huron villages and hospitals. The significance of missionaries whose fingers and thumbs were cut off for all their efforts—particularly Goupil as a deaf man who may have used his hands to communicate—is not lost on Catholics who use sign language. Pope Urban VIII read accounts of Jesuit missionaries in Canada with great interest. He thought of Isaac Jogues as a living martyr and granted him a dispensation to celebrate Mass without a thumb and index finger, once exclaiming, "It would be shameful that a martyr of Christ be not allowed to drink the blood of Christ."[10]

Thanks to Abbé Jogues, René Goupil was finally able to consecrate his life as a brother in the Society of Jesus before he died. One day during their captivity, he said to Jogues: "God has always given me a great desire of consecrating myself to His holy service by the vows of religion in His Holy Society; till now, my sins have rendered me unworthy of this grace; yet I hope that our Lord will accept the offering I wish to make Him now, and to take, in the best manner I can, the vows of the Society, in the presence of my God and before you."[11] Jogues readily assented, and Goupil

---

9. Jogues, *Narrative of a Captivity among the Mohawk Indians,* 63.

10. Francis Xavier Talbot, *Saint among Savages: The Life of Saint Isaac Jogues* (San Francisco: Ignatius Press, 2002), 350.

11. Jogues, *Narrative of a Captivity among the Mohawk Indians,* 63.

pronounced his vows with care. Soon afterward, while treating Mohawk patients in a cabin set up as a hospital, an elder Mohawk man happened to see Goupil affectionately make the sign of the cross over a small child in his care. The Mohawk believed that conversion to Christianity and abandonment of their native religion could cause them to cease to exist as a people, so Goupil's sign of the cross was, to them, a life-or-death threat. Because of this, the Mohawk council decided to execute him: they commanded a young brave to kill him, which he did by approaching Goupil with a hatchet concealed under a blanket, then striking him a mortal blow to the back of the head. Jogues quickly administered last rights as Goupil lay dying, and Mohawk youngsters dragged his body into a ravine to be devoured by dogs, foxes, and crows. Jogues later found and buried his friend's skull and a few bones, but the river had swept away most of the remains. Jogues himself survived long enough to escape with some Dutch traders a year later, but as soon as he was able, he returned to the Hurons of New France and to martyrdom at the hands of the Iroquois.

Today, the Shrine of the North American Martyrs in Auriesville, New York, protects the entire ravine as a reliquary of Saint René Goupil and honors Isaac Jogues and six other Jesuit martyrs along with Saint Kateri Tekakwitha, a Mohawk Christian from the village of Ossernenon and the first person born in North America to be canonized as a saint. There can be no clearer example of colonial-era missionary zeal for souls than these Jesuit martyrs, who were so eager to lay down their lives in the process of evangelization, even to the point of torture and martyrdom.[12] Today, René Goupil is venerated widely among Deaf Catholics in North America, who never fail to recognize that he was a deaf man who died because he made a sign with his hand—the sign of the cross. Ironically, Jogues's narrative reveals that Goupil believed, until impending death, that he was unworthy of membership in the Society of Jesus. His own words suggest a belief that his deafness, because it rendered him unable to complete the novitiate, was a result of his own personal sins.

12. Emma Anderson explores some of the questions surrounding the apparent eagerness for death of the North American martyrs, the lives and deaths of Native American Catholics and non-Catholics evangelized by the Jesuit missionaries, and the history of the veneration of these saints (in *The Death and Afterlife of the North American Martyrs* [Cambridge: Cambridge University Press, 2013]). While some of her investigation emphasizes a lack of lasting, popular veneration for the North American martyrs, it is worth mentioning that the Deaf Catholic community's appropriation of René Goupil is a clear example of expansion in the martyrs' veneration. Moreover, the Deaf Catholic community focuses not so much on any suspected desire on Goupil's part to die for his faith in order to gain heaven but rather his eagerness to evangelize and to serve God through the Society of Jesus, never counting the costs and accepting any and all hardships.

In addition to Goupil, a second late-deafened martyr is gaining devotion among Deaf Catholics interviewed for this book. Saint Manuel Barbal Cosan (or Jaime Hilario, as he was called in his religious order) is one of eleven canonized martyrs of the Spanish Civil War. He entered the minor seminary in Urgel, Spain, in 1910 when he was twelve years old, but the headmaster promptly sent him home when he developed a hearing loss. Persistent in the pursuit of his religious vocation, Cosan was overjoyed when the De La Salle Brothers accepted him into their novitiate at the age of nineteen. He taught school for sixteen years before progressive deafness, in the absence of a sign language community, forced him into a role requiring very little communication. For the remainder of his years, he served the order as a gardener.

After the Spanish Civil War broke out, during a period of enforced secularization, fascist forces captured and imprisoned Cosan with others in his order. When his captors brought him before the People's Tribunal in 1937, Cosan's lawyer advised him to say that he was only a gardener, but he refused to deny that he was indeed a Christian Brother. Consequently, he was condemned to death. As he was led to execution, he told those around him, "God be blessed! In heaven I shall pray a great deal for all of you. What more could I ask for than to die, when my only crime is that I am a religious and that I have worked for the Christian education of youth?" After the gunmen fired, they were astounded to find Cosan still standing, only slightly wounded, with arms crossed over his chest and eyes raised to heaven. The gunmen ran away shouting "A miracle!"— but the commander, infuriated, walked directly to Cosan and shot him five times at close range.[13] Pope John Paul II canonized him, along with eleven other martyrs of the Spanish Civil War, on November 21, 1999.

For Deaf Catholic communities around the world, it is comforting and encouraging to have these saints as part of their Catholic heritage. De Sales's catechetical use of sign language and the brave martyrdom of Goupil and Cosan are iconic examples of faith for hearing and deaf people alike. However, none of the saints in these stories provide a cultural role model of faith for deaf individuals whose primary mode of communication is sign language. De Sales is an inspiring example for missionaries and educators of deaf people like those described in the remainder of this chapter, but little is known about Martin, who benefited from de Sales's charity, pastoral attentiveness, and holiness. Rather than identi-

---

13. "Sanctity amid the Sounds of Silence," *Our Sunday Visitor* (January 12, 2003): 12.

fy with de Sales as a teacher, a deaf person might naturally put himself in the place of Martin, whose traditionally interpreted role is receiving instruction and protection from a saintly bishop who has learned sign language for his benefit. As for Goupil, his role was to use his healing hands to evangelize with the Jesuits in the New World, despite rejection from their seminary because of his deafness. Such stories show the love of Christ in action, but the roles they imagine for deaf people are contextualized by the hearing, speaking culture in which the stories take place. Eventually, the development of sign language education and early deaf missions would contribute a variety of new role models for Deaf Catholics, including consecrated life and holy orders. In fact, the very order that initially rejected René Goupil's religious vocation, the Society of Jesus, would be one of the first to admit congenitally deaf men in the twentieth century.

Religious Orders with Traditions of Serving Deaf People

Just as saints provide human role models for individual Catholics as they live out their Christian faith, the church as a whole offers an abundance of models for understanding its mission as the people of God. In the Second Vatican Council's Dogmatic Constitution of the Church (*Lumen Gentium*), one such model speaks to the role of religious orders and their diverse traditions of service: "As on a tree which has grown in the field of the Lord, various forms of solidarity and community life, as well as various religious families, have branched out in a marvelous and multiple ways from this divinely given seed."[14] At the dawn of the nineteenth century, as religious orders in the Western world developed new ways to order their members' lives of consecrated service, certain branches of the church's growing family tree inclined toward traditions of service to deaf people. As *Lumen Gentium* would explain of religious orders in general, these orders contributed as much to the spiritual progress of their hearing members as they did to the welfare of those they served.

It is no exaggeration to say that some religious orders—Dominican Sisters, Sisters of St. Joseph, Canossian Daughters of Charity, Gualandi

14. Vatican Council II, Dogmatic Constitution *Lumen Gentium* (hereafter, *LG*), no. 43 (November 21, 1964), in *The Sixteen Documents of Vatican II*, trans. N.C.W.C. (Boston: Daughters of St. Paul).

Mission for the Deaf, the St. Vincent de Paul Society, Jesuits, Redemptorists, and several others—participated in the Catholic enculturation of deaf people in the most creative sense. As these orders formed relationships with groups of deaf people throughout Europe and the Americas, they fostered the existence of deaf culture and sign language by helping deaf people come together from dispersed and isolated conditions. Men and women with religious vocations contributed to Deaf Catholic heritage by founding schools for deaf children, making religious rituals and prayers more inclusive, providing job training, enabling civic participation, and encouraging marriages between deaf people who used sign language. Many ultimately became fluent in sign language themselves, and over time the people they served welcomed them as adopted members of the deaf community.

It was comparatively rare that a diocesan priest would be able to engage in deaf ministry or education full time, because he had so many regular pastoral and parochial duties, and many bishops were slow to assign a priest to full-time ministry of the deaf. Furthermore, because deaf people were a small minority and widely dispersed, most parish priests encountered very few deaf people in their parish. As a result of these conditions in parish life, the language barrier for deaf people caused many simply to avoid attending any religious services. All of this made deaf people practically invisible to most parish priests.

In contrast, religious orders were founded in response to a need in society or in the church. Often, religious orders were oriented toward responding to underserved groups of people, and this tendency made them more involved than parish clergy in the development of new services for populations of Catholics and non-Catholics. In other words, active orders of religious men and women (as opposed to cloistered, contemplative communities) developed new apostolates through evangelization and works of mercy. Frequently, members of religious orders lived and worked with poor or marginalized populations, serving them directly by providing health care or education. The same happened when religious orders began to serve the deaf community in the eighteenth and nineteenth centuries. More than other Catholics, men and women in religious orders could live immersed in the language and culture of deaf children and adults, sometimes for a few years, but in exemplary cases for a lifetime.

What was it about these religious orders that led men and women to

devote the whole of their lives to serving deaf people, often in isolated
and impoverished conditions? To answer this question, it is best to start
with the general population's view of deaf people during the era under
consideration. In 1896, Mr. L. W. Reilly wrote a description of the deaf
population for the *American Ecclesiastical Review* that provides a clear
picture of both the discriminatory (perhaps oralist) attitudes about deafness and the abandonment commonly faced by deaf people because of
their language difference:

The condition of the uneducated deaf-mute is pitiful. Walled in by silence, solitary, ignorant, unable to communicate with his kind except by sounds and harsh
cries, treated as a pariah that is a shame and burden to his family, shut out from
the enjoyments of refined society, incompetent to earn a decent living, hopeless
of a career of distinction, untaught by religion, he grows up little better than an
animal, dwarfed in soul, stunted in intellect, caring only for physical comforts,
envious of more fortunate men, malicious, spiteful, bitter, and consumed with
silent discontentment for the fate that has made him as he is. Unless religion
brings to his aid fortitude to bear his cross in patience, and grace to make a virtue
of necessity, his affliction is apt to be a hindrance to the attainment of his end
here and hereafter.[15]

For men and women with a religious vocation for acts of mercy or the
saving of souls, this kind of language—pernicious as it may seem to modern readers—could only be a call to lay down one's life to save desperate and suffering human beings who were so clearly among "the least of
these" brothers and sisters (Mt 24:40). In religious orders of the nineteenth century, radically self-sacrificing individuals were ready to do just
that, and their devotion was not wasted on the grateful and often indus-
trious deaf community.

It would be difficult, perhaps even impossible, to introduce every
Catholic religious order that developed traditions of service to deaf people during the eighteenth and nineteenth centuries. Such a list would
undoubtedly leave some orders out, as there is no one central listing of
historical schools and ministries for deaf apostolates around the world.
Points of cultural contact between the church and the deaf community
sprouted up when and where the need arose, through charity or for purposes of education. In a historical overview such as this, the necessity of
choosing representative examples limits a sense of the great variety and

---

15. L. W. Reilly, "The Education of Catholic Deaf-Mutes in the United States," *Ecclesiastical
Review* 14, no. 4 (April 1896): 289.

scope of religious traditions of service to deaf people. A clearer picture of Deaf Catholic heritage can only develop as historians continue to expand and connect these examples.

In Europe, one of the most notable orders to begin serving deaf people during the nineteenth century is the Gualandi Little Mission for the Deaf (known in Italy as the Piccola Missione per i Sordomuti). The Gualandi Mission is unique in that it was founded specifically to meet the needs of the deaf apostolate, and this remains its sole purpose today. For this reason, it is a good example of how religious orders responded to the needs of deaf people and how the Deaf Catholic community, in turn, developed with the help and influence of these orders. The idea for a Gualandi Little Mission for the Deaf was born in 1849 during an encounter between a twenty-year-old deaf girl, Carolina Galuppini, and the future founder of the mission, Padre Giuseppe Gualandi, a young diocesan priest from Bologna who was only twenty-two at the time. During a Mass for First Communion, Gualandi observed Carolina, who was much older than the other girls taking part in the sacrament, looking lost and confused. Gualandi began to understand that Carolina and others like her were socially and educationally isolated by the language barrier of deafness, and therefore unschooled in their religion. After visiting a Catholic oral school for the deaf in Modena, Gualandi decided to dedicate his life's work to the education and evangelization of "deafmutes" in his own diocese of Bologna, and his bishop graciously encouraged him. There were several Italian oral schools for the deaf already in operation, most of them begun by religious orders that were active in other ministries as well. Gualandi received his training as a deaf educator at the Pendola Institute in Siena, which was founded in the early 1820s. In 1850, Guiseppe Gualandi and his brother Padre Cesare Gualandi founded the Gualandi Institute, the mission's first school for the deaf in Bologna. The school used a variety of methods but, after 1872, focused on the oral method that prevailed in Italian deaf education at the time.

In 1872, Gualandi's mission started two religious congregations, one for women and one for men, both approved by Cardinal Carlo Luigi Morichini of Bologna. Since its official establishment as a religious order, the goal and spirit of the Gualandi Little Mission of the Deaf was to foster the intellectual, moral, religious, and social education of deaf people. Toward this goal, the rule of the order required every member to consecrate "all his intelligence, his energy, and his activities, that is, his whole self, for the love of God and the salvation of souls of the deaf." The order served the spiritual welfare of deaf people through daily prayers, educational institutions, catechism, and pastoral assistance. In their practice of spirituality, members strove daily "to see in deaf people, as in the least and suffering among our neighbors, the person of Jesus Christ who teaches that whatever we do to the least of our brothers and sisters, we also do to him."[16]

The Gualandi brothers extended their mission in the nineteenth century by establishing an institute in Rome in 1884 and another in Florence in 1885, while the sisters began a school for deaf-blind children in Guilianova. As was often the case in European nations, each of these schools eventually received full funding and recognition from the government. As in other European nations where schools for the deaf were founded in this period, the very presence of the schools encouraged the development of deaf communities in their respective cities. Brothers of the Gualandi Little Mission were sent to learn the educational methods of Abbé l'Épée and Abbé Sicard in France, and the mission began to incorporate their philosophy of "learning through the eye." For the most part, their schools retained oral methods in the classroom but, eventually, the Gualandi Mission grew to include social services, job training, and adult ministry in Italian sign language as natural extensions of their support for the deaf community. By the early twentieth century, the congregation for men (called the Fathers of the Little Mission for the Deaf today) had furthered their missionary reach by starting a school for deaf children in Brazil, and the Sisters of the Little Mission for the Deaf founded the Benevento Institute for the Deaf in the Philippines, which still has several outreach activities in Manila, Naga, and Cebu.[17] Eventually, the order welcomed deaf members and volunteers, coming full circle in their mission to include deaf people fully in all aspects of the life of the church.

In the United States, the development of deaf ministries by Catholic religious orders took place in a very different cultural context than those in the Catholic nations of Europe and their colonial areas of expansion. In the United States, the work of Catholic religious orders was part of a

16. "Goal and Spirit of the Mission," Gualandi Mission for the Deaf, http://gualandimission.blog spot.com/2009/05/goal-and-spirit-of-mission-1.html.

17. Franco Zatini, "Istituto Gualandi per i Sordomuti e le Sordomute in Bologna, 1850," Storia De i Sordi, accessed June 30, 2017, http://www.storiadeisordi.it/2005/10/26/1850-istituto-gualandi -per-i-sordomuti-e-le-sordomute-in-bologna-casa-madre/.

larger trend that included the widespread expansion of Protestant evangelism and, as a result, stiff competition with Protestant denominations for the hearts and souls of deaf people.

Compared to Protestant deaf communities, the Catholic Church in America was late in encouraging deaf adult faith communities who wished to worship together in sign language—and therefore late in developing deaf religious vocations. The Episcopal Church ordained congenitally and culturally deaf priests in the United States in the United States decades before deaf priestly vocations became possible in the Catholic Church. The first deaf Episcopal priest was the Rev. Henry Winter Style, a student and parishioner of Rev. Thomas Gallaudet, who had begun St. Ann's Church for the Deaf in New York in 1852. Style was ordained a deacon in 1876, and in 1884 he became the first Deaf Episcopal priest in America. He established All Soul's Church, a congregation for deaf people in Philadelphia, in 1888. Both he and Gallaudet are commemorated in the Episcopal calendar of saints found in the Book of Common Prayer. During the 1890s, a second deaf pastor, Rev. J. M. Keohler, succeeded Style at All Souls Church and began regular missionary excursions throughout Pennsylvania. The 1880s and 1890s include many such examples: Rev. B. O. Dantzer, a deaf man who grew up in a Catholic family in central New York, converted from Catholicism to the Episcopal Church so that he could fulfill his priestly vocation in the growing Protestant Deaf community. There he was welcomed and able to perform all the duties of his office, including preaching and pastoral ministry in sign language. The Rev. Job Turner, also deaf, led missions in sign language throughout Virginia and adjoining states. Rev. J. H. Cloud, also deaf, did the same in Missouri.[18]

These nineteenth-century Protestant pastors and missionaries had the time and the means for full-time service to the deaf community. In addition to holding religious services in sign language, they kept track of all the deaf people living in their territories, invited them to reunions and revivals, found them employment, and empathized with them as deaf adults and fluent users of their native language—all remarkably like the work of a minister assigned to work with an immigrant community. Beginning in 1881, they organized their efforts and shared methods at a biennial meeting, the American Conference of Church Workers among the Deaf. In light of this developing inclusion for deaf people in Protes-

18. Reilly, "The Education of Catholic Deaf-Mutes," 292.

tant America, the time was sorely overdue for Catholic pastoral leaders who could communicate with deaf people in the language they used in their own homes and communities.

However, the first step toward evangelizing and developing a Deaf Catholic community in the United States would not be deaf clergy or preaching in sign language. As in Europe, the first step was the establishment of Catholic schools for deaf children. Protestant Deaf communities in nineteenth-century America were thriving: they baptized adult believers and ordained deaf clergy. For Catholics, however, it was schools—almost all of them founded by religious orders—that developed the deaf apostolate by providing religious education and pastoral care. Like "common school" education for hearing children across the United States, the curricula of public schooling for deaf students was fueled by a desire to produce good citizens schooled in reading, writing, and arithmetic; however, public schooling was often morally aligned to teach civic virtues that were derived from the prevailing Protestant social values of the day. In mainstream schools and schools for deaf students alike, this often included overt anti-Catholic indoctrination. American Catholic schools for deaf children ensured a future for educated deaf adults who remained connected to their community through Catholic religion and culture. Some schools used oral methods of education, while others had begun to use sign language in the classroom following the lead of pioneering educators such as Abbe l'Épée, Rev. Gallaudet, and Laurent Clerc. Among the most fruitful in numbers of students served was the Congregation of the Sisters of St. Joseph, who founded schools in St. Louis, Boston, California, and two in New York State. Because of their broad influence on deaf ministry in the United States, the Sisters of St. Joseph will be treated at length in the next chapter.

Even during the peak of their existence, the regions served by U.S. Catholic schools for deaf children were limited to densely populated cities on the East Coast and in the mid-Atlantic and Midwest. In spite of this geographic limit, a simple list of religious orders that founded these nineteenth or early twentieth-century schools is enough to suggest a Catholic social movement toward meeting the needs of the deaf community and including them in the life of the church: The Society of the Daughters of the Heart of Mary (Nardines) ran the Ephpheta School in Chicago, along with St. Joseph School for the Deaf in the Bronx (New York City) and St. Mary Institute for Deaf Mutes in St. Paul, Minnesota. The Sisters of Charity of Seton Hill in Greensburg, Pennsylvania, founded De Paul Institute for the Deaf. The Sisters of Charity of Cincinnati (an offshoot of Saint Elizabeth Ann Seton's community) founded St. Rita School for the Deaf. In Baltimore, the Mission Helpers of the Sacred Heart founded St. Francis Xavier School for the Deaf, and this same order established San Gabriel School for the Deaf in Puerto Rico. Other orders that founded U.S. schools included Sisters of St. Francis of Assisi in Milwaukee (St. John School for the Deaf); the School Sisters of Notre Dame in New Orleans and Cincinnati; the Sisters of the Holy Cross in Notre Dame, Indiana; and the Sisters of Loretto in Kentucky. Religious orders in Canada also participated in the movement to educate deaf children. The Sisters of Providence and the Little Sisters of Our Lady of Seven Sorrows ran a school for the deaf in Montreal, and the Congregation of the Clerics of St. Viator, who participated in St. Joseph's School for the Deaf in the Bronx, also started a school for deaf boys in Montreal, Quebec.

Some religious orders that founded schools for the deaf in eighteenth- and nineteenth-century Europe and America have detractors in deaf history, especially because of their use of certain educational methods that remain a source of controversy. Like the earliest saints remembered for their service to deaf people, the first religious orders with strong traditions of deaf ministry viewed deafness as a disability in the long-held conventional way, rather than as a language or cultural difference. The tendency in nineteenth-century education, in general, was to segregate children with learning differences in separate "asylums" or residential institutions. This removed them from the culture of their homes so that deaf children often became detached from their families of origin. Harsh educational methods, especially in schools that demanded and enforced oral-only communication, left many deaf adults with memories of frustration and a sense of failure in the classroom. Most of these negative effects occurred in schools where there was forced oralism and a misunderstanding of natural methods of communication that many deaf people develop with each other—making loud, non-speech sounds that they may or may not hear, banging furniture to make vibrations, or touching others more than hearing people do in the process of communication. Much of the strictness in deaf education stemmed from faulty perceptions and received prejudices of these natural aspects of communication that occur when deaf people are brought together. For example, an 1886 article on St. Joseph's Institute for Deaf Mutes in New York noted, "In the uninstructed deaf mute certain instincts of an animal nature incline to strong development, and it takes long and patient training and teaching to bring them under habitual restraint."[19]

Regardless of methods used in the classroom, however, religious orders helped to facilitate and preserve Deaf Catholic culture—to redeem it, even—as alumni of the schools tended to keep in close contact, gradually forming lasting communities that wished to share and perpetuate their Catholic faith in sign language. Unfortunately, most U.S. Catholic schools for deaf children faced problems that were finally insurmountable. Unlike their counterparts in predominantly Catholic countries like France or Ireland, few American Catholic schools for the deaf received state support. With the exception of three schools founded by the Sisters of St. Joseph, one in Boston and two in New York State, Catholic schools for deaf children operated solely from charitable contributions and tuition—and students were never turned away, even when parents could not afford to pay tuition. In addition to these financial problems, a shortage of trained teachers caused several schools to close their doors. Finally, most of these schools could not overcome their financial hardships and teacher shortages, and by the 1950s most had disbanded, especially the residential schools.[20] Only three thriving Catholic residential schools for deaf children survived into the mid-twentieth century: St. Rita's in Cincinnati, St. Mary's in Buffalo, and St. John's in St. Francis, Wisconsin.

As the needs of deaf children became more widely recognized in Europe and North America, diocesan priests and, in time, lay pastoral workers began to include deaf adults in the established life of local churches. In some areas, religious orders formed long-lasting relationships with dioceses that contained large populations of deaf people, and permanent Deaf Catholic communities with strong sign language resources developed in those places. By the twentieth century, ministry carried out by religious orders in North America and several European nations progressed to include not only schools for deaf children but also cultural programs for adults and opportunities for frequent fellowship in sign language. This, in turn, created further opportunities for local deaf communities to grow and develop. Marriages among Deaf Catholics

19. "St. Joseph's Institute for the Improved Instruction of Deaf Mutes," The Catholic Charities of New York, *The Catholic World* XLIII, no. 253 (September 1886): 815–16.

20. Mary E. Stone and Joseph P. Youngs, "Catholic Education of the Deaf in the United States, 1837–1948," *American Annals of the Deaf* 93, no. 5 (November 1948): 470–78.

took place with more frequency, and a Deaf Catholic way of life began to take root.

As deaf ministry moved into the twentieth century, religious orders would follow this same pattern of deaf education and missionary development in Latin America, Africa, and pockets of India and Asia. Many of these orders, like those described in chapter 3, were associations of highly capable and well-educated Catholic women. As a next step, and sometimes simultaneously, traveling missionary priests—usually also members of religious orders—began to organize mission trips and retreats, visiting several dioceses per trip in regions where parish churches had no sign language services. As generations of young deaf adults graduated from Catholic schools, and as more immigrant populations arrived in North and South America from European nations, the expanding Deaf Catholic apostolate continued to develop in several regions around the world. Developments in public deaf education and Protestant deaf evangelism also helped to raise awareness about deafness, and this in turn expanded Catholic awareness about the often-invisible needs of deaf people in their parishes and dioceses.

The next two chapters offer examples of specific Catholic traditions of service to deaf people from the eighteenth to the early twentieth centuries, especially those that developed ministries in sign language. First, we turn to stories from the daily lives of religious sisters who established active deaf ministries (especially, though not exclusively, in the form of schools). Then, we take a close look at two orders of priests with strong traditions of mission work in sign language, Jesuits and Redemptorists. Through the efforts of these orders to address the needs of deaf people, models of Deaf Catholic life would expand from hearing people almost exclusively to people who communicated the faith in sign language.

CHAPTER 3

Women in Deaf Ministry

During the Industrial Revolution, the hardworking heroes of Catholic deaf education were undoubtedly women in religious orders who devoted their lives to serving this population. As historians of women's history have often noted, roles for women expand during times of crisis and when there are opportunities for economic and social development. Historical periods of depression, disease, food scarcity, and immigration all presented a demand for religious women specializing in education, social services, and health care. Because the language disparity of deaf people was so difficult to overcome, this population was often among the poorest and most marginalized members of society during times of economic and social crisis. For this reason, during the eighteenth, nineteenth, and early twentieth centuries, Catholic bishops and priests frequently called upon groups of religious women—who greatly outnumbered men in Catholic religious vocations for much of Christian history—to develop social service programs and education for deaf children and adults.[1]

Most of the orders profiled here lived and worked in Europe or North America, but religious sisters also developed educational institutions for deaf children in non-Western regions, some of which will be covered in later chapters. Each of these orders founded schools or charitable social services and devoted their lives to running them, often without ongoing financial support from church or government. Moreover, they routinely

1. By 1920 in the United States alone, approximately ninety thousand women in over three hundred separate religious communities worked in education, health care, and social services during the nineteenth century. By the mid-twentieth century, their number had doubled. For an excellent account of religious sisters during this period of American life, see Carol K. Coburn and Martha Smith, *Spirited Lives: How Nuns Shaped Catholic Culture and American Life, 1836–1920* (Chapel Hill: University of North Carolina Press, 2017).

did so in the face of biting poverty and harsh living conditions in industrial cities. In their bravery and devotion, these women laid the ground-
work that, in time, would enable Deaf Catholic culture to grow and to
flourish. Truth be told, this short chapter cannot do justice to the tremendous part religious sisters played in deaf history, and there remains
much work for historians in developing a complete picture of their role
in the development of deaf culture and heritage.

Many a Catholic school graduate tells stories of a stern nun or sister
who kept perfect order, perhaps even with a wooden ruler, in an over-
crowded classroom of forty or fifty hearing third graders. Religious sisters in deaf education likewise earned a reputation for being strict, but
almost always for the sake of their pupils' survival in the mainstream
hearing world. With few exceptions, they devoted almost all their resources to their students. They were also generous with their methods,
sharing new pedagogy with others who wished to start schools for the
deaf in their own regions or abroad. For example, a community of the
Sisters of Charity of Nevers (one of the many daughter organizations of
the Sisters of Charity of St. Vincent de Paul) were the primary educators
at the Institute for Deaf Girls founded in Bordeaux, France, in 1786. This
Institute was a large residential school for girls from all over the country,
founded by Jérôme-Marie Champion de Cicé, archbishop of Bordeaux.
The school's first director, Abbé Sicard himself, traveled to Paris to receive training as a deaf educator from Abbé de l'Épée. He then trained
the Sisters of Nevers using l'Épée's methods at the Institute in Bordeaux
until 1789, when he succeeded l'Épée as director of the National Institute
for the Deaf in Paris. Orders of French sisters like this one would, in turn,
train many international sisters who came to learn l'Épée's and Sicard's
successful methods of educating deaf children. As we shall see in chapter
4, the Sisters of Nevers at Bordeaux also became an early inspiration for
the first "deaf-mute" Catholic priest, a development that would give the
world an example for deaf leadership and enculturation in sign language.

The Dominican Sisters of Cabra in Ireland

A particularly successful example of missionary activity and fruitful
enculturation evolved from a nineteenth-century partnership between
French and Irish religious sisters. The dream of Fr. Thomas McNamara, a
Vincentian priest, became a reality in 1846 when Mary Vincent Martin

and Magdalen O'Farrell, two Irish Dominican Sisters of Mercy from the township of Cabra north of Dublin, traveled to France to learn methods of educating deaf children from the Daughters of the Bon Sauveur (another offshoot of the Sisters of Charity of St. Vincent de Paul). The Irish Dominican sisters brought with them their first two deaf pupils, Agnes Beedam and Mary Anne Dougherty, and set out for the Le Bon Sauveur School in Caen, France. There, in addition to learning French sign language from the French deaf students and their educators, the sisters followed the ancient monastic tradition of painstakingly copying by hand and translating into English a hefty dictionary of sign vocabulary, along with descriptions of how to use these signs in sentences that mimicked spoken-language grammar. Through the Dominican sisters' educational mission work, the resulting verbal descriptions of signs influenced both secular and religious vocabulary in sign languages all over Europe and the Americas, and eventually in Australia, Africa, and Asia as well. Later, the Dominican Sisters of Cabra added their pupils' own native Irish signs to the manuscript, rounding out a uniquely Irish vocabulary of signs that represented an early form of Irish Sign Language and, later, some English sign dialects.

That same year (1846), the Dominican sisters returned to Cabra and opened St. Mary's School for Deaf Girls. The newly trained instructors tutored fifteen pupils daily in a sitting room in the Dominican sisters' residence. This number grew to ninety by 1848, requiring a new school building. A second Vincentian priest, Fr. John Burke, was appointed chaplain of the school in 1851. He further established the sisters' "Cabra Method" of language training based on his own studies of l'Épée, Sicard, and the Caen language program of signs used in the order of spoken English. In 1857, he established a second institution, St. Joseph's School for Deaf Boys, administered and run by the Christian Brothers.[2] The influence of these schools on Irish Sign Language was formative. Against the oralist advice of the 1880 International Congress on Deaf Education in Milan, the Dominican sisters in Cabra did not ban sign language or the employment of deaf teachers, and as a result, Irish Sign Language and Irish deaf culture have a traceable history infused with strong Catholic heritage, even while the rest of Europe and much of America experienced what deaf people now call the "dark age" of oralist education.

---

2. Noel P. O'Connell, "A Tale of Two Schools: Educating Catholic Female Deaf Children in Ireland, 1846–1946," *History of Education* 45, no. 2 (2016): 188–205.

Sign language was used for instruction at both schools until 1946 when they finally began to incorporate oralist methods. Even today, deaf men and women in Ireland have dialectical differences in their sign language traceable to the Catholic schools' separation by sexes.[3]

By the late nineteenth century, the Irish Dominican sisters added vocational programs in sewing and lace-making for the girls, as well as a teacher-training program that contributed to an international influence rivaling that of French educators of the deaf around the world. In 1875, Sister Mary Gabriel Hogan—herself a former pupil of St. Mary's and the first profoundly deaf nun to take vows at Cabra—completed this teacher training program before traveling to New South Wales, Australia, where she established the Wanrath School for the Deaf. In 1890, two Irish Dominican sisters, Sister Patrick McQuillan and Sister Augustine Hayden, in cooperation with the School Sisters of Notre Dame from Milwaukee, established the Chinchuba Institute for the Deaf in Louisiana—the first residential school for deaf pupils south of St. Louis. The Dominican sisters' influence continued into the twentieth century as Mother Nicolas Griffey initiated a degree program in Deaf Education at the University College Dublin in 1957; Mother Nicholas also expanded international ties between Deaf Catholic communities as a founding member of the International Catholic Foundation for the Service of Deaf Persons (discussed in part II).[4] Although deaf ministry in Cabra has passed mostly to the leadership of deaf laypeople today, the sisters' influence can still be felt in the schools, as well as in the broader context of Deaf Village Ireland (DVI), a deaf-run complex at the original site of nineteenth-century deaf ministries. Unique in its scope, the DVI offers visually accessible, open-concept spaces for religious, community, sports, heritage, and educational activities, providing a range of facilities for deaf and hearing people in a bilingual setting (Irish Sign Language and English), all under deaf leadership.

The sisters in Cabra performed heroic acts of mercy and charity during dire periods of Irish history, many of which the Deaf Heritage Society at Cabra has preserved. Without the sisters, literally thousands of children could have died in poverty, and Cabra would never have

3. "Irish Sign Language," Ethnologue Languages of the World, accessed January 23, 2019, https://www.ethnologue.com/language/isg.

4. Mother Nicholas Griffey published an autobiography of her years of service to the Irish Deaf community, *From Silence to Speech: Fifty Years with the Deaf, Dominican Sisters* (Dublin: Dominican Publications, 1994).

evolved into the influential center of deaf culture that exists there today. During the nineteenth-century potato famine, many families placed
their deaf children in the sisters' residential school because there was no
food for them at home—if there was a home. Their families were starving
and broken. Many young minds were educated by these sisters, and many
young lives were saved. Their acts of mercy and social service are comparable to a later order of sisters who, in the twentieth century, devoted
their lives to working with deaf people in Manchester, England.

The Sisters of Evron in Manchester

The Sisters of Charity of Our Lady of Evron trace their origins to the
Mayenne province of France, where a young widow named Perinne Bru-
net founded a Vincentian-influenced society of women who consecrated
themselves to God while teaching and serving the poor. In the early years
of the twentieth century after the French separation of church and state,
the order expanded its horizons by sending groups of sisters to found
missions in other countries where there was a need for their services. In
Manchester, England, the sisters crossed paths with one of the most influential English apostles of deaf ministry, Canon Charles Hollywood,
and this fortuitous encounter yielded a tremendous outpouring of charity that resulted in improved standards of living for many in the deaf community. The example of the Sisters of Evron serves as a small but accurate
snapshot of the lives religious sisters led as they served Deaf Catholic
communities during times of crisis and pervasive poverty.

Charles Hollywood was ordained a priest in the Diocese of Salford
in 1960, but only after he had been rejected from the seminary in the
Diocese of Armagh, where it was discovered he had a hearing loss. Fortunately for the deaf community, the stone that was rejected became a
cornerstone in Salford, as Hollywood became one of the rare diocesan
clergy to focus on deaf ministry full time (his story appears in full in
chapter 6). It soon became apparent that Hollywood would need a great
deal of help to carry out his plans for expanding and improving deaf services in the diocese. In 1964, he advertised for a housekeeper for a newly
created hostel for elderly deaf people. One of the applicants for this job
asked if her sister might come along when she came to apply. Hollywood
thought it was a little strange for the woman to bring her sister along just
to apply for a job, but it was harmless enough, so he said that would be

fine. When the women arrived, the "sister" stepped out of the car in a black-and-white religious habit: she was Mother Superior of the Sisters of Charity of Evron. Hollywood and the Mother Superior began negotiations immediately and soon three young sisters arrived to begin work in the hostel. In time, there were new vocations to the order in Manchester, enhancing their work in both the hostel and the diocesan Deaf Catholic Club.[5] The sisters' mission and the growing Deaf Club that accompanied it moved several times in the diocese after its founding, but in each location, the growing community of sisters devoted themselves to religious education and works of charity on behalf of the deaf people of Salford. They visited the homes of deaf people to offer support, helped them find employment, and provided a place to live for those who were homeless or had multiple disabilities. Hundreds of deaf people lived in Manchester during this period, and the sisters greeted them at the Deaf Club with good cheer and hospitality, making enormous tubs of tea using stockings instead of tea bags. Like sisters in other orders with traditions of deaf ministry, the Sisters of Evron improved their credentials for social work by attending college courses and obtaining professional licenses. This paved the way for full recognition by government social service providers, but it also ensured a steady income from outside counseling that would support their primary work with deaf people. Achieving these credentials could be expensive, but the deaf community "gave back" by supporting the sisters in full solidarity. House-to-house collections were a primary source of income. Once, one of the sisters was arrested because she was unaware that collecting donations required a permit. "Before I left the station," she said, "I had a few good pounds from the police."[6]

The Sisters of Saint Joseph in America

In America, the Congregation of the Sisters of St. Joseph were among the first to gather and educate deaf children. This order was founded in the seventeenth century in Le Puy, France by Father Jean-Paul Médaille, a Jesuit missionary and close friend of St. Vincent de Paul. As Médaille envisioned it, this order existed "to perform all the spiritual and corporal

5. Terry O'Meara, interview by Marlana Portolano, St. Joseph Deaf Center, Manchester, England, July 9, 2016.

6. Sr. Maria McCreedy, interview by Marlana Portolano, St. Joseph Deaf Center, Manchester, England, July 10, 2016.

works of mercy of which woman is capable." The highly general scope of this charism led the Bishop of St. Louis, Missouri, Joseph Rosati (a Vincentian) to ask the order's superior to send several Sisters of St. Joseph from Lyon, France, in 1836. "The Sisters of St. Joseph will do anything," he was told. Their mission in St. Louis would be the education of deaf children from all over his diocese, at that time a vast territory from the Mississippi River westward throughout the territory of the Louisiana Purchase.

In a nation where anti-Catholic prejudice was pervasive and Catholic education was as yet largely undeveloped, the task of serving poor deaf children seemed to fit the Sisters of St. Joseph's aim of undertaking merciful works that others would not dare to try. After five harsh weeks at sea and a long steamboat ride up the Mississippi River, six Sisters of St. Joseph from Lyon arrived in Carondelet, just outside St. Louis. To their surprise, there was a need for religious sisters to travel in plain clothes to protect them from hostile encounters (less than two years before their arrival, Protestants had plundered and burned an Ursuline convent in Massachusetts).[7] Borrowing vocabulary from French Sign Language, the sisters began teaching in a small log cabin on the banks of the Mississippi River. With the help of a $2,000 annual appropriation from the Missouri State Legislature for children's tuition (approximately $50,000 today), ministry slowly grew. The most renowned administrator of the convent in Carondelet was Mother Mary Borgia, an expert in sign language and the education of deaf children who headed the congregation for over thirty years at the turn of the century. By 1908, the sisters purchased a school building and established residential housing for students sent from across the nation to attend the institution that is now called St. Joseph Institute for the Deaf—the first Deaf Catholic school in the United States. The congregation and their methods of educating deaf children spread rapidly, and between 1836 and 1889, forty-nine sisters arrived from France to educate deaf children in America.

As news of their success with deaf children spread, other bishops in the United States and Canada asked the Sisters of St. Joseph of Carondelet for professionally trained sisters to develop their dioceses' own deaf ministries (and other services as well). Soon the Sisters of St. Joseph had communities in several different North American cities, and some

---

7. Coburn and Smith, *Spirited Lives*, Introduction, 1–12.

of these satellite communities also sent out groups of sisters to still more dioceses needing help.[8] After training in Caen, France, three Sisters of St. Joseph transferred in 1857 from St. Louis to Buffalo, New York, explicitly to establish a school for the deaf. However, because the sisters had no external government or church support, it was necessary to start a regular (hearing) day-school that charged tuition before they could even begin work with their first four deaf pupils. By 1862, with help and support from Bishop Timon of Buffalo, they were able to steadily grow St. Mary's School for the Deaf, eventually receiving permission from the state legislature to allow children to live on campus as county beneficiaries. Hundreds of children were enrolled at any given time on their twenty-three-acre campus.

In 1847, at the request of Bishop Francis Patrick Kenrick of Philadelphia, a Sister of Saint Joseph named Mother Saint John Fournier arrived in that city to begin deaf ministry. She had trained with the Sisters of St. Charles in St. Étienne, France. After a slow start in Philadelphia, the sisters began religious education classes for students at the Philadelphia School for the Deaf and for other deaf children and adults in the area. Mother Arsenia Bradley began conducting these classes at the Cathedral Chapel, where she had unusual permission from the public school to take Catholic residential students on Sundays for Mass and instruction—as was their right under the Constitution's First Amendment.

One of these students, Bridget Hughes, became the order's first deaf vocation. After making a novena to St. Joseph one evening in her process of discernment, Bridget received a letter from a family friend, Archbishop James Frederick Wood. He wrote, "I want you to place yourself in my hands and I will make you a Sister of St. Joseph. God wants you to come to Philadelphia where there is no one to work for the deaf-mutes." She was deeply moved and surprised since it was the first novena she had ever made to St. Joseph. Afterward, Bridget—now known as Sister Patricia—entered the novitiate for the Sisters of St. Joseph and made her vows on August 16, 1880. Immediately she began teaching with Mother Arsenia at the Cathedral of Saints Peter and Paul in downtown Philadelphia. The first class of fifteen made their First Communion that year. Two new catechetical centers for deaf children opened shortly after, and diocesan priest Father P. M. Whelan instructed the adults in a hall a few doors

8. Coburn and Smith, *Spirited Lives*, Appendix VI.

away from one of the centers. All of this instruction, for both children and adults, was in sign language as these Catholics' native and primary language. Eventually, with the help of Sister Patricia's patient promotion with the bishop, the Archbishop Ryan School for the Deaf was founded in Philadelphia by four Sisters of St. Joseph in 1912.[9] From 1899 to 1994, the sisters also served as staff members at the Boston School for the Deaf.

For the first fifty years of their work in America, all the Sisters of St. Joseph used a method that combined sign language and speech training, with lipreading used when appropriate. However, in 1870, Professor Alexander Graham Bell trained two of the sisters in St. Louis in "visible speech," after which the order gradually dropped the French sign language method in favor of an oral method. By the turn of the century, the Sisters of St. Joseph became mindful of "best practices" recommended at the Milan Conference along with technological advancements in hearing assistance devices. At that time, the sisters made a dramatic shift in their educational method from using sign language in the classroom to teaching children how to listen and imitate speech. While controversial in retrospect, especially for those in the deaf signing community today, this significant change once again established the Sisters of St Joseph as leaders in current trends of deaf education. State schools were springing up across the country at the time, and many of these retained sign language later into the twentieth century, although Catholics often considered state schools spiritually dangerous because of strong anti-Catholic bias in the early twentieth century. By encouraging the active involvement of Catholic parents in their educational program, the Sisters of St. Joseph were among the first educators to offer family-centered early intervention for deaf infants and preschoolers, advances in telecommunications, and, most recently, curricula and methodology focused on cochlear implant rehabilitation. Today, a Catholic day school in this tradition, the Archbishop Ryan Academy for the Deaf in Philadelphia, offers a thoroughly bilingual and bicultural program in American Sign Language and spoken and written English. Over the years, deaf education grew and changed in many ways through the influence of the Sisters of St. Joseph of Carondelet, and the sisters' programs kept up with developments in deaf education.

9. Anthony Russo, *In Silent Prayer: A History of Ministry with the Deaf Community in the Archdiocese of Philadelphia* (Garden City Park, N.Y.: Square One Publishers, 2008), 10–26.

Other North American Churchwomen
in Deaf Ministry

The Ephpheta School in Chicago was particularly important to Deaf Catholic heritage. Here both religious sisters and Catholic laywomen played founding roles. In 1884, Mrs. Nancy Jones called a meeting of several prominent Catholic ladies in Chicago after learning that her housekeeper's deaf daughter had no Catholic school to attend in the city. With the Jesuit Father Arnold Damen and Redemptorist Father Henry Meurer, they proposed to open an institution for the moral, mental, and industrial training of deaf youngsters. The school began that autumn, and the Daughters of the Heart of Mary took charge of operations. By 1886, the need for a boarding school became apparent, and the school moved into St. Joseph's Home and set up accommodations for boarders, where the annual average enrollment was over one hundred by the turn of the century. By 1913, the school listed nearly eight hundred deaf children. In addition to a regular common school curriculum, the girls learned mechanical drawing, wood carving, sewing, needlework, cooking, and housekeeping. Boys learned trades, including stone cutting, wood carving, and printing. The students also helped to write, illustrate, and print *The Voice of the Deaf*, a newsletter for Deaf Catholics with subscribers in several states where residential deaf education had begun to form sign language communities.[10] In each American diocese where Deaf Catholic schools developed, lasting deaf communities grew, and a population of Catholic families and individuals who needed ongoing religious services in sign language naturally followed. The same patterns were developing in deaf communities in Canada.

One Canadian order deserves special mention for efforts to promote religious vocations for young women who were deaf. In 1887, the Sisters of Providence in Montreal, Canada, built a novitiate house at the Montreal Institution des Sourdes-Muettes to establish a new branch of their community especially for deaf women. They named it the Little Sisters of Our Lady of Seven Sorrows (SSND).[11] The founding of the Little Sisters was a result of the longstanding Catholic administration of public schools and social work in the province of Quebec, combined

---

10. "A History of the Parishes of the Archdiocese of Chicago" (Observance of Centenary of the Archdiocese, 1980), Deaf Catholic Archives, College of the Holy Cross, Worcester, Mass.

11. In French: Sœurs de Notre-Dame des Sept Douleurs.

with the late nineteenth- and early twentieth-century trend of creating separate institutions or sanitariums for persons in different categories of physical and mental ability. In some ways, these sisters faced marked discrimination based on their deafness. Like some other communities of the day, they were called the "Little Sisters" to indicate a subordinate role in the strongly hierarchical structure. Although they were not cloistered, the Little Sisters were highly dependent on the Quebec Institute for the Deaf, hardly ever leaving the segregated deaf community encapsulated by the school and the order. The order did not allow them to take perpetual vows as the hearing Sisters of Providence did but instead required deaf sisters to renew their temporary vows at the end of each five-year period.[12] Despite these limiting conditions, the contribution these sisters made to Deaf Catholic religious vocations are among the most fruitful of the religious orders that have welcomed deaf women or men.

The 1950s were a time of expanding membership in women's religious orders in North America, and at its peak, there were sixty Little Sisters of Our Lady of Seven Sorrows, all of them deaf. Most of the sisters were Canadian and used Quebec Sign Language, a derivative of French Sign Language, but a few sisters came from the United States, including Dorothy Steffanik and Elizabeth Kass, who continued with gusto in U.S. deaf ministry well after the institute disbanded.[13] The sisters had a rigorous schedule of daily prayers and devotions, and they assisted in classroom activities and various expositions and school fairs, including the annual banquet in honor of Saint Francis de Sales, patron saint of deaf people. For thousands of deaf children who passed through the Montreal Institution des Sourdes-Muettes, these women represented a model of life, at once Catholic and culturally deaf, and consecrated for prayer and service. When the institute closed in 1976, the members dispersed and took up the new challenges of individual lives and callings. Many of the sisters met this challenge creatively and some became lay leaders in their new Deaf Catholic communities.[14]

Not only these mentioned, but several other orders of religious sisters helped establish lasting Deaf Catholic communities across Europe and the Americas and, later, in every continent where the church expanded

---

12. Dorothy Steffanic, interview with Marlana Portolano, St. Francis of Assisi Deaf Catholic Church, Landover, Maryland, August 3, 2016.

13. Sister Elizabeth Kass continued as a Sister of Charity of Providence of Western Canada, ministering in Canada until her death in Edmonton in February 2018.

14. Stéphane D. Perreault, *One Community—A Sign of the Times: The Sisters of Our Lady of Seven Dolors*, trans. Gloria Keylor (Montreal: Carte Blanche Editions, 2007).

its missionary influence. The Mission Helpers of the Sacred Heart, for example, made deaf ministry a priority for their order in 1892, just two years after they established a residence in Baltimore. There they started St. Francis Xavier School, and in Puerto Rico, they founded San Gabriel School for the Deaf. In Hong Kong and in Singapore, the Canossian Daughters of Charity were especially influential. The roles and contributions of these and other religious orders figure prominently in chapters ahead. In each case, regional pockets of deaf people with their own native sign languages developed deep roots, consequentially needing the support of religious services and social gatherings that would nourish members of this language minority in the security of their cultural home—the Catholic Church. Without a doubt, it became the Church's responsibility to ensure continued religious services for these communities of mature, independent, and capable Deaf Catholic adults, whose spiritual and cultural life had benefited from the work of such dedicated women.

Religious orders of men also contributed to the missionary transformation of deaf culture in striking ways as well, often working together with religious sisters in the context of deaf ministry. In the next chapter, we turn to several such men who gave up the promise of careers in the hearing world to become part of an often isolated and overlooked deaf community. Examples of Jesuit and Redemptorist work with deaf people will illustrate several important advances in Catholic ministry and enculturation using signed languages. However, the Jesuit and Redemptorist traditions cannot represent all the diverse religious orders of men with traditions of service to deaf people. Orders such as the Oblates of Francis de Sales, the Dominican Missionaries of the Deaf and Disabled, and others also had strong traditions of service to and with deaf people, and many of these will figure prominently in part II. Often these consecrated individuals worked side by side with parish and diocesan priests as well as laypeople in the deaf apostolate. Beginning in Catholic schools or with pastoral work in state schools, this transformation often proceeded to the stage of traveling missionary work as soon as word of their sign language ministry spread in a given region. As a natural development from these missionary aims, priests and brothers secured a place for deaf culture to grow by helping to found missions and centers with established chaplains of the deaf community. Eventually, these orders would contribute some of the world's first deaf priestly vocations, men who would, in turn, become important models for sign language ministries and deaf leadership in the church.

CHAPTER 4

Missionaries at the Margins

In the second half of the nineteenth century, deaf culture grew rapidly
in Europe and the United States as government-funded schools for deaf
children became sites of language and cultural development for deaf people. The first government-funded school of this type in the United States
was the American Asylum for the Education of Deaf and Dumb Persons in Hartford, Connecticut (now called the American School for the
Deaf). Thomas Hopkins Gallaudet was principal of the American Asylum from 1818 until 1830, and it was there that Gallaudet's deaf teacher,
Laurent Clerc (himself a Deaf Catholic educated in the Parisian National Institute of the Deaf), taught all subjects in sign language. As Clerc
and Gallaudet shared their teaching methods, deaf children in boarding
schools across the nation could benefit from visual communication and
consequently began to learn as quickly and easily as most hearing children learn through spoken languages. However, sign language schools
did not end deaf pupils' communication difficulties outside of school.
Deaf children often lived in these residential schools—whether public
or parochial— year-round until the age of eighteen or twenty, visiting
their families only on major holidays. Many deaf young people felt more
at home at school than with their parents and siblings, who in many cases
could not communicate at all in sign language. Through close association
and shared language and experiences, these young deaf people became
part of an educated minority group.

It did not take long before graduates of residential schools for the
deaf began to form communities of sign language users outside of school.
Because these graduates were increasingly well educated, they were more
involved in public life than deaf people generally had been in previous

eras. In 1864, the National Deaf-Mute College (later known as Gallaudet University) began to offer federally funded higher education for qualified deaf students in Washington, D.C., and soon a steadily growing number of young adults attended the first institution founded specifically to grant college degrees to deaf graduates. The late nineteenth century also brought new employment opportunities for deaf people, especially in factories in industrial cities. Waves of immigrants in the United States, particularly from Catholic countries like Ireland, Italy, and Poland, expanded the general population and therefore the deaf population. In growing local sign language communities, Deaf Catholic adults sought places to socialize and worship together. Many married other Deaf Catholics and passed on their religious traditions and sign language to second and third generations of Deaf Catholics (including hearing children who grew up bilingual and bicultural). Because of these educational and occupational shifts for deaf people, a need arose for Deaf Catholic community centers, as well as religious retreats and missions in sign language.

During this exciting era of sign language growth in North America, as more and more deaf communities needed chaplains who could sign, two large religious orders began to evangelize Deaf Catholics with particular zeal—namely, the Society of Jesus (Jesuits) and the Congregation of the Most Holy Redeemer (Redemptorists). Though many other orders or diocesan clergy participated in deaf ministries, it is certainly true that Jesuits and Redemptorists provide especially abundant examples of mission work with this newly identified language minority. It may even be argued that the contributions of particular men in these orders were integral to the development of a distinct Deaf Catholic culture in Catholic residential schools, missions, and diocesan communities. Moreover, traditions of deaf ministry in these two orders would pave the way for some of the first culturally deaf men—some of them Jesuits and Redemptorists themselves—to enter the Catholic priesthood in the second half of the twentieth century.

The Jesuits: God in All Things

The Society of Jesus is the largest single religious order in the Catholic Church today, and as such it has a long and storied history. The founder of the order, a Basque nobleman and soldier named Ignatius of Loyola, discerned a religious vocation while recovering from wounds sustained during the battle of Pamplona in 1521. His "Formula of the Institute of the Society of Jesus," accepted in 1540 by Pope Paul III, characterizes the broad purpose of the order to defend and propagate the faith by means of preaching, lecturing, ministering, retreats, education, and "any works of charity, according to what will seem expedient for the glory of God and the common good."[15] The charter echoes Ignatius's military background by requiring from members absolute loyalty to accept assignments anywhere in the world, under any extreme conditions, as soldiers of God. From its founding, the order has been characterized by international missionary work (like that carried out by Saint René Goupil), advocacy for human rights and social justice, as well as education through the development of schools and colleges. Because the early years of the society correspond-ed with the Council of Trent (1545–1563), Jesuits were deeply involved in countering the Protestant Reformation throughout Europe. In their teach-ing and research, they focused on teaching the gospel as well as classics of Western culture and, in particular, the arts of rhetoric and preaching.

In 1773, after various political and ecclesiastical conflicts, the Society of Jesus was suppressed throughout Europe and its colonial holdings in the New World. As a result, the order had to leave many of its outposts and missions and new vocations halted. After Pope Pius VII restored the order to its activities in 1814, the society experienced a period of tre-mendous growth. It was during this period that the order developed a tradition of deaf ministry, beginning in the United States. Ultimately, the way Jesuits reached the hearts and souls of deaf people was through preaching in sign language.

Saint Ignatius of Loyola taught that the reformation of the church began in the heart of the individual. To this end, he authored a series of Spiritual Exercises intended to be used for reflection and prayer during four-week spiritual retreats. The spiritual discipline practiced by Jesuits, known as Ignatian spirituality, is drawn from Ignatius's life and writings, which culminate in a scriptural contemplation on "finding God in all things." Jesuits are known for cultivating this mindset in every area of life. In Jesuit spirituality, God can be found even in those things that appear lacking in beauty or blessings. How, one might ask, would this charism of their founder be applied to ministry with deaf people?

15. Ignatius of Loyola, "Formula of the Institute of the Society of Jesus," *The Constitutions of the Society of Jesus and Their Complementary Norms: A Complete English Translation of the Official Latin Texts*, vol. 15 (Saint Louis: Institute of Jesuit Sources, 1996), 3–4.

During most of Western history, human deafness was defined neg-
atively, as the absence of communication through hearing and speech,
rather than positively, as the presence of other attributes such as gestural
communication. Early Jesuit interest in deaf ministries predictably reflects the mainstream perspective on deafness as a medical condition.
From the seventeenth through the nineteenth centuries, Jesuits primarily
defined deafness not as a lack of hearing, but rather as a lack of speech
communication, and therefore emphasized speech training and oral
methods. For example, a seventeenth-century Italian Jesuit named Fran-
cesco Lana Terzi became interested in deafness through his scholarship
in natural history and physics. He wrote a treatise entitled *Prodromo dell'*
Arte Maestro (1670), in which he described a method of teaching the
deaf to speak through lipreading and imitation of mouth shapes. In the
eighteenth century, a Spanish Jesuit philologist and missionary in Latin
America, Lorenzo Hervás y Panduro, wrote a history of the social and
philosophical foundations of deaf education, containing a prominent
section on methods for teaching lipreading, writing, and speech together
as connected language arts.

Perhaps because the order was so focused on preaching and rhetoric,
oralism seemed, at first, the logical approach to deaf education and religious access. Whether they intended it or not, early Jesuit missionaries
(like other oralists who advocated speech training to the exclusion of
sign language) may have unwittingly helped perpetuate the misleading
concept that deafness was punishment for sin. If deafness is defined as
the absence of an essential faculty of human nature (that is to say, the
absence of language), then deafness may seem unnatural—or even a punishment for personal sin. By the time Catholic missions in established
deaf communities began in the nineteenth century, Jesuits were cultivating a more fruitful understanding of deafness, one that rejected the lack
of speech communication as punitive suffering and instead emphasized
the many spiritual and social gifts that deafness calls forth. This approach
reflected the Jesuit charism of finding God in all things and, at the same
time, invited an attitude of appreciation for sign language. Deafness, to
these later Jesuit missionaries, could be a condition of life through which
God might reveal his goodness.

Fortunately, American Jesuits in the early modern era left a record of
deaf missionary activity by actively publishing academic reports of their
work. Two sources offer a particularly vivid picture of work with deaf

people in sign language. First, prominent Jesuit scholars and missionaries recorded their efforts in the *Woodstock Letters*, published between 1872 and 1969 at Woodstock College west of Baltimore, Maryland. Second, the National Catholic Educational Association published the proceedings of its annual convention from its inception, and from 1907 until 1949, a special "Deaf Section" met when the regular conference was in session.[16] Jesuits doing work with the sign language community frequently published research in these proceedings.

It is difficult to identify all the Jesuits who worked with deaf people in these years, both because they rotated assignments and because of a self-effacing and communal quality in their written reports. Such is the case with one G. A. H., SJ, identified only by his initials in an 1887 *Woodstock Letters* article. This unnamed priest fondly relates the successes and failures of a "little mission" at a state school for the Deaf in Frederick, Maryland. The mission was established in 1881 by Father Francis Barnum, SJ, who spent most of his time learning sign language from his first pupil before he could even begin to teach the catechism. As the little mission grew, boys and girls met in separate classes once a week, and the school's principal remarkably allowed Jesuits to use rooms in the school building for instruction. These classes resulted in an offshoot mission for Deaf Catholic adults in Baltimore, a deaf-led group started by one of the first pupils at Frederick. This Baltimore Deaf Catholic community was a clear example of deaf-led missionary activity and Deaf Catholic culture. Children's catechism and sacramental preparation in sign language developed into a mature expression of lasting Catholic culture in small deaf communities composed of single people and married couples with children (both hearing and deaf) fluent in sign language.

At the Maryland School for the Deaf, a succession of Jesuits acted as catechists, but the mission often faced cultural challenges. The problem, this missionary relates, was that "The Deaf-Mute likes his teacher, is devoted to him, and is always diffident when he sees a new man.... As soon as you have some influence on the deaf, I mean to say after two or three years, you are taken away, and it is just the time you can realize that your work is not fruitless." In this careful way, the author argued to his Jesuit superiors for the necessity of fixed chaplains for deaf schools and

16. The "Catholic Deaf Mute Section" of the National Catholic Educational Association did not meet in 1926, 1928, or for a six-year period between 1934–39. In 1940, it resumed annual meetings under the name "Deaf Education Section."

communities. Catechists, he writes, "have never been wanting," yet this "moving on to pastures new" had been the reason that "very little fruit has been reaped by us in this portion of the Lord's vineyard." The author's tactful complaints illustrate two primary difficulties in the evangelization of deaf people at this time: First, a child may not have acquired any language at all in the home, either spoken or signed, until the age of eight or nine when his hearing parents sent him to the state boarding school. As a result, the child's language often remained severely delayed even into adulthood, and higher or more abstract levels of understanding, while still possible, became much slower and more laborious to acquire.

The second obstacle was the thoroughly Protestant environment of the schools themselves, where Catholic children were required to attend Methodist or Episcopal religious services with the other students. By the mid-nineteenth century, public schools, in general, were often organized and run by Protestants who, like Reverend Thomas Hopkins Gallaudet in Connecticut, saw no reason to separate religious instruction from the rest of the curriculum. No wonder one Maryland School for the Deaf pupil, after three years of sign language catechism, asked Father Barnum whether God was a Methodist or a Catholic. This point is more emphatic in the *Woodstock Letters* report: "The Protestants are educating the Deaf-Mute boys and girls, and making every effort to attach them to themselves, and they succeed only too well. They have societies, and social gatherings and clubs, and Bible classes, and lectures, entertainments, festivals and what not—and we have—well, just about nothing. Our Catholic Deaf-Mutes are losing their faith and are growing up a generation of unbelieving children."[17] Instead of merely complaining in the face of such a daunting situation, however, the Jesuit author presents this condition eagerly as an invitation to missionary action and intercessory prayer—a fresh opportunity to reap a "rich harvest." In fact, in the absence of ecumenical cooperation, Protestant competition only seemed to whet Jesuit piety and energize their evangelization.

The Archdiocese of New York offers an especially clear example of how the Jesuit tradition of ministry in sign language developed in the nineteenth and early twentieth centuries. The first Jesuit to work with the Deaf Catholic community in New York was Father Michael Costin, a Canadian whose first assignment after his 1872 ordination was to estab-

17. G. A. H., SJ, "Missionary Work at the Maryland School for the Deaf and Dumb," *Woodstock Letters* 16 (1887), 201–5.

lish the press that produced the *Woodstock Letters*. Once a noted professor of chemistry and mathematics at Fordham University, Costin gave up his teaching duties because of poor health, which doctors attributed to malaria and heart disease. Not one to be idle, Costin turned his attention to a new apostolate: deaf children at St. Joseph's School for the Deaf in New York City and its offshoot campus in Throggs Neck. Both campuses were new residential schools for deaf students founded by the Daughters of the Heart of Mary (the Nardines), one in 1875 and the other in 1877. Costin became a highly proficient signer and undoubtedly taught and preached in sign language with the clarity for which he was admired as a preacher in spoken English. In addition to the education of children, Costin ministered to a group of deaf adults who had begun to come together as a congregation in New York City. These adults were graduates of various Catholic schools for the deaf in Buffalo, Montreal, and Cabra in Ireland, as well as from New York School for the Deaf in Fanwood.[18] He gave himself unreservedly to working with this community for a few short years until his death at age forty-six. According to Costin's obituary, he remained vital in the deaf community right up until his untimely end, "displaying more energy than could have been supposed possible in one suffering so constantly."[19] The Jesuit tradition of deaf ministry in New York started by Costin continued with his successors in the part-time chaplaincy at St. Joseph's Institute, including Fathers Joseph Stadelman, Joseph Rockwell, and most notably, Michael McCarthy.

Father Michael McCarthy is especially remarkable because of his unusual assignment to serve as a permanent chaplain for the deaf community in New York. Like many of his confreres, McCarthy first learned about Jesuit ministry with deaf people while completing his junior studies at Woodstock, near the Maryland School for the Deaf, but his entry into deaf ministries did not come until later. Like many hearing people who have a passion for deaf ministries, he would come to it through a deeply personal connection to sign language. In 1900, after an illness, McCarthy himself became deaf at the age of forty-one—so severely deaf that he could only understand loudly shouted conversations (body-worn hearing aid technology was primitive and not widespread at the time). Fortunately, he had already begun to learn sign as his second language

18. Thomas F. McCaffrey, "History of the Apostolate of the Catholic Church to the Deaf in the Archdiocese of New York" (master's thesis, Fordham University, 1943), 15–17. More about this group of Deaf Catholic laypeople appears in chapter 8.

19. Obituary of Father Michael Costin, *Woodstock Letters* 13 (1884): 234.

while teaching at Holy Cross College in Massachusetts and Fordham University in New York. With his characteristic Jesuit manner of seeing God in all things, McCarthy refused to perceive the onset of his disability as a setback. Instead, with a missionary spirit, he decided to enter deaf culture, embracing the opportunity to serve the spiritual needs of the deaf community as one of their own. Because of this choice, even though he was late-deafened, Michael McCarthy may, in fact, be the first Catholic priest who was both medically and culturally deaf—or at least what we might call "bicultural" and bilingual in both English and sign language. He certainly set an early precedent for cultural deafness in the priesthood, and his identification with the needs of the deaf apostolate was apparent in the abundant growth of his ministry. The difference between Father McCarthy and, later, congenitally deaf priests in the twentieth century was simply that no one would suggest McCarthy was "a deaf-mute" because his first language for over forty years was spoken English.

Ultimately, McCarthy received an assignment to work exclusively in the deaf community at St. Francis Xavier Church in New York City. There, he united two groups of lay Deaf Catholics that had developed independently in the area, the Mutual Benefit Society and the Xavier Union. After meeting separately with each group, he suggested an integration of their plans and purposes into one organization, the Xavier Ephpheta Society. The united plan was a great success, and the Jesuits incorporated it in 1913. The Xavier Ephpheta Society went on to manage two Sunday schools for deaf children in the city, each stationed in churches near the city's two residential state schools for deaf students. Father McCarthy expanded service to Deaf Catholics by teaching sign language classes at St. Joseph's Seminary in Yonkers, New York, and securing seminarian volunteers to teach catechism. The Xavier Ephpheta Society became known across the country and overseas through a monthly periodical for deaf readers, *Ephpheta* magazine, published by McCarthy under the management of a deaf lay editor, John F. O'Brien. The magazine and McCarthy's frequent mission trips and retreats around the country were instrumental in the birth of various Ephpheta centers that began to spring up around the United States, following the model of the Xavier Ephpheta Society.[20]

In an effort to evangelize the adult deaf community beyond regions

20. McCaffery, "History of the Apostolate of the Catholic Church," 21–23.

served by his missions and retreats, Father McCarthy also published *Ephpheta: A Prayer Book for the Deaf*, the first book written specifically for a readership of Deaf Catholic adults. The book emphasized the story of Jesus encountering the deaf man chapter 7 of the Gospel of Mark. It quickly sold four thousand copies in two editions, fortifying a strong tradition in Deaf Catholic culture of praying for spiritual understanding through the story of Mark 7. Like several of the Sisters of St. Joseph and, later, the Redemptorists, McCarthy regularly presented his work and shared methods at annual Deaf Section meetings of the Catholic Educational Association. He was elected chairman of this group of colleagues in deaf ministry.

As he grew to understand his flock of over five hundred adult Catholics throughout the city, McCarthy was always expanding his knowledge and experience of sign language and its contexts. In 1912, he participated in one of the earliest international gatherings of deaf people, the World Deaf Congress in Paris on the bicentennial of Abbé l'Épée's birthday. During the late 1800s and early 1900s, McCarthy not only preached in sign language twice per month at St. Francis Xavier, he also traveled in a monthly rotation that took him to meetings of the adult deaf community at the Knights of Columbus Institute in Brooklyn and St. Joseph's Institute in Westchester. During the last two decades of his life, he became well known internationally in deaf circles for his preaching and retreats, which his 1915 obituary describes as signed and spoken simultaneously with "perfection rarely equaled" and with "a grace that captivated deaf congregations and won their hearts to virtue and to God."[21] Not until 1925 would another priest (also a Jesuit, Father Michael Purtell) serve the Diocese of New York as a full-time chaplain for Deaf Catholics. In the meantime, a surprising number of diocesan priests—at least sixteen— had begun to learn sign language and were able to step in as occasional substitutes until more Jesuits (Fathers Hugh Dalton and John Egan) were assigned to serve as part-time chaplains for the Xavier Ephpheta Society and the large deaf community of New York City.[22]

Another city with a strong Jesuit presence in deaf ministry was Chicago. In 1882, two priests in Chicago, Father Arnold Damien, SJ, and Redemptorist Father Henry Meurer, were called to attend to a dying man

21. Obituary of Father Michael McCarthy, Deaf Catholic Archives, College of the Holy Cross, Worcester, Mass.

22. McCaffery, "History of the Apostolate of the Catholic Church," 28–29.

who lacked religious instruction because of his deafness. They found the task of communicating with this man to meet his spiritual needs so difficult that they petitioned Archbishop Freehan to found a Catholic school for deaf children in the archdiocese. Miss Eliza Starr, the foundress of the Ephpheta Society in Chicago, took an active interest in the project and secured donations for a school building. The school opened in 1884, with classroom space provided by the Jesuit fathers in their residence. A succession of Jesuits were chaplains at this school: John Condon, Joseph Prince, Paul Ponzighone, Henry Dumbach, Ferdinand Moeller, Patrick Mahan, Francis Senn, Joseph O'Brien, and Charles Hoffman.

Father Ferdinand Moeller is of particular interest, both because of his scholarly efforts pertaining to the education of deaf children and for his lifelong ministry to and advocation for deaf adults. After completing his seminary education in Frederick, Maryland, he spent seventeen years teaching poetry and physics at St. Ignatius College in Chicago, where he also began work with deaf people. When he was assigned assistant pastor of Holy Family Church in Chicago, he committed all his spare time to the pastoral care of the deaf community. To draw attention to the plight of deaf people in the church, he spoke at every opportunity at educational conferences, missions, and once at the first American Catholic Missionary Congress held in Chicago in 1908. With Father Michael McCarthy, SJ, from New York, Moeller also attended the International Convention of the Deaf in Paris in 1912. Wherever he was transferred—St. Aloysius Church in Kansas City, Missouri; St. Joseph's parish in St. Louis; and finally, St. Mary's parish in Cleveland—Moeller continued to carry out his work among Deaf Catholics.[23] In 1917 he published a comprehensive history and current description of education for deaf children as a *Catholic Encyclopedia* article that is still a useful summary today.

Father Moeller's brother, Henry Moeller, was archbishop of Cincinnati from 1904 to 1925. During this time, the brothers worked together on a petition to Rome to institute an annual international day of recognition for deaf people and hearing members of the deaf community in the Catholic Church. They also requested a papal blessing for members of the Deaf Catholic community in the United States, along with a ple-

23. "Father Ferdinand A. Moeller, SJ," in *Lineage: A Biographical History of the Chicago Province* (Chicago: Loyola Press, 1987), 15–16, Deaf Catholic Archives, College of the Holy Cross, Worcester, Mass.

nary indulgence for any Catholic who worked for the salvation of the deaf during their lifetime for at least one year. On June 13, 1910, their petition resulted in a letter from Pope Pius X bestowing the blessing, the day of recognition, and the indulgences requested.[24] For many years afterward, Deaf Catholics in many countries celebrated Ephpheta Sunday as a feast day on the Eleventh Sunday after Pentecost (usually in August) when the gospel reading was Mark 7, the story of Jesus' encounter with the deaf man. Ephpheta Sunday (along with any special acknowledgment of the church's blessing for those who do deaf ministry) officially discontinued in 1965, when the Second Vatican Council changed to a three-year cycle of Sunday Scripture readings. However, deaf people in some places, Australia for example, still annually celebrate this special day, and many in the broader Deaf Catholic community still retain hope of restoring Ephpheta Sunday as a special day for Deaf Catholics in all nations.[25] In the 1940s, one of Father Moeller's successors in deaf ministry in Chicago brought the tradition of Ephpheta Sunday to a fruition of great abundance. Father Charles Hoffman, SJ, engaged Cardinal Samuel Stritch to preside over a historical gathering of Chicago Deaf Catholics at Holy Name Cathedral. The large celebration was a conspicuous event that attracted much public attention: one thousand Deaf Catholics from around the area attended the Mass and six hundred and fifty attended the communion breakfast. Father Hoffman was delighted because he knew that the entire city would now be aware of the deaf apostolate that had struggled so long without a voice in the mainstream.

Father Hoffman had entered the Jesuit novitiate in 1901 in Missouri, but, like so many other priests during this period, he began his apostolate to the deaf community while studying theology in St. Louis. In this city, two little girls from St. Joseph Institute taught him the Hail Mary in sign language. Mother Mary Borgia, of the Sisters of St. Joseph, and Father Patrick Mahan, chaplain at St. Joseph Institute, continued Hoffman's

24. *Catholic Educational Association Bulletin*, 7, no. 1 (1910): 435–36. It is worth noting here that Pope Pius X had already granted an indulgence of 100 days for anyone who prayed a particular "Prayer for Deaf-Mutes," and that deaf people themselves could, for the purpose of these or any indulgences, pray "by signs or mentally, or they may be read over without articulation" (as stated in Ambrose St. John's *The Raccolta or Collection of Indulgenced Prayers & Good Works* [London: Burns and Oates, 1910], 13, 169). The history of these earlier indulgences has not been explored, but interestingly, the published date of their institution was 1906, the same year Charles La Fonta entered the Assumptionists and went to Jerusalem on pilgrimage. Thanks to Audrey Seah for this observation.

25. "Deafness Is a Gift from God: Ephpheta Sunday Celebrations," *The Catholic Weekly*, Sydney, Australia, last modified August 26, 2016, accessed July 7, 2017, https://www.catholicweekly.com.au/deafness-is-a-gift-from-god-ephpheta-sunday-celebrations/.

lessons in sign language, and soon he was both proficient and passion-
ate about deaf people and their language. While teaching high school in
St. Louis from 1919 to 1933, he continued to develop his work with the
deaf community part time, focusing especially on the needs of the adult
deaf community. In 1938, Hoffman was appointed full-time chaplain
of all Deaf Catholics in Chicago, becoming a city-wide pastor of this
cultural group. He celebrated Masses, baptisms, confirmations, and
weddings; he received confessions and administered Extreme Unction
anywhere in the large city where Deaf Catholics needed him. At the Chicago Ephpheta Center, he organized card parties, picnics, dances, and
silent movies. In 1936, he gave a remarkable retreat, in which he gave four
daily presentations in sign language for eight consecutive days, a feat that
would send a less inspired man to bed from physical and mental exhaus-
tion. He was known to bring lapsed Deaf Catholics back to the church
after years of public schooling. As his confrere Father David Walsh once
said of him, "To the deaf in St. Louis and Chicago for years and years,
Father Hoffman was the Catholic Church."[26]

One of the saddest events in deaf history, from a cultural point of
view, was also one of the most difficult experiences in Father Hoffman's
life. When Mother Borgia was replaced at St. Joseph's Institute in St.
Louis by a superior who believed in "pure oralism" and the suppression
of sign language, Hoffman grieved mightily for the Deaf Catholic community. "If we remove the signs," he said, "we cut off the child from the
priest and from Catholic teaching." At the dedication of a new building at St. Joseph's Institute, he came prepared to interpret a speech by
Archbishop John Glennon, but he was told, "As long as you continue
to sign, we never want you on our property again."[27] The influence of
oralism, once the method of seventeenth-century Jesuit educators of
deaf children, had become a major obstacle for this Jesuit who had come
to understand that the only way to reach assemblies of deaf people was
through preaching in sign language.

The growing American Jesuit tradition of evangelizing the deaf community in sign language attracted several more Jesuits during the first
half of the twentieth century. In the 1930s and 1940s, Jesuit Brother Paul
Rosenecker contributed to the expansion of deaf ministry by teaching

26. "Hoffman, SJ," in *Lineage: A Biographical History*, 27–30, Deaf Catholic Archives, College
of the Holy Cross, Worcester, Mass.
27. "Hoffman, SJ," in *Lineage: A Biographical History*, 28

sign language classes to Jesuit scholastics at St. Andrew-on-Hudson in Hyde Park, New York. Brother Rosenecker, as he explained it, had learned sign language as his first language. His "parents were deaf-mutes, and all their friends were deaf-mutes, and he had to learn it for these two very good reasons."[28] At the peak of dactylology, or finger spelling, classes at St. Andrew-on-Hudson, there were twenty-five Jesuit juniors who were fluent, ready, and willing to communicate with deaf signers wherever their future assignments might take them. For practice, they advertised to local deaf communities and then took turns preaching once a month in the school hall of St. Peter's School in Poughkeepsie. In Canada, too, visiting Jesuits such as Father E. Klippert, SJ, helped the St. Francis de Sales Deaf Society in Toronto become one of the most active and robust Deaf Catholic groups in North America.

In the Jesuit missionary field, Father Joseph Stoffel began ministry with the deaf community in the Philippines in the 1930s. By the 1970s, Father Freddy Alphonso contributed to further international expansion of sign language ministries by founding deaf services in India. In short, the work begun by American Jesuits in this field began an expanding tradition of deaf ministries that would continue to extend the boundaries of sign language use and deepen its intersection with Catholic culture. This tradition, guided by the Jesuit penchant for finding God in all things, would eventually contribute two of the earliest ordinations of congenitally deaf priests fluent in sign language. Joseph Bruce, the first congenitally deaf man to become a Jesuit priest, was ordained in 1981, and Paul Fletcher became the first in England in 1997. Their vocation stories figure prominently in part II when we turn to post–Vatican II developments in Deaf Catholic culture.

The Redemptorists: Bringing the Gospel to the Most Abandoned

Saint Alphonsus Liguori is often credited with saying, "I have never preached a sermon that the poorest old woman in the congregation could not understand." Deaf people, who may find it impossible to understand almost any sermon in a mainstream congregation, would put

28. Philip McGovern, SJ, "The Dactylology Bulletin," Weston College, Massachusetts, April 15, 1944, Deaf Catholic Archives, College of the Holy Cross, Worcester, Mass.

this claim to the test. In 1749, with approval from Pope Benedict XIV, Liguori founded a religious order that would eventually strive to meet the needs of the deaf community in several parts of the world. The Congregation of the Most Holy Redeemer (CSsR)—known as the Redemptorists—was established to minister to poor sheepherders and farmers in the area surrounding Naples and Amalfi, Italy.[29] These people, the founder wrote, were

the most in need of spiritual help, as frequently they have no one to administer to them the Holy Sacrament or the Word of God; their plight is such that many, for lack of apostolic laborers, reach death's door without knowing anything at all of the necessary truths of the faith. This is because the number of priests who dedicate themselves expressly to the care of the poor farmers is few, due to the expense involved and, even more, to the trouble such a work entails.[30]

Much the same could be said of Deaf Catholics in every part of the world, even today, for whom priests who can and will administer the holy sacraments and the Word of God in sign language have been hard to find, due to the expense and trouble of learning a new and different language for such a small (though pervasive) population. Primarily, Redemptorists are known for their founder's charism of evangelizing and ministering to people on the margins—those who are most isolated and abandoned by society, especially those who have never had the opportunity to hear the gospel. Given the isolation of deaf people in society and their categorical lack of experience with "hearing the gospel," it seems natural that Redemptorists would be attracted to this dispersed and neglected group. They are also known for a certain unrelenting enthusiasm in evangelization, a quality that is apparent in their historical dedication to assembling and developing a culturally Deaf Catholic apostolate.

The Redemptorists first began ministering to deaf people in the United States in the 1880s, as a part of their missionary activity among European immigrant populations in the newly-formed parishes of Midwestern and Southwestern states. As mentioned above, the first Redemptorist who championed the cause of the deaf population was Father Henry Meurer, who helped found the Ephpheta School for the Deaf in Chicago in 1884, in partnership with Jesuit Father Ferdinand Mo-

29. CSsR stands for Congregatio Sanctissimi Redemptoris.

30. Alphonsus de Liguori, "Petition to the Pope for Approbation of the Institute and Its Rules," *Constitutions of the Congregation of the Most Holy Redeemer*, translated from a Spanish version of the Italian original, published in *Spicilegium Historicum* 17 (1969): 220–23, Redemptorists International, accessed June 14, 2017, http://www.cssr.com/english/whoarewe/constitutions.shtml.

eller and with the support of both the Daughters of the Heart of Mary and the Ephpheta Society, a charitable association of laypeople. To raise funds for the new school, Meurer appealed to notable parishioners at St. Alphonsus Church in St. Louis (known as "the Rock"), whose membership included notable and civic-minded individuals such as Ellen Ewing Sherman, the wife of Civil War General William Tecumseh Sherman. Father Meurer had been Mrs. Sherman's confessor at the church, during the time that he was leading a small ministry for deaf people in the region. So began a persistent Redemptorist tradition of deaf ministry that would lead to international expansion of the Deaf Catholic apostolate in surprising ways.

The first American Redemptorist to preach in sign language was reportedly Father Benedict Lenz, a prolific preacher and polyglot who evangelized immigrants in many languages, including English, German, Italian, French, Spanish, and Portuguese. The addition of sign language to this list shows a forward-thinking and multicultural understanding of deaf people, not only as a category for medical concern and social welfare but as a genuine language group. While he never engaged in deaf ministry more than part-time, Lenz would have a formative influence on one of the most energetic and prolific evangelists of deaf people, Father Daniel Higgins.[31]

Higgins was a native of De Soto, Missouri, who began his career as a mathematics professor at St. Joseph Seminary in Kirkwood, near St. Louis. Around 1908, while he was teaching at the seminary, Higgins happened to observe some children on a streetcar having an animated conversation in sign language. He was so impressed that he paid a visit to their teacher, well-known deaf educator Mother Mary Borgia of St. Joseph School for the Deaf, to begin learning this form of communication. A few years later, Higgins's friend and former classmate Father Benedict Lenz invited him to help with a new mission for deaf people in New Orleans. It was from Lenz that Higgins first learned the art of preaching in sign language. In his words, "Lenz would sit in the front pew and give me the signs for the words I did not know." Although he would eventually match his mentor Mother Mary Borgia in ministerial dedication and productivity, Higgins never specialized solely in work with deaf people. In New Orleans, Higgins first worked as a professor and a parish priest. He had a strong belief

31. Kristine Stremel, "Carrying out a C.Ss.R Tradition," *DenverLink, The Redemptorists/Denver Province* 4, no. 6 (November/December 2011).

that a priest should be for everybody, not just for one cultural group in any given region. However, Higgins became well known and beloved in the deaf community for giving missions coast to coast throughout Canada and the United States. It might be five hundred deaf people in old St. Francis Xavier Church on West 16th Street in New York; a family of four in Ellensburg, Washington; or an isolated Canadian Native American deaf boy who had never been to school.[32] Like other missionaries who served this apostolate after him, Higgins often took trips to visit state schools for the deaf, many of which had no access to catechism or Sunday Masses for year-round residential students who were Catholic. Wherever he went, he also gave talks at seminaries and religious houses to bring more priests into this neglected area of ministry.

When Higgins was a young man, before he entered the seminary, he wanted to be a clown and an acrobat. With charisma as magnetic as any stage actor's and a talent for mime, Higgins found rhetorical delivery in sign language a natural way to express his preaching vocation. In this elocutionary tradition, he became a willing teacher of other priests and laypeople who worked with deaf people. In 1923, he produced a pictorial dictionary of sign language, *How to Talk to the Deaf.* He used a simple cut-and-paste method to reproduce pages of black-and-white photographs of himself making signs, over which he drew arrows for movement and direction. The book was a major step forward from earlier sign language dictionaries, including those compiled by influential French and Irish educators. Earlier sign language dictionaries contained almost entirely written descriptions of signs without pictures. In the United States, three other sign language glossaries addressed sign language specifically for use in Catholic deaf ministries. One was simply a typewritten carbon copy of textual descriptions of signs by an unnamed Sister of St. Joseph that circulated at the turn of the century; next, Father Michael McCarthy, SJ, published a small booklet called *Religious Terms: 101 Signs* (1914/5); and J. Schuyler Long included a short appendix of "Distinctively Catholic Signs" in his nonreligious book *The Sign Language: A Manual of Signs,* with a few photos of Father Ferdinand Moeller, SJ, who provided the information on these signs.[33]

32. St. Louis Province Centenary booklet, St. Louis Province, Deaf Catholic Archives, College of the Holy Cross, Worcester, Mass.
33. These early Catholic sign language dictionaries are in the Deaf Catholic collection at the Archive of College of the Holy Cross in Worcester, Mass.

Higgins's dictionary, on the other hand, contained photographs for every entry and included many more pictures of signs than these other works. Although it contained considerably fewer entries than the several hundred text-only descriptions in early French and Irish Sign Language dictionaries, Higgins's visual dictionary left much less room for misinterpretation or mistakes in making the signs. He correctly judged the developing technologies of photography and image reproduction to be a better match for sign language, existing as it did in spatial, nonverbal modes only and, therefore, without any transcribed or written form. It was certainly of more use to deaf people themselves. As the only work of its kind for many years, the book was influential not only in Catholic ministries but also in the secular world. Actress Jane Wyman used it to learn her lines when she played a deaf woman in the 1948 film *Johnny Belinda*.[34]

A notable case of Redemptorists and Jesuits building on each other's work in deaf ministry centered on Higgins's popular book. After accepting an assignment at the Catholic Center for the Deaf in Boston, Jesuit Brother Paul Neuland felt that a supplementary guide and curriculum of exercises were needed for classes of seminarians using Higgins's *How to Talk to the Deaf*. In 1933, he wrote and published *Learning the Signs*, a companion to Higgins's dictionary with an emphasis on the fundamentals of preaching and sacramental preparation in sign language. Neuland provided what is perhaps an overly optimistic introduction: "It will not be too much of a burden on any priest to add the deaf to his care, for to learn the signs will take but a short time—even a few weeks or months will give at least a moderate ability in preaching through the dactylological idiom."[35] For a readership of ministers who wished to communicate with deaf worshipers, his guide introduced the mechanics of sign language and grammatical parts of speech. Articles (a, the) are never used, he explained, and pronouns are indicated by pointing in the direction of the people indicated. Possessive pronouns are formed by pressing the flat palm toward that person or people. Other parts of speech, such as propositions, conjunctions, and verb tenses, are not present in Higgins's dictionary, so Neuland explained how to sign them in English glosses (there are no pictures in his book as there are in Higgins's). His knowl-

34. Stremel, "Carrying out a C.Ss.R Tradition."
35. Paul A. Neuland, SJ, *Learning the Signs: A Companion to Father Higgins's Dictionary "How to Talk to the Deaf"* (New York: James Donnelly Publishing, 1933), 8.

edge of grammar is much the same as late twentieth-century linguistic descriptions of American Sign Language as a complete human language.

Like his Jesuit commentator, Higgins himself was undoubtedly ahead of his time in accepting sign language and deaf culture, rather than attempting to evangelize deaf people in a second language that they might never learn with proficiency. Descriptions of his sign language preaching suggest that Higgins did not communicate in what came to be known as "Signed English." Signed English is a pidgin form of sign language in which the communicator speaks out loud and uses signs in English word order to accompany his voice—"pidgin" being the term linguists use for makeshift communication between users of two different languages with no language in common. Instead, Higgins used deaf people's own visual-spatial grammar, the natural language now called American Sign Language (ASL). Higgins's conscientious use of ASL grammar is confirmed by his own descriptions in a letter to the editor of a Deaf Catholic community newsletter in the early 1950s:

So many priests and others do not seem to know that our sign language is an ideographic language and not a wordy language. It has an idiom, as other languages have. It uses signs, gestures, acting, impersonating, expression and lends itself to pictographic or pictorial communication of ideas. It makes use of signed words and spelled words only when needed. If a wordy preacher wishes to sign his sermon to the deaf, he should ... fit his sermon to the simplest English language and [translate that] into the ideographic language of the signs.[36]

Contemporary histories of the deaf surprisingly overlook the forward-thinking nature of this approach, which Higgins used as early as the 1920s. Only in the late 1960s would academic linguists begin to accept ASL as a genuine language, but Higgins was already a master of ASL in its genuine form decades before the first academic dictionary of the language would appear.[37] Not even state schools for the deaf were using this approach in the 1920s. Most used lipreading, and, if they used signs at all, it was Signed English in the word-order of spoken language, not this very different, three-dimensional arrangement and grammar.

Higgins explained this visual and spatial grammar best in *How to*

---

36. ICDA Newsletter clipping, 1950s, Deaf Catholic Archives, College of the Holy Cross, Worcester, Mass.

37. In 1965, William Stokoe, an English professor at Gallaudet College, would publish the influential *Dictionary of American Sign Language on Linguistic Principles* (Washington, D.C.: 1965). It prompted the switch to ASL instruction (from mostly lipreading) in all the U.S. state schools for the Deaf.

Talk to the Deaf. As an example, he gave his readers this colorful passage in English: "Long ago, a man was standing on the gable end of a very high house. Suddenly the man toppled over sideways and fell from his elevated position to the ground. The distance of the fall was so great that his body made several complete turns, over and over in the air before he struck the ground. He was dashed to the ground flat on his back and died within a few moments." To translate this little story into the language of deaf people, Higgins explained, the signer would use signs for the following nouns and verbs, along with certain whole-body movements:

1. "Past" (hand being pushed backward to denote "long time past"), "House," "Tall" (signed slowly to indicate the great height of the house, with the eyes following as if looking up the side of a building of great height).
2. "Male" (for "man"), "Stand" (made locally so that the inverted "V" fingertips are standing on the gable point of the "house" just signed).
3. Then the inverted V falls to one side quickly and whirls over and over slowly to indicate a great height. The hand descends slowly during these turns, but the last part of the fall is quickly straight to the ground as all objects naturally seem to fall. The right hand comes to a rest with a jerk, to show the sudden shock, and is surprised to indicate that the victim fell on his back.
4. "Death" (signed slowly to indicate that death is not instantaneous and then followed by "Finish" to tell that all is over.) The expression of the face, in keeping with the ideas, adds much to the fullness of the expression.[38]

Even with this one gloss as an example, readers could easily understand why pictorial representation is preferable and more accurate as a method for learning ASL if no fluent teacher were available to demonstrate it in person. In addition to his visual dictionary, Higgins began to put out manuals for confessors and theologians in the 1920s and '30s, and these included essential prayers for catechism such as the "Examination of Conscience," the "Our Father," and the "Hail Mary." Higgins circulated these manuals widely so that any priest who needed to work with deaf people would be able to learn at least these prayers in sign language. As a missionary, Higgins knew that these prayers were important information and merited broad dissemination: the title page of his pamphlet reads, "The pictures on page one and two interpret the truths which every Christian must know and believe under pain of mortal sin." The Redemptorists were in the business of saving abandoned souls, after all, and it was this charism that motivated all of Higgins's work in deaf culture.

38. Numbers have been added to highlight Higgins's visual phrasing and poetic expression.

A small band of Redemptorists stationed in their Saint Louis Province—then a vast expanse covering everything west of the Mississippi, more than half the United States—followed Higgins into this new apostolate. In 1930, one of these men, Father Joseph Heidell, had damaged his vocal cords with overzealous preaching and, as a result, lost the power of speech for over four years. He could manage only a whisper. During his "silent" period, Heidell became interested in ministering to deaf people as a way to continue his vocation of preaching. Using only Higgins's book *How to Talk to the Deaf*, he set out to learn the language on his own. Three years later, his efforts paid off when he was assigned to work with the deaf community in Lafayette, Louisiana. He soon acquired a large following among deaf people in the region, and his fame spread. Groups of Deaf Catholics in several Southern states began requesting his ministry in sign language. By the late 1930s, he had a regular circuit of missions, retreats, and sermons that took him from New Orleans to Austin, Laredo, San Antonio, and Houston every month. Several times per year he would visit the state schools for the deaf in Arizona, Arkansas, Oklahoma, Mississippi, and Colorado. His traveling mission work once took him as far west as San Francisco. Traveling as much as thirty thousand miles per month, mostly by train, he was given the nickname "the Pullman priest." A Des Moines issue of the *Catholic Register* reported that Heidell was one of "a small band of priests, headed by Father Higgins of Chicago and Father Godfrey Reilly, CP, of Baltimore, working throughout the country to aid these people whose only other contact with the Church is provided by Catholic laypeople teaching in state schools."[39] Because these men were influenced by Higgins's style of sign language preaching, it is probable that they, too, used the idiom of deaf people themselves and not merely signs strung together in English word order. This would certainly account for Heidell's popularity in deaf communities throughout the South.

Other Redemptorists who gave much of their lives to deaf ministry during this period include Father Charles Heing, who dedicated forty years to this apostolate, and Father Julian Grehan, who became interested in deaf ministry when his own hearing began to fail early in his priesthood. Grehan regularly traveled thousands of miles between St. Alphonsus "the Rock" Parish in St. Louis, Holy Redeemer Parish in

---

39. George Kelly, "Apostle to the Deaf Travels 30,000 Miles Every Year," *The Messenger*, May 15, 1942.

Detroit, and missions in the Diocese of New Orleans. Both these men deserve more coverage in this narrative, but much research remains to be done on their contributions. By midcentury, a core group of fifteen or more priests was doing this work, at least part time, in their own parishes or provinces around the continent of North America. Almost half of these were Redemptorists. Father Stephen Landherr had a Deaf mission in Philadelphia, Father John Gallagher in Buffalo, and Father Raymond Kalter in Detroit. These Redemptorists were well known for their missionary work with deaf communities in various parishes, schools, and dioceses.

Father Stephen Landherr of Philadelphia is a particularly strong example of the Redemptorist charism in action with deaf people, since he was one of the rare few able to work full time with the deaf community. Although Landherr was thirty years younger than Father Higgins, he had met the venerable old man in professional contexts relating to the deaf community. Some sources attribute Landherr's interest in deaf ministry to one of Higgins's talks at Mount St. Alphonsus Redemptorist Seminary in Esopus, New York. In any case, the two became admirers of one other's work, and both were eventually part of the group that began, in 1907, to meet annually in the Deaf Section of the Catholic Education Association. Papers and meeting minutes are published in the proceedings and provide a strong record of Catholics doing ministry, running schools, teaching catechism, and providing social services for deaf children and adults. The 1941 program provides a good sampling of topics that were then a major concern to those in deaf ministry. For example, Higgins spoke on "The Writing of Confessions," Landherr on "Study Clubs for the Deaf," Joseph Heidell, CSsR on "A Catholic Missionary to the Deaf and the State School," and Sister M. Janet, CSJ on "Building a Religion Vocabulary."[40] Five out of nine of the presenters were Redemptorists.

Unlike Higgins, Landherr preferred to sign in English word order. Still, like his senior confrere in deaf ministry, he had good reasons for the methods he chose, demonstrating that deafness is never a one-size-fits-all condition. In any case, Father Landherr's method of signing did not seem to diminish him in the eyes of the deaf community in Philadelphia. In practice, this method was clearly distinct from the oralist approach advocated in most schools for the deaf at the time. In a 1944 interview

40. *The National Catholic Education Association Bulletin*, Deaf Section, 38, no. 1 (August 1941), 5.

for the *St. Anthony Messenger*, a reporter asked him "Don't you believe in lipreading, Father?" "Certainly, I do," Landherr replied,

It has accomplished great things. Once in in England I discovered a Jewish youth who could read lips in two languages, Hebrew and English. But lipreading is a long, slow, difficult study. At best it is seventy-five percent guess work. And many pupils are incapable of becoming good lip-readers. Why should a teacher insist that a not-too-apt child read lips and produce vocal speech that only his tutor can understand? In a fraction of the time expended on such study that same child could have learned sign language. Isn't a good sign reader preferable to a poor lip-reader? Once in England I chatted with the principal of a school for the deaf. I asked her what method was being used. "Lipreading of course. My pupils detest the sign language." However, her back was to the window and she could not see what I saw. In the school yard outside those same pupils were signing away to their heart's content. I believe, as do most priests who work among the deaf, that the middle course is best. That is, the combination method, use of both lipreading and sign language. That is why we always preach two sermons simultaneously.[41]

Landherr acted from this "middle course" philosophy during his entire career as a chaplain for the deaf community in Philadelphia. He spent the last twenty-six years of his life in this role, not only at St. Boniface Church where he was stationed, but all over the archdiocese, and with only public transportation to take him from place to place.

A sampling of how Father Landherr spent his days as a minister to Deaf Catholics is as enlightening as it is exhausting, and it provides insight into what others in this apostolate also did with their time. He interpreted for deaf people in courts and hospitals; taught sign language to seminarians and to the general public; preached missions to deaf people nationwide; organized the Philadelphia Catholic Guild to Aid the Deaf; began the Philadelphia chapter of the International Catholic Deaf Association; conducted retreats for Deaf Catholics; counseled and comforted parents of deaf children; prepared deaf couples for marriage; and published a periodical for the deaf community called *The Spokesman*. He also helped establish diocesan programs in Camden and Newark, New Jersey; in Wilmington, Delaware; and beyond. He helped deaf adults fill out their income tax forms, compose letters, and make phone calls, and he interpreted at movies. He collected hearing aids for free distribution.

---

41. Father Stephen Landherr, interview, *St. Anthony's Messenger* newsprint clipping, issue unknown, 1944, Redemptorist Archives, Baltimore Province, Philadelphia, Pa.

He regularly provided catechism at the Philadelphia School for the Deaf and started a small job training program for carpentry and leather work in the city. As Father Anthony Russo, another Redemptorist and his successor in Philadelphia, put it, Landherr's love for his work and his people and his God were "such that he never took a vacation."[42] So devoted and prayerful was Father Stephen Landherr that, after his death, his nephew started gathering all the materials necessary to start a case in Rome for his sainthood. When he arrived in Philadelphia, Father Russo seriously considered moving forward with the Landherr case for sainthood but decided against it, because it would have been very time consuming, and the deaf community needed full-time care immediately because the large and active apostolate Landherr developed.[43]

Father Landherr often told insightful stories about how difficult it can be for a deaf person to receive the Eucharist because of all the ways communication can break down. Here is a sample:

I recall a seminarian I was instructing. He tried to sign "You are about to enter the Holy Sacrament of Matrimony." Instead he said, "Holy Sacrament of Hamburger." But that wasn't nearly as bad as the Canadian missionary who wanted to sign "I hope that during this mission you will all go to Confession." Actually, he signed "I hope that during this mission all of you will go to jail." Not all mistakes are on our part. After one of my mission sermons in Boston I was accosted by a very excited young lady. "Father," she signed, "since when may we eat meat on Friday? I was so surprised to see you sign that we could." Of course, I set her straight. You see, the excited young lady had let her gaze wander for just one second, but in that instant she had missed my sign for "not" and consequently had got the wrong impression. It tires the deaf and hard of hearing to concentrate for long on hands or lips. The least distraction and they lose the whole meaning of a sentence. For that reason, all our sermons are brief, never more than a half hour.[44]

Deaf Catholics today still easily recognize these errors described by Landherr as a symptom of the ongoing shortage of priests who are fluent in sign language. Aspiring ministers to the deaf too often need to sign in religious contexts early in their sign language education, before they have experienced sign language immersion, when they may not be fluent enough to communicate with competence. As in Landherr's time, sign

42. Anthony Russo, *In Silent Prayer: A History of Ministry*, 45.

43. Anthony Russo, interview by Marlana Portolano, October 29, 2016, Redemptorist Baltimore Province Archives, Philadelphia, Pa.

44. Father Stephen Landherr, interview, *St. Anthony's Messenger*, newsprint clipping, 1944, Redemptorist Baltimore Province Archives, Philadelphia, Pa.

language skill development remains a strong argument to assign long-term chaplains for deaf communities today.

After Landherr, several other Redemptorists would play leading roles in the development of the worldwide Deaf Catholic community, including later missionary developments in South America, Africa, and Asia. Father Eugene Oates, CSsR, would advance the cause of sign language in every diocese in Brazil. In the early post–Vatican II years, as vernacular translations of the Mass became available and American Sign Language was gaining wide linguistic acceptance, Redemptorist Fathers John Gallagher and David Walsh led the establishment of sign language ministries in every diocese in North America. Finally, as with the Jesuits, the Redemptorist tradition of deaf ministry would result in one of the world's first culturally deaf priests, Father Cyril Axelrod of South Africa, a prolific Deaf Catholic evangelist in several countries in Africa, Asia, and Europe. His ministry is described at length in chapter 11. These Redemptorists and others, with their Jesuit and diocesan counterparts, were essential participants in Deaf Catholic culture during the second half of the twentieth century. It is no exaggeration to say that missionary work and language-related scholarship in these two orders helped facilitate the growth of sign languages—not only in North America but also in several nations around the world.

CHAPTER 5

A French Forerunner

Charles La Fonta was born on March 1, 1878, on a spacious estate just outside of Bordeaux, France. He was the fifth child of Lucien La Fonta and Hélène de Gaujel, a wealthy couple who spent half the year in a fashionable neighborhood in Paris and the other half at Lagrange, their country estate equipped with its own chapel. Charles was a small boy with a thoughtful manner who was inspired early by the prayers and daily Masses of his Catholic childhood. As a preschooler, he liked to pretend he was celebrating Mass. He prepared everything on a table with respect, carefully imitating the priest at the altar. His mother, who cherished the hope that one of her sons might have a priestly vocation, gave him a toy chalice, ciborium, and cruets. She even made a missal and embroidered a chasuble for him. Madame La Fonta was pleased to encourage her son's budding piety, but she felt a twinge of regret all the while. She thought it a matter of fact that her son would never become a priest because he was born deaf. She could not imagine how his life would later inspire deaf men on four continents to become Catholic priests.

Although not widely remembered, the ordination of Abbé Charles La Fonta (1878–1927) is one of the most important moments in Deaf Catholic history: the first substantiated case of a culturally deaf Catholic priest. Because he was born deaf and educated in schools for the deaf, La Fonta was no missionary but an early "native" of deaf culture called to the priesthood during the formative years of sign language education in France. Like Laurent Clerc, La Fonta had ties to Abbé Roch-Ambroise Sicard, who began his work as an educator of deaf students in Bordeaux, where he was the director of a government-funded school for deaf girls known as the National Institute for Deaf-Mutes of Bordeaux. The Sisters of Nevers who ran this school also tutored Charles La Fonta as a boy. Sicard had studied sign language education under Abbé l'Épée at the school for deaf boys and girls that had become famous for l'Épée's methods, the National Institute for Young Deaf (Institut National de Jeunes Sourds de Paris).[1] Sicard adapted l'Épée's methods for his school for deaf girls in Bordeaux and, after l'Épée's death, left his position in Bordeaux to become director of the National Institute for Young Deaf in Paris. Not many nineteenth-century educators of the deaf, not even these two great men, would have considered their work missionary in the sense of spreading the gospel to those who had not received it before. France was, after all, already a Catholic country, and schools for the deaf were considered social services or charitable organizations for profoundly handicapped children. However, because of his unique perspective as the first congenitally deaf priest, Charles La Fonta was ahead of his time. He understood that deaf people who used sign language needed a priest with whom they could identify as one of their own.

La Fonta's story sets a pattern for deaf priestly vocations that others would follow—but not until decades later. When he first perceived a call to the priesthood, he did not think it was possible for a deaf man to become a priest. However, through the support and faith of teachers of the deaf, religious sisters, priests, and friends, he boldly embraced his vocation as a calling of the Holy Spirit. For the sake of this calling, he endured fifteen years of daily speech training, French and Latin language development, humiliating struggles for accommodation in the seminary, and months of waiting while officials in in Rome considered whether a deaf man, whose speech might be unclear, should serve as a priest. While this arduous route to Catholic priesthood was groundbreaking, La Fonta's Catholic religious vocation remained less influential and less visible in the public eye than Laurent Clerc's role as a secular leader of deaf education in the United States. Moreover, Anglicans and Episcopalians had been preaching in sign language for over twenty years in the United States, and these denominations had ordained deaf ministers.[2] Catholics, on the other hand, considered priestly ordination out of the question for

1. After 1791, when the French legislature approved government funding for the education of deaf children, several government-funded French schools for deaf students were called "National Institutes"—sometimes the "National Institute for Deaf-Mutes" or, like the school in Paris, "for Young Deaf," and always with the name of the school's location appended.

2. See Otto B. Berg, *A Missionary Chronicle: Being a History of the Ministry to the Deaf in the Episcopal Church, 1850–1980* (Hollywood, Md.: St. Mary's Press, 1984).

a deaf man for many reasons. Ironically, deafness was not the most important reason. The church accepted other physical disabilities (poor vision, for example) in candidates for the priesthood. The more important
obstacle for a deaf man was the presumption that he would not be able to
speak—at least not clearly enough to pronounce Latin words with perfect clarity in the Mass. The very nature of language itself, as the church
understood it in La Fonta's time, called into question a deaf man's ability
to learn language from childhood. As most of La Fonta's contemporar-
ies understood it, language was equivalent to speech. Because La Fonta
was "deaf-mute"—the designated term for a born-deaf person—church
authorities would deem it impossible for him to produce clear speech in
either French or Latin.

Charles La Fonta, however, was prepared to meet the challenges
ahead. Because he went through seminary education as a deaf man in
entirely hearing, speaking environments, La Fonta's priestly formation
took years longer than that of Protestant ministers or hearing Catholic
seminarians. His speech training alone extended his priestly formation
by many years. Essentially, he had to learn how to imitate a well-educated
hearing person's pronunciation flawlessly in both spoken Latin and
French without ever having heard the words of either language.

The Struggle for Acceptance

How often has there been a saintly person whose spiritual greatness
passed forgotten and buried in musty archives? Given the presumable
modesty of a saint, it may be common. Most writers of biography wish to
avoid the label of hagiography, but it is hard to avoid a glowing description of piety and self-sacrifice in the life of Charles La Fonta. His story
is lovingly preserved in a book written by his older sister.[3] His life story
would in fact have been buried and forgotten had this book not been
safeguarded by religious orders that specifically served the deaf community. Placed in the hands of a few inspired boys in the years following its
publication, it contributed to the first appearances of culturally deaf vocations on three continents. Although his life story is not widely known

3. Quotes are excerpted from Mme. Raoul de Chaunac-Lanzac, *Un Miracle de la Foi: Un Sourd-
Muet Devenu Prêtre—A Miracle of Faith, A Deaf-Mute Becomes a Priest* (Paris: Society of Orphans
Apprentices, 1930). As presented here, the quotes are from an English translation in manuscript by
Joseph D. Gauthier, SJ, Deaf Catholic Archives, College of the Holy Cross, Worcester, Mass.

beyond the world of Deaf Catholics, La Fonta is undoubtedly important as a precursor in the phenomenon of deafness in the priesthood. His life archetypically represents prejudices and obstacles faced by many deaf men with priestly vocations who came after him.

The La Fonta family had deep connections in the Catholic clergy, and in fact one of Charles's cousins was the Archbishop of Rouen. One of his older brothers also had been born deaf, and Charles benefited from the experience his family had with the older boy. Their mother began training with Charles when he was a toddler. She assigned certain educational tasks to one of the Sisters of Nevers at the Institute for Deaf-Mute girls in Bordeaux, and she also did articulation and lipreading exercises with him herself for an hour each day until he was four. By the age of eight, Charles began to study French with a teacher while his mother continued daily lessons in articulation and pronunciation. Although there were no hearing aids at the time, Charles's rapid progress in speech indicates both the tremendous amount of time his mother spent on preschool intervention and the possibility that he had some residual hearing. His sister writes:

The Superior of the Institute for Deaf-Mutes, Mother Angelique, encouraged the young mother, and Sister Philippe outlined the program of studies. In Paris, Mlle. Dubois obtained softer tones in the voice by another method. With such teachers, Charles's pronunciation became clear, articulate, and soft. Charles understood everything and made himself understood. In the way he shared in a general conversation, one would never have imagined that he was deaf. Furthermore, he led the same life as his brothers and sisters.

Although Charles had to develop great concentration to work longer and harder than his hearing peers at school, he was well adjusted and accepting of his deafness. When he was fourteen years old, he told his sister, "I do not ask for a cure. I would not want Our Lady to make that a condition for becoming a priest." Even at this young age, Charles knew that he could set a precedent for deaf priestly vocations after him.

In his preparation for college, La Fonta studied mathematics, history, and English. The priest who served at his family's estate for nine years, Abbé Chalier, taught him Latin. He enrolled in the University of Bordeaux in 1898 when he was twenty years old and completed his studies with honors. In 1899 he attended the Institute of Agriculture at Beauvais, where he always sat in the front row. His sister writes, "He lost none of the lecture, following the movement of the lips with great concentration, thus using his eyes to replace his hearing. Then he would borrow his neighbor's written notes, enlarge on them, and if need be he would go to the professor for further clarification." In July of 1901, he graduated second in his class. By the time he was twenty-seven, the desire to become a priest was foremost in La Fonta's mind. Unfortunately, he faced almost unanimous opposition because of turn-of-the-century preconceptions about deaf people and the general mislabeling of "deaf-mutes." These deep-seated misunderstandings led to a common belief that a man born deaf would not be able to perform valid sacraments as a priest.

In philosophical terms, there were (and are) three keys for the validity of a sacrament: a valid minister with proper intention, valid form (words that signify the required meaning) and valid matter (material such as bread, wine, water, etc.). The proper intention of an ordained priest was generally assumed, and valid matter (*res*) was simple enough to ensure. However, in a case like La Fonta's, valid form (*verba*) would be subject to great scrutiny. Catholic doctrine asserted that during the celebration of the church's sacraments, the priest acted *in persona Christi* (in the person of Christ), especially while pronouncing the Latin words of certain prayers. Especially during the Eucharistic prayer, the Church took great care to fulfill Christ's saving action in a theologically correct manner. Although Jesus did not speak Latin during his Last Supper but rather Aramaic (or possibly Hebrew), for centuries the church used a blended combination of gospel passages as the words of consecration. Without any intention to preserve a verbatim gospel text, a process of gradual development over the centuries resulted in an established Latin Mass which the church standardized as a fixed, written text. During Council of Trent (1545–1563), Pope St. Pius V had specified by his Papal Bull *De Defectibus* (On Defects) that if the priest were to take away or change anything from the form of consecration of the Body and the Blood, and by this change the words would not have the same meaning, the sacrament would not be confected. If he should add or subtract anything that would not change the meaning he would confect it but would be guilty of very grave sin.[4] In addition to stringent requirements for clear speech, by the early twentieth century the valid form of the Latin Mass had developed to include not only the text of the words to be spoken but also rubrics, which were precise instructions and norms. The

---

4. Council of Trent, "Concerning Defects Which May Occur at Mass," no. 18, in *The Introductory Matters of the Roman Missal of 1962*, ed. Christopher R. J. Ruder (Columbus, Ohio: 2009).

rubrics included what the priest must say aloud and what quietly, in what tone the words should be spoken, and which parts should be sung during solemn High Masses. All these conditions contributed to the theological and canonical necessity for proper pronunciation, especially the words of consecration during which the divine action of transubstantiation would occur. High standards for ecclesiastical Latin and the exacting practice of rubrics ensured that the Mass was not only filled with reverence and beauty but also that it was correct and uniform wherever in the world it was celebrated. Many historical conditions, from the Protestant reformation to the Enlightenment, contributed to a reductive reliance on rubrics, and by La Fonta's time these rules were often interpreted with rigid scrupulosity.

A lack of proper pronunciation would have been an obstacle not only for the celebration of the Eucharist but of any sacrament. "Hearing confessions" in a conventional rite of reconciliation would have been impossible for a priest who could not hear at all, but provisions might be made for a penitent to confess by writing. The more problematic question was whether a deaf-mute priest would be able to say the Latin words of absolution properly. For all these reasons, the church took great care not to ordain a priest who would likely have imperfect speech. Beyond theological and canonical impediments, there were also ministerial obstacles for a deaf candidate to the priesthood. Priests were ordained to minister to the church as a whole or at least to all of the people in a candidates' diocese or in the regions of service for a given religious order. A "deaf-mute" man's inability to pronounce words clearly in French would generally prevent his ministering to people in a French-speaking diocese, and the church would resist ordaining a priest to serve only a small minority such as deaf people. In short, La Fonta's superiors and the officials in Rome would be predisposed to turn down his request for ordination before he even had a chance to prove himself.

He applied to several religious orders. The Benedictines and the Jesuits were categorical in their refusals, the former because of the centrality of chanting of the divine office to their way of life and the latter because of the importance of preaching in their constitution. Both orders insisted it would be impossible to make an exception. A religious order might admit him, he was told, but only as a lay brother. The Augustinians of the Assumption (or Assumptionists), however, considered the possibility that he might make a choir vicar—an administrative position in support of cathedral activities. They agreed to a trial of three months "because there was a certain anxiety about the difficulties that might arise from the infirmity. And yet, there was also the fact that a religious vocation should not be thwarted." La Fonta wrote to his mother:

You see that our prayers have not been fully answered. We just continue to pray with great patience. The Consultors feel it is better not to pursue the request for the priesthood at this time. They feel it would be better to wait a little while so that I can learn to pronounce perfectly and thus make a better impression on the examining bishop, who might happen to be very exacting.

With perseverance, La Fonta entered the Assumptionist novitiate in 1906 and was allowed to take the religious habit, but he endured a great deal of anxiety about whether he would be accepted into the priest-hood—so much so that he reversed his earlier desire not to have a cure:

Dear Mother, I'd do anything to help you bear this cross. I have made a novena asking for the healing of my ears. Please ask the little deaf-mute girls of [the Catholic school in] Bordeaux to pray for this intention. Should the Assumptionists decide not to keep me, I would be deeply sorrowful and would be loath to accept the separation.... I will certainly suffer many contradictions and many criticisms.

In April of 1913, his case was examined in Nice, where he made such a good impression that the bishop, Monsignor Henri-Louis Chapon, sent him to Rome immediately to ask for a dispensation. Unfortunately, World War I broke out in 1914, while he was waiting there for a review of his case, and he had to return to Bordeaux. Because of his deafness, La Fonta was not allowed to enlist in the French medical corps, but he was permitted to care for the sick and wounded in the infirmary set up at the National Institute for Deaf-Mutes near his home.

Finally, an answer came. In spite of the prayers, the cardinals who studied the case all gave a negative answer without giving a reason for their refusal. The superior of his order told La Fonta that such a dispensation had never been granted and could not be granted unless the person were cured. When La Fonta heard this result, he did not give up. He expressed his conviction that the Pope would have the final say "and one word from him would indicate God's will." Again he wrote his mother:

The answer was not a surprise to me. The cardinals must have thought that the deaf-mute in question, although better trained than most, could not possess the necessary aptitudes nor a suitable pronunciation. They must have said: *Ma nono tutti matti!* They are all mad! Not having seen me, they based their decision on generalities.... If the Roman congregations persist in their refusal, in order not to create a precedent, then the only way to know God's will is to speak to the Holy Father himself.

But how would such a humble young man be able to appeal to Pope Benedict XV himself?

In May of 1916, when he was thirty-eight years old, La Fonta met Canon Jean-Pierre Rousselot, professor of linguistics at the Sorbonne, who helped him continue to correct and perfect his pronunciation even this late in his adulthood. In addition to inventing both the theory and the practical system of phonetics that are now standard for teaching reading in Western public schools worldwide, Rousselot was well connected in influential circles of society. He had been the personal tutor of another deaf pupil, Princess Henriette of Bourbon, sister of Empress Zita, the wife of Emperor Charles of Austria. Canon Rousselot began to champion La Fonta, introducing him to his friend Cardinal Andrieu Gaspari. In addition to Gaspari, Rousselot's acquaintance led to a meeting with Cardinal Billot, who recommended that La Fonta come back to Rome immediately. Cardinal Louis Billot, who was about to have an audience with Pope Benedict XV, said that he would speak directly to the Holy Father about La Fonta's case. When this transpired, Billot explained that the case did not depend on the Holy Office but on the Congregation of the Sacraments. Everyone involved in the case assumed that this congregation would be an easier and quicker route for La Fonta than direct papal dispensation. However, this congregation refused to furnish a solution. Their deliberations may have been complicated by the first major codification of canon law, begun under the papacy of Pope St. Pius X and promulgated under Pope Benedict XV in 1917. Under this new code, the Catholic Church explicitly prevented the ordination of any man "impaired in body who cannot safely because of [a defect] ... conduct ministry at the altar."[5] While the 1917 Code of Canon Law did not explicitly mention deaf men, several commentators on canon law specified deafness as one of those defects that made ordination impossible. Under these conditions, even if La Fonta would be able to meet the

5. 1917 CIC 984, in Edward N. Peters, "Canonical Developments Culminating in the Ordination of Deaf Men during the Twentieth Century," *Josephinum Journal of Theology* 15, no. 2 (2008): 427–28.

criteria for a valid Mass, he could easily run the risk of illicit ministry at the altar. Undeterred and full of persistence, La Fonta decided to deliver a direct petition of appeal through his Superior General, along with his examiner's full report, in order to allow the Pope to give his own final decision based on complete evidence. Of course, the answer did not come immediately.

In 1918 a consultant was sent from Rome to examine La Fonta's pronunciation and variations in tone of voice. Mme Chaunac-Lanzac explains, "Mgr. Minghini, very much interested, inquired about the way his mother had trained him and then understood why it was so easy for him to complete his studies. He left with a friendly smile saying, 'I hope the Holy Father will accept you.'" In February of 1919, La Fonta was summoned to Rome after more deliberation, reports, and correspondence. He traveled there with his superior on a religious pilgrimage along with sixty war widows, stopping to pray at holy sites along the way. Finally, on November 23, an answer came, and it was favorable. After fifteen long years of waiting, La Fonta, his family, and his order were overjoyed. The event was announced in Paris on January 15, 1920:

In spite of an infirmity which placed an insurmountable canonical impediment to his desire to become a priest, he has been admitted to the clerical state.... The decision takes on the form of a particular instance, yet it is a new approach to the principles involved. This is the first time that this kind of a problem has been submitted to Rome, and the solution overthrows all actual ecclesiastical jurisprudence used to solve questions of this kind. However, similar cases will not necessarily be solved in the same way, because, although the question of law will no longer be an obstacle, the questions of fact will still have to be examined carefully.[6]

Specifically, the wording of La Fonta's papal indult imparted the privilege of pronouncing in a low voice, as well as a stipulation that at first La Fonta should celebrate Mass in private, *contrariis quibuscumque non abstantibus*—the contrary not being out of question over time.

Abbé Jean-Marie (his new religious name) was forty-two years old and had worked for decades to perfect his pronunciation so that he could say the words of the Mass clearly. This delay and struggle were largely because of general preconceptions about "deaf-mutes." All it would have

6. The announcement appeared in the Assumptionist's "Family News." The original of this document is housed in the Assumptionist Archives in Rome, Italy. Special thanks to Audrey Seah at the University of Notre Dame University for her persistent research efforts.

taken is an earlier in-person interview to disperse these preconceptions, but La Fonta's patience and perseverance were unshakable. Fr. La Fonta was ordained on June 29, 1921, with his mother and siblings in attendance. His restrictions on public Masses were lifted almost immediately when it became apparent that he performed every function perfectly and spoke flawlessly. This decision illustrates the complexity of debates about deafness in the priesthood from the beginning: because of the many variables—physiological, social, and cultural—deafness in future candidates for the priesthood would need to be considered on a case-by-case basis. However, there was no denying that La Fonta had broken a major barrier. What Jesus said to the deaf man in the Gospel of Mark, the church had said to deaf men with potential vocations: Be opened!

The way for others was opened by Fr. Jean-Marie La Fonta's ordination, but it was the prayerful perseverance and long-suffering faith of this gentle man that would begin to open the prejudiced mindset of French society concerning deafness and religious ritual. La Fonta's greatest handicap was not his inability to hear but rather the misconceptions of society about deaf people in general. Once he had broken through this barrier, he began immediately to minister to the deaf in France. As the first congenitally deaf priest, La Fonta helped show the world that it was possible for some profoundly deaf people to master languages and any subject matter studied by hearing people. But perhaps more importantly, he showed the world that deaf people have a need to use their personal talents and strengths by giving back as full members of society and of the church.

La Fonta, the Deaf Evangelist

By the time he was ordained in 1920, Abbé La Fonta was well prepared to minister broadly, both in spoken language to hearing people and in sign language to deaf people. Perhaps most significant from the point of view of Deaf Catholic history, La Fonta's sign language homilies were almost certainly the first ever delivered to assemblies of deaf signers by a congenitally deaf priest. Whatever fruit Abbé La Fonta's ministry produced for hearing people, the fruit of his deaf ministry was more significant, both during his lifetime and beyond.

After his ordination, Abbé La Fonta made ministry to the deaf his constant, driving work as a priest. Mme Chaunac-Lanzac reports that on the day of his ordination on June 29, 1921, the new priest prayed: "Dear Lord, I will be your priest. I shall also be the deaf-mutes' priest, teach them your commandments, and lead them on the way to you." Only two days later, La Fonta visited the deaf students at the Institute for the Deaf at rue de Manille, Paris. He joined the children on the playground and talked to them about how happy he was to be their priest. After this school, he visited others, including the National Institute for Deaf girls in Bordeaux and the Institute for the Deaf in Poitiers. At every school, the children were delighted to greet the priest who was a "deaf-mute" like themselves. In his work with the deaf in France, Fr. La Fonta traveled constantly and worked tirelessly for the remainder of his life. There is a particular drive that imbues pastoral workers and ministers enculturated to the language and the isolated conditions of deaf communities today, and it was much the same in La Fonta's time. Judging from the way he selflessly gave himself to communicating the faith to deaf children in Catholic schools, La Fonta clearly possessed this gift, which is surely none other than a charism for language and preaching, combined with a pressing apostolic zeal. The urgency came from a knowledge that sign language was simply overlooked or even disdained by people and institutions in hearing culture.

La Fonta knew that the deaf community in France needed a culturally deaf priest, because he had experienced the lack of communication with the church that deafness entailed, even after growing up in Catholic schools where oral education in spoken French was the first concern. It was the addition of communication in sign language that had been missing—the true connection to those in the deaf community for whom the visual was the first and most natural mode of communication. For some, it may even have been the only mode of communication. For today's Deaf Catholics and perhaps for anyone with an understanding of enculturation in deaf mission work, it is a great irony that La Fonta had to endure thirty years of perfecting French and Latin pronunciation to utter the words of the Mass in private where only God could hear him— and all the while his bishop and the Roman congregations approving him showed no interest whatsoever in his ability to communicate directly with people who needed him, people in the very midst of French life who had literally never heard the gospel. Because sign language is not a spoken or written language, it did not register in the realm of human languages to the culture of the church in France or in Rome. Remarkably, in the context of society at large, sign language did not yet register as a true language even to La Fonta himself.

Although sources do not say much about his methods of preaching and evangelizing, one question arises in terms of his mode of communication: Did Abbé La Fonta speak to the deaf with his well-trained voice or did he use sign language? The answer is surely that he used both, as well as some unvoiced lipreading in the natural manner of deaf signers today, adapting his communication to the language needs of his audience. The school La Fonta had attended as a child, the Institute for Deaf-Mutes in Bordeaux, was a branch of the famous school founded in 1760 by Abbé l'Épée, the first champion of sign language in deaf education. Although he also stressed oral methods, l'Épée's philosophy that deaf education must show through the eye what other people learn through the ear would have enabled him to communicate with deaf students in their own vernacular outside of the classroom, where a more personal evangelization took place. After his early education at the Institute, La Fonta knew both spoken French and Old French Sign Language (as it is called today). What a tribute it must have been when, for a centennial celebration in honor of Abbé Sicard, the president of the French Society for the Advancement of Deaf-Mutes requested Abbé La Fonta as the celebrant for Mass.[7] In his first public Mass, the assembly heard his perfectly trained voice speak the words of prayer for his benefactor. But for students and graduates of Sicard's school, it was La Fonta's example as a deaf role model that brought honor to people like them, especially his ability to communicate visually and share their identity as deaf people who could be fully mature in their Catholic faith. There was, of course, no way for his deaf apostolate to appreciate La Fonta's meticulously trained speech.

In 1924, Fr. La Fonta obtained permission to receive the confessions of deaf people—again, a precedent that may not have benefited deaf people beyond his small community until much later in the twentieth century. La Fonta then offered the church's sacrament of reconciliation to Deaf Catholics in their own language, to most for the first time. Again, the actual methods of communicating the sacrament are not recorded, but surely the penitents saw the Latin words of absolution on La Fonta's

7. Paul Deschanel, President, Association pour l'avancement des Sourds-Muets, letter to Ernest Boudoy, Procuror Général des Augustins de l'Assomption, April 11, 1922, Assumptionists Archive, Rome, Italy. Special thanks to Audrey Seah for her persistent research efforts.

lips and, more importantly, understood them in his accompanying vernacular signs—an advantage most hearing penitents lacked at the time.
Without this sacrament, many deaf people would not have been able to
receive the Eucharist and therefore were deprived of spiritual sustenance
and the life of their church community. (Although Catholics were instructed to refrain from receiving the Eucharist only if they experienced
themselves as being in a state of mortal sin, it was common practice and
belief at the time that Catholics went to confession before receiving
communion.) La Fonta also gave religious conferences in sign language
to deaf adults who were former students of the National Institute. His
service to the deaf grew as his priestly life progressed:

At a reunion in Poitiers, Jean-Marie gave the homily at Mass. He spoke very
distinctly and used sign language. Everyone understood him and appreciated
the things he spoke about. His love for the deaf could be seen in everything he
did. Jean-Marie knew only too well the needs of the deaf-mutes. They needed
to be accepted in society, to overcome the sense of rejection, to be at peace with
themselves.

In addition to his religious services, Fr. La Fonta spoke out about education for the deaf. Although he used and appreciated sign language, he
was also an advocate of new scientific and technological advances that
might assist the deaf to understand the spoken word, to read languages
based on the spoken word, and to speak to people in hearing society. In
July 1926, he wrote a paper for the General Assembly of the Association
for the Deaf in Nantes in which he advocated oral methods for educating the deaf: "After leaving school the students will be able to learn sign
language which will allow them to communicate with each other at a
distance. Lip reading can only be learned if the teacher avoids as many
gestures or signs as possible. It requires too much attention focused on
the lips and their movement." Of course, it was his own experience that
taught him the work and sacrifice needed for deaf children to even have
a chance at developing a complete, internal model of French and its spoken grammar.

It is interesting that La Fonta supported so wholeheartedly the more
German and English method of oral communication and lipreading, to
the exclusion of the revolutionary French method of signs and speech,
at least in the classroom. His life was a product of the controversy over
methods in deaf education. Signs, for La Fonta, were not for learning
the French language, but without La Fonta's privileged childhood and

private tutoring well into adulthood, many deaf children simply failed to reach his level of spoken and written language. Learning French was difficult for deaf students who had to focus on oral language and its written counterpart through the often-indistinguishable shapes of the lips and tongue. This took complete—and often forced—focus and training daily for years in childhood and adolescence, while hearing children spent time learning history, science, and religion. Many linguists would argue that French is more difficult to lip read than English because more French vowels are visibly indistinguishable, but for the sake of illustration, a simple list of such words in English makes the difficulty clear: *mat, pat, bat, mad, pad, bad, mitt, pit, bit, bid, bed, med, pet, met*, and *bet* are all visibly indistinguishable. Inconveniently, even number pairs can be a problem, such as *seven/eleven, thirteen/thirty, fourteen/forty*, and so on. Contrary to the presumption of most hearing people, the typical deaf person did not (and still does not) read lips better than the typical hearing person, who unwittingly picks up some lipreading by constant exposure to the combined auditory-and-visual reception of spoken languages. Like most deaf people, La Fonta found signs more useful and natural for communicating ideas at a distance or for communication between deaf people themselves. Preaching or other oratory from a podium in a large assembly, for example, was impossible to receive through lipreading alone.

In all of his work with the deaf community, La Fonta supported inclusion and integration into society, which certainly was the reason for his support of oral education. As his sister wrote of the Deaf Catholics in his ministry, "He loved them because he knew their needs, and he became closely associated with them.... In the short span of his priestly life, Jean-Marie planted the seed. He never knew the growth that followed. It was left to others to nurture the apostolate he had begun." As the first deaf man to be ordained a Catholic priest, La Fonta's life had been a long road of faithful struggle, self-sacrifice, study, and painful elocutionary training, all in the hope of eventually becoming a priest who could serve the Deaf as one of their own. After his ordination and only a few years of this demanding work, La Fonta's health began to fail. On February 19, 1929, he died peacefully at home, surrounded by his family. He was fifty-one years old. As a newsletter for Deaf Catholics in Paris reported, "All the deaf, regardless of denomination, learned with real interest of the success of this exceptional deaf man who passed the difficult examination that the church demands to serve Christ under the surplice, the stole, and the chasuble. From this point of view, Abbé La Fonta surpassed the deaf Episcopal priests of the United States."[8]

Attending his deathbed, La Fonta's sister suggested that, as a priest, one of his nephews should replace him. He nodded agreement, but then added, "May my death call forth a new deaf-mute priest, for they truly need one."

8. Henry Gaillard in *La Gazette des Sourds-Muets*, quoted in *The Silent Advocate* (newsletter of St. Rita's School for the Deaf, Cincinnati) 6, no. 3 (December 1927).

CHAPTER 6

Brazilian Apostles

Brazil, the fifth-largest country in the world in both territory and population, is a land of great diversity. Brazilian history spans ancient tribal nations, sixteenth-century conquistadors, colonial expansion, an enormous African slave trade, violent political upheaval, democratic reformation, and massive twentieth-century waves of Portuguese, Italian, German, Arab, and Japanese immigration. With a population that is 65 percent Catholic, Brazil currently contains the largest Catholic population of any single nation. Such rich ethnic and economic diversity has given birth to vibrant metropolitan cities—São Paulo and Rio de Janeiro—but also to widespread poverty and social exclusion, especially in rural areas. Today, Brazil remains a developing nation where access to medical technology and social services can be scarce in places. Perhaps partly because of this, the country contained an unusually large deaf population during the late twentieth-century mission activity described in this chapter, and it is even larger today. Studies by the Brazilian Institute of Geography and Statistics show that 9.8 million Brazilians suffered from hearing loss in 2011. This number represented 5.2 percent of the Brazilian population, 2.6 million of whom are deaf and 7.2 million of whom are hard of hearing. In 2017, the World Health Organization reported that over half a million Brazilian children, ages newborn to fourteen years, had at least moderate hearing loss.[1]

1. The 2011 study was made by IBGE, the Brazilian Institute of Geography and Statistics, in conjunction with the World Health Organization. The numbers are in the process of being reevaluated and may in fact be higher. The World Health Organization website regularly publishes revised, up-to-date global estimates on the prevalence of hearing loss. See *Global Costs of Unaddressed Hearing Loss and Cost-Effectiveness of Interventions,* Geneva: World Health Organization, 2017, https://apps.who.int/iris/bitstream/handle/10665/254659/9789241512046-eng.pdf;sequence=1.

For an example of Brazilian scholarship on the social impact of deafness, see Lys Maria Allenstein Gondim et al., "Study of the Prevalence of Impaired Hearing and Its Determinants in the City

After Portuguese, Brazil's second most-used language is Libras (from *Língua Brasileira de Sinais* or Brazilian Sign Language). The National Congress of Brazil recognized Libras as an official language in 2002, when its use became mandated in education and government services. The linguistic and cultural development of Libras and its widespread use across Brazil owe much to Catholic missions and deaf ministry during the twentieth century, which is the subject of the present chapter. By the count of some linguists, three million users of sign language (deaf and hearing) reportedly live scattered throughout the country today— an astounding number compared to the 271,700 sign language users in the United States; the 327,000 users of British Sign Language throughout the world; and perhaps only 100,000 users of French Sign Language (perhaps because of the availability of advanced hearing aid technology and cochlear implant use).[2] It is possible that these demographics are somewhat inflated by the reports of sign language advocates. However, because of the country's large population combined with its religious history, it is clear that Brazil's Deaf Catholic community is the largest in any one nation, and for that reason Brazilian deaf heritage is immensely important in Deaf Catholic history.

Much of the Deaf Catholic faith community across Brazil owes its existence to two priests who spent several decades ministering to deaf people all over the country. First, Father Vincente Burnier, a native member of the Deaf Catholic community in Brazil, became the second-ever congenitally deaf man in the world to be ordained a priest. With him worked a hearing American Redemptorist missionary, Father Eugene Oates, who was born and grew up in an especially fruitful cradle of deaf ministry, the city of St. Louis, Missouri. At times separately and at times partnering together, Fathers Burnier and Oates celebrated Mass in Libras, led retreats and missions as traveling missionaries, and started deaf services in several dioceses across the nation. They established methods of sacramental instruction for deaf Brazilians, advocated for better education for deaf children, and lobbied for civic privileges such as driver's licenses for deaf drivers. Furthermore, the language of Libras may not have reached its current broad acceptance in Brazilian society without

---

of Itajaí, Santa Catarina State, Brazil," *Brazilian Journal of Otorhinolaryngology* 78, no. 2 (March/April 2012): 27–34.

2. These statistics are published, and frequently updated, in *Ethnologue: Languages of the World*, 17th ed. (2017), an online database of scholarly data on the world's thousands of living languages, accessed January, 2019, www.ethnologue.com.

linguistic scholarship and cultural advocacy spearheaded by these two men. They each played an essential role in the lives of deaf Brazilians during a time when deaf education in the country was shifting from a long tradition of oralism to Libras and bilingualism. For these contributions to Deaf Catholic history, Father Vincente Burnier and Father Eugene Oates are rightly called Brazil's apostles of deaf ministry.[3]

The First Brazilian Deaf Priest

A year after Charles La Fonta was ordained in France, Vincente de Paulo Penido Burnier was born in the small but thriving industrial city of Juiz de Fora, Brazil. The Penido Burnier family was well known for their traditional Catholic way of life, and young Vincente had many relatives who were priests, including several uncles and two brothers. His older brother, Jesuit priest John Bosco Burnier, was martyred on October 11, 1976, in the prelature of São Felix do Araguaia. During a time of political unrest in the Amazon interior, Father John Bosco Burnier was shot by police while defending two native (Indian or *mestizo*) women who were being raped and beaten. With such an exemplary Catholic family, it is no wonder Vincente hoped for a vocation to the priesthood, but like five of his nine siblings, Vincente was born deaf. As Father La Fonta had experienced in France, the presumption in Brazil was that all "deaf-mutes" were unfit for the priesthood. It was assumed that a man who was born deaf could not speak well enough to carry out ecclesiastical duties, particularly the celebration of Mass. For this reason, young Vincente Burnier believed he might never be able to follow in his brothers' and uncles' footsteps and become a priest, but he was determined to try.

After a rigorous primary education at the National Institute for the Deaf in Rio de Janeiro and several years of private speech therapy, Saint Anthony Catholic School admitted Burnier at the age of sixteen. At that time, the school had only twenty-one students, and he was the youngest and the only deaf student. He later explained, "My first surprise was discovering that in addition to Portuguese language, there was a compulsory course in Latin. I had the challenge of studying Latin for six years before I passed exams."[4] Eight of the twenty-one students in his class

---

3. Much historical work remains to be done on deaf communities in Brazil. This chapter relies on many sources from personal testimony, archives still in formation, and internet records from the deaf community.

4. Antônio Campos de Abreu, "Monsenhor Vicente de Paulo Burnier" (historical presentation

were not able to pass exams, but finally Burnier managed to pass and was approved for the Major Seminary of Saint Joseph in Rio de Janeiro to study theology and philosophy, where he took his first advanced seminar in 1941. He graduated in 1947, but there was still the matter of requesting a papal dispensation for his deafness. His bishop, Don Justino José de Santana, wrote a letter to the Vatican, but that was not enough to draw serious attention to his case. His request was delayed for three years because of ever-more stringent interpretations of the 1917 Code of Canon Law. In the meantime, Burnier began to work in an administrative position as archivist of the Archdiocese of Juiz de Fora.

In 1950, Archbishop Justino had to travel to Rome to report on activities of the Juiz de Fora diocese. He decided to take Burnier with him so that the pope might converse with him in person and perhaps decide in his favor. When they arrived, Archbishop Justino called on Vincente's brother Father John Bosco Burnier, who was already in Rome at the time, and the three men requested a private audience with Pope Pius XII the next day. Upon entering, Vincente knelt and begged the Holy Father, "Please, may I be ordained?" The Holy Father lifted him up and told him, "Wait and see." Then, to Archbishop Justino, the Pope said, "He already speaks well, but we need to study this particular case before we give the answer."[5]

During the months he remained in Rome, Vincente was subjected to several rigorous tests in various ecclesiastical colleges, all of which he passed with patience and endurance. Finally, on January 31, 1951, the young man went to the Salesian residence in Rome to pray. It was the feast day of Saint John Bosco, the Salesian priest and educator for whom his brother was named. There, as he recounted later, Vincente Burnier asked for the saint's intercession: "Saint John Bosco, I have prayed every day, but today is my last day to pray about the decision of Pope Pius XII. I will not have to wait anymore, because today he will make his decision. I pray it is a positive one." Two days later, he attended a Mass during which his brother took his perpetual vows as a Jesuit. As he greeted John Bosco Burnier and congratulated him, the future martyr returned his brother's congratulations and gave him the news that Pope Pius XII had granted permission for Vincente's ordination. Before leaving Rome, the

for Feneis, the Federación Nacional de Educación e Integración de Sordos, 2009), based on personal testimony/interviews and archival resources in formation, provided to me by the author, a culturally deaf historian, native user of Libras, and cofounder of Feneis (established 1987). Quotes translated by Patrick Mahicka.

5. Campos de Abreu, "Monsenhor Vicente de Paulo Burnier."

two brothers went to thank the Holy Father. Vincente spoke to the pope, and the Holy Father promised to pray for him on the day of his ordination, which was set for September 22, 1951, back in Juiz de Fora.[6]

In an interview with a reporter some years after his ordination, Burnier said that he dared to consider a vocation because of a French book he had read about a congenitally deaf man who had become a priest.[7] This book, of course, was the biography of Father Jean-Marie La Fonta written by his sister. Without that precedent, Burnier may never have considered it possible even to request a dispensation. In fact, Father Burnier considered the book on La Fonta so important that he translated it into Portuguese himself, so that other Deaf Catholics in Brazil might know it was possible for a deaf man to have a religious vocation in the church.[8]

For Vincente Burnier, admission to the seminary and priestly formation had required clear speech and an ability to absorb class material without the help of specialized support services. Only at the end of the twentieth century did professional interpreters become a possible accommodation in wealthier Western countries, and even today there is no guarantee of funding for interpreters in seminary education. For many deaf aspirants to the priesthood, this would effectively be an obstacle based on language difference and cultural assumptions. Even into the late twentieth century, most of the world's culturally deaf priests believed this obstacle insurmountable until they happened to meet a priest who was either deaf or fluent in sign language. Fortunately, Vincente Burnier was confident enough in his verbal and written language skills to pursue a seminary education once he learned that at least one deaf man had successfully become a priest. While his deafness was congenital and profound, and while he naturally communicated with other deaf people in Libras, Burnier also knew many of the languages of Brazil's diverse population, including Portuguese, French, Italian, German, and (after his seminary education) he could also read Latin.

As Father La Fonta had done before him, Father Vincente Burnier began to minister to the deaf community in sign language immediately after his ordination. By the time of his death in 2009 at the age of eighty-eight, Burnier had been a priest for fifty-seven years. All of that time he

---

6. Campos de Abreu, "Monsenhor Vicente de Paulo Burnier."

7. Obituary, "Morto il Decano Dei Sacerdoti Sordi," *Newsletter della Storia dei Sordi,* no. 712 (September 9, 2009), accessed May, 2017, http://www.storiadeisordi.it/articolo.asp?ENTRY_ID=2113.

8. Campos de Abreu, "Monsenhor Vicente de Paulo Burnier."

worked to include Brazilian deaf people in the sacraments and the life of the church, as well as to improve their social status and living conditions. Between 1965 and 1977, together with Father Eugene Oates, CSsR, Father Burnier founded eighteen pastoral centers and missions throughout Brazil, as well as in Argentina and Uruguay, initiating an international South American ministry for Deaf Catholics. Throughout his work with the deaf apostolate, his greatest hope was the development and refinement of sign languages as true native languages of deaf people. In his own words, "Our greatest concern for the benefit of the deaf should be this: To correct, to improve, and to better the expressive power of the sign language in order that all those who did not have the good fortune of completely attaining the use of pure oral language may obtain the great happiness of being able to live integrated among themselves through greater mutual understanding and brotherly love."[9]

Because of his constant, hands-on involvement in the deaf apostolate, not just as a "missionary from the mainstream" but as one of their own, Father Burnier was beloved in the deaf community. Now ten years after his death, Brazilian Deaf Catholics are still in the process of gathering stories and documents about his life to create a Monsignor Vincente de Paul Burnier memorial library. He is remembered for visiting all the deaf communities in Brazil regularly by bus or even on horseback, where he would preach, celebrate weddings, and offer confessions, using Libras as much as possible. The coordinator of Pastoral Care of the Deaf in the Archdiocese of Juiz de Fora said of Burnier, "He lived to catechize the deaf, was the pastor of this excluded people. His death leaves a void that is impossible to measure."[10] All of this he did while also serving as archivist of the Metropolitan Curia in the city of Juiz de Fora. North American Deaf Catholics were also inspired by Burnier during his visit in 1953 to the fourth annual gathering of the newly formed International Catholic Deaf Association in Detroit, Michigan. Before his visit, most deaf people in North America were not aware that a Deaf Catholic priest had ever been ordained. He created a sensation at the conference by communicating in sign language and celebrating a solemn high Mass in Lat-

9. Vincente de Paulo Penido Burnier, "History of Sign Language in Brazil," in Harry Hoemann, Eugene Oates, and Shirley Hoemann, *The Sign Language of Brazil*, English Edition (Mill Neck, N.Y.: Mill Neck Foundation, 1981), 23.

10. Conferencia Nacional dos Bispos do Brazil, "Mons. Burnier: Falece Primiero Padre Surdo da America Latina," Storia dei Sordi, July 24, 2009, http://www.storiadeisordi.it/articolo.asp?ENTRY _ID=1625.

in, proving to the deaf community of North America that it was indeed possible for a deaf man to become a Catholic priest.[11]

The Redemptorist Tradition of Deaf Ministry Continues in Brazil

Only a year after Father Eugene Oates (or Eugênio as he was known in Brazil) was ordained a Redemptorist priest, he accepted a missionary assignment in the Brazilian state of Amazonia, a region long fraught with political unrest and extensive poverty. In an undeveloped area, far from the fine Catholic schools attended by Father Burnier in São Paolo, Father Oates first encountered poor and isolated Brazilian deaf people. In the town of Manaus, there was a residential school for children with all kinds of disabilities—some were blind, some were physically or developmentally disabled, and some were deaf.[12] He began to visit the school regularly and to seek out deaf adults in the surrounding area. When he witnessed the poverty and separation of Brazilian deaf people from society firsthand, he resolved to help them expand their native sign language, develop deaf social services, find employment, and become active and contributing citizens in their home regions. To facilitate this work, he aimed to help dioceses establish thriving and connected Deaf Catholic communities across Brazil.

From 1946 until 1977, Father Oates undertook several mission trips which served a double purpose: to minister to the isolated Deaf Catholics on the margins of Brazilian society and to further his trailblazing research on regional differences in Brazilian sign language. In reality, the first aim depended upon the second, because broader linguistic knowledge of Brazilian sign language was needed to help enculturate deaf people, both into Brazilian society and into the rich religious heritage that was their birthright as baptized Catholics. In 1946, when Father Oates began his work in Brazil, academic knowledge of sign languages and their dialects was still so new that he was surprised to learn that sign languages differed from nation to nation, much less from region to region within the same country.

11. Colette Gabel, "The Birth of the I.C.D.A. and Its Progress" (1959), graphic-illustrated booklet, ICDA History section, Deaf Catholic Archives, College of the Holy Cross, Worcester, Mass.

12. Eugene Oates, CSsR, "The Apostolate amongst the Deaf," *Mission Renewal Program* (Maryknoll: September 11, 1977), 2–3, Deaf Catholic Archives, College of the Holy Cross, Worcester, Mass.

Father Oates's interest in deaf ministry began when he was attending the minor seminary in St. Louis, Missouri. One of the Redemptorist missionaries who worked in the deaf apostolate (perhaps Daniel Higgins or Julian Grehan) gave a talk to the seminarians. It made an impression on Oates, who later recounted this missionary's words: "Why don't you multiply your priesthood? Learn another language and you can be a priest two times over." The missionary suggested a similarity between the deaf population and Mexican immigrants in Texas, Arizona, New Mexico, and California—that is, language minority groups that usually had no priest to help them because of a shortage of priests who knew their language. "Some of you will be working there later on, so why not pick up Spanish," this missionary told the seminarians, "Or you can learn the sign language of the deaf and be able to communicate with them and help them ... even if it's only spelling out the prayers by the manual alphabet for a poor dying deaf person."[13] With two other seminarians, Oates began to study sign language fifteen minutes per day in his free time. He learned everything he could about sign language and deaf education from other missionaries and no doubt from the Sisters of St. Joseph, who often would allow seminarians to observe classes at their school for deaf children, which was still using sign language at the time.

As a Redemptorist missionary, Father Oates had a deep commitment to bringing the gospel to this most abandoned population on the fringes of Brazilian society. The principal problem of deaf people, as Oates saw it, was not so much a lack of hearing as a lack of communication in general. As he constantly explained to other missionaries and to Brazilians themselves, one could help deaf people overcome many of their difficulties in society just by learning how to communicate with them. As he continued to study regional differences in sign language, he often worked closely with Father Vincente Burnier, who was essential both to his research (because of his native knowledge of Brazilian sign language) and as a Deaf Catholic role model in the pastoral care and cultural development of Brazilian deaf people. The two priests would travel to different areas of the country to establish deaf services and, at the same time, further Oates's research on Brazilian sign language. The many dialects of sign language in Brazil had not yet been standardized by widespread use, and Libras was not yet officially known by this name or recognized as a language at all. It would take decades of work by Father Oates and other

13. Oates, "The Apostolate amongst the Deaf," 3–4.

advocates before the official acceptance of Libras as a national language in Brazil.

With sponsorship from the National Institute for the Deaf in Rio (supported by the U.S. Agency for International Development as part of the Brazilian Ministry of Education),[14] Father Oates authored a comprehensive dictionary of Libras, entitled *Brazilian Sign Language*, first published in 1969. The vocabulary contained in this book is a synthesis of signs used by deaf communities in six regions of Brazil. Photographs of one thousand two hundred fifty different signs correspond to five thousand words, including several Portuguese synonyms for each sign. Proceeding on the principle that approximately one thousand words of any language is a functional vocabulary, he gathered certain signs from the deaf people in each region who had the most language competency. As he compiled the book, he consulted with representatives of the deaf community to choose a single best sign for each concept he wanted to include. Not only did the book become a standard text for teaching Libras to missionaries, educators, and hearing friends and family members of deaf Brazilians, it also contributed to the development of Libras vocabulary for the whole of the Brazilian deaf community. It offered deaf Brazilians new signs to augment and enrich each region's original vocabulary and helped to ensure that Brazilians from different parts of the country could communicate with each other in the same language. Oates's dictionary was the first of its kind in South America and is still considered groundbreaking work. His years of extensive research, carried out as a natural extension of an evangelization based on cultural dialogue and greater understanding, were an important step toward standardizing Libras as an official language in Brazil.

As travelling missionaries in the early years, Fathers Oates and Burnier would seldom spend more than two weeks in a city or town. When they arrived, they would go out into the community to gather up deaf people for the celebration of Mass in sign language. They walked the crowded streets and mingled in bars, asking about deaf residents and watching for people using sign language. When they found deaf people, Oates and Burnier would sit and chat with them in sign language about their problems, then invite them to a place that had been set aside as a temporary "mission"—often in a local home or outdoors in a yard, where they would begin the work of catechizing the deaf community in the

14. Oates, "The Apostolate amongst the Deaf," 6.

immediate area. They used visual adaptations in their liturgy as much as possible. While visiting a Maryknoll Mission Renewal conference in New York in 1977, Oates explained some of these adaptations. He and Burnier often used a slide projector, stopping to explain pictures that had some connection to the meaning of different parts of the Mass. For example, before the offertory, he would show pictures of a wheat field, a bakery with bread coming out of the oven, Christ multiplying the loaves and fishes, and the Last Supper. "I explained how we eat bread for our bodies to have strength and life and how Jesus promised to give us the Bread of Life, He Himself in Holy Communion," Oates told fellow missionaries, "As I offer up the Hosts the deaf extend their hands, symbolizing the paten, and they offer up their prayers privately, offering to God the host in union with the priest, offering up their lives, the joys and sorrows and all they have."[15]

At weddings of deaf couples, Father Oates would have the bride and groom kneel before the altar, where he would tie their joined hands together with a ribbon, the same color as the dress of the bride. While an altar boy held the Bible, Oates would translate into Libras the words of Genesis: that a man shall leave his mother and father, join his wife, and with her become one flesh. Then, he had the couple give Holy Communion to each other, facing each other and holding the chalice together as they each drank from it in turn. "They have given the Sacrament of Matrimony to one another," Oates explained to his fellow missionaries. Afterwards, the couple would light candles from the Easter candle, and he would explain the meaning of the Easter candle in Libras "and talk about the fire of love and God's grace and life, which they share." It is well worth noting the forward-thinking efforts of Oates and Burnier, considering that these missionaries to deaf people were making liturgical adaptations in Libras well before the Second Vatican Council encouraged widespread liturgical renewal and certainly before sign language was officially approved for use in the Mass.

In most of his teaching and preaching, Oates used a mixed mode of communication, speaking and signing at the same time. It was this method he advocated for use in schools for deaf children across Brazil. "In this way," he explained, "the deaf can often read some of the words on the lips and pick up the rest by means of the gestures. When there's a doubt as to what was said, the hand alphabet or writing on a pad can

15. Oates, "The Apostolate amongst the Deaf," 5–6.

be used."[16] Although he encouraged the use of Total Communication and mixed modes of speaking and signing for hearing missionaries and teachers who wished to communicate with deaf people, Oates was well aware of the naturally spatial grammar in the visual language of deaf people. "They use a more abbreviated form," he told colleagues, "a sort of telegraphic communication of ideas." While articulation and tone of voice lend beauty and power to rhetorical and poetic expression in spoken languages, Oates explained, it is a certain rhythmic movement of the hands, arms, and body, as well as precise facial expressions, which mark expert delivery in Libras.[17]

As he continued to learn Libras from Brazilian deaf people themselves, Oates published several works both to educate deaf people about the Catholic faith and to promote awareness of the plight of deaf people among hearing Brazilian Catholics. Most notably for deaf Brazilians, he developed catechetical materials, including a booklet on the Ten Commandments in sign language and a book of prayers entitled *In Silent Faith*, published in 1971. He adapted the contents of *In Silent Faith* for an instructional film by the same title to teach essential Catholic prayers in Brazilian sign language. In 1980, although retired from full-time ministry with deaf Brazilians by that time, he continued to pass on his expertise by participating in an ecumenical project to produce the first Portuguese-language book describing the history, uses, and cultural contexts of Libras. A collaboration of a diverse group of religious and secular people—Lutherans and Catholics, men and women, North and South Americans—resulted in an essay collection, *The Sign Language of Brazil* (1981).[18] Both Father Burnier and Father Oates contributed chapters to this important book.

In addition to these academic pursuits, Father Oates also helped deaf people in Brazil make great strides toward full participation as citizens of their country through persistent advocacy. With the Sisters of St. Joseph in St. Louis as a model for educational practices, he set out to help ensure deaf children's right to an education in Brazil. To prevent delays in language development, he advocated for early enrollment for deaf preschoolers in one of the ten Catholic schools for the deaf or in the few state (and one federal) oral schools which were scattered across the coun-

---

16. Oates, "The Apostolate amongst the Deaf," 5–6.
17. Oates, "The Apostolate amongst the Deaf," 5–6.
18. Harry Hoemann, Eugene Oates, and Shirley Hoemann, *The Sign Language of Brazil*, English Edition (Mill Neck, N.Y.: Mill Neck Foundation, 1981).

try. "Brazilian parents," he once told a reporter, "often believe that they have deaf-mute children as a punishment from God, so they treat them indifferently."[19] Father Oates encouraged such parents to participate in early educational intervention for their deaf infants and children, especially advocating for Portuguese speech therapy and lipreading practice as early in a deaf child's education as possible. Father Oates was an advocate of early oral education for deaf children, but not to the exclusion of sign language as the language of deaf families and the deaf community. Wherever he went, he assured Brazilians that deaf people had a normal human capacity for learning language and that through greater development of bilingual language resources (sign language and Portuguese), their deaf children could be full participants in society. Often, the deaf community and those who served them faced great financial setbacks. During the years of Father Oates's ministry in Brazil, government supported schools for the deaf suffered many steep cuts in annual funding provided by the state, making his task of advocacy that much harder—and the foundation of Catholic ministries and Deaf Catholic communities that much more important.[20]

For several years, Father Oates tried to convince authorities at the Brazilian National Transit Council that deaf people were as capable of driving an automobile as hearing people. Despite the fact that deaf people could already receive a driver's license in several other countries, including the United States, Japan, and throughout Europe, Father Oates could not convince the Brazilian authorities that deaf people would not endanger themselves and others on the road. Finally, in the early 1970s, the development of air-conditioned cars proved the authorities wrong about deaf drivers. Father Oates presented them with a description of air-conditioned cars. He argued that, like deaf people, hearing motorists in air-conditioned cars would not hear any sound coming from the street. The National Transit Council waited three more years to be sure there would not be a rise in traffic accidents because of air conditioning in cars, but ultimately they finalized the decision, and deaf people were able to pursue the legal process of getting a driver's license in Brazil.[21]

Over the course of more than thirty years in Brazil, the many fruits of Father Oates's work in the deaf community encouraged rich develop-

19. "Fé Silencia," *E Leia VEJA*, November 22, 1972.
20. "Fé Silencia."
21. "Padre Eugênio Oates: 32 Años de Trabalho Junto Aos Deficientes Auditivos," *Satuário de Aparecida* (December 13, 1991): 5.

ment in Deaf Catholic culture and accelerated development of Brazilian sign language through the facilitation of community gathering places, social and educational programs, and accessible worship in sign language for deaf Brazilians. As of 2019, there have been organized national, regional, and diocesan meetings of Deaf Catholics in the country for over twenty-three years.[22]

As Father Oates began to expand deaf ministries in Brazil, he focused especially on the education of seminarians who might eventually be able to carry out this work in their own Brazilian provinces. In any given year, he would conduct dozens of seminars and retreats in several Brazilian states, both for lay people and for those in religious orders, especially those who would be engaged in the pastoral care of deaf people. In addition to using the sign language dictionary and catechetical materials he had developed, Father Oates taught seminarians about the social and economic needs of deaf people, suggesting ways to integrate them into the life of a parish and the broader community. To serve the religious needs of all the Deaf Catholics in Brazil, Father Oates believed that at least one hundred and fifty pastoral workers would need training in this ministry. In 1990, he made a documentary about deafness in Brazil to help with this training. Entitled *Sheep without a Shepherd*, it featured the president of the Brazilian National Conference of Bishops, Bishop Luciano Mendes de Almeida, speaking about problems facing deaf people throughout the country. Bishop Almeida remained a great advocate of Deaf Catholics in Brazil, encouraging and supporting Father Oates and Father Burnier in their many sign language projects. On many occasions, the bishop expressed his thanks to Oates's Redemptorist Provincial in the United States for "the precious collaboration of Father Eugênio Oates in the pastoral care of the hearing impaired in Brazil."[23]

The Legacy of Deaf Catholic Brazil

The geographic expansion of deaf missions in South America, for which Father Vincente Burnier and Father Eugênio Oates planted the seeds, follows the pattern of deaf ministries' growth in North America and Europe during the early twentieth century. In the United States and

22. Conferência Nacional dos Bispos do Brasil, http://www.cnbb.org.br/site-do-80-muticom-ja-esta-no-ar/

23. "Padre Eugênio Oates," 5.

Great Britain, the same pattern of expansion happened, for the most part without widespread awareness of Deaf Catholic ministries in these other parts of the world. Today, every diocese in Brazil offers interpreted Masses and Catholic liturgy in Libras. On an even more basic level of enculturation, the very language of deaf people in Brazil, Libras, owes much to the inspired missionary work begun by these two priests and carried out through the development of deaf ministries in the church. Father Burnier's and Father Oates's examples also inspired a notable successor in deaf ministries, Father Wilson Czaia, the second deaf man to be ordained a priest in that country, who now offers weekly Mass in Libras in the Archdiocese of Curitiba and traveling missions in sign language throughout the country.

The influence of one deaf priest becoming the inspiration for other deaf men (who may not have believed it possible to pursue a priestly vocation) is true to the spirit of the deaf apostolate as it grew into a broader community of connected ministries in countries around the world. As Father Wilson Czaia said of Father Burnier in his eulogy: "There is much to say about this great man; however, we have no words to express our deep gratitude for his life, vocation, and mission. The example of his life, his way of overcoming obstacles, motivated me to try to do the will of God through his teachings. Now I feel more responsible than ever as a pastor to the Deaf. They are now orphans of a spiritual father. As the second Deaf priest [in Brazil], I can say that Monsignor Vicente was a great inspiration for me as an affirmation from God for this special mission."[24]

24. Sordos Catolicos, "Murió Monseñor Vicente Burnier, primer sacerdote sordo de América Latina," Testimonios y Trabajos de Catequesis para Personas Sordas, accessed May 2017, http://www .sordoscatolicos.org/Pagina%20de%20Sacerdotes%20Sordos%20Vincente%20Burnier.htm.

CHAPTER 7

English and Irish Apostles

An energetic grandmother with joy in her eyes is telling the story of her engagement to be married, her whole body girlishly animated with sign language. Yes, she recalls, she knew Canon William Hayward. The canon had celebrated the marriage of Denise and her husband and baptized all three of their children. It happened this way: when Denise was a child, she had a difficult time in a hearing school. Fortunately, her parents happened upon a religious brother, a missionary, who was leading a program at a hearing parish. When he met Denise, he recognized that she was deaf and told them about the work that the Sisters of Charity of Our Lady of Evron were doing with deaf people in their community. The family went to meet the sisters, who brought Denise and her parents to see Canon Hayward. He conversed with the little girl for a while, then told her parents to enroll her in Royal Cross School for the Deaf in Preston. "What about Boston Spa?" her mother asked. St. John's School in Boston Spa was the Catholic school for the deaf in west Yorkshire, founded in 1870 by the Daughters of Charity of St. Vincent de Paul. Denise's parents, however, were not religious people. No, Hayward told them, Boston Spa would spend more time on religion than they wished. He advised them to send Denise to Royal Cross Primary School in Preston. At nine years old, she would be a late starter there. "But when you reach the age of twenty," Hayward instructed, "I want you to come back here and become a Catholic."

Denise completed her education at Preston and, as directed, made an appearance at Canon Hayward's Deaf Centre soon after her twentieth birthday. Immediately he recognized her and began catechism, and just as Hayward had advised, Denise became a Catholic. Once that was accomplished, he chose a husband for her. One day after Mass, the Canon introduced her to a young man at the Deaf Centre, saying, "Denise, this is Tony Harris. You two are going to get married." Denise and Tony did get married in a short time, and Canon Hayward himself presided. "That was fifty years ago. We've been very happy," recalls Denise, emitting sounds of delight that punctuate her signs as her husband stands nearby, nodding agreeably. "We loved Canon Hayward. He always said, if you have any problems, you come to me. But he was a very strict man. He laid down the law."[1]

According to the Deaf Catholic community in Manchester, England, and the Sisters of Evron who still serve them, this was not the only case of matchmaking by Canon William Hayward. As the first in three generations of priests who served St. Joseph's Deaf Catholic community, Hayward undoubtedly played the time-honored role of patriarch, for whom matchmaking would have been but one traditional duty. Described by many Deaf Catholics as a second father to them, Hayward had an approach to deaf ministry that was equal parts missionary work and devoted guardianship. The ministry of Hayward and the two generations of priests succeeding him in Manchester—first Charles Hollywood and later Terry O'Meara and Peter McDonough, in partnership with the Sisters of Evron—offer a particularly clear case study of the developments in Deaf Catholic culture during the twentieth century. Often founded by strong-willed yet widely loved men of the World War I generation, twentieth-century Deaf Catholic communities in Europe and the Americas went through a pattern of change that enabled deaf people to have greater self-determination. A gradual emergence of social inclusion took place alongside the slow growth of acceptance and support in the broader culture. All of this contributed to a Deaf Catholic culture that was rich with tradition and becoming more mature in the gifts it brought to the church and to the community. By the 1970s, the community at Manchester fostered not only deaf religious vocations where there had been none before but also Deaf Catholic liturgy in sign language, a greater awareness of international connections among Deaf Catholics, and fuller religious and civic participation for deaf adults. The stories handed down from each generation of ministry speak for themselves about this transformation in Deaf Catholic culture.

1. Denise Harris, interview by Marlana Portolano, interp. Mary O'Meara, Hollywood House and Deaf Centre, Manchester, England, July 10, 2017.

Father Hayward Knows Best

In 1920, the year that Abbé La Fonta was preparing for ordination in
Paris, William Hayward was a young British soldier just returning from
war. Like La Fonta, Hayward struggled for acceptance in the seminary as
a deaf man, and like La Fonta he had a unique understanding of the deaf
community, making him an important forerunner of deaf culture in the
priesthood. Unlike his French counterpart, however, Hayward has the
distinction of spending almost his entire priestly life ministering directly
to Deaf Catholics, giving all his abundant energy to this vocation for
forty-seven years. As a teenager, Hayward had wanted to be an Anglican priest. He began studies at a theological college, but when World
War I broke out he interrupted his studies to serve as an infantryman,
eventually taking part in the Battle for Hill 60 in Belgium. While off
duty, he would visit Catholic churches and attend Benediction in the
local farming community where his platoon was stationed. At the age
of nineteen, Hayward contracted meningitis and was sent back home to
England. The disease left him profoundly deaf and unable to complete
his studies for the Anglican ministry.

Following his discharge from the army in 1915 and subsequent dis-
missal from the Anglican seminary, Hayward remembered his attraction
to Catholicism and began instruction for reception into the Catholic
Church. Unfortunately, his family did not agree with this decision, and
he was left for a time without financial means. "Your religion is not in the
Anglican Church but in the pub!" his father angrily told him.[2] Seeking
a job to support himself where people would accept his disability, he
found a position as a lay teacher of deaf boys at St. John's Catholic School
in Boston Spa. Hayward immediately became immersed in the life and
needs of the students. When he spoke to a religious sister at the school
about the boys not receiving enough religious education, she urged him
to pursue his former vocation, this time in the Catholic Church. "The
boys need a deaf priest," she said, "Why not you?"[3]

Hayward wrote to Bishop Joseph Cowgill in Leeds, who managed
within a year to obtain permission from Rome for Hayward to enter any
seminary that would accept him. But when he applied, every seminary

2. Jack Gee, "Canon Hayward," personal remembrances, Deaf Catholic Archives, College of the
Holy Cross, Worcester, Mass.

3. Terry O'Meara, interview by Marlana Portolano, Bowie, Maryland, July 10, 2016.

rejected him because of his deafness. Finally, a friend who was visiting Oscott College explained Hayward's plight to the rector. Monsignor Parkinson invited him for an interview and on a rainy Saturday evening, Hayward arrived at the rectory door, wet and nervous. When Parkinson answered the door and greeted him in the dim light, Hayward was not able to understand his speech. Parkinson wanted to send him back to his teaching job at Boston Spa immediately, but a storm prevented him from leaving the rectory until Monday morning. Over the weekend, Hayward conversed with the rector for a long time one on one, winning Parkinson's respect with his camaraderie, determination, and religious concern for the deaf community. They developed a strong rapport, and by Sunday the rector had accepted Hayward as a seminarian at St. Mary's College, Oscott.

Not much is recorded about Hayward's experience in the seminary, but certainly it helped that he already had a clear voice. Unlike Charles La Fonta in France, he could demonstrate to Bishop Cowgill that his speech was much the same as a hearing man's and his deafness was therefore not a defect which might invalidate sacramental form under canon law. On December 17, 1927, after a slightly extended period of study, Hayward became (most likely) the first deaf man ordained a priest without a papal dispensation. Finding an appointment for a deaf priest in Leeds was not easy, however, and none came for a long time. Finally, while visiting a friend in the Diocese of Salford a year later, he found a job as chaplain for the Alexian Brothers in Newton Heath. He was prepared to serve in any way he could, but he did not give up on his dream of serving as a priest in the deaf community.

On the afternoon of Good Friday in 1929, a classmate of Hayward's brought him to visit the president of the St. Vincent De Paul Society in Ancoats, a neighborhood near downtown Manchester. After just a few hours of negotiation, the Society agreed to sponsor a mission for Deaf Catholics and appointed Hayward its chaplain. The Sisters of Charity at Ancoats made part of their monastery at St. Joseph's Convent available for this purpose. They called the mission St. Joseph's Mission to the Catholic Deaf and Dumb and laid out its aims: to provide for the special needs of this population, improve religious instruction for deaf adults, and expand the deaf community's reception of the sacraments. The Catholic education of deaf children was to be a special part of the Mission as well, since Catholic parents were concerned when their deaf children had to attend non-Catholic schools. The plan also included a social club where the deaf community would be able to attend lectures, games, and leisure activities.

In a short time, the mission prospered and had to move to a larger building in Old Trafford, where it thrived despite bombing in the Manchester Blitz during World War II. Members of the Deaf Catholic community supported each other during these and other difficult times, and Father Hayward fostered the community's development by providing a wide variety of educational and social activities in sign language. He also had a commitment to growing and developing the broader Deaf Catholic community in Great Britain, so he began to take mission trips several times each year. As a traveling missionary, he helped to gather together pastorally neglected Deaf Catholics from all over England. He helped establish Deaf Catholic communities in London, Glasgow, Newcastle, Preston, Liverpool, and Birmingham, and he began to foster a stronger, more connected deaf identity among them. When he returned to the mission in Manchester, like a true apostle he always brought news and stories of the faith to share in sign language. Over time, strong connections between diocesan centers grew in the British Deaf Catholic community.[4]

Personal accounts of the members of the Centre in Ancoats recall Hayward as an energetic shepherd whose first concern was always the spiritual well-being and clear understanding of his deaf flock. Each week he arranged hard-backed chairs in a semicircle around the fireplace and chatted with them informally. Because reading English was difficult for many of the community members, chatting about the newspapers enabled them to keep up to date on what was happening in the world before television and, in that way, to participate more fully as British citizens. Afterward, he showed silent films—Charlie Chaplin, Charlie Chase, Harold Lloyd—or a film of himself delivering a sermon in sign language. Noting the usefulness of film for conveying knowledge and information to deaf people, Hayward became an amateur filmmaker himself. He directed and filmed several of his own silent films in British Sign Language, the first of their kind in Great Britain. One community member remembered a film about Saint John of Vianney, but many of the films documented group trips or pilgrimages. Often people in the

4. Bernard Hatton, "Life and Work of Canon Hayward" (manuscript), Deaf Catholic Archives, College of the Holy Cross, Worcester, Mass.

deaf community had an interest in history, so Hayward would arrange group tours to sites in Matlock, Morecambe, and towns in Wales. Everyone was asked to pay him for coach fare, but as one man remembered it, "He always lost some money because many times deaf people changed their minds and crossed their names off the list. The Canon had a war pension, so he was able to afford something. He had a big heart." This same member of the community remembers the way Hayward took time to explain even scientific matters to members of the community:

He loved astronomy and he explained a lot about the stars, the sun, the moon in the sky. In fact, he used it to teach us something about God. For instance, I remember he explained the atom bomb that was dropped in Hiroshima in Japan. He drew the earth, England one end of the globe, and Japan the other side of the globe. He explained the power of the atom bomb. Then he drew the Sun, it was a lot bigger than the Earth. Then he drew the flares from the Sun. The flares were huge, much bigger than the Earth. The Canon explained that the flares were a lot more powerful than the atom bomb dropped on Hiroshima. He said, "But God is a lot bigger than the Sun, and a lot more powerful than the Atom bomb or the flare."[5]

When Father Hayward celebrated Mass, the deaf assembly could not see his face, as he was facing the altar in the usual form of the pre-Vatican II ritual. But at the end of Mass, he always turned around and preached or explained a few things about the Mass in sign language. His benedictions in sign language often drew a crowd of nearly a hundred Deaf Catholics.

Canon Hayward's care with evangelization and explaining the faith to deaf people was patient and persistent, even when communication had to take a variety of slower modes. One deaf man from St. John's School in Boston Spa became furious at him for wasting time doing "church things" with deaf people. Father Hayward surprised onlookers with his calm manner. He brought the man to his office and spent time listening to him and typing back and forth with him on a typewriter. A few weeks later the man completely changed his attitude at the Deaf Centre and began to participate fully with the others. To facilitate this kind of teaching in both evangelization and catechesis, Hayward wrote a "plain English" catechism for deaf adults in 1948, *Faith and Love through Christ*. The book was influential in British and Irish Deaf ministries for many years—not only in deaf circles but for children or adults for whom English literacy was a challenge.

5. Gee, "Canon Hayward."

In many ways, Hayward encouraged the people in St. Joseph's community to be like a family, and he took very seriously his role as their spiritual father. At times he was criticized for having too controlling a pastoral style, but he never apologized for having an abundance of confidence and assertiveness. Once a teacher who was visiting St. Joseph's stormed out, shouting, "That man is a little Hitler. He is a megalomaniac!"[6] Speculations about the cause of this outburst aside, Hayward always put his personal traits to use in the service of an overlooked population that had little support for self-advocacy at the time. The success of St. Joseph's Centre seems to confirm this need in the early years of its mission. "I have to blow my own trumpet," he told a member of the community, "If I don't, nobody will know anything about deaf people or be aware of the work that is being done for deaf people."[7] Eventually, his nonstop drive and vehement temperament wore Hayward down. He was a manic smoker and consumed three packs of cigarettes per day, an over-the-top habit fueled by his abundant energy and intensity. But as the apostle Paul suggested of himself, Hayward's weaknesses, though apparent, were the other side of his strengths. Hayward channeled every available minute into living with his flock and walking with them on their spiritual journey.

As many in the deaf community of Manchester recall, Canon Hayward's whole life was given over for the good of deaf people. His love for them reminded them of the all-encompassing love of a father, and through him they learned to love the gospel and the person of Jesus. He entered their world through sign language and community building, making their every concern his own. He helped them build their own Deaf Catholic community and stayed with them every step of the way. Although he was forceful and practical in his fight for fair treatment of deaf people, everyone who knew him saw that he was also a deeply prayerful man. He made everyday life at St. Joseph's Mission a model for living a Christian life in community. Every Sunday night after Mass, he organized a "whist drive," which was a social event during which people played cards and enjoyed tea, cakes, and prizes. Hayward organized these events much like a large family gathering, and he used them as an opportunity to preach about the family of Jesus, Mary, and Joseph. At

6. Terry O'Meara, Panegyric at the Funeral Mass of Canon Charles Hollywood, Saint Patrick's, Livesey Street, Manchester (April 10, 2003), Deaf Catholic Archives, College of the Holy Cross, Worcester, Mass.

7. Gee, "Canon Hayward."

ten o'clock, he would tell everyone to go home, but a few would linger, chatting in sign language with each other. Looking through the window, they would see Canon Hayward pacing his room and reading a prayer book, perhaps the Divine Office, sometimes until midnight. The St. Vincent de Paul brothers who worked in Manchester often said he resembled St. John Bosco in his devotion to the Holy Family and his ceaseless work. He also embraced his role as a moral shepherd and protector, making himself a buffer for aspects of mainstream culture that, in his judgment, might be detrimental to the Deaf Catholic community. On one occasion, one of Hayward's friends brought a popular new invention—a television—to the club. This friend knew shorthand, so he jotted down everything the programs said and then repeated it for Hayward to lipread. He promptly pronounced it a lot of rubbish, and no television was purchased for the club. Some of his actions are surprising from a modern point of view, but generally the people made no fuss about his tight rein.

Hayward did not, however, wish to keep Deaf Catholics in isolation. Even in the 1950s, Deaf Catholic communities and associations in different countries had begun to reach out to each other, and Hayward made sure that the British Deaf community had knowledge of and communication with these other Deaf Catholics. If there were better ways to provide access to the sacraments and the life of the Church, he wanted to know about them, especially if they made use of sign language. In 1954, he attended a conference in Newcastle, where he defended the religious use of sign language against educators of deaf children like Alexander Ewing, a professor of Deaf Education at the University of Manchester. Ewing and his followers were rapidly expanding a medical approach to deafness in England, along with a corresponding oralist philosophy that eliminated sign language and focused on amplification of residual hearing, speech therapy, and daily practice of lipreading. Lipreading, Hayward asserted, was good and useful, but it was of little use in Christian liturgy. If a large assembly could not see the presider's lips, they would have to bring binoculars to church on Sunday. It was a practical assessment from a practical man.

Hayward expanded his use of sign language in church services and religious education in 1954. That summer, he was the guest of honor at the New York City conference of the International Catholic Deaf Association (ICDA) in the United States, where American Deaf Catholics honored him with enthusiasm, as yet having no ordained deaf priest in their own country. He visited deaf schools and clubs and was impressed with the American openness toward sign language, especially its use in the Mass for hymns and homilies. After his trip, Hayward founded a chapter of the ICDA in Manchester. He began to use more British Sign Language (BSL) during the Mass, and he encouraged the congregation to do their responses in sign language instead of only watching as they had before. Every Thursday evening, he would roll out a blackboard, write prayers and other passages on it, and translate and explain them in sign language. In practice, he used sign language both to teach religion and to teach English as a second language. Sometimes he would even write out English nursery rhymes so that he could explain, in sign language, the importance of sound and rhyme to the meaning of English phrases. If there were no British sign for something, he would borrow the American sign. For example, the sign for "Virgin" is the same today in both ASL and BSL: the signer sweeps the hands over the head in the ASL finger spelling for the letter V, even though BSL has a different finger alphabet. However, as a matter of principle, Hayward insisted on using BSL rather than ASL in his British deaf ministry. His awareness and appreciation of the distinct local culture of British deaf people motivated him to preserve BSL as both a better mode for deaf people's access to religious services than lip reading and as a cultural good for British deaf people.[8]

During his last years, Hayward received a great deal of support and encouragement from Bishop Henry Marshall of the Diocese of Salford. When Marshall was a parish priest in St. Anne's, Ancoats, during the early years of Hayward's ministry, the two had become friends. Marshall had learned to finger spell in those early days specifically to communicate with Hayward. In 1955, he named Hayward a Canon of the Diocese of Salford in recognition of his work with deaf people, and he continued to show a great interest in St. Joseph's Mission for many years. As Hayward's health began to fail, the bishop grew concerned that he would not be able to find a priest with the right combination of sign language skill and dedication to succeed the canon. It would be hard to fill Hayward's audacious shoes, but finally a young priest appeared who also had a hearing loss and who was having difficulty getting an assignment because of it. Charles Hollywood came to join the mission in July of 1960 when he was twenty-six years old. After his arrival, Canon Hayward's health

8. Bernard Hatton, "Life and Work of Canon Hayward."

deteriorated rapidly, and he died two-and-a-half years later on January 9, 1963, at the age of sixty-nine. His successor said that, at the end of his life, Canon Hayward had more commitment to his faith, to the priesthood, and to his apostolate than many priests do on the day of their ordination.[9] He had given his life to the Deaf Catholic community of England, opening a way for many after him who joined with deaf people in their struggle for full inclusion in the life of the church. He was truly an apostle of Deaf Catholic culture.

Canon Hollywood: Self-Sacrificing and Humble Leader

The successor to Canon Hayward at St. Joseph's Mission for the Deaf very nearly did not become a priest. Charles Hollywood hoped to prepare for ordination in a diocese near his hometown of Armagh in Northern Ireland, so he went to St. Patrick's College in Maynooth, Ireland, to study for the priesthood. However, the seminary in Maynooth was overenrolled in those years with over a thousand students. In 1956, when Hollywood was in his second year of study, a medical report revealed that he had a hearing loss, so the Diocese of Armagh simply dismissed him from formation.

The young man was devastated as he tried to discern where to turn next in his vocation. On a trip to Liverpool, a chance meeting with a Daughter of Charity brought him to Salford Diocese, where Bishop Marshall had been searching for a second priest to direct St. Joseph's Mission. He was surprised to find that at the mission, his deafness was not a disabling obstacle but instead a gift that led him back to his priestly vocation. Bishop Marshall sent him back to the seminary in Maynooth with the promise of a placement, and he was ordained in 1960. For two years, he was an assistant and understudy to Canon Hayward, but the canon's health deteriorated rapidly. Soon Hollywood, still in his twenties, was shepherding the dynamic but demanding Deaf Catholic community on his own. He had only been at St. Joseph's Mission for about a month when Hayward scolded him with characteristic vehemence, telling the young man "Get on your bike and get on with the job!" Hollywood said that the old man's admonition ignited a motor in him that sputtered a

9. O'Meara, Panegyric for Canon Charles Hollywood.

few times but never quit. For years after Hayward's death, whenever he had an important decision to make, he would ask himself "What would Father Hayward do?"[10]

Although he was destined to earn the same honorable title of canon, Hollywood was as unassuming and humble as Hayward had been extroverted and attention-seeking for the sake of his beloved deaf apostolate. While his energy and devotion to the deaf community matched his predecessor's, it was clear that Charlie Hollywood had no agenda of his own. He did not seek to gather people around himself, but rather, as Vicar General of Salford Mark Davis described it, "He wanted to gather people round Christ and quietly disappear. His aim was the communion of the church, not the Charles Hollywood foundation."[11] The deaf community at St. Joseph's Mission welcomed him, and he was soon beloved for his ceaseless dedication, cheerful personality, and penchant for Irish storytelling. Some liked him especially because his signed homilies were short, but his aim was always to direct all attention to the Eucharist. He attributed whatever success the ission had to the community's daily holy hour spent in adoration of the Blessed Sacrament. However, Hollywood was more than a prayerful and beloved pastor; he became an astute manager and gifted professional networker for the deaf community. Under his direction, the mission grew in size and recognition, and on national and international fronts he led the establishment of several key organizations important both to the deaf people of England and to the development of a global Deaf Catholic community.

Under the direction of Charles Hollywood, the Deaf Catholic community experienced some growing pains as St. Joseph's Mission expanded its facilities and moved through several different addresses in the city of Manchester. In 1964, Miss Edwina Henesy, a benefactor of the mission, died, and her sister offered £10,000 to establish a home for deaf children as a memorial. Hollywood explained to her that what Manchester really needed was a residential home for deaf adults. Once this new arrangement was accepted, he immediately began to plan and organize a new residential home, to be called Henesy House. He knew that the home would need a residential manager but was uncertain where to turn for help. The first thing he did was to advertise for a housekeeper. When

10. O'Meara, Panegyric for Canon Charles Hollywood.
11. Mark Davis, Homily, Mass for the Reception of the Body of Rev. Charles Hollywood, Saint Patrick's Livesey Street, Manchester (April 9, 2003), Deaf Catholic Archives, College of the Holy Cross, Worcester, Mass.

a mature woman in her seventies applied for the job, Hollywood was uncertain about her ability to do much more than cook and tidy up, but he needed someone immediately and hired her on the spot. Once hired, the lady asked if her sister might stay at the residence for a little while, and Hollywood thought, "Well, why not?" and agreed. The next day, the housekeeper's sister appeared—wearing her habit! She was Mother Henrietta Redmond, Provincial of the Sisters of Charity of Our Lady of Evron. Father Hollywood explained his needs to Mother Henrietta, and the Sisters of Evron (as they are known today) came to run the residence in November of 1965—first Sister Martha Savage, and later Sister Maria McCreedy, Sister Pauline Nolan, Sister Margaret Mary McDonough, and others. In the decades that followed, the mission grew rapidly. For four years Henesy House remained in the neighborhood of Old Trafford; then it moved to Deansgate for several years where the sisters established a residential hostel for deaf adults; then in the 1970s both the sisters and the hostel's residents moved again to Denmark Road, where the original St. Joseph's Mission had begun. All the while, the number of Deaf Catholics who worshipped in the community expanded through plentiful Irish immigration, and the sisters, Father Hollywood, and a third priest appointed to the mission in 1975, Father Terry O'Meara, continued to meet their needs.

Bishop Patrick Kelly accommodated the growth of St. Joseph's Mission by moving the Deaf Centre and its religious and lay residents to its current location, St. Patrick Church in downtown Manchester. The spacious church building was built in 1937 to replace the small, historic church built there in 1832 after the British Parliament fully enacted Catholic Emancipation. On the wall above the altar of the large church, a painting of St. Patrick himself in his missionary travels from England to Ireland welcomes the many Irish people in the parish who share the building with the deaf community, many of whom also have Irish heritage. In the large rectory next door, Hollywood and O'Meara lived in one residence as a religious community, together with the Sisters of Our Lady of Evron, for thirty years. Eventually the community expanded to nine religious sisters (including Sister Joan Hayward, who joined the order after her brother Canon William Hayward's death) and a handful of priests who were part of the deaf apostolate.[12] Henesy House also moved here, and a new residential home for Deaf Catholics was built in 1989.

12. O'Meara, Panegyric for Canon Charles Hollywood.

Canon Charles Hollywood's style of leadership and professionalism changed deaf ministries in Great Britain in several ways, as his ministry responded to the changing social climate of the times. St. Joseph's Community and Henesy House began to take on a more respected and professional character, garnering the attention of bishops and social service professionals. He took a keen interest in government-administered social services for deaf people and others in need, and he was one of the founding members of Catholic Welfare Societies in the Diocese of Salford. He was a certified social worker, and he encouraged all the priests and sisters who worked with him at the St. Joseph's Mission to pursue advanced degrees in social work. This penchant for professionalism and a developing network of community support also characterized Hollywood's evangelical efforts. He played a leading role in the establishment of the Association for Catholic Deaf of Great Britain and Ireland. Moreover, in the interest of helping deaf people everywhere to overcome the exclusion they historically faced as a group, Hollywood did not stop with Salford diocese or even with Great Britain. In 1980, to encourage an international Deaf Catholic community that would support both social and religious inclusion of deaf people, one that would enable them to fulfill their rightful role as full and visible members of the church, Canon Hollywood and Father Terry O'Meara began to form an international foundation for the service of Deaf Catholics.

The International Foundation for the Service of Deaf Persons (ICF) had its first official meeting in 1986, at a conference on religious education for deaf people in Leuven, Belgium. Hollywood led a group of chaplains, pastoral workers, catechists, and others working in countries around the world to promote the religious formation and pastoral care of deaf people. Based on the resolutions of an international conference organized by the Dominican Sisters of Cabra in 1971, the foundation aimed to make people aware of the difficult position of deaf people in the life of the church and "to bring the riches of their vocation with others in the Church and society so as to achieve a fuller expression of Eucharistic communion."[13] Two hundred Catholics involved in deaf ministry attended the 1971 international conference, held in Dublin, with representatives from Africa, Australia, England, Germany, Ireland, the Netherlands, and the United States. Among the resolutions was an appeal to

13. International Catholic Foundation for the Service of Deaf Persons, "Our Mission," accessed August 11, 2017, https://www.icfdeafservice.org/about.

the conference of bishops in each nation, which would advise one bishop in each country to take responsibility for the spiritual welfare of the deaf community. The foundation advocated for continued attention to the pervasive nature of social isolation and language differences of deaf people, which would require translation and special liturgical adaptations in each nation in order to include them in worship. In the years after its inception, Hollywood directed and organized several international ICF conferences and symposia at which pastoral workers and scholars shared professional and cultural information about Deaf Catholics and their needs. After Hollywood's death, Father Terry O'Meara continued as director of ICF and organizer of its international conferences. ICF is certainly one of Hollywood's greatest legacies. A more developed account of the foundation and its more recent activity supporting deaf people and Deaf Catholic culture around the world appears in chapter 12.

Although Hollywood made substantial contributions toward the development of an international deaf apostolate as it began to take shape in the twentieth century, the contribution he considered his most important work was the Eucharistic Prayer for Deaf People in British Sign Language, prepared in collaboration with his friend and advocate Monsignor Patrick Kelly (later bishop of Salford and then archbishop of Liverpool). After Vatican II concluded in December 1965, Deaf Catholics became keenly interested in the development of vernacular Masses and liturgy for modern language communities—in particular, for sign language communities. Two days after the close of the council, Pope Paul VI granted permission for the priest and the people to use sign language at Mass.[14] The Council had clearly recognized the great importance of the Eucharistic prayer in the Mass and advised that all the lay faithful should take an active part in it. Naturally, this involved participation in the prayer as a direct communication between the priest (acting in the place of Christ) and the assembly. Documents of Vatican II emphasized that the nature and circumstances of each assembly should be considered so that people would be able to communicate, not in a rote manner, but in mind and heart. The Dogmatic Constitution of the

14. See Concilium for the Implementation of Constitution on the Liturgy, "Private Reply," December 10, 1965, in *Canon Law Digest VI: Officially Published Documents Affecting the Code of Canon Law 1963–1967*, T. Lincoln Bouscaren and James I. O'Connor (Milwaukee: Bruce Publishing, 1969), 552–53; International Commission on English in the Liturgy, *Documents on the Liturgy 1963–1979: Conciliar, Papal, and Curial Texts*, ed. and trans. Thomas C. O'Brien (Collegeville, Minn.: Liturgical Press, 1982) DOL n. 274. Referenced in Edward Peters, "Canonical and Cultural Developments Culminating in the Ordination of Deaf Men," *Josephinum Journal of Theology* 15, no. 2 (2008): 427–43.

Church (*Lumen Gentium*) renewed the call for all Christians to exercise participation in the Eucharist as both a right and a duty because of the great dignity of baptism. Knowing all of this, Canon Hollywood began work on a Eucharistic prayer that priests could easily sign when there were Deaf Catholics in an assembly.

Submitted to the Catholic Bishops' Conference of England and Wales in 1977 by Canon Hollywood and Monsignor Kelly, the Eucharistic Prayer for the Deaf was intended for parish priests (presumably hearing ones). Some parishes were already employing interpreters to great benefit. However, interpreters at the time were not plentiful—and not always carefully trained in either sign language or theology. Their signs could be inexact or misleading for deaf people in the assembly. Even very good interpretation drew attention away from the priest and toward the interpreter—the only person communicating in a language the deaf assembly could see and understand. Development of a Eucharistic prayer in sign language was a logical step towards preventing confusion about the priest's acting "in the person of Christ" during consecration. To make it possible for busy parish priests to learn how to use signs while simultaneously speaking the words of the English text, Hollywood simplified the written language into very plain English.

Canon Hollywood's new Eucharistic prayer, as a glossed written form, was shorter than the conventional form and simpler in its diction. The purpose of the simplified text was to accommodate the hearing priest who must sign in tandem with the words—not, as readers unfamiliar with deaf ministry might suppose, "to bring the language down"[15] to the deaf faithful (who were far more competent in sign language than the simplicity of an English gloss could suggest). The team composed both signed (video) and printed text forms of the Eucharistic prayer, so that it might "reasonably be signed even by a part-time chaplain" without much previous knowledge of sign language. This prediction proved to be true, as use of the Eucharistic Prayer for the Deaf spread to several parishes in England, where it is still in use today. The prayer was a tremendous advance in ministry to deaf people, especially for those Deaf Catholics who could not travel to larger diocesan centers where Deaf Catholic culture was more developed and integrated. It also proved successful in Manchester's own culturally Deaf Catholic community, where celebrants were flu-

15. "Background Note," *Eucharistic Prayer for the Deaf,* Catholic Bishops' Conference of England and Wales (May 23, 1992), https://www.liturgyoffice.org.uk/Resources/Rites/DeafEP-note.pdf.

ent in sign language and fully adapted to the deaf community's language and culture. There, Charles Hollywood, his successors Father O'Meara, and later Father Peter McDonough, skillfully translated the prayer into British Sign Language (BSL) so that deaf people could not only participate in the Mass but also appreciate the profound meaning of the Eucharist through the visual beauty and nuance of skillfully executed BSL.

As it was accepted by the British bishops, the "Background Note" of the Eucharistic Prayer for the Deaf contains some phrases that might strike a sour note among deaf people today if taken out of context. An unknown author added the prayer after Hollywood submitted it to the bishop's conference and its origin remains unknown. It reflects an understanding of deafness that was still in its infancy and a view of sign language that linguists would later prove false. In particular, the note includes a statement meant to explain the simplified nature of the English text:

The deaf cannot listen attentively as hearing people do. They cannot even make their acclamations with the same facility.... The Eucharistic prayers of the Roman Rite employ a language that is complex, abstract and highly stylized with every word carefully balanced against another. In contrast, the language most suited to communication with the deaf is simple, concrete and very direct.... Sign language, properly so called, is a much less systematic collection of individual shorthand gestures, some of which vary from place to place but which nevertheless provide the chief means of communication among a large number of deaf people. The adaptation of the language of liturgical texts for use with the deaf has to take into account the restriction imposed on the expression of ideas by those commonly understood signs and gestures.[16]

Any deaf person who reads these words is bound to feel their sting: the beliefs expressed in this "Background Note" are unfortunate echoes of older biases and falsehoods about deaf people and their level of intelligence. In all likelihood, such a note was needed in 1977 to receive approval from bishops who were still largely uninformed about sign languages and deaf culture.

Today, readers of this note have the benefit of seeing, in hindsight, the broader historical context and development of signed languages. The note was written before linguists had studied and documented British Sign Language (BSL) as a complete—and quite complex—language, and it was therefore seen by mainstream culture and the church as a simplified gestural "shorthand" or accompaniment to spoken and written En-

---

16. "Background Note," *Eucharistic Prayer for the Deaf.*

glish. In fact, sign language itself was in various historical stages of development in different regions of England at the time, especially where oral education was the dominant practice in schools. In those regions, users of signs accompanied by English speech may not have demonstrated the level of language competence found in users of voice-off BSL as a natural human language. In 1977, for people committed to oral deaf education and for hearing ministers without much enculturation in the British deaf community, it was accepted that signs were simply an inferior accompaniment to the "real" language, spoken and written English.

The British Eucharistic Prayer for the Deaf, as Canon Hollywood wrote it and Bishop Patrick Kelly approved it, is really an English gloss for on-the-spot translation into a signed language that has no written form. Only when the celebrant signed the prayer did a visual "text," a translation in British Sign Language, appear as an act of communication. However, this in no way discredits Canon Hollywood's achievement. His was the first successful attempt to gain the Church's approval for a Eucharistic prayer delivered in sign language and therefore received by deaf people solely through the sense of sight.

The deaf assembly of St. Joseph's Deaf Centre had no trouble "listening attentively" as Canon Hollywood signed the Eucharistic prayer in their own language. Of course, hearing members of the same assembly, if they were present, still needed spoken English to understand. It was the first time in history that a Eucharistic prayer had been approved not only for a visual language but also for delivery in two languages by one priest simultaneously. The resulting doubling of languages, only possible because of the purely visual mode of sign language and the contrasting audible mode of English, may have been awkward at times in the hands of a priest who was not expert in BSL. For Deaf Catholics and those who ministered to them, however, even awkward communication was much better than no communication at all. The Eucharistic prayer in sign language was a new opening of channels of communication worthy of comparison to Pentecost. In the hands of a celebrant like Hollywood, who was thoroughly enculturated in the language and customs of deaf people, the prayer took on the depth and nuance of near-native idiom. It was no longer a rigid gestural accompaniment to a spoken or written language with a linear grammar. From this text, a BSL-fluent celebrant could translate the Eucharistic prayer into the three-dimensional syntax of sign language in all its natural grace and beauty.

Cannon Hollywood was keenly aware, as he wrote for an ICF conference in 1991, that the contributions deaf people could make to liturgy and communal prayer were much greater than mere gestural accompaniment to spoken and written English texts. He knew that demonstrating a Eucharistic prayer in pure sign language, not simultaneously mixed into a pidgin so that hearing people could understand, would demand greater training for celebrants (and also for interpreters, because BSL-fluent celebrants were rare). It would necessarily require the use of film or video in the future. As he taught in conferences and workshops for ministers to the deaf, a radically simplified English text could not compare to the dynamic meanings of coded body language, the depths and nuance of facial expression, the exact specificity of direction, and range or speed of hand shapes in native-deaf sign languages.

In presentations at ICF conferences and for audiences who acknowledged the existence of complete sign languages and deaf culture, Hollywood encouraged wholehearted advocacy for liturgy in these languages. The oral methods of British deaf education were highly advantageous for a few, Hollywood often said, but did very little for others. The deaf community and their educators had done their best to enable deaf people to join the hearing world and compete with it on hearing terms. But finally, it was time for the church to meet the deaf community on its own terms and to accept a share in the deaf community's unique charisms and fruitfulness. Hollywood emphasized to the growing international deaf apostolate that wherever deaf people achieved full and active membership in the church, they had the potential to contribute to the richness of its life, much like "young churches" in Africa and Asia and missions of ethnic groups that had been different from the church's European cultures. "They have a charism," he wrote, "which can enrich the life of the Church for deaf and hearing people alike. It is a firm conviction of many, that Liturgy is an area where the dynamic Deaf faith-community can make a substantial contribution. They need help to make their contribution; but it will be well worth the effort of relevant practitioners—liturgists, theologians, and whoever, with the patience and commitment to work along with the Deaf people in this manner. There is a treasure here, hidden in a field."[17]

17. Charles Hollywood, "Visual Dimensions of (Prayer and) Liturgy," in *Seeing Is Believing: Proceedings from the Fourth International Catholic Conference on Religious Education of the Hearing Impaired* (Manchester: Henesy House, 1991), 51.

Canon Hollywood died on April 2, 2003, after forty years of service to Deaf Catholics, but the spirit of his work in England and beyond continued in the vision and practice of several members of St. Joseph's community. As Manchester faced the challenges of the upcoming new millennium, there were ongoing changes and developments. Both deaf culture and the church's vision of the role of laypeople were developing, and this would give rise to new opportunities for cultural evangelization and leadership. A new, deeper understanding of the changes prompted by the Second Vatican Council had begun to take root in deaf ministry.

The Third Generation: A Good Team

By the late twentieth century, St. Joseph's Mission began to incorporate liturgical changes that put into practice the spirit of documents promulgated at the Second Vatican Council. In 1965, shortly after the conclusion of the council, Pope Paul VI had given permission for the use of sign language in the Mass, and this occasioned serious thought about the design of spaces and religious rituals for people who use their eyes but not their ears to communicate and to worship. These liturgical directives—centered as they were on vernacular language and greater participation of laypeople in the liturgy—led to significant changes at St. Patrick's Church in Manchester.

In 1989, Father Terry O'Meara redesigned the interior of the spacious church for the language needs and visual culture of the deaf community. In the back of the building, he designed a large second-level social hall connected by an open balcony to a sweeping view of the historic sanctuary and altar. This connection between sanctuary and social hall seemed at first unorthodox to many parishioners, but soon it was clear that the design was a true reflection of the deaf community's full membership and inclusion in the church. It remains so today. Father O'Meara's open-concept design was an inspired reenvisioning of how the church could enable deaf people to "Be opened!" in new ways—and how deaf people were opening up the church in return. Finding the right space has often been a problem in the history of deaf ministry, for financial reasons and because deaf people need open, visually accessible spaces. The history of the multiple moves of Manchester's deaf ministry over the years illustrates this perennial challenge, as well as the pastoral team's vision in using space well, both for the deaf community and for those who served them.

One sign that an evangelized community has reached a fruitful maturity of Catholic enculturation is the appearance of religious vocations from within the community. In its third generation of leadership, a young deaf man who had grown up in St. Joseph's Deaf Catholic community felt a call to the priesthood. Peter McDonough, whose parents were both Deaf Catholics and who had looked to Canon Hayward as a role model, was ordained in 1982 by Pope John Paul II in a ceremony at Manchester's Heaton Park, with hundreds of deaf people in attendance. Although no longer active in the clergy, McDonough has been an important and authentic leader in deaf ministry and is currently secretary of the Catholic Deaf Association of Great Britain. He has followed Canon Hollywood's example of working internationally with several Deaf Catholic communities, and he has authored a book to inform hearing Catholics about the Deaf Catholic community in Britain.[18] When asked about his work with Canon Hollywood and Father O'Meara, McDonough is quick to say it was "a good team." Deaf and hearing clergy, together with the Sisters of Evron and lay volunteers both deaf and hearing, continued the work of inclusiveness at St. Joseph's Mission that Canon Hayward had begun. McDonough served the Deaf Catholic community for twenty-seven years as priest and later as pastor of St. Patrick's Church, during which time he also completed university coursework in the field of Deaf Studies. He attributes appreciation for his own linguistic and cultural identity as much to Canon Hollywood and Saint Joseph's Centre as to his education in deaf culture.

Today St. Joseph's Mission continues its services to the Deaf Catholic community in BSL—including liturgy, baptisms and funerals, preparation for sacraments, pilgrimages, conferences, as well as home visits to sick and bereaved people. Several Sisters of Evron still live in the large house adjacent to St. Patrick's Church. The center's focus is deaf people whose native language is BSL, along with their hearing family members who sign. In addition to the culturally deaf environment of St. Joseph's community, four pastoral satellite areas have been established as part of the bishop's outreach for Deaf Catholics in other parts of the Salford Diocese. Mass is celebrated using the Eucharistic prayer in British Sign Language once a month in each location. The program functions as part of the diocesan Department for Social Responsibility, and it actively participates in national and international organizations for the service of

18. Peter McDonough, *Deaf Resource Pack* (Manchester: Catholic Deaf Association, 2017).

deaf people. Also on the property is the newest Henesy House facility, used today as a state-funded social service for elderly and profoundly handicapped individuals. So many of Manchester's deaf people have integrated into society that a dedicated deaf residential facility is no longer a necessity. The center shares its vision and philosophy with Catholic bishops in Britain and abroad, as well as ecumenically with the Anglican Communion.

It is especially remarkable that St. Joseph's Centre witnessed three generations of chaplain-directors who were deaf themselves—the most recent, Peter McDonough, being a Deaf Catholic whose native language is BSL and who grew up in the Deaf Catholic community to which he would return as a priest and, later, after leaving active ministry as a priest, as a pastoral worker. As the deaf community's Catholic culture grew to be an integral part of their deaf culture and heritage, it became clearer that the greatest resource for evangelizing deaf people would be deaf people themselves—not in isolation from the hearing mainstream but as role models for those who serve the deaf community. McDonough explains this realization well with understanding from both deaf and hearing cultures:

It is essential that we get rid of the common misconception or myth that Deaf people's lives are impoverished, that they have limited language or understanding of the world, are unable to grasp complex ideas or abstract notions, and that they are unspiritual. The first thing we have to do is recognize and reaffirm that Deaf people already have their own language, and it is usually [hearing people] who are unable to communicate with them using their language. It is a stark fact that nothing short of becoming fluent in sign language will do. This is one of the reasons why the best ministers to other Deaf people are Deaf people themselves. We must acknowledge their wealth of life experience, and even spiritual experience. We must utilize this as a starting point.[19]

By the first decade of the twenty-first century, St. Joseph's Centre had begun to show a very clear turn to the leadership of deaf people themselves, including the leadership of laypeople in the deaf community, while at the same time fostering the expansion of Masses signed by hearing priests. In this turn to lay leadership, new and different vocational roles opened for Deaf Catholics as well as pastoral workers who serve the deaf com-

19. Peter McDonough, "Collaborative Ministry in the Deaf Vineyard," International Catholic Foundation for the Service of Deaf Persons Conference, Mexico City (August 2003). Manuscript provided to me by the author.

munity. A similar pattern of growth and development happened in the course of the twentieth century in the United States, to which we turn in chapter 8.

The three generations of leadership at St. Joseph's Catholic Deaf Centre are a striking case study of Deaf Catholic cultural development in the twentieth century. Moreover, the work of sisters, priests, and pastoral workers at St. Joseph's Catholic Deaf Centre illustrate how deaf ministries responded and evolved as part of the community they served. From Canon Hayward, the protective father figure of a disadvantaged and marginalized group of deaf people; to Canon Hollywood, humble but dynamic advocate and social organizer; to Terry O'Meara and Peter McDonough, new servant-leaders of a self-conscious cultural group with their own recognized language and culture[20]—the history of St. Joseph's Centre illustrates a process of enculturation that progressed from mission work, to community development, to leadership springing from the community itself.

20. On March 18, 2003, British Sign Language (BSL) was recognized by Parliament as a language.

CHAPTER 8

Deaf Leadership in North America

The twentieth century was a renaissance for deaf culture in many parts of the world. In the United States, hundreds of deaf people had been gathering for National Association for the Deaf (NID) conventions since 1880, and this association grew dramatically during the twentieth century. In many other countries as well, deaf people formed civil and human rights organizations to advance their causes and promote full accessibility in public life. In 1951, the first multinational organization for deaf people was established: the World Federation of the Deaf (WFD), which held its first congress in Rome, where representatives from twenty-five different national associations for deaf people gathered together. Secular associations like these worked to ensure that deaf people had the knowledge, resources, and strategies to advocate for their own civic and human rights. It was during this period that the American practice of capitalizing the term Deaf as a cultural designation solidified in writings on deaf history and culture.[1] All of this, combined with a renewed democratic awareness inspired by the American Civil Rights movement, led to a veritable awakening in deaf culture in the West. Culturally Deaf Catholics, too, were quick to note that an organized social movement could lead to positive change. Many felt that organizing an international association for Deaf Catholics would embody a growing spirit of unity around

1. To explore foundational works on deaf culture during this period, see the recommended reading list at the end of part II. For an analysis of the origins of capitalizing the term "Deaf" to distinguish deaf culture from medicalized terminology, see Brenda Jo Brueggemann, *Deaf Subjects: Between Identities and Places* (New York University Press, 2009). She identifies a 1972 *Deaf Studies* essay by James Woodward, "How You Gonna Get to Heaven if You Can't Talk to Jesus?" as the most commonly cited origin (in *How you Gonna Get to Heaven if You Can't Talk to Jesus: On Depathologizing Deafness*, James Woodward [Silver Spring, Md.: T. J. Publishers, 1982]).

the world for deaf people eager for full participation in the church.

This chapter traces the development of the International Catholic Deaf Association (ICDA) as an organization supporting Catholic leadership "for the deaf, by the deaf" in North America and internationally. The narrative begins with two precursors of national and, later, international deaf-run Catholic organizations. First, educators, missionaries, and chaplains who were mostly hearing and who worked with deaf communities began gathering in a special section of the American Catholic Education Association's annual conference in 1907. This special interest group exchanged ideas and discussed best practices for the religious education, evangelization, and community development of culturally Deaf Catholics. At the same time, local deaf-led Catholic associations were growing in major metropolitan areas in North America where there were large deaf communities; as a result, Deaf Catholic laity began to evangelize their own deaf communities, especially through catechism and sacramental preparation. In 1949, several metropolitan Deaf Catholic associations in Canada and the United States came together to found the ICDA as a Canadian-American service association. At that time, hearing pastoral workers and educators who had been meeting for over forty years at the Catholic Education Association (later National Catholic Educational Association) left that organization and began to meet at ICDA conventions with the deaf people. The two sides of this longstanding relationship in deaf mission work—the deaf apostolate and those who served them—began to blend as a community within the church.

This merging stimulated unprecedented growth and fruitfulness in North American Deaf Catholic culture. In the later years of the century, as the church began to incorporate the recommendations of Vatican II into church life and liturgy, the Deaf Catholic community in North America would witness deaf-led leadership training, spiritual retreats in ASL, deaf catechists and deacons, the first deaf priestly vocations in the United States, and even complete Masses in ASL. The new impetus for social organization in the deaf community and the growing use of ASL in deaf social gatherings would lead North American Deaf Catholics to a strong, self-conscious awareness of their cultural attributes. Because these early organizations were a powerful validation of deaf culture, Deaf Catholics began to see sign languages and American Deaf Culture in a new way—as human goods and gifts from God, meant to enable connectedness with fellow Catholics instead of causing separation from them.

Networking in Deaf Ministry at the
Catholic Education Association

Early in the twentieth century, Catholic missionaries, educators, and pastoral workers began meeting as professionals to share methods and develop materials for deaf people. In 1907, a special "Deaf-Mute Section" began to meet at the annual conference of the Catholic Educational Association. The meetings of these educators and ministers, almost all of them hearing clergy, fulfilled a need that deaf-led organizations such as the ICDA would also encounter: the need to share ideas and strategies for catechizing and enculturating Deaf Catholic communities. Reflecting on some of the challenges facing this apostolate, Thomas Galvin, CSsR issued a "Battle Cry" for deaf ministry at the 1910 CEA conference:

If you have tears to shed, prepare to shed them now. The condition of our Catholic deaf-mutes is most deplorable, the most saddening of any class of people in this country.... They are intelligent.... They know what ought to be done for them. They are willing to remain Catholics. For years they have been pleading for priests, for schools, for recognition; but their pleading has been unheard in the din of battle. They are intelligent readers of newspapers and periodicals, both Catholic and non-sectarian. They are, therefore, well informed about things general and Catholic. They see rising up all around them Catholic institutions for every human indigency, but nothing being done for them.[2]

With oratorical vehemence, Father Galvin exhorted his fellow priests and religious sisters to sound a bugle call and "hurry to the rescue of our helpless fellow-soldiers, the Catholic deaf-mutes of America." The "Deaf-Mute Department," as Galvin called this group of Catholics in deaf ministry, acted quickly: for several decades afterwards, the Proceedings of the Catholic Education Association contain a growing collection of papers documenting educational and mission activity all over the country.

In 1927, the Catholic Education Association changed its name to National Catholic Educational Association (NCEA) and moved its headquarters to Washington, D.C., in proximity to secular agencies for education. By 1920, NCEA conference proceedings reflected tremendous developments for Catholic educators of deaf children (who used mostly oral methods) and for cultural missionaries, especially Jesuits and Redemptorists (who used sign language to evangelize deaf communities).

2. Thomas Galvin, CSsR, "A Call to Action: A Plea for Deaf-Mutes," *Proceedings of the Catholic Educational Association* (Columbus, Ohio: Catholic Educational Association, 1910), 439.

By the 1940s, the "Deaf-Mute Section" of the NCEA exhibited an impressive range of participants and approaches, as well as a sustained effort to record new developments and analyze advances in Deaf Catholic ministry. Father Everett McPhillips, who ministered to the deaf community in Providence, Rhode Island, and the Redemptorists Joseph Heidell and Eugene Gehl gave several presentations on how to teach catechism to children in state-run, residential schools for the deaf. There were presentations on specific issues such as building religious vocabulary in sign language, study clubs for deaf adults needing continuing education, and the writing of confessions for the sacrament of reconciliation. Redemptorists and Jesuits who ministered to deaf communities, such as Patrick Mahan, SJ; Charles Hoffman, SJ; Daniel Higgins, CSsR; and Stephen Landherr, CSsR all participated in these gatherings. There was strong representation from the faculty of Catholic schools for deaf children in St. Louis, New York, and Chicago, and from the staff of diocesan and archdiocesan Deaf Centers of Boston, Buffalo, Detroit, Cleveland, New York, and Philadelphia.

American Ephpheta Societies

An essential precursor to national and international deaf-run Catholic organizations were local Deaf Catholic clubs and associations that came together in large dioceses. These organizations sprang up in many metropolitan cities in the United States and Canada as graduates of Deaf Catholic schools and religious education programs began to seek each other out for fellowship, ongoing faith formation, and advocacy in church life. Any of the North American dioceses with large deaf populations—Montreal, Milwaukee, Cleveland, Detroit, St. Louis, or Buffalo, for example—could serve as a case study of how regional associations strengthened the Deaf Catholic community at a grassroots level. Several church historians, most with backgrounds in deaf ministry themselves, have undertaken local Deaf Catholic histories.[3] The Deaf Catholic apostolate in the Archdiocese of New York is a particularly strong example of deaf-led evangelization, because New York's Deaf Catholic clubs expanded to active chapters in other cities. The Xavier Ephpheta Society,

3. See, for example, Anthony Russo, *In Silent Prayer: A History of Ministry*; Dolores Beere, *History of the Catholic Deaf, Archdiocese of Detroit* (Detroit: Archdiocese of Detroit, 1984); Anthony Schuerger, *History of Deaf Ministry in the Diocese of Cleveland*, manuscript, Deaf Catholic Archives, College of the Holy Cross, Worcester, Mass.

as it came to be known, had many starts and stops in its early years, as did many diocesan Deaf Catholic associations and clubs. Two perpetual challenges caused many setbacks: financial troubles and difficulty securing long-term appointments of clergy who could use sign language.

The first deaf-organized gathering of Catholics in the Archdiocese of New York met in 1880 in response to an invitation by James O'Neil, a graduate of the New York Institute for the Deaf in Fanwood, New York. The fifteen Deaf Catholics who met were mostly graduates from Fanwood but also some from the Montreal Institute of St. Viator, St. Mary's School in Buffalo, and the Cabra School in Ireland. First, they had the privilege of electing a delegate for the first meeting of the National Association of the Deaf (NAD), to be held in Cleveland, Ohio, on August 25, 1880. Second, they welcomed Father Michael Costin, SJ, whose knowledge of the manual alphabet had earned him a chaplaincy for the entire deaf community of the Archdiocese of New York.[4] The newly founded group dubbed themselves the Catholic Literary and Benevolent Union. As Father Costin's knowledge of the deaf community grew, he responded to the interests of this growing group of Deaf Catholics—all users of sign language. The deaf-run Catholic Literary and Benevolent Union met at St. Francis Xavier College, where Costin would celebrate Mass and expand his sign language skills. Within a year, the group had elected a lay president, John McNally, and established a schedule of literary readings, debates, and public lectures.

After the untimely death of Father Costin in 1884, Archbishop Michael Corrigan assigned a new chaplain, Father Alfred Belanger, CSV, to care for the spiritual needs of deaf people in the archdiocese.[5] Belanger continued Costin's support of the Deaf Catholic laity by helping the group organize frequent meetings at churches around the city. Finally, Belanger secured the use of a parish-owned house on East Fourteenth Street. This house would be devoted exclusively to the Deaf Catholic community, who at this time adopted the new name "The Infant Savior Mission" (after the name of the parish). Unfortunately, financial troubles prevented its continuing at this location. A further blow to the new organization occurred with Father Belanger's superiors transferred him to Canada, leaving New York's Deaf Catholic community with neither a spiritual director nor a place to gather.

4. See chapter 4, pp. 74–75.
5. The Viatorians (CSV) ran a school for deaf boys in Montreal, Canada.

Keenly aware of the need for a priest who knew their language, the Deaf Catholic community of New York set out, in 1893, to recruit one. Two recent graduates of St. Joseph's Institute for the Deaf went to St. Francis Xavier College to visit the Jesuits, who had taken an interest in the deaf club at its founding in 1880. Their explanations must have been convincing: over a hundred notices were soon sent to Deaf Catholics that meetings would resume at St. Francis Xavier. In 1893, under the direction of Father Joseph Stadelman, SJ, this renewed group organized as the Xavier Deaf Mute Union. Father Stadelman served as a chaplain for three years, during which he improved his sign language skills and often invited missionaries and notable preachers to address the assembly through interpreters. As word spread about his signed sermons on the gospel readings each Sunday, more in the Deaf Catholic community began to come to Mass.

In 1893, Stadelman's superiors reassigned him to the Catholic Society of the Blind; however, in his place, they soon assigned Father Michael McCarthy, SJ, whose prolific work with the deaf community is described in chapter 4.[6] In the meantime, another deaf community leader, Miss Nora Joyce, had launched a second, dues-paying organization for Deaf Catholics called the Mutual Benefit Society. Although this society had beneficial objectives, members of the Xavier Deaf Mute Union feared it might cause division in the already-dispersed deaf community. At a meeting of officers representing each deaf-led group, Father McCarthy facilitated an integration of their missions and policies into a single organization, one that would have far-reaching effects in Deaf Catholic history: the Xavier Ephpheta Society.

Finally, New York had a stable, united apostolate of Deaf Catholics with a permanent priest moderator who was fluent in sign language. The Xavier Ephpheta Society thrived, and deaf leadership grew. Among the articles of its constitution was a single clause laying out the society's purpose as being simply "the spiritual and material benefit of deaf-mutes in time of sickness and the support of deaf-mute Sunday Schools."[7] In the spirit of this mission, the society established catechism classes at the two residential state schools for deaf students in New York, with society members taking the role of catechists. To expand the pool of seminarians interested in deaf ministry, Father McCarthy taught sign language classes

6. See chapter 4, pp. 75–77.
7. Ephpheta Society for the Catholic Deaf Golden Anniversary booklet, New York, June 8, 1952.

at St. Joseph's Seminary in Yonkers. The society also organized entertainment for the deaf community, distributed religious literature, and accomplished many works of charity for sick and needy deaf people in the city. Their constitution designated that a Mass should be offered for all living members on Ephpheta Sunday on the day when the gospel passage describes Jesus' encounter with the deaf man. Ten years later, Pope Pius X would make Ephpheta Sunday the patronal feast of deaf people all over the world.

As the society grew, several satellite groups of Deaf Catholics began to meet in locations convenient for monthly or bimonthly worship services and religious education classes. The first of these was the Brooklyn de l'Épée Society, whose early discussions of Deaf Catholic history led to an organized campaign for a statue to honor Abbé Charles Michel l'Épée, the great Catholic teacher of the deaf and promoter of sign language. The society's periodical, *Ephpheta* magazine, spread the word about plans for the statue and published requests for donations to fund it. When Father McCarthy attended the 1913 National Association of the Deaf (NAD) meeting in Cleveland, he made the Xavier Ephpheta Society's case for a l'Épée statue to the broader deaf community of the United States. The plan was well received by Catholic and non-Catholic deaf people alike. In 1930, the Third World Congress of Educators of the Deaf was held in Buffalo, and three thousand educators and deaf community members attended. During this event, the NAD presented St. Mary's School for the Deaf in New York with an impressive bronze statue of l'Épée, sculpted by Eugene A. Hannon, a deaf man who began his study of art at St. Mary's.[8]

As Deaf Catholic culture began to flourish in the United States, Deaf Catholics and those who served them began to print and distribute newsletters and magazines to connect the deaf apostolates nationwide. In time, such publications became another notable area of deaf leadership in the Archdiocese of New York. In 1900, James F. Donnelly, a deaf man from New York City, founded a monthly periodical called *The Catholic Deaf Mute*. Donnelly learned printing at the New York Institute for the Deaf (Fanwood), where his teachers early recognized his talents, and the Catholic Literary and Benevolent Union elected him secretary while still in school. He started *The Catholic Deaf Mute* when he was thirty-nine,

8. "Ephpheta Society for the Catholic Deaf," booklet, n.d.

after he learned firsthand the importance of a broadly circulating newspaper for evangelizing the deaf community. For thirty-three years, Donnelly edited and set type for the paper by himself at home, page by page,
then carted the printing forms to the printer in a baby carriage. When
his wife learned the trade, she took over setting the type, and their eight
children helped with folding and wrapping. The paper quickly developed
a national circulation and had subscribers overseas as well.[9]

Ephpheta magazine, established by the Xavier Ephpheta Society in
1912 with Father McCarthy as editor and John F. O'Brien (a deaf lay-
man) as business manager, was a successful deaf-run periodical. Until it
was discontinued in 1919, the magazine helped to encourage the development of Ephpheta Societies in several different cities. Several different newsletters then circulated to Deaf Catholics in New York between
1900 and 1930. In December of 1933, when illness forced James Donnelly to resign his editorship of *The Catholic Deaf Mute*, Father Michael
Purtell, SJ, the new archdiocesan moderator for the New York deaf community, took up editorship of that publication and renamed it *Ephpheta*
after the Xavier Ephpheta Society, merging the history of these two notable New York publications in Deaf Catholic history. The newly named
periodical ran until 1971. The only other periodical for Deaf Catholics
at the time with both a national and international circulation was *Our
Young People*, established by St. John's School for the Deaf in Milwaukee
and printed by students in that school from 1891 to the mid-1920s.

The International Catholic Deaf Association

By the mid-twentieth century, Deaf Catholic laity in the United States
and Canada were fully engaged in creating broader and stronger connections, and they had been evangelizing the deaf community for several
decades. Usually, Deaf Catholics and hearing priests or educators shared
leadership of most local Deaf Catholic organizations during the early
twentieth century, but by the 1940s there was a widespread commitment
in the Deaf Catholic community to prioritizing deaf leadership. At the
local level, highly motivated laypeople organized their connections, encouraged deaf people to participate in the sacraments, and pursued an

9. Thomas F. McCaffrey, "History of the Apostolate of the Catholic Church to the Deaf in
the Archdiocese of New York" (master's thesis, Fordham University, 1951), Deaf Catholic Archives,
College of the Holy Cross, Worcester, Mass.

active role in church life even when Catholic parishes and schools could not or would not provide interpreters. Expanding the pool of marriageable Catholic young people who were competent in sign language was also a serious concern, one that helped to fuel the expanded organization of Deaf Catholic fellowship and culture. Within a few decades, this emphasis on lay leadership and participation would blend with a new drive for civil rights and social justice in mainstream America.

In 1949, Deaf Catholics in Canada and the United States formed an alliance of scattered diocesan associations and ministries. The International Catholic Deaf Association (ICDA) was created to be a fraternal service organization for deaf men and women. In the 1950s and early 1960s, the ICDA reached its peak of individual participation when over two thousand seven hundred active members belonging to fifty chapters in American and Canadian cities—though records indicate that membership grew significantly in subsequent decades because of new group membership categories. In addition to promoting Catholic devotion and social justice among deaf people, the ICDA aimed to educate Deaf Catholics about their faith and to make the sacraments—especially the Eucharist and reconciliation—available directly from priests who were fluent in the native language of deaf signers. For Deaf Catholics, the founding and rapid development of the ICDA—from a congress of Canadian-American Deaf communities in 1949 to a fully international association in the '50s and '60s—is a story that imparted a cultural history and identity. As an institution the ICDA provided needed validation and practical solutions for deaf church members excluded from parish activities, catechism, and even the sacraments. Eventually, the association would touch the lives of deaf people across six continents.

Members of the ICDA preserved its history in two booklets that illustrate the visual character of deaf culture: *The Birth of the International Catholic Deaf Association: Ten Years of Progress* by Colette Gabel (1959) and an expanded edition of this history by Michael and Frances Preston, *The Journey of the ICDA from 1949 to 1989*. Gabel's contribution is similar in composition to a graphic novel (it is, in fact, a graphic historical narrative) with hand-drawn illustrations in panels. It contains an interesting and relevant post-script for those puzzled by this format:

Some readers may find this a strange book. It was put together entirely by deaf people. It is about the deaf, by the deaf and chiefly for the deaf.... The English text may seem odd to you in places, the sentence structure awkward at times, but we were warned not to be ruthless in our corrections but to keep intact as far as possible, the native charm of the deaf idiom.[10]

The book presents the history of each ICDA convention as a visual narrative, with a self-conscious aim of preserving these stories in a form that later generations of Deaf Catholics might use as they recount this history to each other in sign language. Some panels highlight hearing chaplains, deaf board members, and guest speakers with short biographical sketches in idealized drawings resembling the 1950s comic book style of Lil' Abner or Prince Valiant. As in the world's oral cultures prior to widespread use of print and writing, it was most often storytellers who preserved historic events in Deaf Catholic culture by memorizing them in narrative form and retelling them in person during trips to visit other deaf communities.

The 1950s were a momentous decade for the ICDA, as each convention brought new developments for the spread of Deaf Catholic culture in the broader deaf community. The first ICDA convention was held in July of 1949 at the King Edward Hotel in Toronto, Ontario. Eleven priests (all hearing) and about one hundred laypeople (mostly deaf) were present at this convention. Each of the seven U.S. priests who were present was known for missionary work with deaf people in various parishes, schools, and diocese-based communities that were isolated and largely uninformed of each other's activities until the ICDA connected them.[11]

The participants gathered and acknowledged their ambitious aim "to unite all the Catholic Deaf associations in the world into one central body," an organization that would advocate for the unmet needs of deaf adults, including spiritual welfare, material needs, and education for their children.[12] Deaf lay delegates attended from Buffalo, Rochester, Brooklyn, Boston, Providence, Philadelphia, and Detroit in the United States; and Ottawa, Montreal, Halifax, and Windsor in Canada. These founding members decided that the organization would be a "natural meeting place for priests and laity, once a year arranging a convention wherein hundreds of deaf meet with priests dedicated to this task to discuss matters of interest to the deaf, make preparations for the improve-

10. Colette Gabel, "The Birth of the I.C.D.A. and Its Progress" (1959), graphic-illustrated booklet, ICDA History section, Deaf Catholic Archives, College of the Holy Cross, Worcester, Mass.
11. The seven priests from the United States were Godfrey Reilly, CP; John J. Watson; Raymond Kalter, CSsR; Everett McPhillips; Thomas Cribbin; G. B. Hauser; and John Gallagher, CSsR.
12. Gabel, "The Birth of the I.C.D.A. and Its Progress."

ment of work among the deaf and offer solutions to the problems concerning them." A board of seven deaf laypeople, men and women, were elected as executive officers, including Marcel Warnier, president; James Coughlin, Mary Garland, and Frank Meyette, vice-presidents; Nicholas Wojcik, secretary; Mary Pontus, financial secretary; and William McGovern, treasurer. The second convention was scheduled for the Hotel Statler in Buffalo, New York in 1951, with Father John Gallagher, CSsR, a hearing priest with only two years' experience serving the deaf community, as chairman.

At this second convention, the ICDA began a tradition of preaching in sign language at Masses during the conventions. This was important to the deaf community on many levels, since at-home members might only receive interpreted readings and sermons or (in the great majority of parishes) no sign language at all. Interpreters facilitated a degree of inclusion, but they were still a third party and sometimes not even Catholic, which undoubtedly influenced translation. For these reasons, the very presence of an interpreter served to highlight the fact that deaf attendees had no direct communication with the priest. Without priests who could preach in sign, interpreted homilies were (and still are) important as the primary form of preaching for Deaf Catholics. However, as with the development of BSL preaching in Great Britain, interpreted homilies and religious activities in the United States did not include deaf parishioners with the fullness of communication that ASL vernacular would eventually provide.

Even at these early conventions, the ICDA secured a bishop or archbishop to celebrate Mass for the event at the host city's cathedral. One of the hearing ICDA priests who could sign would interpret the bishop's sermon. At the 1951 convention, Father Joseph A. Burke, Auxiliary Bishop of Buffalo, celebrated Mass and preached a sermon at St. Joseph's Cathedral, which Father Stephen Landherr, CSsR, interpreted into sign language. Unfortunately, the content of the sermon was not recorded. At the 1952 convention in Boston, however, Archbishop Richard J. Cushing spoke of discernment of a full range of adult vocations for deaf people, urging them on as equal disciples of Christ. He exhorted the assembly as directly as he could, while Father Stephen Landherr interpreted the sermon:

Overcome your handicaps and take up your assignments in life. As members of the mystical body of Christ, you have a duty to change the face of the earth. You have a handicap, but we all have a handicap; whether it be mind, body, or soul, it makes no difference. Sooner or later everyone encounters a handicap in life. As an important part of Christ's army on earth, you must all follow your vocation in life. If you don't, no one will do it for you![13]

Most early convention sermons, like this one, addressed the deaf assembly but were composed and delivered in spoken English. One of the priests or pastoral workers who ministered in the deaf community would then interpret in sign language. At the 1951 convention, Father Daniel Higgins, CSsR, of De Soto, Missouri, pushed the boundaries of this convention, preaching a sermon directly to Deaf Catholics in their own sign language at the chapel of St. Mary's School for the Deaf. Unfortunately, ICDA members did not record whether the sermon was voice interpreted or if Higgins himself voiced while he was signing. What is certain is that, for many in attendance, Higgins's sermon was the first they had ever received directly from a priest in sign language.

Father Higgins authored some of the earliest published manuals on religious sign language in the United States. During his lifetime (1876–1959), Higgins gave many missions coast to coast throughout Canada and the United States. He was a natural performance artist with an animated and dramatic style of sign language preaching, as suggested in a memorial tribute: "His special gift was not his command of sign language but his understanding of movement, pantomime, the creativity of those magnificent hands that could do magic, mold chalices, make rosaries. His sermon outlines resembled a set of stage directions as he moved his characters around for visual effect."[14] If some of his sermons were composed with English words, those words were a distant second to his understanding of how space, movement, and visual shapes of the body and hands would create a dynamic sense of meaning for viewers attuned to the visual mode. Higgins's performance-like delivery is one style of sign language eloquence that has remained a rhetorical tradition of the Deaf Catholic community. Through his mastery of ASL, he became an active part of Deaf Catholic culture and contributed to the preservation and development of preaching in ASL as a respected rhetorical tradition.

As the ICDA grew throughout the 1950s, its all-deaf board of directors developed more services in compliance with its mission. Wherever Deaf Catholic centers were already in place, delegates helped the deaf

13. Gabel, "The Birth of the I.C.D.A. and Its Progress."

14. "Unusual Man: Daniel D. Higgins," in *Let Us Now Praise Great Men: A Centenary Tribute to All the Redemptorists Who Made the St. Louis Province, 1875–1975* 14: 1–7, Deaf Catholic Archives, College of the Holy Cross, Worcester, Mass.

community to form ICDA chapters. Toronto became Chapter One and Boston Chapter Five, and new applications for chapter membership came in each year. Among the services developed during the 1950s were a bimonthly newspaper, fundraising to finance sign language classes for seminarians, and the planned creation of Catholic Deaf Centers in every diocese. Established chapters began training a deaf lay apostolate to foster the spiritual well-being of deaf people, especially the poor. A home for elderly deaf people was developed in Milwaukee, and in 1956 the ICDA began facilitating a national adoption service to find signing deaf parents for orphaned deaf children. In 1951, the ardent new organization received a letter of praise and Apostolic Blessing from the Holy See.

At the 1953 ICDA Mass in Detroit, participants had yet another reason to rejoice: Father Vincente Burnier from Brazil celebrated the Mass; he was the only Catholic priest living at that time who had been born profoundly deaf. Before this convention, most Deaf Catholics believed it impossible for a deaf man to become a priest. However, they soon discovered that Father Burnier was an accomplished speaker and lip-reader. He celebrated Mass as any other priest did, in Latin, though of course most of the people in the assembly had never heard Latin, just as they had never heard English. With amazement at Burnier's achievement and the joy of belonging to a nationally recognized group of Deaf Catholics, the assembly quieted their hands as Father Burnier processed down the aisle toward the altar. During Mass, many prayed their rosaries and looked up periodically to see Father Burnier at the altar with his back turned, just as many hearing Catholics did before Vatican II. At the appropriate time, someone stood to read the Scripture readings out loud. At home, Deaf Catholics may have followed along in their missal at this point, but English was often not a deaf person's strong suit. At the ICDA Mass, they watched with rapt attention as Father Stephen Landherr from Philadelphia stood next to the lector and interpreted in sign language. It may have been the first time some of them experienced Scripture readings in a language they could fully understand. Finally, Father Burnier mounted the pulpit and addressed his sermon to the deaf assembly—in sign language! His topic was the presence of Christ in the Eucharist for all, both those who could hear the Word and those who could only see it. At that moment, language barriers dissolved, and the work of the Holy Spirit must have been palpable in the people, in the sermon, and in the sacrament. Those in attendance then easily understood: what had been missing in their parish churches was not just their sense of hearing but the understanding and fellowship of other Christians.

In 1953, the ICDA continued its mission of evangelizing the deaf community, especially Deaf Catholic children living away from home in state schools. Marcel Warnier, ICDA president, organized a research bureau to investigate the number of Catholic pupils in state schools for the deaf, with an aim of discovering which schools had access to chaplains or catechists and who supported these roles financially. The organization nurtured a keen desire to make the Catholic faith accessible to deaf children and, at the same time, to preserve sign language as a cultural good for this next generation. To this end, the ICDA actively promoted sign language among seminarians by circulating publications and flyers. As a result, Richard Bowdren, professor of dactylology at St. Joseph's Seminary in Dunwoodie, New York, trained a large class of seminarians in sign language communication.

As ICDA membership grew, its executive officers further developed the organization's mission and bylaws. Through an improved definition of purpose and better communication with deaf members, the ICDA created and continually augmented a sense of identity for Deaf Catholics. Active members visited the sick in hospitals and their homes, gave instruction to prospective adult converts and to Catholic children in public schools for the deaf, and encouraged fallen-away Deaf Catholics to practice their faith. ICDA's robust membership led to new activities, such as a sports committee for athletics, especially bowling leagues and basketball tournaments for deaf youth. Members created the ICDA Mission Fund to pay for retreats or signed sermons in areas where deaf people could not afford to pay for a signing retreat master, and chapter leaders organized pilgrimages for deaf adults to visit sites such as Rome and Lourdes, France. In support of the organization's aim to integrate Deaf Catholics with the broader church, a research committee began to document the need for more priests to serve deaf communities' spiritual welfare. The committee took as its guide the words of Father John La Farge, SJ, "Let the public know who you are, what you do and why you do it, and the public will respect you, and justice will be done." The ICDA took this to heart: "This is precisely what the ICDA asks for: justice. Our aims are reasonable: more priests with more time to work for the deaf. More Centers. More schools. In order to save souls from being lost and to make weak souls strong."[15]

15. Gabel, "The Birth of the I.C.D.A. and Its Progress"; La Farge also quoted here.

The fervor of lay deaf leaders in the ICDA, with the help and vision of the organization's first chaplain, Redemptorist Father John Gallagher, ignited deaf people to active participation in church life across
North America. In turn, this publicly visible activity of the ICDA often
drew attention to deaf people from the mainstream press and Catholic
newspapers alike. Interest in deaf ministry grew as a result. Between 1945
and 1960, over thirty priests assigned to deaf ministry provided pastoral care around the United States. In their publications and newsletters,
the ICDA showed great esteem for the priesthood as a sanctified and
self-sacrificing role. Members were urged to pray for priests who served
the deaf (all of them hearing at this time). A persistent problem in the
1950s was that, despite the ICDA's efforts to spread sign language, only
a handful of priests who served the deaf apostolate had even basic competence in sign language.

Nevertheless, the leadership of these priest moderators was essential
in the early years of the association. At the 1956 ICDA convention in
Milwaukee, a record number of thirty-seven priests involved in the deaf
apostolate convened to issue a statement on "The Religious Education
of Deaf Children." Although there was not a single deaf person among
them, the ICDA looked to these priests to represent their interests in
the broader church on issues in deaf education and social justice. The
1956 statement encouraged Catholic men and women to enter the field
of deaf education and urged all major seminaries to offer sign language
classes. At the time, the ICDA advocated a method combining sign language and lipreading, similar to the signing that accompanied religious
education for Deaf Catholics in Britain during this period. It is important to note that the ICDA's position on combining sign with spoken
English was not tenacious oralism but, rather, a move toward including
more sign language than schools for the deaf were using in the 1950s. In
an era when oralism and the forced suppression of natural, gestural communication were still the norm, this mixed mode combining signs with
spoken language was an advancement in the human right of unimpeded
communication for deaf people.

The ICDA's 1956 statement on religious education acknowledged
that "since the greater part of a deaf person's life will be spent in the company of those who hear and speak, every deaf child should be given as
much training in speech and speech reading as he can absorb." However,
the statement also insisted on special religious education classes for deaf

children, since "it is normally impossible for a deaf child to receive a satis-
factory knowledge of his faith when he is compelled to attend catechism
classes with children who have normal hearing." These classes, ICDA
specified, would be better offered in sign language, since "The majority of deaf, regardless of educational background, use the sign language
among themselves as an easy and certain medium of communication."[16]
In a move that must have shocked many oral-deaf educators at the time,
the board of directors published recommendations to accept and standardize sign language and to suit the method of communication to the
needs of particular deaf children and adults, rather than force the use of
one method because of its prevalence in schools. By publicly embracing
this important aspect of deaf culture, the ICDA—and by extension, the
Catholic Church to whom it belonged—were far ahead of state schools,
who did not embrace the Total Communication philosophy until the
late 1960s into the 1970s.

All of these developments and ICDA's advocacy for deaf participation in church life led to growth in the association. The tenth anniversary
convention of the ICDA in 1959 was the largest gathering of Deaf Catholics to date. Over one thousand members were present in Cleveland,
Ohio, more than attended the twenty-fifth National Association of the
Deaf convention in 1960 (the civil rights association for deaf people, already fifty years old at the time).[17] This ICDA convention was the largest
gathering of Deaf Catholics ever convened in the world to that date. The
organization had grown to include chapters in fifty cities—forty-three in
the United States, four in Canada, and three in Great Britain, with the
densest number of Deaf Catholics from the Northeast and Great Lakes
areas. During this peak year, there were 2,672 active individual members
(with dues fully paid), 117 "Life Members," and 75 priest moderators in
the organization. Self-consciously promoting the Mass in sign language,
ICDA documents exclaimed, "The ICDA has seen a spiritual growth
commensurate with its growth in influence all over the Catholic Deaf
world.... In all these years, without any doubt, adult Catholic Deaf
have seen in their own language a far greater interest in the spread of the

16. Gabel, "The Birth of the I.C.D.A. and Its Progress"

17. The "Proceedings of the Twenty-Fifth Convention, National Association of the Deaf," printed in the August 1960 edition of *The Silent Worker* (Knoxville, Tenn.: National Association of the
Deaf) does not include the number of attendees for this historic meeting, which included delegates
of several state associations of the deaf for the first time. The convention gathered 51 representatives
from 29 states to represent 9,276 deaf members, and attendees in the general assembly numbered in
the "hundreds" (3).

visible signs [Mass and sacraments] of the Church than ever before in history."[18]

During its second decade, the ICDA continued its mission to unite Deaf Catholics in an active religious association. Father David Walsh, a Redemptorist priest who became the organization's chaplain in 1960 and its official missionary in 1962, led an effort to establish deaf services in every North American diocese. Recognizing the importance of both public and private schools for the continuation of ICDA's mission, Father Walsh began this effort with a renewed focus on religious education. Walsh prioritized reaching out to known Catholics who taught in state-funded residential schools and recruiting these teachers, hearing and deaf, to lead catechism classes for Catholic pupils. In 1960, continuing in the tradition of the Catholic Education Association's annual "Deaf Section" gatherings, he began to organize and lead annual religious education workshops for pastoral workers from across North America. In agreement with ICDA's mission, Father Walsh actively encouraged the use of sign language in religious education and in celebrating the sacraments, and he successfully recruited several religious sisters to the cause of deaf ministry. A role model in deaf religious education for many years, he was himself a skilled and expressive signer.

Called the great Apostle to the Deaf in his obituary (as Hayward had been in Great Britain), Father Walsh traveled widely as part of his duties as ICDA's official missionary.[19] Walsh was a celebrity for Deaf Catholics during the 1950s and 1960s. Through newsletters, signed storytelling, and convention keynote addresses, they eagerly followed his progress as he drove a van far and wide, across the United States, Canada, and Mexico, evangelizing Deaf Catholic communities who had requested him to lead a mission or retreat. As former chaplain Father Jerry Trancone put it, deaf people would "come out of the woodwork" to see him preach.[20] Everywhere he went, he visited the local bishop with local deaf leaders accompanying him. If there were no priest or pastoral worker assigned to deaf ministry in the diocese, Walsh would seek the bishop's agreement to appoint someone. As ICDA founded more chapters across the United States and Canada, the association more fully represented the Deaf Catholic community in North America. Between 1961 and 1971, the as-

18. Gabel, "The Birth of the I.C.D.A. and Its Progress."

19. *Chicago Tribune*, August 17, 2005.

20. Fr. Jerry Trancone, then-director of Deaf Ministries for the Archdiocese of Washington, interview by Marlana Portolano, Silver Spring, Maryland, December 15, 2015.

sociation added almost forty more chapters in as many cities.[21] Many
had existed as small deaf-led organizations or communities since early
in the century and were only now describing themselves publicly as a
cultural group. In their growing sense of deaf cultural identity, members
increasingly saw the ICDA as an official stamp of recognition for Deaf
Catholics as a cultural apostolate within the church.

After centuries of being invisible, an auspicious time in church history was dawning for Deaf Catholics. Part II of the book will examine civic
and religious changes in the lives of deaf people during the last decades of
the twentieth century—a veritable renaissance for sign language and deaf
culture. Because of the strong foundations laid by dedicated deaf lay leaders and sign language-proficient missionaries, a new and unprecedented
era of fruitfulness in deaf ministry lay ahead.

21. Michael and Frances Preston, *The Journey of the ICDA from 1949 to 1989* (Silver Spring, Md.:
International Catholic Deaf Association, 1989), 130.

Recommended Reading
for Part I

The following works provide deeper context in the field of deaf history. A second list focusing on late twentieth-century deaf culture appears at the end of part II. Readers may view video resources in signed languages at the companion website, http://icfdeafservice.org/beopened.

Introductions to Deaf Studies

Gallaudet, Edward M. *Life of Thomas Hopkins Gallaudet—Founder of Deaf-Mute Instruction in America*. New York: Henry Holt, 1888.
————. *History of the College for the Deaf, 1857–1907*. Washington, D.C.: Gallaudet College Press, 1983.
Neisser, Arden. *The Other Side of Silence: Sign Language and the Deaf Community in America*. Washington, D.C.: Gallaudet University Press, 1990.
Padden, Carol, and Tom Humphries. *Inside Deaf Culture*. Cambridge, Mass: Harvard University Press, 2009.
Veditz, George. *The Preservation of the Sign Language*. Washington, D.C.: Gaulladet University, 1913. Film.

Historical Overviews

Baynton, Douglas C. *Forbidden Signs: American Culture and the Campaign against Sign Language*. Chicago: University of Chicago Press, 1998.
Burch, Susan. *Signs of Resistance: American Deaf Cultural History, 1900 to World War II*. New York: New York University Press, 2004.
Fraser, Benjamin, ed. *Deaf History and Culture in Spain: A Reader of Primary Documents*. Washington, D.C.: Gallaudet University Press, 2009.
Gannon, Jack R. *Deaf Heritage: A Narrative History of Deaf America*. Washington, D.C.: Gallaudet University Press, 2012.

Nomeland, Melvia M., Ronald E. Nomeland, and Trudy Suggs. *The Deaf Community in America: History in the Making.* Jefferson, N.C.: McFarland Publishing, 2011.

Shea, Gerald. *The Language of Light: A History of Silent Voices.* New Haven, Conn.: Yale University Press, 2017.

Van Cleve, John V. *Deaf History Unveiled: Interpretations from the New Scholarship.* Washington, D.C.: Gallaudet University Press, 1999.

————. *The Deaf History Reader.* Washington, D.C.: Gallaudet University Press, 2007.

Part II

―――――――

New Deaf Evangelization

CHAPTER 9

Deaf Catholics after Vatican II

I don't mean to push aside hearing people and the good they've done for the deaf, but I think the deaf should accept more responsibility for the ministry of their own people.—Father Thomas Coughlin, first culturally Deaf priest ordained in the United States, quoted in the *St. Anthony Messenger*, 1981.

In both civic and religious realms, the second half of the twentieth century brought dramatic transformations in what came to be known in the United States as Deaf Culture. The Civil Rights movement revolutionized the way minority groups saw themselves in society, and deaf people demanded their own rights using vocabulary and strategies borrowed from civil rights activists. At the same time, the theological significance of the Second Vatican Council (1962–1965) encouraged the church to reexamine communication among Catholics all over the world. Deaf Catholics and those in deaf ministry were intensely interested in these changes. In areas where Catholicism had become well established in deaf communities, ministry moved beyond its pioneering and missionary stages. Pastoral leaders who came from, rather than to, the Deaf-World began to take center stage as equals with and, often, role models for their hearing counterparts.[1] The institution of vernacular Masses corresponded with more frequent and more accurate use of sign language by hearing

1. In ASL, "Deaf-World" is a signed term for the deaf way of life.

167

clergy and, increasingly, by deaf clergy as well. By the end of the century, developments in technology and communications had helped to usher in a new era of connection among deaf people as a language community in society and in the church. Finally, Deaf Catholics could envision a time when evangelizing "to the deaf" as an underprivileged group could cease to be a role reserved for hearing educators, pastoral workers, and interpreters. Instead, hearing participants in Deaf Catholic life could serve alongside their deaf brothers and sisters in Christ, benefiting from spiritual gifts that only the deaf community could bring to the church.

Perhaps most exciting for the future of the church, the turn of the twenty-first century saw the first deaf ministries in Asia and Africa and expansion of deaf ministries in Latin America, where deaf people frequently still do not have access to hearing aids or new communication technologies. The narrative profiles in Part II illustrate not only the global diversity of deaf people in the church but also their common human gift of sign language and the growing international connectedness of deaf people as a cultural group in the church. These advances in Deaf Catholic culture did not come easily, and in truth the church has only begun to include this population, present in every nation of the world. Serious problems, even crises, continue in the new millennium, but the legal and social advances that took place for Western deaf people during the late twentieth century have paved the way for further evangelization in countries where deaf people still have precious few rights as citizens and as human beings.

Sign Languages as True Languages

Rapid development in sign languages, both in the field of linguistics and in practical or artful communication, was undoubtedly the most important condition for advances in twentieth century Deaf Catholic culture. Without a more accurate understanding of ASL as a complete human language, American Deaf Culture may never have achieved recognition as a language minority, and ASL may never have entered Catholic liturgy. For the key milestone of linguistic recognition, ASL was privileged to lead the way and thus to serve as a precedent for other national sign languages.

The acceptance of ASL as a genuine language rather than a substandard gestural accompaniment to English had far-reaching effects on Deaf Culture in the United States and abroad. Much of the credit goes to William Stokoe, an English professor who joined the faculty of Gallaudet University (then College) in Washington, D.C., in 1955. As Stokoe closely observed deaf students using extensive ASL outside of class, despite educational practices that required them to speak and lip-read, he became convinced that ASL was a true and complete human language definable in linguistic terms. In 1960, Stokoe published his findings in the first modern linguistic treatment of a signed language as a scholarly monograph entitled *Sign Language Structure*.[2] Five years later, with his Gallaudet colleagues Dorothy Casterline and Carl Croneberg, he published the groundbreaking *Dictionary of American Sign Language on Linguistic Principles*. This formal recognition instilled validation and confidence in the American Deaf community as citizens and communicators. As canon lawyer Edward Peters puts it, "While Deaf people always knew their sign languages were real languages, watching the hearing world come to recognize that fact had an energizing effect on the Deaf community's self-confidence. The pride that the Deaf had long felt in their language(s) and communities could finally be expressed."[3]

Today, according to the World Federation of the Deaf, about seventy million people in the world claim a signed language as their first language. Linguists have shown that natural signed languages exhibit all the structural properties of other human languages and that they originated independently of spoken languages within their own linguistic family trees. For example, American Sign Language (ASL) and British Sign Language (BSL) have very little vocabulary in common, but ASL shares many signs with French Sign Language (LSF) because French educators and missionaries founded schools for deaf students in the United States during the nineteenth century. While sign language is not a universal system as many hearing people mistakenly believe, there are universal features in any signed mode of human communication. Because it is spatial and related to the human body, certain gestural aspects of signed communication depend on biological norms—pointing, direction, and the reach of the arms (technically, indexical and spatial indicators). Because of these transcultural and basic anatomical features, users of different

2. William Stokoe, "Sign Language Structure: An Outline of the Visual Communication Systems of the American Deaf," *The Journal of Deaf Studies and Deaf Education* 10, no. 1 (January 2005): 3–37.

3. Peters, "Canonical and Cultural Developments Culminating in the Ordination of Deaf Men," 249.

sign languages typically learn to communicate with one another more quickly than users of unrelated spoken languages that do not make use of the body to convey spatial or directional ideas. The communication that results from negotiation between different sign languages is not a complete language but rather a simplified pidgin; nevertheless, as deaf people from different countries began to organize international gatherings in the late twentieth century, this type of signed communication came to be called International Sign Language.[4]

From the late 1980s to 2016, several national sign languages besides ASL gained linguistic recognition as true native languages of deaf people, including Australian Sign Language (Auslan), British Sign Language (BSL), Brazilian Sign Language (LIBRAS), Thai Sign Language, Uganda Sign Language, and many others. The number of linguistically complete sign languages continues to grow in the twenty-first century. It is important to note that these are naturally evolved languages. They differ from artificial systems or derivative sign systems, which were created by educators or missionaries to represent spoken languages (for example, Manually Coded English or Signing Exact English).

Instead of using the three-dimensional, kinetic grammar of natural sign languages, derivative systems attempt to use signs in the temporal word order of a spoken or written language. Derivative systems are still common in public school classrooms today, especially in mixed modes of signing simultaneously with spoken language. It is no surprise that mixed modes have appeared frequently in deaf ministries through the ages, especially where deaf and hearing people worked side by side. Like other Christians, Deaf Catholics are people of the book, and they rely on knowledge passed down in carefully codified language through print. Several situations illustrating these mixed modes—and the controversy surrounding them—appear in part II.

Advocates of Deaf Culture who value strong ASL often malign derivative sign systems. While it is true that derivative systems are linguistically incomplete and often awkward, historically they helped to achieve acceptance for the use of signs in education and in mainstream culture. It would be an error to deny any "cross-pollination" with spoken languages

---

4. McKee, Rachel, and Jemina Napier, "Interpreting in International Sign Pidgin: An Analysis," *Journal of Sign Language Linguistics* 5, no. 1 (2002): 27–54; and Ted Supalla and Rebecca Webb, "The Grammar of International Sign: A New Look at Pidgin Languages," in *Language, Gesture, and Space,* International Conference on Theoretical Issues in Sign Language Research, eds. Karen Emmorey and Judy S. Reilly (Hillsdale, N.J.: Erlbaum, 1995), 333–52.

at all in the history of signed communication. Just as spoken languages grow and change by borrowing from each other, contact with spoken and written languages has an ongoing influence on signed communication, and derivative systems have played a part in the historical development of sign languages. A fair list of borrowings would include finger spelling, translated vocabulary, and perhaps even categories of knowledge that did not exist before print and literacy—even the idea of grammar itself. By the same token, some translated ASL phrases (such as the "Deaf-World" already mentioned and a few other ASL idioms) have travelled into English vocabulary, and the study of signed languages has taught linguists many new things about language as a human phenomenon.

One practical outcome of linguistic recognition of ASL was the re-introduction of signed communication, especially mixed modes, into the classroom and the quick spread of signs as a norm for the education of deaf students. Until midcentury, the oralist teaching methods championed at the 1880 International Congress of Deaf Educators in Milan were the dominant methodology of the twentieth century.[5] Prior to 1960, several new oralist schools were founded in the United States and Europe, and some major oralist schools founded in the nineteenth century (such as the Clarke School in Massachusetts and St. John's in England) continued to flourish and spread their influence. Deaf histories (from a deaf cultural perspective) are often bitter about this "Oralist Dark Age," and there are good reasons for this attitude among signing deaf people. Many deaf senior citizens today remember having to sit on their hands in school and communicate solely by speech, lip reading, and residual hearing (if they had any). No sign language communication was allowed in the stricter schools, even for play or social purposes among the deaf children. A few children did well with this method and gained higher reading levels than they may have with sign alone, but more often children did not gain competence in either language, spoken or signed. Literacy levels among deaf children and adults remained low.[6]

In 1964 the United States Congress issued the Babbidge Report, which concluded that, based on low literacy rates and a lack of communication skill in deaf high school graduates, oral deaf education in U.S.

---

5. See chapter 1, pp. 35–38.

6. For a complete account of English language learning for deaf students in the United States prior to 1960, see John V. Van Cleve and Barry A. Crouch, *A Place of Their Own: Creating the Deaf Community in America* (Washington, D.C.: Gallaudet University Press, 1989); Harlan Lane, *The Mask of Benevolence: Disabling the Deaf Community* (New York: Alfred A. Knopf, 1992).

schools had been a dismal failure. Many in the deaf community consider the Babbidge Report an acknowledgment of the superiority of signed communication in deaf education and a major advance for deaf people and Deaf Culture. Because of the Babbidge Report and the linguistic scholarship of Stokoe and others, oralism in deaf education declined dramatically in the 1970s and 1980s. In the United States, almost all state schools for deaf children began to carry out instruction in sign with English as a second language, primarily through text and, if it benefitted the student, speech therapy. A corresponding heyday came about for American Deaf Culture as schools for deaf children began, once again, to hire deaf teachers with native ASL signing skills. Unfortunately, English literacy levels did not improve.[7] The only consistent predictor of higher literacy levels was for deaf students who were the children of deaf adults: these had a complete first language (ASL) to begin with, so their ability to learn a second language (English) for reading was greater than those who had very little language before starting school.[8]

During the late 1960s, deaf teacher and administrator Roy Kay Holcomb attempted to find a middle ground in the battles over methodology by coining the term "Total Communication." Total Communication was not a method but rather an educational philosophy in which each child could use the communication method that worked best for that child's individual needs. If a student learned better with ASL or with pidgin signed English, that mode of communication would be used for teaching and learning; if a student did well with an oral approach, that method would be used. The philosophy caught on and rapidly spread through schools across the United States, representing the first break from the rigidly oral approach that had dominated deaf education in the first half of the century. Much of the Deaf Catholic community in the United States were advocates of Total Communication during these years, and the nation's remaining Catholic schools for the deaf all used some form of it. Unfortunately, in practice, Total Communication often

7. See, for example, Barbara Luetke-Stahlman, "Documenting Syntactically and Semantically Incomplete Bimodal Input to Hearing-Impaired Subjects," *American Annals of the Deaf* 133, no. 3 (July 1988): 230–34; Clair L. Ramsey, "Language Planning in the Deaf Community," in *The Sociolinguistics of the Deaf Community*, ed. Ceil Lucas (New York: Harcourt Brace Jovanovich, 1989): 123–146; Peter V. Paul, *Literacy and Deafness: The Development of Reading, Writing and Literate Thought* (Needham Heights, Mass.: Allyn and Bacon, 1998); Peter V. Paul and Stephen Quigley, *Language and Deafness*, 2nd ed. (San Diego: Singular Publishing Group, 1994).

8. See Harlan Lane, Robert Hoffmeister, and Ben Bahan, *A Journey into the Deaf-World* (San Diego: DawnSign Press, 1996); Paul, *Literacy and Deafness*.

disintegrated into a hodgepodge mode of speaking and signing, and both languages suffered.

Throughout these bitter struggles over deaf education methods, the Catholic Church in America was no stranger to ASL, as we have seen in part I. Even before public schools and universities began to accept sign language in the twentieth century, the church was reaching out to embrace deaf people in their own language and culture through the work of missionaries such as the Redemptorist Father Daniel Higgins and the Jesuit Father Michael McCarthy.[9] These missionaries and educators helped prepare the way for the development of signed liturgies and Masses. In 1965, the same year William Stokoe published his *Dictionary of American Sign Language*, Pope Paul VI recognized signed communication (in general) as the vernacular of deaf people throughout the world and gave permission for both the priest and laypeople to sign during the liturgy wherever it was pastorally appropriate.[10] This permission was a breakthrough that opened the way for many advances in the church's understanding of culturally deaf people, and the first attempts to translate Scripture and Catholic worship into grammatically complete sign languages eventually followed. As the Word became fully expressed in the sign languages of different nations, fullness of life in the church became more accessible to deaf people in major dioceses of those nations. Within two decades, signed liturgy, sacramental preparation, and participation in the Eucharist would prompt a full range of vocations for deaf laypeople and enable many in the Deaf Catholic community to discern their true gifts and actively participate in the life of the church.

Civil Rights and Religious Rights

The American Civil Rights movement of the 1950s and 1960s had a profound influence in the lives of Deaf Catholics. As social and educational issues became a focus for deaf people, the Deaf Catholic community began to shift from a narrower focus on religious education, devotion, and sacramental access to a broader, more organized focus on the Catholic social justice tradition. As in the mainstream, church attendance dwindled as society became more and more secular. By the 1970s, however, a

9. See chapter 4, pp. 75–77, 83–88.
10. Michael Preston and Frances Preston, *The Journey of the ICDA from 1949 to 1989* (Silver Spring, Md.: International Catholic Deaf Association, 1989), 36.

smaller but more empowered group of American Deaf Catholics, newly informed by the Civil Rights Movements of the 1960s, emerged as outspoken church leaders.

At times, even these leaders found it difficult to arrive at a consistent concept of Deaf Catholic identity. Conflicting definitions of deafness during this period sometimes caused uncomfortable division: on the one side were those who saw deafness as a disability needing intervention and special benefits and, on the other, were those who saw deaf people as a cultural and linguistic group entitled to full civil rights and, by extension, religious rights and responsibilities. The two approaches were ideologically opposed, but proponents of Deaf Culture strategically promoted both positions. For example, by the early 1970s, pastoral workers for the deaf community began to professionalize. Some North American dioceses began to hire or train disabilities specialists in order to take advantage of new laws protecting deaf and disabled people, including the Rehabilitation Act of 1973. At the same time, groups of Deaf Catholics and pastoral workers organized legal efforts to apply civil rights laws to disabled persons. These efforts met with a mixed reception in the deaf community, since many deaf people identified not as disabled individuals but as a cultural group.

In 1976, canon lawyer Father Richard Ryan made an influential statement at a Catholic Pastoral Week conference for the deaf community in Gulf Shores, Alabama. It combined the professionalism of the newly organized pastoral workers with the language of deaf human and civil rights adopted in the 1960s. Several Deaf Catholics who were present took particular interest in what he said:

Historically, Church tradition has been the attitude of "be kind to the unfortunate, for charity requires this." ... [But] the Church's work with the handicapped is based on justice, not charity. What Vatican II states concerning the essential equality among all men, concerning social justice, and concerning discrimination, applies to the members of the ecclesial community as well as to the civil community.... If justice is really to be put into practice within the ecclesial community, the Church as a community and as individual members "must be prepared to take on new functions and duties" toward minority groups within the Church.

Ryan then listed certain "religious rights" that were "in part owed to Deaf Catholics":

- The right to religious instruction despite smallness in number.
- The right to Mass in their own language.
- The right to confession as they wish.
- Rights that hearing-impaired individuals have to enjoy the assistance of qualified interpreters, especially if it seems impossible to provide priests.[11]

Statements such as these at gatherings of pastoral workers and Deaf Catholics, coupled with the acceptance and expansion of ASL in the United States, inspired a new kind of evangelistic leadership among culturally Deaf Catholics.

In mainstream secular culture in the United States, similar deliberations about the civil rights of deaf people were taking place. In January of 1988, the Congressional Commission on the Education of the Deaf published a report, "Toward Equality: Education of the Deaf," which refuted derivative sign systems and recommended that deaf children receive classroom instruction in linguistically complete ASL as part of the Bilingual Education Act (1968). Advocates of Deaf Culture were encouraged by this development, but two months after Congress' recommendation, the Deaf community made an even greater leap in the public perception of deaf civil rights. As has often been the case, this development took place at an important site for deaf education.

When in March 1988 Gallaudet University's Board of Trustees appointed a hearing person who did not know sign language as president of the University, students and faculty protested for eight consecutive days in what came to be known as the Deaf President Now movement. In narrative accounts of deaf history, Deaf President Now was a defining event that would rock the Deaf-World for decades to come. In multiple rallies, marches, and press conferences, college-age protesters took an unequivocal stand against the perceived control of deaf people by those who were not deaf. As a result, I. King Jordan, a psychology professor and Gallaudet's Dean of Arts and Sciences, was named the first deaf president of Gallaudet University. Jordan was a late-deafened man who used a mixed mode of signing and speaking when he communicated; nevertheless, Deaf ASL users celebrated the change as a victory. With a deaf, signing man of any caliber at the university's helm, culturally deaf people were one step closer to widespread recognition as a cultural group and a valid language minority.

---

11. Richard Ryan, "Statement to the Bishops on the Deaf Person in New York State," Pastoral Workers Meeting, 1976, submitted by the Pastoral Workers to the Catholic Deaf in New York State, New York State folder, Deaf Catholic Archives, College of the Holy Cross, Worcester, Mass.

Disabilities Legislation and Deaf Culture

Far from finding a resolution, the quarrel between medical views and cultural views of deafness continued into the late twentieth century. Alongside changes in education and the academic acceptance of ASL, new medical legislation affected the lives of deaf people, including Deaf Catholics. In the 1980s, a widespread trend toward the medicalization of disabilities encouraged the development of new laws in many countries. The World Health Organization's International Classification of Impairment, Disabilities, and Handicaps (IC-IDH) strongly influenced new definitions of disability and the criteria for classifying them, as well as medical policies and standards. For example, in 1990 China passed a Law on Protection of Disabled Persons, with Article 45 establishing that "all citizens … have the right to material assistance from the state and society when they are old, ill or disabled." The term "disabled persons" was (and often still is) used to indicate people with a wide and disparate range of conditions including "visual, hearing, speech or physical disabilities, intellectual disabilities, psychiatric disabilities, multiple disabilities and/ or other disabilities." This medicalized approach was equally strong in the West, and it was sometimes troubling to the deaf communities in the United States and Europe, who were struggling to define themselves as a viable cultural and language group rather than people needing monetary handouts and government support because of a medical condition. Fortunately, the medical model drew significant new attention to the problems of deaf people. However, in the deaf community, attention to the needs of deaf people ultimately shifted to a focus on civil rights— arguably a more culturally determined category.

The deaf community in the United States received a civil rights boost in 1990 when President George H. W. Bush signed the Americans with Disabilities Act into law. The Americans with Disabilities Act ensured protections for disabled persons that were similar to the 1964 Civil Rights Act with its protections against discrimination based on race, creed, or sex. Expanding the work of the Civil Rights Act, the Americans with Disabilities Act required employers to provide reasonable accommodations to employees with disabilities and established mandates for accessibility accommodations in public facilities. Although it would not be fully implemented for over a decade, the Americans with Disabilities Act contributed to a rapidly changing approach to deaf people in mainstream public life. In 1995 Great Britain passed their own Disability Discrimination Act, and activists in several other European countries undertook disabilities rights movements during the 1990s, many of which resulted in specific legislation benefiting deaf people.

However, these changing perspectives were not always uniform, even inside Deaf Culture. While the benefits of the Americans with Disabilities Act were a tremendous help for the advancement of deaf rights and deaf access to public resources, the medicalized emphasis often frustrated those in the deaf community who had begun to define deafness as language-based and cultural. In public discourse about Christian deaf apostolates, for example, many ministers in Catholic and Protestant churches began freely combining the language of civil rights (in support of a suppressed minority) with the language of medicalized disability. At times, the two ideologies caused conflict in the progress toward deaf people's sense of identity and self-sufficiency, but each aided the advancement of deaf people in public life in different ways. In retrospect, the deaf community's selective use of these opposed identities, for maximum benefit in different contexts, was often expedient and politically astute.

Despite any benefit these combined terminologies may have had for deaf communities, any appearance of homogeneity in the United States deaf community would not last long. In the decades following the Deaf President Now protest, public school districts in the mainstream expanded a variety of deaf education options, proliferating the choices for families with deaf and hard of hearing children. The Individuals with Disabilities Act, fully adopted in 1990, required that students be able to attend schools with the "least restrictive environment." In 1992, the Americans with Disabilities Act was fully enacted, outlawing obstacles to accessibility in both education and employment. By the end of the twentieth century, a wide variety of deaf education programs were available in public school districts. Schools advised families to choose a program—whether ASL, oral-aural, signed English, Total Communication, Cued Speech, or a combination of these—that best suited the needs of their individual child, taking into consideration his or her cause and severity of deafness, family situation, and cultural background. Rapid advances in hearing aid and cochlear implant technology began to change the demographics of Deaf Culture once again. By the turn of the twentieth century, most parents chose to place their deaf children in their local school district so they could live at home with their families. Enrollments at residential state schools, once the wellspring of American Deaf culture, began to shrink, and education in European countries similarly began to offer a variety of approaches from which parents of deaf children might choose. As a result, the demographics of Deaf Culture began to change rapidly on both sides of the Atlantic. Today, over 50 percent of babies who are born profoundly deaf in the United States receive a cochlear implant. Furthermore, that percentage is growing rapidly and does not take into consideration the many older children and adults who opt to receive an implant.[12]

For those who struggled to preserve sign language and Deaf Culture earlier in the twentieth century, these new developments often appeared to be one more step in the powerful drive of hearing culture to dismantle Deaf Culture and ASL and make them obsolete. Even today, some supporters of American Deaf Culture feel that the widespread use of cochlear implants and the popularity of mainstream education for deaf children are nothing less than cultural genocide. Many Deaf people understandably express strong fears—one might even say existential fears—of losing their language and culture. Users of native ASL work hard to preserve their language, especially those in Deaf families and at traditional sites of Deaf Culture such as Gallaudet University. Still others believe that the Deaf-World is changing as it expands to include new forms of access in the mainstream, new cultural developments, and ASL-English bilingualism. As always, the deaf experience is not one size fits all.

The Claggett Statement

In 1984, a landmark ecumenical event occurred in deaf religious history, one often cited as a theological basis for the deaf rights movement of the twentieth century. The Board of Missions of the Mennonite Church invited a group of prominent deaf and hearing Christians from many different denominations to pray together and to discuss how recent developments in liberation theology could inform the growing deaf rights movement. Ministers, deaf cultural advocates, and ASL linguists met for five days in June at the Claggett Center, an Episcopal retreat property in Adamstown, Maryland. The group called themselves Christians for

12. U.S. Department of Health and Human Services National Institute of Health, *NICDC Fact Sheet: Cochlear Implants*, updated 2011, https://www.nidcd.nih.gov/sites/default/files/ Documents /health/hearing/FactSheetCochlearImplant.pdf.

the Liberation of the Deaf Community, but since then they have simply been called the Claggett group. Deacon Patrick Graybill, a prominent teacher and actor, was the only deaf founding member as well as the only Catholic present at the group's first meeting. The following summer, Father Raymond Fleming, a deaf priest from Rochester who was involved in deaf ministry, became the second Deaf Catholic in the group.

The Claggett group took inspiration from the popular liberation theology movements of the 1980s, especially those developed by Latin American Roman Catholics in countries where politically motivated violence had terrorized indigenous populations. In their own country, they also saw American Civil Rights activists as role models who demanded social justice for oppressed minority groups. Looking to these social movements as examples, the group wished to address church leaders about wrongs done to deaf people. As a civil rights strategy, the Claggett statement is similar to another argument addressed to church leaders, "Letter from a Birmingham Jail," by Martin Luther King Jr. Like King, the Claggett group wanted to proclaim the message of Jesus as a message of welcome and freedom for all people, including those who had suffered cultural or ethnic suppression. The participants agreed that deaf people did not need liberation from being deaf but rather from social exclusion and cultural oppression. They stood against institutions that denied deaf people clear visual communication, and they asserted that sign language, like any group's native language, is essential to Deaf people's identity. Unfortunately, churches had been among the institutions that historically excluded deaf people by not welcoming their native language. Most deaf people did not attend church because they could not understand the spoken language used in worship.

On the last day of the second gathering, participants drafted the Claggett Statement, an ecumenical document that boldly asked churches to reflect on their contributions to the oppression of deaf people. The statement begins with a profession of shared Christian faith, followed by a summary of a variety of experiences of hearing loss and the historical development of a shared Deaf culture. The document claims that, historically, the church had emphasized works of charity toward deaf people as a disadvantaged group and that this charitable perspective helped to perpetuate misunderstandings in society at large. The participants argued that, although linguists had finally accepted ASL as a true human language, the misunderstandings of society had not suddenly changed.

Because linguists and educators did not see sign languages as valid languages until the late twentieth century (many around the world still do not have legal recognition), deaf people whose first language was sign remained marginalized in most of Western society. The document presented to the religious community evidence of ongoing struggles endured by deaf people as they sought inclusion, linguistic recognition, and cultural participation in churches. This interpretation of the church's role in deaf history flowed from a desire to recognize the presence of paternalism and colonialism in deaf lives.

Much of the language of the Claggett Statement may seem jarring and confrontational to readers unfamiliar with deaf history, but the statement's most provocative accusations derive from ASL linguistics and deaf cultural studies. In effect, these disciplines gave deaf people a deeper understanding of their own culture and a strong desire to defend it politically. For example, most ministers to deaf people tended to see oral education, Signed English, and Total Communication, not as compromises, but rather as small steps forward in deaf enculturation and inclusion. The Claggett group, on the other hand, defined them as systematic methods of forcing deaf children to behave more like hearing people, thereby denying them a healthy sense of identity with members of their own language group. The statement argued that poor ASL interpreters and hearing teachers in residential schools were symptoms of the broader problem of deaf people's marginalization as a cultural group. Furthermore, the statement claimed that even though most signing deaf people marry within their language group, they still did not believe "that their indigenous language is really a 'language,' but rather an inferior, make-do form of communication," because hearing teachers, audiologists, and other professionals had taught them so.

Christian churches, Claggett Statement participants agreed, were guilty of upholding and perpetuating these same hurtful conditions. For example:

Many deaf people reject the church because its representatives have been as oppressive as their teachers and therapists. "Religion" has become one more place where deaf people feel they are told to stop being "deaf" and try to be "hearing." They must try to fit into hearing forms of worship with its hearing emphasis on music, its wordy English liturgies, and its love for ancient phrases—all through an interpreter they frequently cannot understand. Unfortunately, even in the separate deaf churches and/or programs, there has been little development of indigenous worship forms that reflect the experience of deaf people. All of this has led to alienation and/or superficial involvement in the Church. Clearly the situation has not encouraged any real understanding of God and the message of Jesus. Exceptions exist, but unfortunately the exceptions are far too few.[13]

The statement then issued a very serious accusation: "The Church generally has not looked upon deaf people as a potential gift or resource to the broader Christian community" but has instead considered deaf people to be handicapped and "intellectually and morally inferior, unable to learn properly and/or spiritually inhibited by the lack of an adequate language." In effect, the Claggett Statement issued a bracing and direct fraternal correction to church leaders, accompanied by a call to correct the problem of deaf people's marginalization in public worship.

Finally, and perhaps most importantly, the document called on deaf people themselves to "develop indigenous forms of worship" that could convey the prayer and devotion of the deaf Christian community. They announced that the Holy Spirit was leading deaf people to pray together publicly and to translate the Bible into different national sign languages. Without the gifts of Scripture, prayer, and liturgies in sign language, the Body of Christ would remain broken and fragmented without deaf members, and it was up to deaf people themselves to call the church to wholeness by making their linguistic and spiritual gifts known to the larger church. While some of the accusations of the Claggett Statement may still sting, especially to hearing people who devoted their lives to ministry with deaf people, the advice it offered about liturgy and forms of worship in ASL were points well taken and would bear fruit in the years to come. From a rhetorical perspective, the statement boldly takes the prophetic tone of a jeremiad, a form with a notable American tradition spanning back to Jonathan Edwards's "Sinners in the Hands of an Angry God" and much used by civil rights activists. From a Deaf cultural point of view, the direct language of the Claggett Statement is also an example of how "deaf speak straight"—an ASL idiom for the characteristically candid communication among people in Deaf Culture. Overall, the statement represents a painful but eventually fruitful stage in a long process of expanding the relationship between the church and the deaf community. For many Deaf Catholics, it was the initiation of a much-needed process of reconciliation for harms done to deaf children and adults in society at large, including, unfortunately, in the church.

13. "The Claggett Statement," *Sojourners Magazine*, March 1985. 30–32.

The Claggett Statement was published in both ASL (in video form) and English (in the March 1985 edition of *Sojourners*) and it spread rapidly, not only in North America but internationally as well. Its influence was widespread and lasting in the deaf community, and timelines of major events in deaf history now commonly include it. The broader Deaf Catholic community found the influence of the statement alternately empowering and divisive. For several years after the statement's publication, the National Catholic Office of the Deaf participated in an ecumenical Deaf Ministry Committee composed of representatives from fifteen different denominations who met annually to develop resources. As a response to the Claggett Statement, the committee distributed a brochure containing the following statement of hearing church workers' observations:

We are aware that, despite years of ministry efforts, perhaps less than 10% of the Deaf community are churched. Many of us who have worked in deaf ministry now see that:

- We have lacked the linguistic ability and cultural sensitivity to listen to the Deaf community.
- We have not recognized the uniqueness of Deaf culture.
- We have made decisions for Deaf and hard of hearing persons.
- We have extended control over Deaf ministry and have imposed a "hearing" perspective on it.
- We have perpetuated a model of Deaf ministry that has had limited success in effectively proclaiming the Gospel.

The group made a public commitment not to speak for deaf or hard of hearing persons and to "stretch current church structures so that Deaf and hard of hearing persons may assume their rightful roles as leaders, envisioners, etc." The committee also worked to recognize the variety of communication preferences among deaf and hard of hearing people and to include more effective ministry for each of these groups, whether their mode of communication was ASL, English-like signs, printed text, or amplified spoken English.[14]

Although it was an ecumenical document rather than a specifically Catholic one, the Claggett Statement certainly had an impact on American Deaf worship and Christian liturgical practices, especially for those Protestants whose congregations are free to create their own worship

14. Deaf Ministry Committee, "It's Time to Listen," brochure, National Council of the Churches of Christ, New York, N.Y.

services. In the context of the Catholic ecumenical movement, it also re-
inforced the cultural identity of some Deaf Catholics as active members
of Deaf Christian dialogue and the Deaf civil rights movement. Not all
Deaf Catholics subscribe to liberation theology as a uniting philosophy
for deaf civil rights; however, the Claggett Statement's call for freedom
from misguided control undoubtedly influenced the Deaf Catholic community as a language-based cultural group. It demonstrated the existence
of continued struggles and growing pains even during the flowering of
late twentieth-century Deaf Catholic culture.

The Flowering of Deaf Catholic
Culture after Vatican II

In ways that the church is only beginning to understand, the Second Vatican Council was the defining religious event of the twentieth century,
and the twentieth-century flowering of Deaf Catholic culture is evidence
of that. Among the documents resulting from the Council, the "Dogmatic Constitution of the Church" or *Lumen Gentium* reaffirmed the
foundational Christian belief that every individual is given particular
gifts for the glory of God and "must complete what God has begun by
their own actions with the help of God's grace."[15] Even suffering, infirmity, and poverty may be particular gifts through which individuals show
the abundant love of Christ, who also suffered that we might have eternal
life in union with him. This renewed emphasis on the dignity of baptism
for each person—and on the church as the whole People of God—was
certainly a primary cause for a changed outlook concerning deaf people
in the church.

In 1978, the Catholic Bishops of the United States responded to this
changed outlook by issuing a "Pastoral Statement on Persons with Disabilities." The statement called for broader integration of persons with
disabilities into the life of the church, especially through increased evangelization and catechesis and full participation in the sacraments. In the
spirit of *Lumen Gentium*, the bishops reasoned that excluding those with
differences, even in passive omission, is to deny the spiritual tie that binds
Christians together. They also encouraged roles in ministry for people
with disabilities. "When we think of people with disabilities in relation

15. *LG*, no. 42.

to ministry," they argued, "we tend automatically to think of doing something for them. We do not reflect that they can do something for us and
with us ... [and] can, by their example, teach the non-disabled person
much about strength and Christian acceptance. Moreover, they have the
same duty as all members of the community to do the Lord's work in the
world, according to their God-given talents and capacity."[16] The statement also called the church to advocate for full participation of people
with disabilities in civic life, overtly linking Catholic moral responsibility
with civil laws in development at the time. The document came at an
opportune moment in Deaf Catholic history, just as the first deaf men
with priestly vocations in the United States were seeking ordination. It
was an exciting time to be deaf and Catholic. While most Deaf Catholics did not appreciate being grouped with "the disabled," insofar as they
were a group with a linguistic and cultural identity, they recognized that
the "Pastoral Statement on Persons with Disabilities" gave them greater
recognition in the family of the church. In the deaf centers of major dioceses, ministers to the deaf community began more frequently to arrange
Masses in mixed modes with both sign language and spoken English.
Deaf Catholics were able to take a stronger leadership role in their own
communities and to help teach hearing pastoral workers how to improve
their connection with deaf members of the Church.

At the level of the Roman Curia, Pope John Paul II instituted the
Pontifical Commission for the Pastoral Assistance to Health Care Workers in 1985 (renamed the Pontifical Council for the Pastoral Assistance
to Health Care Workers in 1988). Its task was "to stimulate the work of
formation, study and action carried out by the diverse Catholic International Organizations in the health care field as well as other groups and
associations which work in this sector."[17] The deliberately international focus of the Curia on issues relating to disability and health care—
arguably a development that sprang from the influence of *Lumen Gentium*—has been a great benefit to deaf people as the deaf community
simultaneously embraced a more internationally connected perspective
through organizations such as the World Federation of the Deaf and various national associations. Since its inception, the Pontifical Council for
the Assistance of Healthcare Workers has organized a network of bish-

16. "Pastoral Statement of the U.S. Catholic Bishops on Persons with Disabilities," United States
Catholic Conference, Washington, D.C., 1978.
17. John Paul II, *Dolentium Hominum* (Establishing a Pontifical Commission for the Apostolate
of Health Care Workers), Apostolic Letter (February 11, 1985), 6.

ops in each nation who are responsible for health care ministry. It keeps a record of Catholic organizations for health care workers and associations serving sick and disabled people in all nations where the church is present—including the International Foundation for the Service of Deaf Persons and other organizations profiled in part II. Since its inception, the council has hosted annual international conferences to promote the pastoral care of sick and disabled people around the world. In 2009, the theme of the twenty-fourth international conference in Rome was "Ephphatha! The Deaf Person in the Life of the Church." Many Catholics involved in deaf ministry see this event, covered in depth in chapter 14, as a defining moment in Deaf Catholic history in the context of the New Evangelization.

Perhaps the most important way for the church to contextualize late twentieth-century changes in deaf culture is through the words of Pope John Paul II as he described the New Evangelization. In his encyclical *Redemptoris Missio* (1990), he advised his flock around the world that "the moment has come to commit all of the Church's energies to a new evangelization and to the mission *ad gentes* (to the nations). No believer in Christ, no institution of the Church can avoid this supreme duty: to proclaim Christ to all peoples."[18] In the encyclical, Pope John Paul II describes three different situations for evangelization: mission *ad gentes*, Christian communities, and the New Evangelization. As the turn of the century neared, it was not difficult for Deaf Catholics to see that evangelization had taken place for them in all three contexts described by the Holy Father. In the missionary years prior to Vatican II, evangelization to Deaf Catholics had been *ad gentes* or "to the nations" who had literally never heard the gospel before because of lack of accessible communications in sign language. Then, as small sign language-using Deaf Catholic communities began to form around the world, the church carried out her activity and pastoral care through ongoing evangelization of these fragile, new communities. Finally, in the late twentieth century, Deaf Catholics themselves began to engage in what John Paul II describes as the New Evangelization, "where entire groups of the baptized have lost a living sense of the faith, or even no longer consider themselves members of the Church, and live a life far removed from Christ and his Gospel. In this case what is needed is a 'new evangelization' or a 're-evangelization.'"[19]

18. *RM*, 3.
19. *RM*, 3.

The term "New Evangelization" pertains to a very specific group of people: fallen-away Christians in Europe and North America. In Africa and Asia, evangelization *ad gentes* helped to establish young, rapidly growing Christian communities with a greater proportion of religious vocations than in the West. Similarly (though on a much smaller scale), Deaf Catholics, as a newly evangelized cultural group, witnessed an increase in religious vocations after 1983, when the revised Code of Canon Law removed disability as an impediment to Holy Orders. Even as mainstream Americans and Europeans saw their number of priests declining at an alarming rate, the number of culturally deaf priests rose dramatically. Before the twentieth century, there were no deaf men in the priesthood whose native language was sign. At the time of this writing, the current count is at least sixteen living deaf priests who use sign as their preferred mode for day-to-day communication, and there are several deaf permanent deacons. This number may seem insignificant, but considering the diminishment of priestly vocations in the West, an increase in vocations for one cultural group from zero to sixteen in the span of thirty years is noteworthy. For those who would listen, the message was clear: Deaf Catholics had much to teach fallen-away, secularized Catholics about long-suffering faithfulness.

Since ministry "by the deaf, for the deaf" is an important development for this cultural group, the chapters ahead shift from the history of ministering "to the deaf" to a focus on the education, vocation, and ministries of church leaders who are from the deaf community and who communicate directly with congregations in native sign language without need for interpreters. These priests and laypeople are helping to extend deaf participation in the church to the full range of sacraments. They represent deaf communities not just in one region but all around the world, including South America, Asia, and Africa. The remaining chapters of part II examine the roles of some of these individuals as skilled preachers, chaplains, founders of beloved cultural centers, and directors of archdiocesan deaf ministries.

CHAPTER 10

A Place of Their Own

In some striking ways, the scattered distribution of deaf people in every nation and their struggle to come together in language communities resembles the exile of an ethnic group.[1] Like Jews, deaf people have struggled to keep their cultural and religious identity; they have cherished their language in the midst of mainstream cultures demanding assimilation; and like other groups who have experienced diaspora—African slaves and Native Americans among them—deaf people often lost their common culture or were forbidden access to their language in schools designed to assimilate them. Unlike other language groups, however, people who use sign languages are dispersed geographically. Unless they grew up with deaf family members, deaf people must first find and encounter other deaf people before they can communicate fluently with each other in a mode that is natural to the realm of their own senses. Throughout deaf history in Western culture, deaf people have often expressed a feeling that they are foreigners in their own lands, and many longed for a place where they could share an identity and a sense of belonging.[2]

Only about 10 percent of deaf children inherit deafness genetically from family members.[3] The rest become deaf because of disease, illness,

1. The title of this chapter echoes an important book on contexts in Deaf history: John V. Van Cleve and Barry A. Crouch, *A Place of Their Own: Creating the Deaf Community in America* (Washington, D.C.: Gallaudet University Press, 1989).

2. For a discussion of "Deaf diaspora" in the context of deaf ministry, see Bob Ayers, *Deaf Diaspora: The Third Wave of Deaf Ministry* (iUniverse, 2004). "Deaf Diaspora" is also a weeklong festival in the United Kingdom that coincides with the International Deaf Day hosted by the World Federation of the Deaf.

3. Ten percent is the most common statistic for deaf children with deaf parents, but this number has been contested. See, for example, Mitchell and Karchmer, "Chasing the Mythical Ten Percent," 138–63.

or accident. Because of this, deaf people almost everywhere start out as a scattered group but are brought together culturally through schools, clubs, religious services, and other places where sign language is used. Until the 1970s in the United States, as we have seen, it was not uncommon for deaf children born into hearing families to attend residential schools from the age of four or five and to come home only for holidays. Close ties formed at these schools, and deaf people often regarded them as a second family, especially when lack of communication at home left them feeling isolated. Schools and churches for deaf people have often been home for the deaf community, places where sign language, history, stories, and traditions were passed from one generation to the next.

Consistent with this idea of a deaf homeland, Deaf Catholics have been concerned with the idea of deaf places and "deaf space." Since the early years of deaf history, commentators have written about deaf people's unique visual and spatial relationship with their environment and each other as natural users of sign language. In 1855, in a treatise that would influence the movement to found Gallaudet College, a deaf activist named John Flournoy developed a utopian vision of a country consisting entirely of deaf citizens. In this tradition of imagining deaf places, deaf people today still refer to the "Deaf-World," a figurative place separate from the hearing world where deaf people are not viewed as foreign or "other."[4] The nature of deafness as a language and cultural difference—one that accentuates the visual and spatial aspects of the human condition—has likewise led to the need for specially designed diocesan Deaf Catholic centers, parishes, and summer camps. In the process of deaf diaspora, dispersed deaf people have undertaken a journey to this new home. For many of the more fortunate ones around the world, this home has been in the church.

This chapter investigates the cultural identity of three uniquely deaf places for Catholics and the Deaf-World at large: Camp Mark Seven in Old Forge, New York; the Detroit Catholic Deaf Center; and the Archdiocese of San Francisco's Deaf Catholic community. In addition to showcasing these places and their roles in deaf history, this chapter introduces several of America's first culturally Deaf Catholic priests, whose leadership at these sites contributed greatly to the flowering of Deaf Catholic culture. Together, these deaf leaders and the deaf people in their community made these places noteworthy models for deaf ministry and deaf cultural evangelization in America and abroad. The

---

4. See Lane, Hoffmeister, and Bahan, *A Journey into the Deaf-World*.

conclusion of the chapter addresses a complementary movement to integrate deaf services into regular Catholic parishes and neighborhood
churches, because hearing churchgoers also need to see deaf people and
know them as part of the Body of Christ. These two opposing impulses
in Deaf Catholic life—creating a place that belongs to deaf people in the
church on the one hand and being part of the larger church as a whole
on the other—still present practical dilemmas for deaf ministries today.

America's Deaf Priests Enter the Scene

Concurrent with the American Deaf rights movement, one particularly visible Catholic trend contributed greatly to the use of deaf space in
Catholic worship: the ordination and ministry of culturally Deaf Catholic priests. In places where both priest and assembly were deaf, distinct
Deaf Catholic worship and cultural expression began to develop naturally. The first culturally deaf priest ordained in the United States was Father
Thomas Coughlin, who was born in upstate New York to deaf, signing
parents in 1947. At Rochester School for the Deaf, he learned spoken and
written English using the controversial Rochester Method, a technique
allowing fingerspelling and oral communication only. In high school, he
attended St. Mary's Secondary School for the Deaf in Buffalo, run by the
Sisters of St. Joseph, where he encountered a religious sister who inspired
him to consider a priestly vocation. Coughlin first applied to the Carmel-
ite order, but they turned him down because of his deafness. He began
to correspond with the Trinitarians without revealing his deaf identity.
When he visited them in person, the Trinitarian vocation director tested
Coughlin's lipreading on the spot by asking how tall he was. When he answered correctly, Coughlin recalled in an interview, "They were surprised
that I was not mute and dumb. They did not have a proper understanding
of a deaf person, and they didn't know what to do with one."[5]

Coughlin was accepted into the Trinitarian order in 1972, only a
few months after receiving his bachelor's degree with a major in English
from Gallaudet College. While in the seminary, Coughlin experienced
isolation and often thought about leaving, but despite these difficulties,
he earned a master's degree in theology from the Catholic University of
America and pursued additional training in counseling and deafness at

5. Janis Johnson, "A Day to Remember Forever," *Washington Post* (May 8, 1977), reprinted in
Listening 1, no. 1 (September 1977).

Gallaudet. The Trinitarians provided an interpreter for his coursework at hearing schools, but it was a lonely time without the enriching talk among classmates that builds community life in the seminary. Coughlin's talent as a communicator would be used only after his ordination, which took place on May 7, 1977, at the Basilica of the Assumption of the Blessed Virgin Mary in Baltimore. Five hundred people were present, mostly Deaf Catholics, at a ceremony conducted in English and sign language.[6]

The Deaf Catholic community celebrated Coughlin's ordination as a major triumph. In interviews, he expressed his conviction that the time was right for a deaf priest who could bridge American Deaf Culture and the hearing world through the inclusiveness of the Catholic Church. This statement rings true, as Coughlin was not the only deaf man who discerned his priestly call in the wake of Vatican II. Two other deaf Americans with priestly vocations entered the scene in the seventies: Father Raymond Fleming (now a diocesan priest) entered the Franciscan novitiate in 1971, and Father Joseph Bruce of Massachusetts entered the Jesuit novitiate in 1974. The 1970s would also see the ordination of the first deaf permanent deacons, Paul Pernecky of Washington, D.C., and Jerome Kiel of Baltimore.

It may seem a contradiction that, just as church attendance across America was decreasing rapidly, there began a rise in culturally deaf priestly vocations that continued into the turn of the century (today there are eight culturally Deaf Catholic priests in North America and a few permanent deacons). Given impediments to the priesthood for deaf men, the cultural suppression of sign language for centuries, and the denial of sign language in education and in the sacraments, it is no wonder it took the church as long as it did to accept deaf men as priests. Yet the first deaf deacons and priests fulfilled and continue to fulfill a pressing need for clergy who are competent in sign language and therefore able to minister to deaf people directly without need for interpreters. As noted by canon lawyer Edward Peters, "Signing deacons and priests, coming from the Deaf community instead of to it, inspire a special pride and devotion among Deaf Catholics akin to that seen whenever indigenous clergy begin serving in cultures once reached only by missionaries."[7]

6. Johnson, "A Day to Remember Forever."
7. Edward N. Peters, "The Ordination of Men Bereft of Speech and the Celebration of Sacraments in Sign Language," *Studia Canonica* 42 (2008): 441.

In 1978, the International Catholic Deaf Association (ICDA) appointed Father Coughlin to be the organization's travelling missionary, a position first held by Father David Walsh in the 1960s. In his column "God, Me and the Van," in ICDA's periodical *The Deaf Catholic*, Coughlin chronicled the mission trips he made for three years, visiting as many as ten cities a month. He first went to several cities in the Midwest, where he led missions and retreats in ASL, visited state schools for deaf children, and offered Mass and the sacrament of reconciliation in sign language. Essentially, he fulfilled the aims ICDA had set forth in the early days concerning a better relationship between Catholic clergy and the deaf community. However, he did so—not by waiting for the church to provide hearing clergy who could sign but by answering a call to priesthood himself. At the same time, his ministry was a witness to the often-overlooked presence of deaf people and sign language in the broader church. Following the role that Father Walsh had developed as ICDA missionary, Coughlin also met with bishops in several dioceses and was interviewed by newspapers in each town he visited, energetically spreading the word about Deaf Catholics' need for access and inclusion.[8]

Descriptions and video recordings of Coughlin's communication from the pulpit echo descriptions of Father Daniel Higgins, who had enchanted assemblies with his dramatic signing style, bringing together large assemblies of Deaf Catholics even before the early years of the ICDA. Coughlin had a special connection with deaf youth. An article in the *St. Anthony Messenger* gives a sense of his style of preaching during a visit to St. Rita Catholic school for deaf children in Cincinnati, Ohio:

No yawning, slouchers or private conversations here: all sit in rapt attention.... The high-schoolers hang on every word that Trinitarian Father Thomas Coughlin recreates for them in sign pictures.... Swiftly, deftly, his fingers flutter and fold in myriad configurations. He fleetingly touches his shoulder, crosses his hands on his chest, reaches heavenward—as joy, sadness, puzzlement, pain, and surprise flit across his face. Before an altar that bears an engraving of a hand signing "I love you," he strides back and forth, dramatizing his message. Through this pantomime, Father Tom brings the gospel to life for spiritually hungry deaf youth.[9]

It was this hunger for meaning and a connection with others that fueled Coughlin, along with deaf Jesuit Joseph Bruce and a small group of other

---

8. *The Deaf Catholic* 28, no. 1: 4–5.

9. Lisa Osterman, "Father Thomas Coughlin—Spreading the Good News in Sign Language," *St. Anthony Messenger* 89, no. 1 (1981).

leading Deaf Catholics, to create a place that deaf people from across North America and around the world might call their own. In Coughlin and other deaf priestly vocations of the 1970s, American Deaf Catholics finally had leaders from among "their own." Similar to diasporic or immigrant peoples, however, Deaf Catholics still had a longing for a dedicated place of their own—a place developed by Deaf Catholics rather than for them as a place apart.

Camp Mark Seven

In the deep pine forest of upstate New York, just north of the village of Old Forge, sits a sprawling summer haven that many Deaf Catholics today consider their second home. Like Gallaudet University, Camp Mark Seven is a uniquely deaf place where generations of deaf people have passed down their language, culture, and religious traditions to younger generations. Camp Mark Seven takes its name from the gospel story where Jesus encounters the deaf man. In addition to serving American Deaf Catholics, the camp has also been an international destination for deaf people from countries as far as Japan and as near as Canada since it opened in 1982—almost a kind of pilgrimage destination. The analogy of diaspora fits the story of Camp Mark Seven well, not least because the nature of this "homeland" is specifically religious.

Camp Mark Seven was originally the Old Mohawk Hotel on the banks of the Adirondack's Fourth Lake. First opened in 1900, the stately hotel had three levels and room for a hundred guests. Even at that time, the nine-acre grounds included tennis courts, shuffleboard courts, and stables. Guests participated in water sports including waterskiing, swimming, and canoeing. Herbert and Carrie Longstaff, the original owners, ran the Mohawk like an exclusive country club. Guests stayed for weeks, if not the whole summer, and the owners conducted interviews of potential guests and required references. Tourists continued to summer at the Mohawk and other Adirondack hotels like it for many years, until the Great Depression made summer-long retreats a thing of the past. After changing ownership a few times, the Mohawk stood empty and unused in a state of bankruptcy by 1980.[10]

That year a deaf woman named Debbie Crno met the recently or-

10. "Former Mohawk Hotel Born as Camp Mark Seven," *Observer-Dispatch*, Utica, New York, July 16, 2009.

dained Father Thomas Coughlin. At a chance meeting in Buffalo, he told her he was on his way to Lake Placid in search of a place to develop a summer camp for deaf youngsters. Crno happened to know about the Mohawk's bankruptcy, so she took him immediately to see the old hotel. For three years, Mark Seven Deaf Foundation, an organization dedicated to moral development and the promotion of religious vocations among Deaf Catholic youth, had been searching for the perfect site to develop a summer camp. The foundation was directed by respected leaders in the Deaf Catholic community including Coughlin himself, Father Joe Bruce, Dorothy Stefanik, Kathleen O'Leary, and Sister Maureen Langton, CSJ. The organization's bylaws clearly deemphasized the attitude of pity toward deaf people that the medical model of deafness encouraged and stressed service from Deaf Catholics as full, adult members of the church. Mark Seven's founders solidified plans for a retreat center and Bible study camp for Deaf Catholics and their families. To encourage more deaf vocations, Mark Seven Deaf Foundation held the first Deaf Catholic Vocation Retreat in 1979. Their search for a place had at times seemed hopeless. Between the four of them, they had already visited over fifty different sites, but the moment they saw the Mohawk Hotel, the Mark Seven Deaf Foundation knew they had found their "pearl of great price."[11]

In bankruptcy court, Mark Seven competed with four other organizations for the purchase and redevelopment of the old hotel. One wanted to turn it into a condominium; others wanted a private club, a big restaurant, and a new hotel. Mark Seven Deaf Foundation explained their humbler plans: they wanted to make a camp for deaf youth. The judge thought it was a good idea. What clenched the deal, however, was that the Mark Seven Foundation bid $75,000 , cash in hand and no loan necessary, to make the final purchase.

How this humble deaf religious organization came by such a sum of money in 1981 is another story. During his three years as the ICDA missionary, Coughlin began a lifelong habit of travel that was both missionary and mendicant, in the time-honored tradition of begging for alms. In his first month, Coughlin visited no fewer than ten different diocesan centers and schools for deaf children in Denver and Colorado Springs, Colorado; Cheyenne, Wyoming; Olathe, Kansas; Des Moines,

11. Father Thomas Coughlin, OP Miss, interview with Marlana Portolano, Camp Mark Seven, Old Forge, New York, August 24, 2014.

Iowa; Salt Lake City, Utah; and Omaha, Nebraska. He also met with a Protestant organization called Deaf Missions in Council Bluffs, Nebraska.[12] Eventually he would travel to Montreal and to Minneapolis, as far east as California, and as far south as Mexico. Everywhere he went, he got to know deaf people and their hopes and needs. As he preached, he told people about the Mark Seven Deaf Foundation's hope for a place where deaf youth could deepen and develop their identity as Catholics in sign language and where they could look to deaf adults as role models in ways that hearing adults could not fulfill—and he asked for donations. By 1980, Coughlin had raised enough money for the Mark Seven Foundation to pay cash for the Old Forge Hotel. With that victory, however, the Camp Mark Seven Foundation's struggles for deaf agency and ownership of the camp had just begun.

"Do you want to know how I felt when I received the key and opened the door of the hotel for the first time?" Coughlin signed during an interview in his residence on the grounds of the camp. "Nauseous! I thought: what have I gotten myself into?"[13] The woods surrounding the hotel were overgrown and encroaching on the building. The electricity, plumbing, heating, and ventilation systems were all in disrepair. The roof was about to collapse. To the surprise and delight of the Mark Seven Deaf Foundation, however, volunteers from all over the country came to transform the property into a thriving camp for deaf and hard of hearing youth. The Deaf Catholic community had been connecting and growing through ICDA and through the work of missionaries like Walsh and Coughlin, and they were ready to embrace Camp Mark Seven as a homestead for Deaf Catholic culture. Coughlin was pleased to take on the role of camp director. From its inception in 1981, he spent summers in residence at the camp and the rest of the year in his religious community.

The camp thrived. Hundreds of deaf children and deaf families, Catholics and non-Catholics, came each summer for programs such as ASL Culture Immersion Week, Deaf Children's Camp, and camps for children of deaf adults. Campers took advantage of the lakeside resort facilities including tennis courts, game room, arts and crafts room, auditorium, and a dining room large enough to seat one hundred eighty guests. They told sign language stories in the fireside lounge and went to

12. Father Thomas Coughlin, OP Miss, "God, Me, and the Van," *The Deaf Catholic* 28, no. 1 (1978): 4–5.
13. Father Thomas Coughlin, OP Miss, interview with Marlana Portolano, Camp Mark Seven, Old Forge, New York, August 24, 2014.

daily sign language Mass in the spacious chapel with its picture window facing a wooded hillside. Father Coughlin, Sister Maureen Langton, and other leaders in the Deaf Catholic community would come and give sign language presentations for the development of the camper's spiritual and moral life in the Catholic tradition. As one camper reported in 1987, "Every morning we had lecture series … about our responsibilities to be good leaders and witness to our faith. They spoke to us about the goodness of God. We had seminars and discussions about our deafness and how we can make good use of our disability to help make our society a better place for others to live."[14]

Unfortunately, a new Trinitarian Provincial felt Coughlin's ministry had become divorced from Trinitarian community life. As a corrective, the provincial proposed the Trinitarians assume oversight of Camp Mark Seven and its related deaf ministry under the new name, Mark Seven Trinitarian foundation. For the executive council members of Camp Mark Seven Foundation, this was an unacceptable solution. From its inception, Camp Mark Seven was meant to be deaf-owned and deaf-operated. With the same impulse that would drive Gallaudet's Deaf President Now movement later in the same decade, the members of Mark Seven's executive council wanted to preserve deaf leadership in order to keep Deaf Catholic culture strong.

With the assistance of a lawyer, the Camp Mark Seven Foundation officially incorporated with a board of directors before the Trinitarians could assume ownership. Camp Mark Seven would remain a place owned and operated by the deaf, for the deaf. The response of the Trinitarians was to require Coughlin to make a choice: either he would lose Camp Mark Seven or forfeit his vows as a Trinitarian. Distraught, he took a leave of absence from the order for six months to sort out his commitments. At the end of that time, he decided that although he was happy with the Trinitarians, the lack of deaf communication with others in the community outweighed his desire to stay. No one in the Trinitarian province made an effort to learn sign language, and he felt like an outsider there as a result. Reluctantly, Coughlin left the order and set out in his search for a new assignment or community, a journey that would eventually lead him to found the Dominican Missionaries for the Deaf, a religious order specifically meant to accommodate men who were deaf or who wished to serve the American deaf community in sign language.

14. *The Deaf Catholic* 36, no. 3 (May/June 1987).

All the while, in spite of moves to many different dioceses, Coughlin continued spending summers at Camp Mark Seven as chaplain and camp director. He even pursued a nursing degree to fulfill a camp licensing requirement for an on-site nurse.[15]

Today, Camp Mark Seven continues to thrive and has earned its reputation as one of the best camps in North America for children who are deaf. It is unapologetically Catholic, and as such it serves an evangelical role by introducing deaf people from all over North America, as well as visitors from abroad, to moral and spiritual development in the Deaf Catholic tradition. In addition to the original cultural immersion camp and camps for children of deaf adults, Mark Seven expanded to include camps for teens, families, and senior citizens. In 2013, Mark Seven added a widely acclaimed film camp that produced several nationally televised music videos, each one expertly choreographed in ASL.[16] Their 2014 rendition of Will Pharrell's top-forty hit "Happy" drew attention to the camp when it went viral on social networking sites.

As a truly Deaf and Catholic place, Camp Mark Seven also became home to Mark Seven Bible Institute in 2006. Founded by Father Thomas Coughlin and Father Matthew Hysell (the first culturally deaf priest in Canada), Mark Seven Bible Institute is a community of scholars, catechists, and other Deaf Catholics who gather once a year to pray and study Scripture in depth. The Institute seeks to provide instruction in sign language and to equip catechists to serve the Deaf Catholic community. Their weeklong gatherings generally include daily *lectio divina* (a traditional Benedictine practice of meditative Scripture reading) and three daily sessions of Bible study led by expert catechists and biblical scholars. In 2015, the institute began negotiations with the American Congregation for the Clergy for official recognition of their program. As an indication of competence in biblical catechesis in ASL, the institute aims to develop a certification for participants. The original aims of the Mark Seven Deaf Foundation, to evangelize the deaf community by developing Deaf Catholic leaders, continue to advance through the education of deaf adults for ministry in their home communities.

---

15. Father Thomas Coughlin, OP Miss, interview with Marlana Portolano, Camp Mark Seven, Old Forge, New York, August 24, 2014.

16. See Camp Mark Seven Film Camp's website, http://www.deaffilmcamp.com/; and also https://www.youtube.com/user/CampM7.

Diocesan Deaf Centers as
Sites of Deaf Culture

Like Camp Mark Seven, several diocesan Deaf Centers have played a key role in the history of Catholics who are deaf and in the Deaf-World in general. From the late nineteenth century, Deaf Catholic centers were places where deaf people could gather as a community, learn about religious formation and civic life, and pass on their history and traditions in sign language. As uniquely deaf places, diocesan centers of Catholic life have also played a role in evangelization—not only for deaf people but also for hearing people who come in contact with the spirit-filled culture of worship in sign language.

Much of the organizational history of these centers was passed on from person to person, mostly orally or in sign language, but by the end of the twentieth century a few members of these communities, both deaf and hearing, had begun to write diocesan histories of Deaf Catholic centers.[17] Diocesan pamphlets and websites often include a brief history of their regional Deaf Catholic centers, and diocesan archives hold the occasional unpublished manuscript of a long-standing minister who worked with deaf people. However, like many local church histories, the stories of these deaf centers often remain in the miscellaneous files of their diocesan office until accidentally discarded. Fortunately for researchers who learn sign language, the nonprint nature of deaf culture ensures frequent storytelling among members of the Deaf Catholic community, contributing to the rich (though no doubt endangered) collective memory of this language group.

While there are many such centers staffed by hearing ministers who have dedicated their lives to the service of deaf people, part II of this book highlights places where a culturally deaf priest ministers to a deaf community. The Deaf Catholic community cherishes these places as models of ministry "by the deaf, for the deaf." Not only do these examples represent a common story for Deaf Catholics but also a variety of deaf experiences in the Catholic Church, including liturgy in ASL, different kinds of preaching in sign language, and ways of incorporating

---

17. Examples of these include Dolores Beere's *History of the Catholic Deaf in the Archdiocese of Detroit*, published as a booklet by the archdiocese in 1984, and Anthony Russo's *In Silent Prayer*. See Anthony Schuerger's unpublished manuscript, "Deaf Catholic Ministry in the Diocese of Cleveland," Deaf Catholic Archives, College of the Holy Cross, Worchester, Mass.

interpreters (both for voice and sign language) in worship. The final two sections of the present chapter profile the Detroit Deaf Catholic Center and the Archdiocese of San Francisco's Deaf parish as two historic places of deaf worship and culture. As elsewhere in Part II, any comparison of these deaf places is not to invite judgment about what kind of deaf center is the best but rather to show how institutional, social, and historical conditions have contributed to the character of each community's Deaf Catholic space.

Detroit Deaf Catholic Center

The history of the Detroit Deaf Catholic Center is a strong example of the pattern of missionary transformation in deaf culture described in part I. The center is one of a constellation of metropolitan deaf centers in a midwestern and eastern geographic region that might be called the "Catholic belt": Montreal, Ottawa, Toronto, Cleveland, Milwaukee, Chicago, Cincinnati, Buffalo, and Philadelphia. In these cities, the deaf population increased because of industrialization and large populations of Catholic immigrants. As deaf people came together, they often fostered hopes for a deaf community center—a place designed with deaf people's visual culture and communication needs in mind, where there would be no anxiety about living up to expectations of the hearing world in ways that hindered deaf communication and understanding.

During the early years of the twentieth century, Detroit attracted many deaf people who came in search of factory jobs. Deaf ministry began in 1914 when the pastor at St. Joseph's Church noticed that these deaf people were a large "flock without a shepherd." Although he was not the first to do deaf ministry in Detroit, Monsignor Henry Kaufmann is considered the founder of Detroit's Deaf Catholic community. Under his direction, the St. Joseph Ephpheta Society began with monthly meetings of forty people at St. Joseph Commercial College on Jay Street, but by the end of the first year it grew to over a hundred members. Father Kaufmann gave religious education classes, facilitated pilgrimages, officiated at weddings, and arranged for sign language missionaries to come for retreats. He studied sign language with Mother Borgia of the Sisters of Carondelet in Saint Louis and in 1924 took a seven-month tour of Deaf Catholic ministries in Europe, visiting Norway, Denmark, Germany, Holland, and Ireland. When he returned, he applied his new knowledge to the inclusion of deaf people in sacramental life—for instance, using written (then burned) forms for the confessions of deaf people, a method later recommended in the *American Ecclesiastical Review*.[18]

An early concern of the Ephpheta Society was to fund an Ephpheta Centre Building for the Deaf Catholics of Detroit. For the first several years of the society's existence, it was difficult to find a place to accommodate their growing numbers. Monthly meetings were held in college and hospital auditoriums. In 1921, the society hosted a large fund-raising bazaar and entertainment event at the Knights of Columbus Hall. Funny visual stunts in the style of Charlie Chaplin characterized the performances, and Father Kaufmann gave a speech on the spiritual needs of deaf people as a neglected population in the church. As a finale, a large choir of deaf performers signed the "Star-Spangled Banner" with musical accompaniment. The event was well attended by both deaf and hearing people, and the society raised over two thousand dollars as a seed fund for their dream of a dedicated Ephpheta Center. A blueprint was drawn up and the prospects seemed high, but events would not go as the society planned.[19]

After devoting twenty-seven years to deaf ministry, Father Kaufmann stepped down from deaf ministry in 1941. After Kaufman, Archbishop Edward Mooney invited a series of Redemptorists to be chaplains for the deaf community. The first was Father Raymond Kalter, a priest with excellent sign language skills. The church bulletin announced, "many old timers who had quit coming to meetings are coming back. They like their little fat priest." As Kaufman had before him, Kalter gave instruction on Catholic doctrine and prayer on the third Sunday of the month, followed by Benediction, a business meeting, and a social in the auditorium of their new location, Holy Redeemer Church on Junction Avenue. Within a year, attendance had grown to over three hundred. In 1943, the archbishop invited the Mission Helpers of the Sacred Heart, a group of sisters with a long tradition of religious education for deaf children in Baltimore, to live in a convent in Saint Elizabeth's Parish. Four sisters set up classes at various sites around the city. Father Kalter was succeed by other capable Redemptorists, including Father Julian Grehan and, for a year, Father David Walsh. The support and participation of Deaf

18. Father Stephen Klopfer, "The Confession of Deaf-Mutes," *American Ecclesiastical Review* 57, no. 1 (July 1917): 78.
19. Beere, *History of the Catholic Deaf*, 1–46.

Catholics in Detroit remained high, so that in 1952 the Detroit chapter of the International Catholic Deaf Association (ICDA) was chosen to host the fourth annual convention. Still, deaf ministry in Detroit was not without its problems, and many of these were caused by issues surrounding how deaf ministry was administered in the diocese.

Diocesan administers have often faced difficulty when deciding where deaf ministry belongs within diocesan structure. In some dioceses, it is placed under cultural ministries, in others, it is placed with special needs or disabilities ministries, and in still others it is considered a branch of catechesis. In Detroit, the CCD (Confraternity of Christian Doctrine) office of religious education oversaw deaf ministry. From the early days of the Ephpheta Society with Father Kaufmann, Deaf Catholics worked hard to raise money for their goal of building a deaf community center. In the 1940's, however, when the chaplain position took on the additional role of moderator for Detroit's ICDA chapter, the director of the CCD office wanted to pay the moderator's salary with money raised by the deaf community. The community opposed this, arguing that they had raised this money for a Deaf Center. While this caused some misunderstandings on both sides, Deaf Catholics of Detroit never lost their hope of having a place of their own.

In 1954, diocesan priest Father Edward Burkhardt was named both assistant director of the CCD office and ICDA moderator to the Deaf apostolate. With one person in both roles, there was less chance of misunderstanding between the deaf and the archdiocese. Many positive outcomes resulted for the deaf community during the 1950s and 1960s, including the development of a Young Catholic Deaf group, a deaf Legion of Mary for charitable work and visiting the sick, and participation in an annual ICDA basketball tournament with teams from other cities. These programs met in various hospitals, schools, or churches throughout the diocese. Despite the lack of a designated Deaf Center, a new chaplain, Father Raymond Ellis, started several helpful programs including a Cana Club for married couples, adult faith formation classes, and a "Boysville Camp" run by the Mission Helper Sisters and seminarians from St. John's Seminary in Plymouth. Father Ellis also spread an interest in sign language among the clergy by teaching classes at this seminary.

In 1965, after Pope John XXIII had given permission for the use of sign language in the Mass, Archbishop (later Cardinal) John Dearden gave Father Ellis permission to celebrate Mass facing the people. For the first time in their lives as Catholics, these loyal and long-suffering people were able to experience the sacrament of the Eucharist and the entire order of the Mass as interactive communication. The effect was an injection of new life among the Deaf Catholics of Detroit. The growth in devotion was notable, and Father Ellis was able to spread a true sense of piety in the community by visiting homes of deaf families and consecrating them in a special devotion to the Sacred Heart. In 1970, Father Ellis and Father David Walsh facilitated the first Cursillo for Deaf Catholics, and several members of the Detroit community took part.[20] Like Father Kaufmann, Ellis was beloved among members of the deaf community and the archdiocese at large, so much so that, at the one-hundredth anniversary of deaf ministry in the Archdiocese of Detroit, Archbishop Vigernon suggested starting a case for his canonization.

Finally, in 1974, Detroit Deaf Catholics' hopes for a place of their own were rewarded. Under the chaplaincy of Father Gary Beuche, the community began to remodel the first floor of an old high school building to use as a center for Deaf Catholics. After sixty years of hard work and frustrations, the Deaf Catholic community of Detroit would have not just a clubhouse but their own parish center. On September 11, 1974, over three hundred people attended the dedication of Saint John's Deaf Center on Fisher Street in Warren, Michigan, just north of Detroit. In 1975, the new St. John's Deaf Catholic Center received a $10,000 bequest from the will of Anthony Japes, the brother of one of the deaf community members. Grateful to the archdiocese for their help with the new parish center, the Deaf Center voted to give the money to the Archdiocesan Developmental Fund. As the center continued in its role in the Detroit deaf community in the 1970s and 1980s, its programs reflected the times—from ecumenical prayer services for Deaf Christians to performances of "Rock Gospel," a group that combined a rock band and four interpreters (including the Catholic and Lutheran chaplains of Gallaudet College).[21]

Since the 1980s, Detroit has become one of the few cities with multiple ASL Masses each Sunday: one on the west side of town at Our Lady of Loretto Church and one at a new location on the east side at Holy Innocents Church. Beginning in 1984, two Oblates of St. Francis de Sales began expanding deaf ministry in Detroit. However, what made the De-

20. See pp. 204–5 for further discussion of Deaf Cursillo.
21. Beere, *History of the Catholic Deaf*, 50–100.

troit Deaf Center an especially important Deaf Catholic place for the twenty-first century was the vocation of a Detroiter who was deaf.

Father Mike Depcik, OSFS, was born in Chicago on January 16, 1970 to deaf parents. The youngest of five deaf siblings and a graduate of Saint Rita Catholic School for the Deaf in Cincinnati, Depcik never had any trouble communicating at home or in school. However, he was not a particularly devout Catholic in high school, and his classmates could never have predicted that one day he would become a priest. Although he learned his catechism and memorized his prayers, he remembers the 1980s classroom experience of Catholic religion as rote and lifeless. It was not until he studied abroad for a year as an exchange student that he found God. During his home stay with a family of evangelical Deaf Christians, he was deeply impressed by their daily prayer and devotion. "Through the faith of these people," he said in an interview, "I was able to truly believe in God and not just repeat the doctrines I had learned by rote from the catechism." He went home determined to leave the Catholic Church once he finished high school at St. Rita's.[22]

By the end of his college experience, however, Depcik would call himself a "born again Catholic." Furthermore, largely because of auspicious meetings with ASL-fluent people, he would discover his call to become a Catholic priest. After graduating from St. Rita's, Depcik studied at Gallaudet University as an education major. While he was there, he met Father Jerry Trancone, director of deaf ministry for the Archdiocese of Washington, D.C., who encouraged him to start attending Mass again. Eventually, he felt drawn back to the church through the persistence of Father Trancone and of several Deaf Catholic students on campus. Pondering these things after a visit to the National Shrine of the Immaculate Conception in Washington, D.C., Depcik read a book about Marian devotions and taught himself to pray the rosary (no one had taught him at St. Rita's). Then, that fall semester in his dorm room bed, he had a dream.

In his dream, Depcik awoke to find himself lying in bed, dressed as a priest. "Wait a minute," he thought in his dream, "I don't remember studying to become a priest! What's going on?" Nevertheless, as the dream continued, he got up and walked to the chapel on campus. As he went, other students waved and greeted him, "Hi, Father Mike!"

22. Father Mike Depcik, interview with Marlana Portolano, Archdiocese of Washington Deaf Center, April 4, 2014.

"What?" he signed back to them, "I'm not a priest!"

"Yes, of course you are. You're going to say Mass for us today!"

"No, I don't even know how to say Mass!" As he went into the chapel in his dream, everyone watched and waved him on, but Depcik ran away.

He was not sure what this dream meant, but that summer he decided to go to Camp Mark Seven to work as a camp counselor and to continue exploring the connection between the Deaf and Catholic worlds. There, Depcik met Father Thomas Coughlin, who inspired him with his dynamic ASL preaching and Deaf Catholic leadership. One of the aims of the Mark Seven Foundation, from its inception, was to encourage religious vocations among Deaf Catholic youth, and Mike Depcik was destined to become one of the first young people to find a priestly vocation with the help of the deaf-run camp. During the summer of 1992, while working as a Mark Seven camp counselor, Depcik's roommate was Father Ken McKenna, an Oblate of Saint Francis de Sales who had served in deaf ministry in Detroit. McKenna told Depcik that because Saint Francis de Sales was the patron saint of deaf people, it would be entirely appropriate for the order to have a deaf priest. In the Fall of 1992, Depcik became a novice in the Oblates of Saint Francis de Sales, and he was ordained in 2000.[23]

Today, Father Depcik leads the Detroit Catholic Deaf Center with two ASL Masses each week, monthly Bible study, adoration of the Blessed Sacrament, rosary circles, senior citizen gatherings, community events, and sacramental preparation. Largely because of Father Depcik, the Deaf Center overcame a period of sparse Mass attendance resulting from Detroit's financial obstacles. In 2017, Depcik's deaf community had grown large enough to reactivate the city's International Catholic Deaf Association (ICDA) chapter—it had been the fourth city historically to have a chapter of the ICDA. Combined, the center's two locations serve approximately one hundred culturally Deaf Catholics each week in person today, but his Sunday morning Mass at Holy Innocents Church is livestreamed on Facebook, reaching hundreds more around the world each week. In addition, Father Mike video records and publishes his homilies on his website, *Father MD's Kitchen Table* (described in chapter 12), reaching linguistically isolated Deaf Catholics all over the United States and around the world. He is also a popular retreat master in Deaf

23. Father Mike Depcik, interview with Marlana Portolano, Archdiocese of Washington Deaf Center, April 4, 2014.

Catholic communities across North America. Under the leadership of Father Depcik, their first culturally deaf priest, the Detroit Deaf Catholic Center has not only persevered in its proud tradition as a deaf place, it has also established a far-reaching online presence, evangelizing without geographical boundaries as well as becoming an iconic model of Deaf Catholic culture for the twenty-first century.

San Francisco's Deaf Parish

The Archdiocese of San Francisco has a rich tradition of ethnic diversity, and its deaf ministry illustrates the richly multicultural and international nature of the New Evangelization. Deaf ministry began in the archdiocese in 1895—when the Sisters of St. Joseph of Carondelet founded the St. Joseph's Home and School for the Deaf east of San Francisco Bay in Oakland, California. During its early years, under Monsignor Michael O'Brien, the center developed a variety of religious, social, and educational services, including religious education classes in sign language taught by Father J. J. McCumminskey, SJ. However, in 1962, the Diocese of Oakland was created as a separately administered area apart from the Archdiocese of San Francisco. St. Joseph's Deaf Center remained in Oakland, continuing services to Deaf Catholics in three different locations. The Diocese of Oakland's administrative approach to Deaf Catholics was from the beginning distinctly cultural rather than disabilities focused. For example, one of the archdiocesan sites for deaf services was Holy Family Ethnic Mission, a multicultural religious center serving Polish, Indonesian, Korean, and Deaf Catholics from 1992 to 2011.

After the new Diocese of Oakland was established, there remained a need for deaf ministry in San Francisco. The deaf community had developed strong Catholic roots over several generations at St. Joseph's Center in Oakland, and they needed a new place to worship and plan community activities. In 1963, Archbishop Joseph McGucken appointed Father Tom Hester as both director of Deaf Ministry and director of the new Cursillo Movement. Hester set up his dual ministry in a vacant church building, St. Benedict the Moor Mission at Bush and Lyon Streets.

Although it stood empty in 1963, the new location for Deaf ministry already had a multicultural history. Named for St. Benedict the Moor—a sixteenth century saint who is patron of African Americans and Africans in America—the church had been a segregated African American mission in the early years of the twentieth century, before the American Civil Rights Movement. The San Francisco Deaf Catholic community thrived in this new location, and soon the Cursillo community was also very active in the shared space. Father Hester immediately set up a schedule of signed Sunday Masses, catechism classes for deaf children, and a deaf-led Society for Deaf Catholics. The two ministries worked together, and hearing Cursillo leaders got involved with the Deaf Catholic community, at one point collecting 480,000 Betty Crocker coupons to purchase a Volkswagen bus so that deaf children all over the city would have transportation to catechism classes. Father Hester and Cursillo volunteers also advocated for deaf people outside of church, for example petitioning the United States Post Office to hire deaf workers.

During the 1960s and 1970s, St. Benedict Center actively became involved in the Civil Rights movement. When Dr. Martin Luther King Jr. led his famous march in Selma, Alabama, St. Benedict's sent a truck full of blankets and clothing for distribution to the needy in Selma, and when San Francisco began an Interracial Home Visiting Program to improve understanding between groups, members of the Deaf Catholic community visited the homes of African American families who extended their hospitality. In 1967, Father Bill Cane became the director of St. Benedict's, and Sister Cleta Herold, PBVM, joined his ministry. Sister Cleta and the several sisters of her community, who lived nearby, named their residence "Ephphatha House." When Dorothy Day, leader of the Catholic Worker movement, visited San Francisco on her seventy-fifth birthday, she stayed at Ephphatha House with the sisters. And in 1972, members of St. Benedict community led the first Western States Deaf Cursillo at the dual-purpose center for the Cursillo and Deaf Catholic communities.

In 1984, through the work of Father Jack McMullen, the Archdiocese of San Francisco granted St. Benedict's community full status as a parish. Father McMullen added several programs that proved vital to the Bay Area deaf community: a summer camp, a job training and placement service, interpreting services, and a Catholic Charities counseling program for deaf persons. In 1990, McMullen died of a brain tumor after sixteen years of service to the deaf community.

In 1993, under the new director, Father Daniel Adams, St. Benedict Parish moved to its present home: St. Francis Xavier Church, a small but beautiful place of worship built during World War II to serve as the

Japanese National Parish. When the U.S. government relocated Japanese parishioners to an internment camp in 1942, several frightened members of the parish stored their furniture in the social hall of their newly built church, the only place they thought might be safe in their absence. St. Francis Xavier's graceful Japanese architecture is a reminder of these origins, and the few remaining members of the Japanese Catholic Society are still there today, sharing the building and their Catholic faith with the Deaf Catholic community of San Francisco.

Since its move to St. Francis Xavier Church, the Archdiocese of San Francisco has assigned three deaf priests to serve the community at St. Benedict's. The first culturally deaf priest ordained in the United States, Father Thomas Coughlin (profiled earlier in this chapter), was chaplain at St. Benedict's from 2002 to 2007. After Coughlin, Father Paul Zirimenya (deaf) took up the assignment, and Father Ghislain Bazikila (also deaf) from the Republic of Congo was also in residence. Such abundant deaf leadership is a flowering of Deaf Catholic culture to celebrate, but another small detail makes this parish a particularly inspiring example of New Evangelization. The current chaplain to St. Benedict's has an uncanny resemblance to iconic images of the parish's patron, St. Benedict the Moor, because Father Paul Zirimenya is a culturally Deaf African, born and raised in Uganda. Through his iconic chaplaincy, the multicultural Deaf Catholic heritage of St. Benedict's Parish reflects the blending of Catholic identities into one community welcoming all people.

When he was six years old, Father Zirimenya began to lose his hearing as the result of a middle ear infection. Hearing loss was gradual and frightening, until he finally became profoundly deaf at the age of fourteen. In the meantime, he learned to speak both English and his native language, Luganda, with the help of speech therapists at his Anglican primary school. Few secondary schools accepted deaf students, but he was able to enroll at a Muslim school for a period of five years. Zirimenya first considered the Catholic priesthood when he was fourteen years old, attending a Muslim school and not even a Catholic. Catholic relatives on his mother's side of the family, combined with a strong, positive presence of missionary development in Uganda's history, led him to contemplate this path. When he transferred to an Evangelical high school and took classes on European history, he found himself seriously considering a vocation to the priesthood. In 1998, he completed a bachelor's degree in social work at Makerere University in Uganda and began to discern

God's direction for his life. While working with an outreach team for the Ugandan National Association for the Deaf, Zirimenya met a Catholic priest who became his spiritual director. Father Aloyse Reiles (a Missionaries of Africa priest from Luxembourg), along with other priests at his university, helped Zirimenya make initial contact with Father Thomas Coughlin, who then invited him to begin his discernment and formation process in New York with the Dominican Missionaries for the Deaf.[24]

Although Zirimenya was familiar with Ugandan Sign Language, it was not until he studied theology at St. Patrick Seminary in Menlo Park, California, that he learned ASL. There he formed a close bond with three fellow deaf seminarians (Shawn Carey, Matthew Hysell, and Ghislain Bazikila) and embraced his identity as a culturally Deaf Catholic priest. Although the seminary's one accommodation for deafness, an ASL interpreter, did not take into consideration the individual language differences and backgrounds of the four deaf seminarians, Zirimenya embraced the challenge and became a leader in the Deaf Catholic community. Those who watch him celebrate Mass and deliver homilies would never guess ASL was not his native language. Graceful in delivery, Father Zirimenya signs the entire Mass and homily at St. Benedict's parish while a voice interpreter translates into English for those in the assembly who need to hear to understand. Like most centers of deaf worship, St. Benedict parish is as inclusive as possible, welcoming everyone and accommodating everyone's needs as best they can. The parish's definition of a deaf community on its website overtly promotes this: "A community that is bound together by a signed language that is visual/gestural in nature and a shared culture. It includes but isn't exclusive to Deaf and hard of hearing adults, seniors, teens and children, all of whom may have either Deaf or hearing family members who can also be considered part of this community."

As the chaplain of St. Benedict's, Father Zirimenya has a unique ability to identify with the diverse members of his community: he has been deaf, hard of hearing, speaking, signing, a minority, and an immigrant. He has experienced the positive outcomes of missionary enculturation in his native country Uganda, and he therefore is an exemplary individual for carrying out a New Evangelization among deaf Americans and immigrants of mixed ethnic and socioeconomic backgrounds. Because deaf education and hearing aid technology lag behind in many non-Western

24. Father Paul Zirimenya, interview with Marlana Portolano, San Francisco, May 29, 2015.

countries, these populations are particularly vulnerable to exclusion from mainstream worship and church life. Spiritually, Zirimenya has a deep concern for poor and homeless deaf people in his parish, with whom he regularly converses. It is evident that the members of St. Benedict Parish love him in return. They are especially fortunate to have a priest who is one of them in so many ways and who can stay with them for the long term, something increasingly rare in the Deaf Catholic world.

Inclusion or a Place Apart?

For deaf people living in the West, the world has become increasingly full of opportunities since the late twentieth century. The 1990 Americans with Disabilities Act ushered in a time of greater inclusion for deaf Americans and other countries enacted similar laws. Local school districts expanded their deaf education programs, and the public and private sectors opened up new employment opportunities beyond the traditional types of jobs sought by deaf workers. Advances in medical technology have also improved deaf people's lives. In particular, the number of deaf children and adults with cochlear implants increased rapidly in the last years of the century, providing, for many, a new kind of access to the world of speech and sound. Yet, in spite of greater integration in mainstream education and the work force, many deaf people still tend to—and need to—gather in groups for the purpose of communicating in sign language. For most deaf individuals, understanding a speech or sermon delivered to a large assembly of hearing people is difficult or impossible and attempting to communicate in social situations with groups of hearing people can induce significant anxiety. Despite high-powered hearing devices, trying to understand spoken language in these situations remains painfully frustrating. Because of this, the deaf diaspora is still happening.

For some dioceses, offering one or two ASL Masses in a designated parish's usual Sunday schedule of mainstream spoken-language Masses helps include deaf people in church life. One outstanding example of this arrangement is the Archdiocese of Boston's Deaf Catholic Community. In this archdiocese, Father Shawn Carey, a culturally deaf priest who grew up in Massachusetts, serves as director of Boston's Deaf Apostolate within the archdiocese's Division of Cultural Diversity, its branch for administering Ethnic Communities rather than disability services.[25] The Boston Deaf Catholic community shares the church building of Sacred Heart Parish with parishioners in the immediate neighborhood. However, in many Catholic parishes, deaf people still find it difficult to negotiate church life in a hearing parish because of their language and cultural differences. Many small, historically deaf parishes and Deaf Catholic community centers still exist—not only in the United States but in countries all over the world, from Europe to Australia, and from South America to Asia. Model parishes like the communities profiled in this chapter take positive steps toward enabling Deaf Catholics to access a full range of sacraments and religious practices. In turn, the deaf community can continue to enrich the whole church by preserving and cherishing their rich Catholic cultural heritage. Moreover, because of the visual nature of deaf language and culture, places of deaf worship are examples of Catholic inclusivity that can be "placed before the eyes" of hearing people, especially through image sharing today's hyper-visual media environments. Through the visibility of deaf places and deaf ministries, either in person or through film media, Deaf Catholics can and do evangelize widely, helping the church establish a broader understanding of Christian belonging for the twenty-first century.

25. Video examples of Boston's Deaf ministry may be found on this book's companion website, http://icddeafservice/beopened.

CHAPTER 11

Love and the Gift of Listening

We all know that the closure of man, his isolation, does not solely depend on the sense organs. There is an inner closing, which covers the deepest core of the person, what the Bible calls the "heart." That is what Jesus came to "open," to liberate, to enable us to fully live our relationship with God and with others. That is why I said that this little word, *"Ephphatha*—Be opened," sums up Christ's entire mission.—Pope Benedict XVI's Angelus message from the 23rd Sunday of Ordinary Time (Year B)

In a literal sense, the story of Jesus healing the deaf man in Mark 7 is a healing story. Yet, for Christians, the image of Jesus laying hands on this deaf man and speaking the word *Ephphatha!* is much more: it is the sacramental image of a human being receiving God's Word. This deeper meaning of the passage is why the church has long used Christ's words and gestures from Mark 7 in the rite of baptism. However, Deaf Catholics know firsthand the isolation and exclusion that can result from emphasizing the physical healing of deafness over the deeper meaning of receiving the Word of God. Sadly, because of their language barrier, children in residential deaf schools have often been cut off from communication with their families and the larger community, including the broader church. Because of their isolation, these children are doubly vulnerable to abuse. During the last two decades, the church has mourned as the media exposed clergy in sexual abuse cases from the 1960s and 1970s. The victims of these crimes, including several former students of residential Deaf Catholic schools, suffered anew with each media frenzy, and the broader church has suffered with them.

The mainstream media often overlooks deaf people because of their language difference, but in 2012, the Deaf Catholic world entered the public eye in a particularly conspicuous way. A critically acclaimed HBO documentary by filmmaker Alex Gibney, *Mea Maxima Culpa: Silence in the House of God*, profiled a devastating case of child abuse at St. John's School for the Deaf in the Archdiocese of Milwaukee.[1] The historic school, founded in 1876 and one of the most successful and beloved Catholic residential schools for deaf students in the United States, became the site of systematic child molestation by Father Lawrence Murphy, then superintendent and chaplain of the school. The most memorable scene of Gibney's film is footage of four deaf men in their sixties giving an account of their school years at St. John's in eloquent, expressive ASL. The boys suffered frequent sexual abuse during the 1960s—in confessionals, in Murphy's office, in rooms darkened to watch films, even in Murphy's personal retreat cabin. The four deaf men interviewed in *Mea Maxima Culpa* reported their abuse at the hands of Catholic clergy to civic and church officials, initiating a still-accelerating chain of events that would expose many similar cases, first in North America, then in Europe, Australia, India, and Latin America. It is a scenario appallingly familiar to readers of the 2002 John Jay Report, the 2009 Murphy Report in Ireland, the 2018 Pennsylvania Grand Jury report, and other documents detailing sexual abuse of minors under the care of priests. However, the film claimed that local church authorities and Vatican officials long ignored these deaf men's attempts to bring Murphy to justice.

The film received positive reviews in major newspapers and periodicals in the United States and Europe; however, reviews in the Catholic press claimed that Gibney's film aimed not to bring Murphy to justice, but rather to smear the church publicly as an institution. The primary point of contention in these differing reviews was the film's attempt to elicit anger about the alleged Vatican cover-up of hundreds of similar cases then familiar to the viewing public from an earlier BBC documentary, *Sex Crimes and the Vatican* (2006). Reviews in the Catholic press were quick to point out that the film lacks coverage of some of the most

1. Alex Gibney, dir., *Mea Maxima Culpa: Silence in the House of God* (New York: Jigsaw, 2012).

important people in the St. John's School story, including public law enforcement who ignored the case and did not press criminal charges against Murphy—and the archdiocesan legal counsel, who did, in fact, interview all the victims and worked aggressively to remove Murphy from ministry.[2] Sadly, the fact remains that Archbishop William Cousins of the Archdiocese of Milwaukee did not pursue prosecution of Murphy in this case, and pleas for justice from deaf alumni of St. John's School were effectively silenced in the meantime.

While Gibney's film appeared sensationalistic to many Catholics in 2012, his documentary did the deaf victims a great service by allowing them to tell their story in native ASL. It is now a sad part of Deaf Catholic history that cannot be ignored. The Deaf Catholic community in North America and Europe were proud of St. John's School for the Deaf and considered it a revered part of their heritage for over a century. St. John's School was a strong example of how the church actively facilitated development of a distinct Deaf Catholic community. The school began in 1876 as an outreach service of Pio Nono College, a Catholic school for music teachers. Father Theodore Bruener, rector of Pio Nono, saw the tremendous need for instruction of deaf pupils in Milwaukee and undertook fundraising for a three-story Italianate building surrounded by acres of forest and farmland. By the 1880s, a series of new directors had expanded the facilities to include workshops where boys at the school learned to make furniture. The production of altars, confessionals, baptismal fonts, statues, and pulpits proved quite profitable, earning over $20,000 in the first year (over $550,000 in U.S. dollars today). Girls were taught by Sisters of St. Francis of Assisi, who developed programs in cooking, sewing, and housekeeping.[3] The school's sixth director, Father Eugene Gehl, expanded distribution of the school's successful periodical for deaf readers, *Our Young People*, to subscribers across the nation and abroad, contributing to the international reputation of the school in the Deaf Catholic community. For decades under Gehl's direction, parents trusted St. John's School as an alternative to public schools for the deaf, which they feared would indoctrinate their children with Protestant propaganda and anti-Catholic ideology. On May 10, 1963, after fifty-four years of service as director of St. John's and

---

2. David Pierre Jr., "Sex, Lies, and HBO Documentaries," *The Catholic World Report*, November 9, 2012, www.catholicworldreport.com/item/1735/sex_lies_and_hbo_documentaries.aspx.

3. M. M. Gerend, *In and About St. Francis, A Souvenir of St. John's Institute for Deaf-Mutes* (Milwaukee: St. Francis, 1891).

a travelling missionary for the deaf community, Father Gehl died, leaving his assistant Father Lawrence Murphy in charge. Impressively, Gehl's grave marker at Saint Francis Seminary Woods Cemetery reads, "Priestly life spent entirely for the deaf."

Father Lawrence Murphy was assigned to St. John's School for the Deaf for twenty-four years, beginning with his appointment as athletic director in 1950 and ending with his resignation in 1974.[4] As viewers of Gibney's film learn, during that time Murphy used the sacred seal of the confessional—and his image in the boys' eyes as a father figure and Christlike authority—to coerce boys at the school into sexually abusive acts. He required over a hundred boys directly under his moral and spiritual care to submit regularly to sexual acts of "education and reconciliation." In what psychiatrists have since learned is an incurable disorder, Murphy believed he was giving them direct experience and understanding of the nature of sexuality and sin.[5] Unlike most of the adults in their home lives, Father Murphy could sign, so the children at St. John's trusted and relied on him. Murphy chose only boys whose parents could not communicate in sign language, effectively isolating them from any way to inform other adults about the abuse. Their language barrier and the ostensible safe haven of the school were an effective trap of silence. Lay staff at St. John's have also been accused in multiple cases.

Even as adults, the victims in Gibney's film demonstrated how this ASL-English language barrier remained a barrier to justice. At one point, the documentary recounts, the men littered the parking lot outside the Milwaukee cathedral with homemade wanted posters while Murphy celebrated Mass inside. Fueled by the spirit of the Deaf Power movement of the 1980s, with its focus on civil rights and protections, these men worked vigilantly for years to attract the attention of lawyers and church officials. Law enforcement would not listen, and it seemed to them that the Vatican ignored them as well. At one point in Murphy's tenure, Father David Walsh, a well-known hearing priest in deaf ministry, visited St. John's to lead a mission in sign language. One of the boys conversed privately with Walsh in ASL, describing what Murphy had done. Walsh immediately confronted Murphy and took the matter to Archbishop Cousins, and although the abuse was not reported to police, the admin-

4. "Can You Turn Deaf Ear to This Plea?" *Milwaukee Sentinel*, April 22, 1962, 1B.

5. Ray Blanchard, et al., "Pedophilia, Hebephilia, and the DSM-V," *Archives of Sexual Behavior* 38, no. 3 (2009): 335–50.

istrative follow-up was swift: Murphy was removed from his position, isolated in his remote cabin, and forbidden to engage in any ministerial role in the Archdiocese of Milwaukee.[6] If the case had come to light just a few years later, laicization (the removal of priestly status) would have promptly resulted, since those found guilty of sexual abuse were often laicized beginning in the 1980s.

It is helpful to put this abuse by Catholic priests into perspective, both in general and for the sake of the Deaf Catholic community. While contemporary readers are appalled by the extent of these scandals in popular media, it is still too early for sociologists, psychologists, and historians to have collected the full range of data necessary to analyze the causes of these problems. In 2004, the John Jay College of Criminal Justice, compiling data on abuse cases from 1950 to 2002, reported that 20 percent of women and 15 percent of men in the United States were sexually mistreated by an adult (any adult) when they were children or young adolescents. The report found that 4 percent of all Catholic priests in the United States were accused of sexually victimizing minors during the years under study, but the percentage was even higher for public school teachers and men in the general population. By far, most sex offenders are not celibate priests but rather married or partnered men. Taking sexual advantage of children and adolescents is a widespread human problem, and therefore it tragically happens in the church. By far the highest incidences of sexual abuse by priests occurred during the 1960s and 1970s, and new cases were almost nonexistent by the 1990s.[7]

Now, seventeen years later at this writing, the number of surviving priest abusers in the John Jay study must be small indeed, although the underlying problem is in need of further study and analysis. For example, the Pennsylvania attorney general's recent Grand Jury Report will no doubt result in many more studies, investigations, changes in priestly selection and formation, and improvements in the protection of minors under the care of priests and religious. Nevertheless, for many victims, it is too late to receive either a meaningful apology from abusers themselves or the satisfaction of judgment and reparations in the form of a criminal charge and sentence. For those harmed by these systemic problems, including the Deaf Catholic community, spiritual healing must

6. Gibney, *Mea Maxima Culpa.*
7. John Jay College of Criminal Justice, *The Nature and Scope of Sexual Abuse of Minors by Catholic Priests and Deacons in the United States, 1950–2002* (Washington, D.C.: United States Conference of Catholic Bishops, 2004).

now come from ongoing, active, and highly positive forms of reconciliation between the church as an institution and the affected people.

The effect of the Lawrence Murphy case on the Milwaukee Deaf
Catholic community was devastating—and Deaf Catholics who felt
connected to this community in other areas also experienced a lasting
sense of betrayal, shame, and anger. Immediately after Murphy was relocated, his assistant Father Donald Zerkel became director, but the school
never recovered from these events, finally closing in 1983, during the period when victims were actively trying to bring Murphy's crimes to the attention of lawyers and police. Adding to the damage were similar stories
of abuse in Catholic schools for deaf children in other North American
cities and across the Atlantic in Catholic schools for the deaf in England
and Ireland. As recently as 2017, another such case of abuse in a Catholic school for deaf children came to light in Argentina. With the brave
first testimonies deaf alumni of St. John's and other victims like them,
the church began a long, hard look at the causes of this outrage and the
need for contrition, healing, and reconciliation. Revelations of abuse,
lawsuit payoffs, and reassignments of offending clergy have now reached
the point of worldwide, systemic crisis in the church. For this reason,
what happened in the wake of Milwaukee's tragedy during the recovery
and healing of the city's Deaf Catholic community sets an important
precedent for the entire church.

Christopher Klusman and the
Shadow of Darth Vader

The life story of Father Christopher Klusman, the only culturally deaf
priest currently serving the Archdiocese of Milwaukee, circulates as oral
history—or, rather, signed history—in the shared knowledge of the deaf
community. In a house just a few blocks from the now-closed St. John's
School for the Deaf lived a family imbued with Catholic faith and ide-
als. This couple, Elaine and Elmer Klusman, celebrated the birth of their
fourth child, Christopher, on August 21, 1976—a birthday which, in
1998, would coincide with the death of the infamous Father Lawrence
Murphy. Like many of his cousins, Christopher Klusman was born profoundly deaf, but because of the multigenerational family precedent, no
one saw this as unusual or problematic; his parents simply began to sign
with him when he was a baby. Perhaps because of this, he began to talk

early and showed a talent for both oral and signed communication from the beginning. Many deaf children, like those in the Lawrence Murphy tragedy, find it difficult to communicate with their non-signing parents, who may lack the opportunity to become fluent signers through frequent socializing with the deaf community. However, Klusman and his parents always had fairly good communication. In an interview, he said he considered them his greatest role models because love of God and family had always come first in their lives. He grew up hoping to become a completely unselfish person, which is what he saw in his mother and father.

When Klusman was a child growing up in the shadow of St. John's, his parents took him to several signed Sunday Masses at the chapel of St. John's before the school closed in 1983. However, he and his family usually went to Mass at a conventional hearing church, Sacred Heart of Jesus parish, across the street from St. John's. There was no interpreter for Mass (they were still hard to come by at the time), but his parents tried to fill him in on what was happening. All in all, Klusman grew up happy and well adjusted during the malignant aftermath of the St. John's scandal, blissfully ignorant of what had happened and the resulting decline in church attendance by deaf people in his hometown. As an adult and an ordained priest, he put it years later in an interview, "It was funny, I knew even then that something was going to happen to me having to do with the Catholic Church. I couldn't really put my finger on it. At that time, it was a bit alienating. But my parents would always go no matter what. They never miss Mass."[8]

Like his hearing sister and two older brothers, Klusman wanted to attend a Catholic school across the street from St. John's School for the Deaf, but this school did not have deaf services. Unlike his siblings, he attended Milwaukee Public Schools, where the deaf program incorporated multiple methodologies and special services into an individualized education plan including sign language, speech therapy, Cued Speech, and oral education. Reflecting on his elementary school years, Klusman recalled working harder on speech than many of his classmates, only to discover years later that many of these classmates were hard of hearing rather than profoundly deaf. In the summers during elementary school, he often spent time with signing friends, further developing his sign language skills. By the time he was in ninth grade, Klusman was able

8. Father Christopher Klusman, interview by Marlana Portolano, St. Roman Catholic Church, Milwaukee, Wis., January 12, 2014.

to mainstream in St. Thomas More Catholic high school. The campus was, once again, in the immediate proximity of St. John's School for the Deaf, but he did not give it much thought. It was exciting to take religion classes as his brothers and sisters had, but there were no interpreters at the Catholic high school. The exhausting effort of lipreading everything left him with little energy to do anything outside of class but study.

After high school, Klusman attended the University of Wisconsin in Madison, where he majored in elementary education. There, he found a close group of deaf friends, and the coordinator of interpreting and deaf services introduced him to more aspects of Deaf Culture. He wanted to join the Newman Center with other Catholics, but unfortunately it was not accessible to him as a deaf student. In general, his college experience was not particularly religious. To continue as a practicing Catholic, he frequently went home on weekends and eventually attended Mass again with his family. However, one year an auspicious event made him wonder if he might have a vocation to become a priest. A friend had mentioned that a former teacher of the deaf and interpreter in Rockford, Illinois, had become a Catholic priest and was leading Bible study groups for deaf people. A small group of deaf friends drove together to attend Monsignor Glenn Nelson's sign language Masses and Bible study group, which met every week during Lent and monthly during ordinary time. What surprised and interested Klusman about Nelson was the way he taught with depth and content. "Often times," Klusman explained in an interview, "a deaf person will go to Bible study and it's so very watered down. People often talk down to the deaf," but Monsignor Nelson was different. Klusman recalls:

I was on fire. We would be chatting about this and that after every session. After several classes and Masses, I felt greatly blessed to have such an opportunity. So I went up to him afterwards and said, "Thank you, Monsignor. I can't explain, but this is exactly what I needed." And—I'll never forget this—he looked right at me and said, "Have you ever thought about the priesthood?" I was shocked. I was like a deer in the headlights.[9]

As an education major, in student teaching, and in the state outreach program for the deaf community, Klusman had already become a strong advocate for deaf youth, but he had never considered the priesthood. He would always tell deaf children that they could do anything they put their

9. Father Christopher Klusman, interview by Marlana Portolano, St. Roman Catholic Church, Milwaukee, Wis., January 12, 2014.

minds to, but when it came to the priesthood, he had thought it not possible, considering the expense of interpreters at the seminary and other obstacles that would inevitably come up. These were the obstacles that kept surfacing in Klusman's mind, but Monsignor Nelson assured him that if God willed it, there was nothing that could stop it from happening.

Klusman began meeting with Nelson once a month for discernment, and very soon, he was considering the priesthood. When he asked his friends at school, "Do you think I would make a good priest?" several responded without hesitation, "Well, of course! We thought all along you were supposed to be a priest." Klusman, it seems, was spiritually deaf to his own call. Others pointed it out to him—in particular, by a priest who himself used ASL in his priestly role, as Klusman would do were he to become a priest. Perhaps his vocation had been evident earlier, in his family and community, but the recent collective memory of Father Murphy, Milwaukee's most famous signing priest, still clouded his community's vision of what might be possible for their linguistically talented and spiritually inclined boy. Finally, he opened to his own gifts and the particular path God had in store for his life.

After he completed his bachelor's degree and gained some work experience, the now twenty-eight-year-old Klusman attended St. Francis de Sales Seminary, just four blocks from his childhood home, followed by Sacred Heart Seminary in Milwaukee. Both schools provided him with ASL interpreters, and he worked with generous classmates who agreed to share lecture notes. Although he did not know it when he began attending Saint Francis de Sales, Klusman later learned that Francis de Sales, for whom the seminary was named, was the patron saint of deaf people and that, coincidentally, they shared the same birthday. If there were any question in Klusman's mind that he was meant to be a priest who could work with the deaf community, these not-so-subtle coincidences erased all doubt. When Klusman finally met a deaf priest for the first time, he was at the threshold of his seminary education. It was the year of the 2005 International Catholic Deaf Association convention in Milwaukee. There, Klusman watched Father Mike Depcik, OSFS, sign the Mass, preach an ASL homily, and chat with him in ASL throughout the conference. Having never seen a deaf man with a priestly vocation, Klusman recalled how strange and wonderful it was to meet this cultural role model from another city.[10]

10. Father Christopher Klusman, interview by Marlana Portolano, St. Roman Catholic Church, Milwaukee, Wis., January 12, 2014.

As the only deaf student in his classes, Klusman found entering social life and casual conversations with fellow seminarians a challenge. However, in the spring of 2005, around the time he was accepted into the seminary, Christopher attended a Deaf Ministry workshop. There he found one close and lasting friend who understood all his trials: Father Carmelo Giuffre, also profoundly deaf, was near the end of his pastoral year at Saint Francis de Sales. After his ordination, Giuffre became Christopher's mentor priest, and for years they met regularly for coffee or lunch to support one another as deaf men with a vocation in common. Together, Father Carmelo Giuffre and Father Christopher Klusman represent two very different experiences of deafness in the Western world today. Unlike Klusman, Giuffre's education and family life were entirely oral and focused on speech and lipreading. He had no exposure to sign language growing up. Fortunately, he was one of the few who did particularly well with this methodology. In 2016 he was appointed share-pastor and administrator to Saint Veronica Congregation in Milwaukee and Nativity of the Lord Parish in Cudahy, an assignment that included overseeing a thriving Catholic school. Giuffre's role required the management of all business in a large urban parish, celebrating Mass and preaching, all the while using lipreading as a primary mode of communication. Because he does not use ASL, Giuffre's deafness remains an invisible disability to his parishioners and to his superiors in the archdiocese, rather than a feature of the language group or American cultural identity of deafness. The archbishop at the time of his seminary formation never considered pursuing a dispensation for Giuffre, because he thought that deafness, as Giuffre experienced it, would not interfere with his service as a priest. Because Giuffre's experiences of deafness derive from the medical understanding of deafness as a disability, it would be a diminishing label to call him "a good deaf priest"—ironically, a description that Klusman embraces proudly. Giuffre wants simply to be a good priest, without the medical or cultural label of the word "deaf." True to his role as pastor of a large parish, he serves almost exclusively hearing families and does it well, winning over individuals, one at a time, who are at first uncomfortable communicating with a deaf person like Giuffre. Parishioners who are culturally deaf and use sign language go to the ASL Masses celebrated by Father Klusman as a special language service just five miles away.[11]

11. Father Carmelo Giuffre, interview by Marlana Portolano, Milwaukee, Wis., January 13, 2014.

In a sense, Father Giuffre is "passing" in a hearing world, while Father Klusman made a different choice—one that fit his family history and style of communication—to identify with Deaf culture and use ASL as his primary language. Yet their mutual appreciation for roles they each play is evident. At Klusman's ordination, which was filmed as a DVD production that aired on Eternal Word Television Network (EWTN), Giuffre eloquently summed up the role Klusman would play as a priest in Milwaukee's deaf culture after the sad history of St. John's. He said to Klusman's parents, "As you watched your son enter the Cathedral and take his place beside you at the Ordination Mass, you suddenly realized what you had done. You bound your son to the cross." Giuffre continued, "Holy Mary, Mother of God, pray for Elaine and Elmer and the family, for despite the difficulties in the priesthood, in the Church and in the world today, their gift of their son Christopher is a sign of hope. A new priest gives us hope. We believe in hope."[12]

One of Klusman's ASL homilies, preached in 2014 at St. Roman Church in Milwaukee on the feast of the Baptism of the Lord, is an apt explanation for the role he has played in healing the Deaf Catholic community in Milwaukee. In the church's theological reading of John's baptism of Jesus, the church sees all three aspects of the Trinity: Jesus the human being in the flesh, the Holy Spirit descending in the form of a dove, and the Father as a voice proclaiming, "This is my beloved son." On this Sunday in 2014, a culturally deaf deacon, David Sommers, rendered the visual scene of the gospel in sign language. Water drenched Jesus' head in the form of fingers trickling over Sommers's own scalp, and the dove, which the deacon embodies in giant form, flaps his arms at full length in a surprisingly graceful image, calling to mind da Vinci's iconic painting of this scene. Then, Father Klusman stood in front of his assembly, a 6:00 p.m. vigil Mass at Saint Roman. About forty-five people were in attendance, most of them deaf but several hearing members of the parish who enjoy attending the ASL Mass, which includes voice interpretation in English. Klusman has a reputation among deaf parishioners for being a great teacher with a charism for joy, both of which shine through his homily Saturday evening. For some people in the assembly, Klusman's visual explanation may have been the first time the story and its symbolic meaning in Catholic tradition were presented in a language that was

12. "Hearing God: Hosted by Robert Dolan with Fr. Christopher Klusman," DVD, EWTN, 2014.

accessible to them. He spent time discussing baptism as a new birth into the family of the Trinity, with God as our father, Mary as our mother, and Jesus as our brother, and he explained how the holy water at church is a remembrance of baptism. Klusman's preaching style made use of his whole body and a significant area of space around him, so that viewers got a clear image of baptism as going down under water and rising up again, similar to being buried and resurrected.

Then Klusman used an example that is familiar to just about every modern person in the Western world: the revelation of Darth Vader as the father of Luke Skywalker in *Star Wars*. Everyone in the assembly, deaf and hearing alike, perked up and began to wonder where he would take this. Predictably, it was a negative example, ending with Luke crying "No!" and denying his parentage in service to the Dark Side. Father Klusman vividly called to mind the famous battle scene, his fingers representing dueling light sabers in an expanded and dramatic sign space. For a moment he was Darth Vader himself, holding four fingers over his mouth from the chin in the sign imitating Vader's mask (his name sign). Then, he abruptly turned his body to signal that he was addressing a contrast in Scripture, as he explained: in the baptism story, Jesus' behavior is the opposite of Luke Skywalker's.

In his explication, Klusman tells his assembly that unlike Luke Skywalker, Jesus proclaims a resounding *Yes!* as he acknowledges his father. His parentage is not the unknown Vader or the past sins of the Father Murphys of the world, but instead, the parentage of every Christian into the family of God through Jesus. It is a message for all nations, he says, even those who have been in exile. In the conclusion of his homily, Klusman explained that, even today, deaf people are often lost in exile like the Israelites before the time of Jesus. Only through Christ can all people, deaf or hearing, able-bodied or disabled, no matter their national or cultural origin, unite in one body of believers through baptism. This application of the gospel message is characteristic for a Deaf Catholic priest teaching a deaf assembly: access and evangelization are often one and the same. However, his example has a poignant message for hearing members of the group—and for Milwaukee Catholics who remember the scars inflicted on the community by the scandal at St. John's School.

Looking Ahead

The scandals at St. John's School for the Deaf and at other Deaf Catholic schools engendered a fear of church in the deaf community that is not unjustified, and yet many Deaf Catholics continue to demonstrate the spiritual gifts of their iconic forbearer in the gospel story—they continue, with resilience characteristic of the Deaf Catholic community, to evangelize and cling to hope. As the church seeks to reconcile with members of damaged communities like Milwaukee's, it is no doubt helpful for clergy to preach the passage in Mark 7 as a call to "Be opened!" to investigations of harm and past secrecy. In a similar sense, *Ephphatha!* also speaks to victims' rights to openly tell their stories. Vulnerable Deaf Catholic residential schools in the West and, eventually, in Asian and African deaf missions where the global church is growing today, will no doubt continue to require this kind of openness, at the same time guarding the vulnerability of victims at deaf schools because of their language barrier.

While purification is part of the answer, in the meantime the church can embrace other paths to reconciliation in both the deaf community and the broader church. The priesthood, especially in America and Europe, has been in crisis since the last decades of the twentieth century. Even since 1970, the total number of priests in the U.S. has fallen from just over fifty-nine thousand to just over thirty-seven thousand.[13] For most of history, the seminary admissions process preemptively excluded a deaf man with no speech or with a voice that was difficult to understand, but now, the church not only accepts deaf men's vocations, but needs them to serve populations of deaf and hearing people worldwide. Because of a growing understanding of deaf people, the church is becoming more inclusive and (some would argue) truer to its theology of love for the poor, redemption of those who are ostracized, and equality in the eyes of God. In this light, it is worth returning to the literal meaning of the image in Mark 7 and how it might continue to open up the sacramental meanings of the passage. Not only does Jesus cure the deaf man's physical deafness, but with the laying on of hands and a single word summing up the mission of the church, Jesus calls the deaf man to evangelize his broader culture and community.

13. The Center for Applied Research in the Apostolate, "Frequently Requested Church Statistics, U.S. Data Over Time," Georgetown University, accessed January 18, 2019, https://cara.george town.edu/frequently-requested-church-statistics/.

Admittedly, the culturally deaf community is a very small minority in the church. How can this obscure, non-print-based culture evangelize the church as a whole? In the midst of America's decline in priestly vocations, deaf men and other men with disabilities have been called forth to become Catholic priests for the first time in history. In these times, the Catholic church needs representatives of faithful but marginalized or historically silenced groups to help lead the way, like the deaf men in Gibney's biopic and like Father Christopher Klusman. The victim-survivors of St. John's School for the Deaf, as the silenced victims of coercion and violation, revealed the abuse of power underlying the very fabric of clericalism in St. John's School. Now, through a change in the story's point of view, the church has an opportunity to become truer to its word.

CHAPTER 12

Signing in the Person of Christ

If you with your tongue utter speech that is not intelligible, how
will anyone know what is said? For you will be speaking into the
air. There are doubtless many different languages in the world
and none is without meaning; but if I do not know the meaning
of the languages, I shall be a foreigner to the speaker and the
speaker a foreigner to me.—1 Corinthians 14:9–11

Contemporary preaching is heir to ancient rhetorical traditions, beginning with the practice of public speaking in Israel, Athens, and Rome,
then passed on to Christians in the writings of notable speakers such as
Saint Augustine, Desiderius Erasmus, Lorenzo Valla, and many others.
Because of the verbal nature of rhetorical traditions, the very concept of
voiceless oratory may strike some people as absurd. In the case of preaching in sign language, however, the resulting composition does not diminish eloquence but rather multiplies the ways nonverbal forms of communication can create meaning. As part of the Mass, a sign language homily
also embodies the Word of God in the flesh and blood of the preacher
in ways that spoken preaching simply cannot. For these reasons, worship
and preaching in sign language are among the greatest cultural gifts Deaf
Catholics bring to the church.

Like any type of sign language communication, sign language worship and preaching can be divided into two basic modes: the mixed

mode of spoken words together with signs and the pure mode of sign language without the spoken voice (commonly called "voice off" as an English interpretation of an ASL sign that resembles turning off a switch at the throat). The division comes directly from the history of deaf culture, and even today this division is the subject of bitter controversies. The first priests to preach in a mixed mode may have been teachers such as Padre Pedro Ponce de León in the sixteenth century or Abbé l'Épée in the nineteenth century. However, it is uncertain whether they preached homilies (or popular sermons) in this mode. The form of communication these early teachers used resembled a pidgin, which is the term linguists use for makeshift communication between users of two different languages with no language in common. In pidgins, the structure comes from one language, vocabulary from the other. In the case of signed pidgins, structure comes from a dominant spoken language, such as English, and vocabulary from the native signs of deaf people. A pidgin is never anyone's native language but, rather, a stage of communication in the process of learning a second language. Pidgin sign language, most often used by hearing teachers and family members, is a makeshift mode of communication that can hinder clarity and meaning in both languages. For this reason, the social and academic status of pidgins is low.

As Catholic worship and preaching in pure (voice-off) sign languages spread during the late twentieth century, preachers who could sign more frequently delivered homilies in true signed languages. Those who advocate preaching only in ASL (rather than a mixed mode) today have sound reasons for doing so. First and foremost, they are preaching in the vernacular of their assembly. Second, the mixed mode of signing and speaking at the same time often creates an awkward form that exists only during contact between hearing and deaf people. The clarity and completeness of one or the other language, often both, will suffer if the preacher does not have years of experience in the mixed mode. Addressing this issue during an interview, one American priest demonstrated his ability to finger-spell "d-o-g" on one hand and "c-a-t" on the other. "It is difficult, but the brain can actually be trained to do two completely different things at once," he said. "Sometimes, for a little while, I find I *can* speak English and sign ASL at the same time."[1] In practice, however, hearing priests who preach in this mode often slip into and out of ASL

1. Father Jerry Trancone, interview by Marlana Portolano, Silver Spring, Maryland, August 26, 2015.

as the dominant language, signing silently for a few phrases and then, a beat later, interpreting verbally. As evidence of the tension between the language of the eye and the language of the ear, those who attempt to do this sometimes speak English in ASL sign order by accident.

There are brilliant exceptions to this awkwardness, however, especially among preachers who have used mixed modes of communication since childhood. In these cases, pidgin sign language slips more easily into a natural, deaf use of space and pictorial representation of scenes. Without a doubt, there are eloquent preachers who use pidgin sign language—most often because of their natural experience with sign language and deaf culture. For these men, the mixed or pidgin mode may be moving closer to a creole—the term linguists use to designate a language that was once a pidgin but has become nativized by groups of fluent users.

Father Thomas Coughlin, the first culturally Deaf priest in the United States, communicates every day in ASL. Yet he has said that his mixed use of speech and pidgin signs in the Mass is a deliberate communication strategy. Deaf people with a variety of language backgrounds and preferences are almost always present in a deaf religious assembly, both those who grew up signing ASL and those educated orally or with Total Communication. In these cases, Coughlin believes using the mixed mode achieves the greatest understanding for the most people. However, in addition to signs in English word order, Coughlin always uses space, body language, movement, and facial expression in what linguists have described as ASL prosody. For deaf native-ASL users, the effect is seamless understanding of the signs. For hearing and deaf assembly members whose first language is English, the effect of this communication is much like a supercharged use of rhetorical gesture or acting. It can enhance Coughlin's spoken delivery, especially for hearing members of the assembly who have trouble understanding deaf speech. However, this level of mixed-mode fluency is rare and seldom seen among hearing preachers, who still comprise most priests and deacons doing deaf ministry today.

Preaching in ASL

Preaching in true signed languages, rather than speaking and signing at the same time, is the gold standard for ministry in American Deaf Culture today, because true signed languages are the native form of communication in Deaf Culture. Native signers are naturally more effective and economical because they are not attempting to accomplish communication in two languages at once. Many native signers rely less on the mime-like enhancements that are common to pidgins (although visual "scene-painting" and mime are always an option in ASL depending on the message and style). Instead, native sign language users exploit the full resources of their language to express a clear, concise, fully illustrated meaning. For Deaf Catholics, worship and preaching in grammatically correct, voice-off sign language fully situates Catholic liturgy within the heritage of the Deaf-World. Most of the time, Deaf Catholics must look to priests or deacons who are culturally Deaf for liturgy and sacraments communicated directly to them in a signed language, or else they must receive the communication secondhand through an interpreter.

For Catholics, receiving the sacramental words of institution directly from a priest acting in the person of Christ, in one's own vernacular language, is an essential part of modern worship. Perhaps even more indispensable is receiving absolution in the sacrament of reconciliation in one's own language since it allows penitents a direct and personal experience of forgiveness communicated one on one.[2] Although there are a handful of hearing priests today who are highly skilled in ASL or another signed language, certainly there is need—even a responsibility—to train more. In the United States, Protestant ministers fluent in sign language still greatly outnumber Catholic priests and deacons who are fluent, and deaf church goers naturally avoid church services where they cannot understand the language.

Adequately describing an ASL sermon in written English is not easy. Using video is the only way to quote directly in the original language. An ASL message can be rendered in spoken or written language only in translation. Moreover, this book is not a resource for sign language linguistics, nor is the author claiming expertise in sign language beyond its relationship to church history, the history of rhetoric, and certain basic ethnographic observations. For these reasons, this book has an accompanying website with video examples of preaching in signed languages (including ASL, BSL, Auslan, Libras, and others) and in the mixed mode.[3] Readers should turn to it for illustrations and information about dioceses that currently offer deaf ministry and Mass in sign language.

2. See Edward Peters, "Video Communication Technology and the Sacramental Confession of the Deaf," *The Jurist* 73, no 2 (2013): 513–538.
3. http://icfdeafservice.org/beopened.

The basic grammar of ASL follows a topic-action signing order, using direction and movement in space to indicate prepositional modifiers. Some ministers may use a written English gloss to "read" a passage into ASL. For example, for the first two verses of the Book of Genesis, one of many possible ASL glosses might look something like this: "LONG-TIME PAST. EARTH NOTHING SPREAD OVER ALL. HERE EMPTY, DEEP, DARK. GOD BLOW OVER TOP OF WATER." However, a gloss is ineffective for anyone who does not already know two things: the full meaning of the original passage and how to communicate the missing information in person using ASL direction, movement, and prosody. Because a gloss is a linear arrangement of written words on a page, it cannot contain much of the meaning ASL signs carry through three-dimensional use of space. Most often, the best sign language preachers stand away from the pulpit or ambo, close to the deaf community, as a pastoral application of "preaching from the chair." This allows for more natural use of direction and space in the signed communication.

The best way to understand ASL worship or preaching is to learn the language and visit ASL services in person. However, being aware of things to watch for may help observers identify certain conventions unique to culturally Deaf church services and oratory. For example, Father Shawn Carey, Director of the Deaf Apostolate in the Archdiocese of Boston, always begins his proclamation of the Gospel as the rubric requires: by tracing a small cross with this thumb on his head, his lips, and his heart to signify "May the Lord be in my mind, on my lips, and in my heart," but unlike hearing, non-signing, priests, Carey also crosses each palm as a way of inviting Christ to be present in his sacred Word proclaimed through the hands of a signing priest. Many Deaf priests (and hearing priests signing the Mass) do the same, because without this gesture the rubric would lack relevant meaning for people who communicate in ASL. At a Mass observed during research for this book, Father Carey engaged in another common ASL convention: a story about growing up deaf. During a homily on the twenty-seventh Sunday of Ordinary Time (Year C), he began by recalling "one of the most popular stories I saw growing up in Deaf school." Hearing people would tell the children, "You know, when there is a big thunderstorm, you should go outside and pray to God that lightning strikes your ear and you become a hearing person." (His visual portrayal of lighting striking his ear was quite dramatic.) "This is actually a popular saying," he told his assembly, adding "but do we want to become hearing? Should we ask God for that?" From here he transitioned into his message about asking God for his will rather than our own will, because we lack an understanding of God's larger plan.[4] While a hearing priest may earn the trust of a deaf assembly by reflecting on stories told to him by deaf friends, there are countless experiences of growing up and living day to day as a deaf person to which only a priest who is deaf can fully relate. So, in addition to fluent ASL language skill using space and the body to deliver his message, Father Carey communicates clearly with his deaf assembly because of a wealth of common experiences and a shared identity.

One of the most loved and respected ASL preachers in America today is Deacon Patrick Graybill. A graduate of Gallaudet University, Graybill grew up in Kansas as one of seven siblings, five of whom were deaf. His eloquent ASL and creative temperament led him to become one of the most celebrated ASL poets in this often-overlooked canon of American literature. He was also one of the founding members of the National Theatre of the Deaf, a company with a continuous history of traveling performances since 1967. Since 1982, he has also become well known in the Deaf world as a Catholic deacon in the Diocese of Rochester, New York. Because of his successes in literature and the performing arts, Graybill is an especially well-known language model and religious elder for Deaf Catholics. His skill with ASL communication has inspired many deaf people to find a place for themselves in the church.

At a weekend retreat for Deaf Catholics in Washington, D.C., in 2015, Graybill exemplified many of the best strategies for teaching and preaching in ASL, all of which contribute to better worship services in this language. On Saturday morning, Graybill announced his theme for his weekend retreat: walking with God. The technique for this session would be a prayerful reading of Psalm 63 using *lectio divina* or "divine reading," a traditional Benedictine practice of focused reading and meditative prayer that many religious orders have adopted. Graybill learned *lectio divina* from his Jesuit spiritual director, Father Peter Monty, a hearing Canadian priest who is fluent in ASL and has worked in deaf ministry for over forty-five years.

Carefully working through Scripture readings prepared retreatants to experience Mass more deeply. For example, Graybill projected a slide

4. Shawn Carey, Homily on the twenty-seventh Sunday of Ordinary Time, Year C, Archdiocese of Boston, October 6, 2013, author's personal video collection.

displaying Psalm 63 on an overhead screen. He explained the tradition of *lectio divina* and that reading very slowly and prayerfully could lead to greater personal understanding and deeper communication with God. At the same time, he assured participants that he knew reading English is not always easy for deaf people. One participant was visibly nervous about having to study written text and openly admitted that reading was always difficult for her. Graybill assured her and the others, that they would look at the text carefully but that they would translate it into ASL together several times. It was okay to let go of the text and focus on getting the meaning from the ASL as it evolved from the group's interpretation and reflection. He worked through the psalm line by line, changing the text's color from black to red on the slide as he parsed each English phrase with ASL questions, explanation, and elaboration. Sometimes a single word, translated into an ASL sign, would spark deeper reflection on walking with God. He left plenty of time for questions and discussion, often signing two or three versions of a line in ASL. Turning off the overhead projector, he asked participants to watch as he slowly signed the whole psalm using the ASL translation—a signed "text"—that they had just constructed together. He asked them to pause for five minutes of silent reflection before they signed it again, one last time, this time together. Finally, he asked the retreatants to go outside for a solitary walk around the beautiful retreat center grounds, thinking about the psalm and talking to God about what it might mean to each of them:

> You are my help,
> and in the shadow of your wings I shout for joy.
> My soul clings fast to you;
> your right hand upholds me.

English idioms in written text are often difficult for deaf people to comprehend. Children and adults learn idioms of their native language through thousands of passively received repetitions in a person's lifetime. Biblical passages are typically full of idioms—both idioms of the original Hebrew or Greek text and, at times, idioms of the translation language used to convey the original meaning. Many Hebrew and Greek idioms (and their translations) emphasize the physical lifeworld of ancient peoples. Native users of ASL immediately understand "the shadow of God's wings" and "your right hand upholds me" as figurative, once they know these are metaphorical descriptions of God. After Graybill made this point clear, he could sign figuratively in the person of God, symbolically and imaginatively embodying God's wings and right hand.

At Sunday Mass in ASL the next day, the readings that had been interpreted in this way were filled with meaning for the signing lectors and the deaf assembly. Anyone, hearing or deaf, can benefit from doing *lectio divina* with Mass readings, but for deaf people who share a non-print language, the practice of group discussion of the text in ASL can add tremendously to the quality of a lector's signed translation and to the deaf assembly's comprehension of biblical texts. For this reason, voice-off programs such as Religious Sign Language Week in the Diocese of Rockford, Illinois, are training clergy, laypeople, and interpreters to practice *lectio divina* in ASL.

In some ways, what makes a good preacher in ASL is the same as in any language. The Sunday gospel reading during Deacon Graybill's retreat was from Luke 9, when Jesus says to his disciples, "If anyone wishes to come after me, he must deny himself and take up his cross daily and follow me."[5] In his homily, Graybill drew on the shared reflection about walking with God during the retreat, but not before beginning with a technique often used by good homilists. He told a story that was so common to everyday experience that anyone could identify with it: a store clerk sold mattresses for a living, and almost every day a customer would come into the store, lie down on every single bed on the showroom floor, mess up all the display linens, and leave without buying anything. The clerk had to clean it up without complaining, day after day. This pain-in-the-neck customer, Graybill explained, was the clerk's cross to bear, and like the good clerk we should not complain about God's will for us. We are often a pain in the neck to God, but he loves us anyway and perseveres. Any listener, hearing or deaf, who had been present at the retreat or not, could identify with a clear and simple story like that.

In the United States, a handful of churches with sizable deaf populations offer ASL Mass at a certain time on Sunday, in the same way a parish might offer weekly Spanish (or other language) Mass for those minorities in mostly English-speaking parishes—or in immigrant communities to preserve the heritage of the group. Unlike Masses in different spoken languages, however, the deaf assemblies attending ASL Masses will not eventually learn to understand spoken English. Long after im-

5. Deacon Patrick Graybill, Luke 9: 18–24, Homily on the twelfth Sunday of Ordinary Time, Year C, author's personal video collection.

migrant populations assimilate and offer Mass in an immigrant language only to preserve heritage, Deaf Catholics will continue to need sign language at Mass. Also, unlike services for foreign-language populations, an ASL Mass with added voice interpreting often attracts a regular audience of mainstream hearing parishioners (in addition to deaf people from all over the diocese). Hearing people at an ASL Mass receive the message in English through a voice interpreter standing to the side and usually using a microphone, while the ASL of the liturgy for these hearing participants becomes an aesthetic enhancement, deepening the experience of diversity in God's family. In some parishes, a priest may well choose to use a mixed-mode style (voice and signs) as a deliberate pastoral and liturgical choice, believing the mixed mode enables the whole assembly, hearing and deaf, to pray together and participate fully. Yet communicating adequately and competently in the mixed mode demands a high level of skill—and weekly preparation—by the priest in two languages.

Because there are only a handful of priests and deacons fluent in ASL, most Deaf Catholic church goers experience ASL in the Mass through an interpreter—the difference being that deaf people cannot benefit from the spoken words of a Mass in the same way hearing people benefit from ASL with voice interpreting. Whether for voice or ASL, interpreters can occasionally be the source of disagreements. For example, during an interview, licensed interpreter Theresa Schmechel discussed the role of female interpreters in signed Masses in Milwaukee. It is Catholic teaching that, because a priest celebrating the Mass acts *in persona Christi* (in the person of Christ), the priest must be male. When a female interpreter is involved, however, the assembly receives a woman's voice or even a woman's body as the medium of God's message. For these reasons, a former archbishop of the Archdiocese of Milwaukee would not allow female interpreters in this role.[6] As a language service provider, an interpreter may even be a non-Catholic, which may cause misinterpretation of key concepts. For example, an interpreter unfamiliar with Catholic traditions might make inappropriate sign choices, such as signing the familiar "sister" rather than the sign for a religious sister or using the sign for a Jewish Old Testament priest instead of the Catholic sign. For these reasons, a qualified ASL interpreter may or may not be a qualified church interpreter.

6. Theresa Schmechel, interview by Marlana Portolano, Milwaukee, January 10, 2014.

Preaching in Pidgin Signed English

For non-native signers, learning ASL as a second or third language takes the same amount of immersion time as any other language. However, even for the most diligent of hearing students, the learning process may feel much longer. The reason is twofold. First, accomplishing the necessary language immersion to develop fluency can be difficult because spoken language is everywhere, but extended ASL immersion is scarce without deaf family members or other built-in contact with Deaf culture. Even those deaf signers who find spoken language uncomfortable or difficult often will add voice to signs when communicating with hearing people, because they know that few hearing people understand ASL. Second, even learners who already have several spoken languages can find it challenging to switch to a visual and spatial mode of language. For hearing priests and deacons in a busy mainstream parish also serving a small deaf community, it may be difficult to spend the time needed in the deaf community to become fluent in ASL.

Does the difficulty of learning ASL make communication impossible for Deaf Catholics in mainstream churches? In the United States, ASL is the ideal language for deaf ministry because it is not a pidgin but an actual language—the deaf community's native language. However, in the absence of clergy and pastoral workers fluent in ASL, there are some intermediate steps toward fuller linguistic access in mixed modes. For new or unpracticed users, the mixed mode can be disastrous, dramatically compromising fluency and meaning in both languages. On the other hand, expert users of Pidgin Signed English, especially those who incorporate ASL prosody and a deaf use of space, communicate better than poor users of ASL. Deaf people themselves often code-switch to a type of "contact sign" that resembles English word order when they are communicating with hearing people. Deaf lectors often communicate Scripture readings in this "contact sign" mode when time is lacking to translate the reading into highly skilled ASL ahead of time, and many dioceses offering ASL or BSL Masses adapt their signed translation to resemble the idiom of the English translation (rather than the natural idiom of the signed language). An example of Scripture reading by an expert deaf user of the mixed mode easily illustrates the benefits of this type of sign language over poorly interpreted readings, with the caveat that only a few highly skilled signers can reach this level of skill in the mixed mode.

Father Joseph Bruce, a deaf Jesuit priest, generally speaks and signs simultaneously in English word order, but his oratorical style clearly aligns with American Deaf traditions of storytelling, dramatic performance, and poetry in sign language. When he addresses deaf assemblies, his homilies contain few long stretches of monologue and often incorporate interactive dialog. For example, he may call a teenager up and sign-and-speak in a one-on-one Socratic dialogue. (The deaf teen most often signs without voice in reply, either not aware that Father Bruce is voicing or simply more comfortable with native ASL.) Or he will call parishioners by name—sign name—then ask questions and include them as communication partners in developing the message. This homiletic form, requiring an active role in communication from the congregation, stands in sharp contrast to homilies at most hearing parishes. In some ways it resembles African American preaching, with its charismatic call-and-response dynamic. However, the purpose of interaction in African American preaching is usually to drum up emotion through the assembly's participation in a rhythmic, ritual dialogue. The purpose of dialogic interaction in deaf assemblies, on the other hand, is to secure clear communication in a visual-spatial mode of language.

Like homilists in any language, Father Bruce often begins with a story from his own life. Because he grew up deaf and attended deaf schools, a deaf assembly identifies with him as someone who understands deaf cultural experiences. During the Second Sunday of Lent (Year C) at St. Francis of Assisi Church in Landover, Maryland, Father Bruce peached a homily on the Transfiguration of Jesus in Luke 9, in which God says from a cloud, "This is my chosen son, listen to him." However, in this Lenten homily, Father Bruce focused on a sign that might stand out for the deaf audience: *listen*. He showed a few different ways to sign "listen" and evoked a few more from the assembly. This kind of list-making is a common trope in ASL. It serves to unite signers who might have different dialects. One sign places a hand next to the ear, as if to hear better. Father Bruce's facial expression—a half-smile, raised eyebrows, and an exaggerated nod—indicated to the assembly a degree of irony. He then asked the congregation if any of them had decided to do something for Lent. Not many raised their hands. Why not take time, he asked in speech and sign, to listen? Only this time he used the ASL sign for "pay attention," two hands held parallel to the sides of the face and moved back and forth toward the audience, like blinders on a horse's bridle. "This means you listen not only to the words of the person but also to another flesh-and-blood person," he explained. The English manuscript of the homily puts it this way, but Father Bruce's delivery is much more interactive than the static words of a written text. He emphasizes that it is the *person* you listen to, not just the *words*, a distinction he makes clear both by his attentive facial expression and by sweeping his hands from shoulder to hip, as if a human torso stood before him. Using sign language amplifies his meaning that a person must be present to listen. The signs, used in a "deaf way," make his meaning more concrete, or at least more visualized, in a scene. He gives examples of people who were good listeners, counting them off on his fingers in the ASL signal for making a list: Mary, who listened to angels; Helen Keller, who could neither hear nor see but listened through touch to her teacher Annie Sullivan; and St. John Vianney, who spent twelve hours a day listening to repentant hearts in the confessional.

Each time Father Bruce perceives that his audience knows something about his examples, he asks them for information and confirmation, drawing out their part in the reasoning and giving them a vested interest in the meaning of the homily. When he judges that the group seems united in agreement, Father Bruce proceeds with his conclusion. He exhorts his assembly to attend to God by listening—not just to his words but to the divine person present to us in signed readings of the Gospel and to individual human beings who make up the body of Christ in the church. Although he uses English grammar and word order, ASL signs are what make clear his focus on the human person of Christ enfleshed in a human body. There is nothing abstract about the person of Jesus in this mode of communication—unless, perhaps, you are a hearing member of the audience with eyes closed, listening to Father Bruce's voice but not seeing his sign language.

Given the background of the preacher and the language experiences of the assembly, there have been and continue to be situations in which the mixed mode is rhetorically the best choice. As more (even a majority) of deaf people in the developed world receive cochlear implants and public- or parochial-school mainstreaming, this may very well be the most comfortable form of signed communication for a large portion of the deaf population. Done well and with an aim toward developing ASL fluency, the mixed mode can provide deaf assemblies with greatly needed direct communication from a signing priest or deacon. It can also be used in cooperation with a skilled ASL interpreter as a third-party mediator for parts of the Mass that are spoken but not signed.

Preaching Online

As electronic communications and internet access have expanded around the world, ministers to the deaf have taken advantage of new media to reach deaf people who are geographically and linguistically isolated. Because of their visual language, deaf people have gravitated toward online communications of all kinds in the new millennium. Signed video Masses, stand-alone homilies, readings for the liturgical cycle, and instruction in prayer and devotion have shown promise for reaching isolated deaf people who have no other means of accessing religious services in their own language, as well as providing opportunities for spiritual enrichment for those who are not so isolated. They also serve the function of an accessible sign language "text" for study and spiritual enrichment. In the United States, various dioceses have websites with videos illustrating Mass prayers, and a program in Great Britain is working on a Catholic translation of the Bible in British Sign Language. Social networking such as Facebook group pages and YouTube video channels have enabled diocesan communities and international associations alike to discuss issues online in a combination of signed and print languages. It is not unusual to encounter a Deaf Catholic person who relies on these online resources as a main form of religious practice and corporate worship today. In cities or towns where there is no signed or interpreted Mass—or where sign language is only available once per month or for special events or missions—Deaf Catholics may turn to video homilies and individual readings of Scripture in lieu of attending a Mass with no sign language.

Preaching in sign language online is common among Evangelical Christians, who also have made particularly strong efforts in producing ASL scriptural resources on video. Organizations such as Deaf Missions, a nondenominational affiliation that has completed an ASL translation of the Bible and an online religious sign language dictionary, are easy for deaf people of all religious backgrounds to find and use online. The Church of Jesus Christ of Latter Day Saints has a similar dictionary of religious sign language online. These video resources, both on the internet and in DVD form, serve as resources for prayer and religious education, as well as for education in sign language for the broader community. In this way, their service promotes sign language and integrates it into mainstream society at large, especially in the context of Christian devotion and religious education. In some ways, the presence of Deaf Catholics competes with the excellent resources available from other religious traditions. Indeed, to engage the dispersed population of Deaf Catholics in a feeling of connectedness and fellowship, it is necessary for Deaf Catholic ministry to be more active online than hearing Catholic parishes and organizations typically are. The focus in this section is how Catholics in Deaf ministry, particularly Deaf Catholics themselves, have engaged specifically in sign language preaching and homiletics.

Originating from Spain's Canary Islands, the video blog (or "vlog") of Spanish Deaf priest Augustin Yanes Valer is a catalog of three hundred thirty-five homilies and other devotions published online between 2007 and 2016, delivered in signed Spanish as Valer simultaneously spoke and signed his homily. In the Spanish-speaking world, Valer's vlog served as a resource for Deaf Catholics in Europe and across North and South America, wherever Deaf Catholics' sign language resembles his own. In addition, hearing ministers learning to sign have looked to Valer's video compendium as a searchable database of topical and seasonal homilies, a type of resource that is scarce in signed languages.

In the ASL-signing world, Father Michael Depcik has become well-known for his vlog, *Father MD's Kitchen Table*, which he created as part of his ministry as an Oblate of Saint Francis de Sales. Knowing from his own experience as a deaf man that many Deaf Catholics live too far to drive to an interpreted or signed Mass, Depcik wanted to make his ASL homilies and some basic teachings of the Catholic Church available where anyone could view them online. Depcik began his vlog when he lived in Chicago in 2008. While working as a counselor for deaf people in Chicago, he met a young man skilled with computers who helped Depcik create an online presence for his preaching and teaching. He learned how to use a simple electronic video camera and the WordPress blogging platform. Since then, he has posted over two hundred homilies, thirty lives of the saints, and two dozen basic Catholic prayers such as the Our Father, Hail Mary, Stations of the Cross, Rosary meditations, and morning and evening prayer. In addition to these catechetical and devotional materials, Depcik has created dozens of informative videos in ASL about Marian devotions around the world. He has also posted news about events in the Deaf Catholic world, along with dozens of sign language interviews with key people in deaf ministry, including Deaf religious and pastoral workers who work with deaf people, primarily in the United States. For his homilies, he dresses as if he were celebrating Mass, but many of the informative or teaching videos were made in the comfortable setting of his kitchen table—thus the name of his website.

Depcik's vlog has been a singular resource both for Deaf Catholic laypeople and for priests and deacons (hearing and deaf) in need of models for preaching in sign language. Priests who have never seen ASL preaching but who need to learn it themselves have used the vlog as an anthology of models, searchable both by subject and by date in the liturgical calendar. The value of culturally deaf models for Catholic homily in sign language cannot be overemphasized. While there is no shortage of books containing collections of homilies and instruction on Catholic preaching for the spoken word, the inexperienced sign language preacher new to deaf ministries faces a daunting shortage of models in an area where he may need much more practice simply to use sign vocabulary and grammar well enough to be intelligible. Many who enter deaf ministry may never get a chance to see a deaf person preach a homily in native ASL in real life, much less learn the language through cultural immersion, and Depcik's vlog demonstrates correct use of religious vocabulary and concepts expressed in this language by a native user.

For Depcik, the vlog is an outreach for his spirituality in the tradition of Saint Francis de Sales. As he explained in an interview, "Often people see me preach on my vlog, and it fits their everyday life. That's what Saint Francis de Sales's spirituality was like in his book *Introduction to the Devout Life*. It's for regular people. A long time ago, people thought that to be holy you had to enter a monastery and become a priest or a nun, and laypeople tried to follow those guidelines for living. But Saint Francis said you can't do that. There are chores, you're busy, and your life gets all messy—that can be holy, too, if you do it the right way."[7] In his homilies on the vlog, Depcik emphasizes basic Catholic beliefs and practices, a clear understanding of Scripture, and examples from the everyday lives of his listeners. Often his homilies use examples from the Deaf experience and point of view, such as problems in the family or in the workplace faced by deaf people. His vlogs are often reposted on other websites, so they also serve as explicit Catholic evangelization in modern culture.

7. Father Michael Depcik, interview by Marlana Portolano, St. Francis Deaf Catholic Church, Landover, Maryland, December 9, 2013.

These online materials can even reach large international audiences. His vlog about the sixteenth-century martyr Saint Paul Miki, SJ, of Japan received a very high view rate, and when he traced the shares, Depcik discovered that it had been posted on a Japanese website commemorating the martyr. Because his vlogs include an audio track with voice interpreting, hearing viewers with English language can also benefit from his homiletic messages.

While preaching online is one way to expand services for Deaf Catholics and to evangelize new deaf audiences, a comparison of Depcik's vlog with his preaching in person demonstrates the strengths and limitations of internet media. Father Depcik's vlog homilies are short and to the point, usually under five minutes, which is ideal for the online format in ASL. A normal adult attention span for long discourses in sign language, without the back-and-forth communication and feedback of an in-person audience, is generally shorter than it is for sign language communication in person. In the first minute of his video, Father Depcik gives a brief retelling or example from the scriptural reading. He does not use much space in his video, just the area in front of his body that fits within the frame of the video image. Even in a small signing space, he can give a full sense of the reading and then preach one strong, clear point about it—often in two or three minutes. Few homilists could do the same with greater skill in any language. In addition, Depcik does not neglect hearing viewers: an English voice-over interprets in a soundtrack, and his sign language is aesthetically beautiful to watch even without ASL comprehension.

In 2018, Depcik began livestreaming Sunday ASL Masses on the Deaf Catholic Community Facebook page from Holy Innocents Church in the Archdiocese of Detroit; the videos quickly gain up to seven hundred views. Here, viewers can see the entire Mass, including readings by lay lectors in ASL. In live media, Depcik signs naturally for a community he has known for many years, so he tailors the style of the homilies to his viewers. The national and even international audience of the vlog requires very general examples and explanations, so that deaf people from any region can identify with the message. At Sunday Mass, however, Depcik's homilies for the same readings are longer, often fifteen minutes as compared to four or five for the video delivery. In person, he moves close to the assembly when he preaches, using a large oratorical sign space and expanding his examples based on the visual cues and feedback from his congregation.

For many geographically dispersed individuals in the deaf community, internet media may be their only access to worship in their own language. However, video is not really a substitute for experiencing the sacrament as part of an active local community. Video and internet communication in sign language point to the existence of deaf ministry and can lead deaf people to seek out a signed or interpreted Mass, but each diocese varies according to the services they can provide.

Communicating through the Body

Which mode of worship and preaching in sign language is the best? Should voice-off, academically "credentialed" sign languages be the only accepted mode, or should the church encourage signers of different skill sets and methods? Even after hundreds of years of sign language education and the development of deaf culture in the church, there are no clear answers to these questions. Standardization of worship in ASL and other signed languages is a work in progress, and the different styles of preaching and worship in sign language bear witness to the difficulty of standardization for a language without a static print form. Even with a media for preserving texts in a given language, preaching styles will always differ because there are—and will be—preachers from many backgrounds.

ASL is among the world's youngest languages, having developed after 1817 at the American School for the Deaf. Any comparison of senior deaf signers with children who grew up schooled in ASL illustrates that the language is still in a process of relatively rapid change. All living languages are, by nature, in a process of change, but standardizing ASL was a challenge until film and video recording became widely available. Because of this, decisions about language use in the Mass should consider the language experiences of the deaf community. As the Constitution on the Sacred Liturgy (*Sacrosanctum Concilium*) communicated, "It is very much the wish of the church that all the faithful should be led to take that full, conscious, and active part in liturgical celebrations which is demanded by the very nature of the liturgy, and to which the Christian people, 'a chosen race, a royal priesthood, a holy nation, a redeemed people' (1 Pt 2:9, 4–5) have a right and to which they are bound by reason of their Baptism.... In the restoration and development of the sacred liturgy the full and active participation by all the people is the paramount concern, for it is the primary, indeed the indispensable source from which the faithful are to derive the true Christian spirit."[8]

Ultimately, any vernacular language used in worship and evangelization should connect people as a community, not put up walls. The most profound spiritual truths of the Christian faith are expressed most fully not through the spoken or written word but through the human body—specifically, Christ's body. In highly skilled hands, both ASL and mixed-mode signed communication have the potential to shift the viewer's focus from a static text to the relationship between flesh-and-blood participants in communion with one another. In sign language preaching and worship, the word is expressed not only through the human voice; in sign language, the word is embodied in and through the human form.

8. Vatican Council II, Constitution on the Sacred Liturgy *Sacrosanctum Concilium* (hereafter, *SC*), no. 14 (December 4, 1963), in *Vatican Council II: Constitutions, Decrees, Declarations*, ed. Austin Flannery (Northport, N.Y.: Costello Publishing, 1996).

CHAPTER 13

Signs of God in Asia and Africa

Now after these things the Lord appointed seventy others and
sent them two and two.—Luke 10:1

Most "Apostles of the Deaf" who contributed to Deaf Catholic history
lived in Christianized countries where the first missionaries arrived from
hundreds to well over a thousand years ago. Sometimes nineteenth- and
early twentieth-century deaf missionary work involved travel to foreign
lands to preach the gospel—particularly when Europeans traveled to the
Americas to start schools or when North Americans traveled to South
America to preach the gospel in sign language. However, in most places,
missionaries brought the Good News to deaf people who lived in the
missionary's own cultural milieu—but in language-based marginalization. Despite language differences, the ideas and cultural practices of
Christianity were not completely foreign to European or North American deaf people of European descent.

In contrast, the proportion of those who embrace the Christian faith
in some countries of Asia and northern Africa is still very small, usually
under 5 percent. Yet it is in these places that Christianity is growing exponentially through new efforts to evangelize. At the end of the twentieth century, the Catholic Church witnessed an important turn to new
missionary fields on these continents. Consistent with Pope Francis's
contemporary language in his apostolic exhortation on the church's mission, *Evangelii Gaudium* or "The Joy of the Gospel," the fruits of these

efforts are multiplying today. Embracing evangelization as the whole activity of the church, Francis writes, "Despite the tide of secularism which has swept our societies, in many countries—even those where Christians are a minority—the Catholic Church is considered a credible institution by public opinion, and trusted for her solidarity and concern for those in greatest need. Again and again, the Church has acted as a mediator in finding solutions to problems affecting peace, social harmony, the land, the defense of life, human and civil rights."[1]

Many Catholics define the New Evangelization as a renewal of faith in traditionally Christian countries where public life is no longer infused with Christian values and religious practice has become hardened, impoverished, or nonexistent. In many U.S. and European parishes, missionaries from newly evangelized communities in Africa and Asia have infused tired and jaded Christian communities with new life. Still, there is tremendous work to be done in parts of Asia and Africa where poverty and the struggle for basic human rights are widespread and the gospel remains unknown. This new era of missionary expansion, with its developments in the very definition of evangelization, is contributing to the ongoing missionary history of Deaf Catholics as a language group in the church.

At the time of this writing, only 3 percent of the world's Catholics live in Asia, the world's most populous continent, but that number is growing exponentially. More people are now baptized annually in China than in all of Europe. During the past four decades, the population of Catholics in South Korea has grown significantly, from 2 to 11 percent. Although Buddhism is still the most widely accepted religion in Korea, and most young people profess no religion, Korean Catholics tend to be well educated and form an important part of their country's political elite.[2] These few and scattered statistics, combined with the endangered place of Christians in the Middle East, provide a meager sketch of the diversity and complexity of Christian lives in countries outside the cultural West. Naturally, this diversity is reflected in the history of Deaf Catholics, who exist in every country where Catholicism exists. Moreover, the mission of the church also concerns deaf people in countries where Catholicism does not yet exist. In these countries, proclaiming the gospel

1. Pope Francis, *Evangelii Gaudium*, Apostolic Exhortation (November 24, 2013), 36.

2. David Willey, "Pope Francis Faces Greatest Challenge Yet in Asia," BBC News, August 13, 2014, accessed February 11, 2019, https://www.bbc.com/news/world-europe-28755656.

in sign language may not be the first step on the missionary agenda, but living the gospel is.

There are several historically recent centers of deaf ministry in Asia, India, and Africa, and a great deal of scholarly work remains to be done on non-western Deaf Catholics in many academic disciplines. This chapter introduces three outstanding missionaries' lives and works and highlights only a handful of these deaf centers. After a brief description of groundbreaking activity in these areas by Father Harry Stocks, the chapter profiles Father Charles Dittmeier's work, especially in Cambodia, where a new sign language is developing as a result of missionary activity. The next two sections describe the ministry of Father Cyril Axelrod, a convert from Orthodox Judaism and a culturally deaf (and later blind) missionary who crossed numerous cultural boundaries against great odds, first in South Africa under apartheid, then in several countries in Asia. The chapter concludes with a look at what might lie ahead for deaf ministries in the twenty-first century.

An Apostle to Deaf People in Asia

The first apostle of the deaf in Asia had a reputation for being rough around the edges. Father Harry Stocks, a native of Scotland, was an immigrant to North America and a member of the Canadian Province of the Congregation of the Holy Cross. In many ways a man of action, Stocks leapt at an opportunity to work with the missionary program Cardijn Community International soon after his 1966 ordination. It was the beginning of a life spent serving the people of India. Stocks became fluent in the Tamil language and fostered a deep commitment to the poor in Bangalore, Karnataka, through his involvement in two large projects: a Cardijn Worker's Centre and a housing project for the homeless. There, he developed a special sensitivity for deaf people among the poor, ultimately dedicating the next forty-two years of his life to championing the deaf community in Asia. As part of this commitment, he built the Technical Training Centre for the Deaf in Bangalore and furnished the institution with modern equipment, enabling graduates to secure jobs in factories for over twenty years.[3]

3. Unfortunately, visitors in 2011 reported that the center's then thirty-year-old equipment, along with the power, water supply, and hostel rooms, were dilapidated and failing, as the center has not been kept up since Stocks's time there. See "Training Centre for Deaf in Shambles," accessed January 4, 2017, Deaf News Forum, alldeaf.com.

While working in India, Father Stocks periodically had to travel to renew his visa, and he turned these excursions into mission trips in other countries in Asia. He was particularly active in Singapore, Sri Lanka, and Hong Kong. Wherever Catholic schools for deaf children had been founded, generally by religious sisters during the colonial era, he would travel and evangelize deaf children and the deaf adult community, as well as the schools' teachers, in sign language. Much like Father Hayward in the early years of deaf ministry in England, Father Stocks had a reputation for speaking his mind, a trait that could make deaf educators wary of his demands. While most colonial schools still used oral education methods, Stocks was convinced that the only way to reach the hearts and souls of deaf people was through their own native sign language. In the late 1970s, Father Stocks began a second Cardijn Worker's Centre in Karwar, Karnataka. His work with the deaf community and with the international worker's movement there led to the involvement of several Indian support organizations, including other religious communities and secular agencies. With other missionaries who worked with deaf people in the 1980s and '90s, Stocks began to hold international Deaf Catholic conferences for Southeast Asians in Malaysia, Indonesia, India, Bangladesh, and Sri Lanka. After his death in 2013, these regional groups of Deaf Catholics continued to meet in international conferences to share their concerns about deaf people's lives, education, and worship in Asia.[4]

In our present focus on the development of deaf-led communities, we turn now to two later missionaries who followed Father Stocks' trailblazing example.

A School-Centered Community in Hong Kong

When Father Charles Dittmeier was ordained in 1970, there were only a handful of priests who worked with Catholic deaf people in the United States. Every year, they would get together as a part of the newly fledged National Catholic Office of the Deaf to discuss deaf ministry. "It was just shop talk," Father Dittmeier recalled, "you know, what signs do you use for 'marriage,' and how do you do marriage preparation. It was a kind

4. Charles Dittmeier, oral history interview by Marlana Portolano, Cambodia via Skype, June 8, 2016.

of support group."[5] At this meeting one year, Father Dittmeier met the unusual Father Harry Stocks, who said any of the priests doing deaf ministry would be welcome to volunteer with him in Banglador. Dittmeier always dreamt of working outside the United States, so in 1985 he asked Bishop Thomas Kelly of the Archdiocese of Louisville, Kentucky, for a two-year mission trip in India. After this first trip, his life would never be the same. When Dittmeier returned, he asked for and received permission to return to Asia as a long-term associate priest with the Maryknoll missionaries.

For his first assignment, Maryknoll sent Dittmeier to Hong Kong. There he became involved with a Deaf Catholic community that had sprung up around graduates of the Canossian School for the Deaf—one of a few schools that the Canossian sisters established in Asia, along with others in Singapore. His aim was to begin community worship services and pastoral counseling in sign language. At the time, there were fifteen or twenty deaf young people who attended Mass at the school. They would sit in the front pews, not understanding the spoken language, while one of the sisters wrote notes about what was being said and passed it down the rows. Each deaf person would read the note and pass it along as the sister wrote another note, until the end of Mass. When they went out for lunch afterward, Dittmeier asked the group, "Did you all understand anything?" Not a thing, they told him. It was then that he decided to provide visual access to worship for these young adults through sign language services.

At first, remembering the more directive style of Father Harry Stocks, the school's principal Sister Theresa Chen held him at arm's length, but Father Dittmeier had a gentler, more diplomatic way of negotiating. He praised her oral approaches, agreeing that the Canossian School had the very best oral education program he had ever seen, but at the same time, Dittmeier admitted his own spoken Cantonese was not very good. He suggested that she continue her fine education in speech and lipreading, but perhaps he could use sign language to get his religious ministry started outside of class. She agreed, and Father Dittmeier began celebrating Mass every week in Hong Kong Sign Language, one of the two main varieties of Chinese sign language used in that part of Asia, which

5. Charles Dittmeier, oral history interview by Marlana Portolano, Cambodia via Skype, June 8, 2016. All quotes and information in this section are taken from this interview unless otherwise noted.

he learned from the deaf people themselves without formal instruction. At first, the deaf community merely tolerated his efforts—after all, the government banned sign language in their school, and most of them thought it must be inferior or even wrong—but more people came each week. Eventually, the diocese allowed Dittmeier and a few deaf ministers working with him to renovate one of the city's old refugee centers, which became the parish church of Hong Kong's still-vigorous Deaf Catholic community. After Dittmeier's initial contract was up in 1992, his Maryknoll superiors asked him to become Area Coordinator for Asia. Even though he was still a priest of the Diocese of Louisville, with his bishop's blessing, he accepted the job and remained a Maryknoll associate.

In 1997, the designated time came for England to hand Hong Kong back over to China. The Western-influenced city had been losing fifteen to twenty thousand residents per year as people fled the uncertain prospects of a Chinese government. Maryknoll knew that those who stayed in Hong Kong would need the security of international friendships, so they asked Dittmeier to stay there and maintain the church's presence as a sign of stability and solidarity. Once again, he asked for an extension, and Bishop Kelly agreed. "But be aware," the bishop said, "you can reach a point of no return." Father Dittmeier realized then that he had already reached that point: Deaf Catholic Asia had become his world.

A New Language in Cambodia

As Father Dittmeier took up his position as Asia Area Coordinator for Maryknoll and his appointment in Hong Kong neared an end, he often travelled to other Asian countries, sometimes for missionary conferences and sometimes to visit Maryknoll missioners on-site. During one of these trips, he met Katjia Merentie, a deaf field worker for the Finnish Association for the Deaf's outreach project in Cambodia. Cambodia is a land of great natural beauty and terrible war-ravaged destruction. In the remote villages of this nation of rice paddies and forests, the average age is under twenty-five because of deaths caused by the Khmer Rouge. Cambodia remains one of the most aid-dependent countries in the world, receiving millions of dollars in foreign aid annually.[6] When Katija Merentie had first traveled around the country in 1996, trying to discover work with deaf people there, she found there simply were no

6. Sebastian Strangio, *Hun Sen's Cambodia* (Bangkok: Silkworm Books, 2014).

deaf services at that time. Cambodia was still in a state of devastation
from the occupation and mass killings committed by the Khmer Rouge.
There were no books, no schools, and no organizations—none of the
things that allow advanced language and culture to develop. Beyond a
limited use of "home sign" (invented signs families use to communicate
basic ideas), deaf people simply worked at home or in the fields, unable
to communicate much even with their own families.[7]

In fact, there was no developed or consistent Cambodian sign language and perhaps never had been even before the devastation caused
by the Khmer Rouge, although confirming this is difficult because of
the lack of deaf elders or signed folk history. After the genocide, no deaf
adults survived to pass on sign language native to their region. According to Father Dittmeier, during the twenty years since deaf ministry began in Cambodia, Maryknoll found only two congenitally deaf senior
citizens. Since the 1990s, however, linguists studying Cambodian Sign
Language found what may be traces of one or more "old Cambodian sign
languages" in the current Cambodian Sign Language. One study claims
that Cambodian Sign Language shows a 42 percent rate of similarity in
basic core vocabulary with Modern Thai Sign Language, perhaps a result
of events during Khmer Rouge rule, when several Cambodian deaf people were in refugee camps in Thailand. This same study is inconclusive
about where the remaining 58 percent of Cambodian signs come from,
as they are unrelated to any other known sign language.[8] However, events
during the establishment of the current Deaf Development Program in
Phnom Penh suggest that missionaries, volunteers, and staff members of
the program encouraged deaf Cambodians to invent and use new signs
"on the spot."

To help restart sign language in Cambodia, during each of her three
trips in the 1990s, Katja Merentie gathered a group of twenty to twenty-
five deaf people in a small room in Phnom Penh and got them to create

7. One American deaf researcher writes, "During fieldwork in 2014–15 I observed encounters
between members of a community outreach team and individual deaf people in villages who had
neither received a formal education nor been exposed to Cambodian Sign Language (CSL). During
these observations, I made connections between CSL signs currently in use and gestures that Cambodians use to communicate gender and familial hierarchy." See Erin M. Harrelson, "SAME-SAME
but Different: Tourism and the Deaf Global Circuit in Cambodia," in *It's a Small World: International Deaf Spaces and Encounters*, eds. Michele Friedner and Annelies Kusters (Washington, D.C.:
Gallaudet University Press, 2015), 202.

8. James Woodward, Anastasia Bradford, Chea Sokchea, and Heang Samath, "Cambodian Sign
Language," in *Sign Languages of the World: A Comparative Handbook*, ed. Julie B. Jepsen, et al. (Berlin: Walter de Gruyter, 2015), 159–76.

signs. She would hold up an object like a banana or a book and encourage them to make a sign for it. This humble start contained the seeds of a modern sign language which, with the help of missionaries and deaf volunteers, quickly evolved into a language they called Khmer Sign Language—now known as Cambodian Sign Language. As Father Dittmeier learned about Merentie's work for the Finnish Association of the Deaf, he began to discern a strong missionary call to serve deaf people in Cambodia—a nation whose three million people are 97 percent Buddhist or nonreligious.[9]

In 1997, Father Dittmeier began his work in Cambodia's Deaf Development Program, at that time a joint venture between the Finnish Association for the Deaf and the Cambodian Disabled People's Organization. In Phnom Penh, there were thirteen staff members, none with a job description and none with any training in working with deaf people. Fifty to seventy deaf people ranging in age from six to fifty sat on the floor of an empty room while an untrained teacher stood at a chalkboard, pointing at a list of written words with a stick. They would learn a sign to pair with each written word, and the teacher would point at each person in turn to stand and repeat the signs by rote. Then they would start over with a new vocabulary list. According to Father Dittmeier, the deaf people had no frame of reference for the written Khmer word and no way of learning the meaning of either the words or the signs from these methods. The signs were never put into sentences and the deaf people were not asked to communicate with the signs they learned, though there may have been some undocumented communication outside of class. The Cambodian Disabled People's Organization had centers like this one in six more cities around the country, and the same methods were used at each site. In Phnom Penh, they held lessons daily; in the provinces, they did it once a month, so their education program was just twelve days per year.

In 2000, the Finish Association of the Deaf, which had been funding the program, decided a term review was in order. To organize this task, they hired Colin Allen, best known today as president of the International Federation of the Deaf. Allen and his team investigated and made recommendations for education and deaf community development, beginning with instruction in Cambodian Sign Language. With deaf ed-

9. "The World Fact Book," Central Intelligence Agency (CIA), accessed January 25, 2019, https://www.cia.gov/library/publications/the-world-factbook/geos/cb.html.

ucation in such a poor state in Cambodia, it is not surprising that the original Cambodian Disabled People's Organization collapsed. After the term review, Maryknoll missionaries stepped in as the local partner with the Finnish Association of the Deaf, and Father Dittmeier became the program's director. When he began, the same deaf people were there, doing the same list of words, who had been sitting on the floor when he arrived in 1997. They had not even gotten through the Khmer alphabet. Overwhelmed with the lack of training, the new management team under Dittmeier closed the education program and brought in two deaf education trainers from Australia. He and his team then trained the Cambodian teachers and reopened the program after three months.

When they reopened for classes, there was a new group of students, fresh and ready to learn. However, it soon became apparent that the teachers could not transfer their new Western skills to daily instruction, having no formal education of this type themselves. The first day after the teacher-trainers left, the teachers used the new methods that the trainers had taught them, but on the second day, they went back to teaching the old way because they did not know how to extrapolate or make their own examples. To address this problem, Dittmeier hired Meghan Young, a deaf woman from Canada who had trained deaf teachers in the Peace Corps, to give the Cambodian teachers more intensive sign language instruction. It was an expensive year. Young knew only ASL and Kenyan Sign Language, so the Deaf Development Center had to hire an interpreter to translate from ASL into spoken English for the hearing staff members. However, the Cambodian hearing teachers did not know English, so they had to hire a third interpreter to translate from spoken English to spoken Khmer before in-depth instruction could proceed. The whole process cost them fifty thousand dollars. Finally, at the end of six months, Dittmeier hired the top six of thirty-seven Cambodian teachers, and the newly trained faculty abandoned previous methods of rote memorization and began teaching part of the day in a large group and part of the day in small groups. They incorporated learning games, role play, and other techniques of language learning proven to be effective in Western education.[10]

To meet the needs of the new Cambodian deaf community and forge ahead with language development, the center started new social services,

10. Charles Dittmeier, oral history interview by Marlana Portolano, Cambodia via Skype, June 8, 2016.

along with a program to promote Cambodian Sign Language both nationally and internationally. At this point, James (Woody) Woodward, a
deaf sign language linguist from Gallaudet University, came to Phnom
Penh with four sign language researchers. Dittmeier had met Woodward
while they both were living in Hong Kong, before Dittmeier moved
to Cambodia and Woodward moved to Vietnam. To carry out his linguistic study, Woodward began visiting Cambodia once a month to
train researchers and document the developing language.[11] Since these
early linguistic and cultural programs began, Cambodia has become a
popular destination for deaf tourists and short-term missionaries from
Western countries. Organizations based in the North Atlantic such as
Deaf Nation, Discovering Deaf Worlds, and Global Reach Out facilitate
deaf study tours and educational exchanges with the intent to empower
Cambodian deaf people with cultural role models in Western Deaf Culture.[12] While short-term visitors can bring false presumptions about the
homogeneity of a "global culture" in the international Deaf World, such
contact has brought needed attention and financial support to the area.

Through the coming together of all these efforts and influences,
Cambodian deaf people in Phnom Penh became a community in earnest.
For the first several years, the Deaf Development Program primarily addressed education and language development, but once this was in place,
the next step seemed apparent: the program needed job training for deaf
people. Deaf-run shops, manufacturing, and even the above-mentioned
tourist industry contributed new opportunities for deaf Cambodians
to learn about the broader world. Civic understanding and participation as citizens naturally followed as deaf people took responsibility for
themselves and sent money home to help support their families in the
provinces. Cultural understanding continued to grow, both on a local
level and in terms of a broader world with different languages in different
countries. People who began with almost no language would sit in class
for the first two weeks, frightened and confused beyond understanding.
As young adults, they had no social frame of reference for understanding
what deafness was. As their language grew, their understanding of the
world around them opened up and grew at an astounding speed. Early in
the program, one young woman volunteer told Cambodian deaf people
that she was from a school for the deaf in Alaska. They looked at her with

11. This trip is documented in Woodward et al., "Cambodian Sign Language."
12. Harrelson, "SAME-SAME but Different," 202.

wonder and signed, "Oh, you have deaf people in your country, too?"[13] By the end of this baptism by fire, participants came to realize that they were deaf and that all the other people in the room were deaf like them.

Sending Them Two and Two

The success of the Maryknoll-led Deaf Development Program has been both a blessing and a strain. The program started in 1997 with only thirteen staff members, but by 2016 it had grown to eighty-six. As the deaf community grew, so too did the program's needs, but there were no other organizations for deaf adults. Fortunately, a French-funded nonprofit organization, the Krousar Thmey Foundation, started a school for deaf children. They began with a first-grade class in 1997, and by 2017 this school served all deaf children up to age sixteen, while the Deaf Development Program continued to serve deaf people sixteen and older. Since there has never been a census of deaf people in Cambodia, the number of prelingually deaf Cambodians is unknown; however, the United Nations estimates that, in general, one person out of every one thousand in the world is born deaf or becomes deaf at an early age. In 2017, the population of Cambodia was sixteen million, making the estimated deaf population sixteen thousand.

To bring dispersed Cambodian deaf people together, Maryknoll missionaries and other volunteers travel in pairs, following the trails of rumor to homes where deaf people may be living with their families. Each team consists of a social worker, an interpreter, and a culturally deaf person who travel as far as they can go by car, then by motorcycle on the dykes between rice paddies, and finally by foot for the last miles until they reach a village. They ask the villagers if there are any deaf people, and generally the response is no, because there is little understanding in Cambodia of the nature of deafness. The Khmer word for "deaf" literally means "not speaking" or "mute," so deafness is defined in terms of speech production rather than reception of sound—as it was in the West before the mid-twentieth century. Eventually, in Father Dittmeier's words, one of the villagers might say, "Well, we've got this one crazy girl who makes all kinds of strange noises. She doesn't listen to her parents and won't do anything they tell her to do." When the field team asks to meet her, sure

13. Charles Dittmeier, oral history interview by Marlana Portolano, Cambodia via Skype, June 8, 2016.

enough, she is deaf. Once they find these people, who are most often completely lacking in language and formal education, the team is faced with the daunting task of persuading mothers and fathers to allow their deaf sons and daughters to leave the safety of home, where they may be needed to watch other children or do household chores.[14]

Using this method, they find eighty to one hundred deaf people per year in the three provinces, and still there are large areas that have not been reached. Cambodian culture classifies most deaf people as having a mental disability, and it is difficult to argue against this because the people have so little education. The deaf team member demonstrates how sign language can impart knowledge and communication that would enable a deaf person to get a job and earn money for the family. Many times, however, they are up against a superstitious or karmic idea that deafness is a punishment for a lack of motivation in one's previous life. This element is disappearing as people in Cambodia become more educated, but there is still a fear of human trafficking. The field team may argue that without language, education, and job skills, their deaf family member will have no way to avoid falling victim to sex trafficking. Finally, the team may be allowed to bring a deaf young person to one of the program's hostels or into Phnom Penh. It is time consuming and expensive, and they are not able to serve everyone because of the numbers of people they have encountered. In addition to the deaf program, Maryknoll also has projects for AIDS victims, internationally displaced refugees, village social services, and moral development and education. "We're driving Maryknoll crazy," said Dittmeier, "They're trying to downsize our presence here."[15]

With so many people needing services, the Deaf Development Program had to create a triage system to determine who got to live in the one-hundred-person hostel in Phnom Penh, who moved to the main center from two smaller satellite hostels in the provinces, and who could use the program as commuters. The hostels accommodate only thirty-five or forty people each. For these residential units, the program prioritizes participants who are taking classes, so deaf people outside of Phnom Penh have little chance of using the job training and other deaf develop-

14. Charles Dittmeier, oral history interview by Marlana Portolano, Cambodia via Skype, June 8, 2016.
15. Charles Dittmeier, oral history interview by Marlana Portolano, Cambodia via Skype, June 8, 2016.

ment services. While the staff and number of buildings has grown since 1997, the program continues to need more help as field research teams learn more about living conditions for deaf people in the provinces.

The Western world is clearly at a different stage of Christian missionary history than Asian nations like Cambodia, but church-led development projects in these areas have much to teach the West about the church's mission and the meaning of evangelization in modern life. Evangelical churches have also come to the provinces, driven by religious zeal and earnest fear for the souls of Cambodian people. According to Father Dittmeier, these churches use every means they can to get Cambodians baptized: they may give everyone fifty kilograms of rice and a Bible, then encourage them all to come to Bible study and Sunday worship services. The government tolerates this for a while, until they start baptizing a whole village of Buddhists. After a few months, these missionaries and their Cambodian converts are devastated to find their churches burned to the ground. Maryknoll, on the other hand, is accepted by the Cambodian government as a productive and helpful organization. Cambodia knows Maryknoll is a Christian group, but Maryknoll is not interested in a baptismal "body count." The difference arises from a different interpretation of Jesus' missionary directive in the gospel of Matthew. Evangelical missionaries are motivated by a nineteenth-century interpretation of Matthew 28 as the "Great Commission," where Jesus commands his disciples to "go and make disciples of all nations, baptizing them in the name of the Father and of the Son and of the Holy Spirit, and teaching them to obey everything I have commanded you."[16] Most Catholic missioners in the early stages tend to focus instead on directives earlier in the text, like Matthew 25, where Jesus separates the proverbial sheep from the goats. The souls who get into heaven, the writer of the gospel warns, will be the ones who feed the hungry, give drink to the thirsty, and clothe the naked.

In parsing the differences between Catholic and Evangelical missionary activity, however, there are larger traditions in play than the interpretation of one passage in Scripture. Ultimately, it is a matter of varying philosophical understandings of the human person. From the Catholic perspective, it is imperative that adults come to the faith in a way that enables engagement through reason and dialogue. Mandatory Bible study or attendance at church services are not required to participate in

16. Mt 28:19–20, New International Version.

the Maryknoll health program, so people understand that this group of Christians wants to help them because they are deaf or because they have AIDS—not because Maryknoll want to convert as many Cambodians as possible. Knowledge of the history and tenets of world religions—of Judaism and Islam and Christianity—is part of Maryknoll's basic education program, as is cultural dialogue and discussion at every opportunity. When a new building is opened in Cambodia, Buddhist monks are always expected to do blessings and exorcisms. The Maryknoll priests of the Deaf Development Program use this as an opportunity to follow up in sign language with their own Christian blessings, explanations, and readings of Scripture. If deaf participants become curious about Father Dittmeier's own religious practices and come to daily Mass, he will celebrate Mass in Cambodian sign language, so they are included in the communication of prayers and blessings. Inquiry sessions are the logical next step.[17] From Maryknoll's perspective, it is important to live out the gospel as examples of Christlike love by first enabling participants to be liberated from the physical and cultural conditions that keep them chained in darkness.

Deafness as a Gift from God— Father Cyril Axelrod

Father Cyril Axelrod is a Redemptorist priest who served as a missionary to deaf communities in Africa and Asia for over forty years. As both a wide-ranging evangelist and a culturally deaf man, Father Axelrod represents a host of intersecting traits in Deaf Catholic culture. In many ways, his ministry embodies the whole arc of missionary history in deaf culture from the founding of Catholic schools at the margins of society to the full participation and active contributions of Deaf Catholics in church life. Because he was born with Usher's Syndrome, Axelrod is also, perhaps, the church's only—certainly its most outspoken—deaf-blind priest. As such, he models a challenge for Deaf Catholics to transform "Deaf power" into Deaf Catholic inclusivity and responsibility. Originally from South Africa, he was born into a family with strong Orthodox Jewish roots, so his vocation story is also a conversion story. Throughout his ministry, Father Axelrod has embodied a message he considers im-

17. Charles Dittmeier, oral history interview by Marlana Portolano, Cambodia via Skype, June 8, 2016.

portant for all people: against all odds, he sees his deafness—and his blindness—not as conditions to lament but as gifts from God.

Father Axelrod's vocation story and his own ideas about the "gift of deafness" show not only how disabilities present new opportunities for cultural understanding but also how they can flower into abundant spiritual gifts through faith and a supportive church community. After many years of building deaf missions in South Africa, Singapore, the Philippines, Hong Kong, and Macau, Father Axelrod completed an autobiography (*And the Journey Begins*, 2005). Written through a combination of tactile communication, sign language, and braille, the events of Father Axelrod's life story illustrate the ways in which deafness can foster individual gifts of spirit for deaf people, while at the same time offering a stunning testimony to the human spirit itself. Axelrod's ministry—and the mature spirituality that grew out of it—call to mind *The Cloud of Unknowing*, in which an anonymous fourteenth-century writer counsels, "You are to smite upon the thick cloud of unknowing with a sharp dart of longing love. Do not leave that work for anything that may happen."[18] Like the author of this spiritual classic, an unrelenting energy and longing moved Father Axelrod forward in his mission work. As he put it in an interview for this book, he believes God wanted him to use an inner sense that would enable him to hear, see, and know God without physical sight or sound. A short personal account of these interviews is in the notes for interested readers.[19]

With a supportive family, Axelrod grew up loving his spiritual tradition as an Orthodox Jew. However, when his parents learned that there

18. *The Cloud of Unknowing*, ed. James Walsh and Simon Tugwell (Mahwah, N.J.: Paulist Press, 1981), 131.

19. Cyril Axelrod, interview by Marlana Portolano, London, July 8, 2016. I was privileged to spend three days interviewing Fr. Cyril Axelrod at his small second-level flat in London. We spent the first day negotiating communication styles. I wasn't used to signing hands-on with a deaf-blind person, and Fr. Cyril's ASL was rusty. His assistant Grace (also deaf) used both BSL and South African Sign Language with him. When Fr. Cyril didn't understand what I had tried to express in ASL, Grace would read my lips and clarify to him in BSL. Day 2 was the serious workday. We recorded what he had to say about his many mission fields in Singapore, the Philippines, Hong Kong, South Korea, and Macau. His ASL got clearer throughout the day, and he was always making sure I understood everything (I did, almost invariably). His communication skills are so good that he can converse with multiple people using different sign languages in one conversation, switching without a hitch between them. On the third day, his assistant could not be present, but we were communicating well by then. He prepared and served lunch for me—an experience I found humbling. After discussing his spirituality for a while, he ceased being an interview subject and began truly to minister to me about the nearness of Christ in our lives. Then, he celebrated Mass with me at his kitchen table in ASL. "Lana, this is like the last supper," he told me, glowing in his happiness. Electronic video files of these interviews may be found in both the Redemptorist Archives in Philadelphia and the Deaf Catholic Archives at College of the Holy Cross in Worcester, Mass.

was no Jewish school for the deaf in Johannesburg, they began to send three-year-old Cyril to St. Vincent's School for the Deaf, a hundred-year-old school run by Dominican Sisters.[20] Understanding his parents' distress that their son would attend a Catholic school, the sisters arranged to teach him about his Jewish tradition with the help of other Jews in the community. Although he did not become Catholic in school, the Dominican Sisters impressed him with their belief that he could do anything he put his mind to. At this school, he learned spoken English and the foundations that enabled him to undertake higher education, both in deaf and mainstream institutions. At the same time, his family founded a hostel for Jewish deaf adults, where they could come and learn about their faith in sign language.

During a series of tragedies, including his father's death, Axelrod began to feel a deep desire to serve deaf people through spiritual leadership, but it was clear that he could not become a rabbi through the current educational routes. Distraught, he wandered into a Catholic cathedral one day. There, he saw the light through a window illuminate a crucifix, and immediately he felt an urgent call to use his specific strengths for the good of others. In his mind, he associated this light on the crucifix with flashing lights he experienced before (unbeknownst to him, as a precursor to his blindness). Afterwards, in a conversation about deafness with a Catholic friend, Axelrod asked if Catholic deaf people needed a priest. "Yes," his deaf friend explained, "Deaf people feel excluded and could only really be included if the priest could use sign language." But when Axelrod asked if he thought he could ever become a priest, his friend "looked startled and signed wildly, 'You must be mad! How can an Orthodox Jew become a Catholic priest? Your family would kill you.'"[21] Despite painful opposition from his family and the Jewish community he loved, Axelrod decided he would go to the seminary. He reflects in his autobiography:

To me it did not feel like choosing to give up one faith for another. It was not, as many people thought, that the love and care I had from the sisters at St. Vincent's School had influenced me to give up Judaism. It is true that their warmth was something very important to me and that my parents, by contrast, had found it difficult to overcome the communication barriers. However, this was

20. St. Vincent's School for the Deaf in Johannesburg, South Africa, is named for St. Vincent Ferrer, a fourteenth-century Dominican preacher renowned for restoring hearing to deaf people.
21. Cyril Axelrod, *And the Journey Begins* (London: Douglass MacLean, 2005), 70.

not the reason. In fact, now I realize the choice I struggled with, through the various phases of my conversion, was really not a choice at all. I have within me, even now, an acceptance of both faiths as equal, harmonious, and complementary, something which maybe is beyond the comprehension and understanding of most Jews and Catholics.[22]

The young Axelrod did not see his conversion as a departure but as a continuation into a new form and development of his Judaic faith. In time he would see his new vocation, in his specific drive to serve deaf people, as a way to bring faithnot just to Jewish deaf people but to deaf people all over the world. He was able to attend Gallaudet University for two years, where he learned ASL and improved his English skills while discerning his vocation. Afterwards, he attended St. John Vianney Seminary among hearing peers back in Pretoria, South Africa. Unlike the easy communication he found at Gallaudet, priestly formation was arduous and involved years of isolated study in his room. It was often difficult for hearing peers or his superiors to understand his inability to participate in class as a deaf man, but finally he was able to pass all his tests. In a gesture that related all the significance of his two blended faiths, Father Axelrod's mother not only came to his ordination on November 28, 1970, she took part in the ceremony, offering her only son to the church. In appreciation, his superiors encouraged him to go home on Friday nights for as long as he could to say the Kiddush with her.[23]

Crossing Boundaries in Africa and Asia

After his ordination, Father Axelrod's first assignment was to develop projects and services for deaf people in several parts of Africa, regardless of their race or creed. With a dedicated assistant, Sister Mannes, who was fluent in both English and sign language, he began work in the black community of Soweto just outside Johannesburg. Coming from a background of white South African privilege, Axelrod was surprised, even shocked, by the poverty of this community. People lived five or ten to a room, with an outdoor toilet shared by two families. Once, giving a memorial service for several black people who had died in a protest over inferior education, four white policemen snatched Father Axelrod's prayer

22. Axelrod, *And the Journey Begins*, 72.
23. A blessing over wine performed by the head of a Jewish household at the meal ushering in the Sabbath.

book and threatened to arrest him. Fortunately, they only gave him a warning, but the scare informed him deeply about the exclusion of black people in South Africa.[24]

Once, to continue work on his speech articulation, he made an appointment with the resident speech therapist at the Baragwaneth Hospital in Soweto. There, in a crowded room, he found fifteen black children. Their parents dropped them off for therapy on their way to work and picked them up eight or ten hours later, even though the children had nothing to do after a thirty-minute appointment. Under apartheid, the children could not get on the wait list for the school for the deaf in Soweto. Father Axelrod pleaded with the government and the church for these children who needed the same opportunities he had as a deaf child growing up. Finally, the hospital emptied a storeroom as a place to start a day school, and an envelope from Rome arrived containing a check for sixty thousand rands (then about $25,000). In October of 1978, forty deaf children, ages two to fifteen, began school in this storeroom, which Axelrod had equipped with desks, chairs, and a blackboard. Because the children came from different ethnic groups, parents and administrators argued bitterly about whether Zulu or another native language should be used in addition to various native sign languages. Father Axelrod pleaded with the government to allow English to be used in schools for black deaf children, so they could have at least one language in common. The answer came back in favor of his request, and this little storage room became the first school in which black South African children received instruction in English—an unprecedented historical landmark under apartheid.[25] Today, the Zizwele School is a large educational and technical complex with over five hundred deaf students.

Axelrod's next task was the improvement of a hostel for black deaf people in Hammanskraal, just outside the city of Pretoria. Boboqweng Hostel for the Deaf, whose name meant "Place of Progress," was a residential home for black deaf people seeking work in the city. There Axelrod faced the challenge of learning not only Xhosa, the tribal language of the people in that part of Africa, but also their sign language. The apartheid policies isolated and marginalized black and mixed-race deaf people of different ethnic groups by preventing them from meeting together

24. Axelrod, *And the Journey Begins*, 151.

25. Cyril Axelrod, interview by Marlana Portolano, London, July 8, 2016; Axelrod, *And the Journey Begins*, 141–47.

and sharing a common language. Against all odds, he was able to over-come these social barriers and found a hostel where deaf people could communicate together in both sign language and English. Continuing to break down barriers, in 1987 he established a multiracial association, Deaf Community of Cape Town, under apartheid. In the ministry of the linguistically gifted Father Axelrod, deafness proved to be not an iso-lating condition, as some in his order may have expected, but rather a unifying principle that transcended tribal and even racial differences.[26] Again and again, his weakness was his strength in Christian evangeliza-tion and in broader community building in the spirit of Catholic social justice.

During eighteen years of ministry in Africa, Axelrod travelled widely to small villages all over South Africa, Zimbabwe, Mozambique, Swa-ziland, and Lesotho. He would meet one deaf person from a particular area and send him ahead to sign the news of his visit to other deaf people. When Father Axelrod arrived, he would find a large gathering of deaf black people waiting for him. He would celebrate Mass in sign language and give whatever pastoral support and encouragement he could. In ad-dition to South African Sign Language, Axelrod carried out his mission in Irish Sign Language, Setswana Sign Language, or one of five other native sign languages of the people with whom he worked.

Finally, after starting several African deaf communities and leading retreats across the United States and in European Deaf Catholic com-munities for many years, the Redemptorists tasked Father Axelrod with a mission that would cross even more challenging cultural boundaries: to develop services for deaf people in different countries in Asia, regardless of race or creed. During an exploratory visit to Singapore in 1980, Axel-rod experienced a vibrant Deaf Catholic culture that Redemptorists had helped to develop in the 1970s. He was fascinated to learn about Singa-porean Catholics, whose language and culture was a mix of Chinese and British colonial heritage. He learned, too, about Zen meditation from Brother Casimir, an Australian Redemptorist who had studied with a Benedictine monk in India. When he discovered there was a deep di-vision between Chinese deaf people who were Catholics and those who were Evangelicals, he decided to undertake a peacekeeping address at a joint meeting of the two groups. Their response was positive and strong.

26. Cyril Axelrod, interview by Marlana Portolano, London, July 8, 2016; Axelrod, *And the Journey Begins*, 148–51.

Axelrod was able to persuade them of the benefits of a united Christian Deaf Club, where deaf people could communicate in sign language and organize together while maintaining respect for religious differences.[27] These positive experiences with Southeast Asian Deaf Catholics inspired Axelrod to continue his missions in Asia, this time in China.

In 1988, the Redemptorists assigned Father Axelrod to work in Hong Kong, where he stayed with Maryknoll missionaries for the first year, including Charles Dittmeier and others. Father Michael McKeiran, who had returned to China after the Communists deported him in 1950, tutored him in Chinese culture, and he studied Cantonese, a very difficult language for a Western deaf man. Despite his struggles with spoken Cantonese, Axelrod loved working with the adult deaf community connected to the Canossian School for the Deaf, and he and Father Dittmeier took many mission trips around Asia, to the Philippines and Taiwan. When he visited Macau, however, he knew he had found a new home for his ministry.

Father Axelrod was especially drawn to the diversity of Macau, with its combination of Portuguese and Chinese culture, as well as its many languages, races, and religions (Christians being a small minority). This complex richness of cultural diversity, combined with widespread poverty, suggested the possibility of cultural divisions he might bridge by developing a new deaf community. The country had no specialist services for deaf people yet in place. So, in 1989, Bishop Domingo Lam, the first Chinese bishop of Macau, accepted his ministry, and Father Axelrod began work there in the center for disabled people, a place where deaf people were served along with blind and physically and mentally handicapped individuals. Under the center's director, a Maryknoll sister from the United States, he developed a small hearing and speech clinic. He had to learn how to communicate with the children, set up a training program, find financial support, hire teachers, and buy equipment; however, when the center's director was recalled to America, his deaf center lost its financial support because the government of Macau considered it an educational facility rather than a social service. He soldiered on with help from Caritas, the Catholic relief and social services organization. By 1991, he had two different deaf centers, each in a room so small it could barely accommodate the dozens of deaf children and adults who

27. Cyril Axelrod, interview by Marlana Portolano, London, July 8, 2016; Axelrod, *And the Journey Begins*, 161–67.

attended, and he had trained a Macau-born speech therapist, teachers, and other staff members. At the end of that year, he negotiated with the government's Social Welfare Department for larger rooms, and a Portuguese lawyer helped him write a constitution for the Macau Deaf Association: The Kai Chung Centre for the Deaf was born.[28]

Father Axelrod worked with the deaf people of Macau, regularly taking mission trips back to the Philippines and Hong Kong, until Portugal returned governance to the Chinese Republic in 1999. Today, the Macau Deaf Association remains an active hub of deaf life in Macau, where it continues to promote and preserve Macau Sign Language, a derivate of Hong Kong Sign Language.[29] Although sign language in Macau certainly received a boost through the ministry of Father Axelrod as their deaf, signing founder, the Macau government requires oralist education and the exclusion of signs in public education. Without continued deaf leadership in the preservation of sign language, this deaf heritage is slipping away. As a result, in 2019 Macau Sign Language has only two hundred adult users and is once again endangered, according to the SOAS University of London's video archive of Endangered Languages.[30]

By the time Father Axelrod left Macau, his Usher's Syndrome had progressed, and his sight had deteriorated to just 3 percent of the normal field of vision. Leaving the Deaf Association in Macau to be self-governing under their new Chinese government, Father Axelrod moved to London, where his field of vision grew narrower and narrower, until he could no longer read or see faces. Understandably, he was devastated. During this dark night, he began to learn how to live as a deaf-blind man: to distinguish streetlamps from telephone poles with a cane and find every item in the kitchen by touch; how to read Braille and how to use the rail system as a blind person. Slowly, he began to feel comfortable with his new skills, even rediscovering his Hebrew through braille. He also began to draw on daily meditative prayer practices he had learned in from Father Casimir in Singapore; in his words, "I began to 'feel' blindness in a new way as the true touch of God upon my soul. I began to make blindness my friend. I could see that I was beginning to gain a new kind of knowledge and understanding and wisdom that I could, in turn, give

28. Axelrod, *And the Journey Begins*, 169–177.

29. Current activities of the Macau Deaf Association are listed on their website, https://mda .org.mo/.

30. "Macau Sign Language," Endangered Language Archive, SOAS University of London, London, England, retrieved January 24, 2019, https://elar.soas.ac.uk/Collection/MPI1029748.

to the world."[31] At that opportune moment in 2001, he received word that he had been chosen to receive an honorary doctorate from Gallaudet University. That trip, as well as the faith others had in him, made him realize once again that what he thought were insurmountable obstacles could be opportunities to evangelize others in new ways. In 2015, Father Axelrod was awarded an Order of the British Empire for his work, and he continues to serve the deaf and deaf-blind communities in London and around the world today at every opportunity.

The Future of Deaf Ministries in Asia and Africa

The three "apostles of deaf ministry" in Asia described in this chapter—Fathers Harry Stocks, Charles Dittmeier, and Cyril Axelrod—are greatly esteemed by the deaf communities they helped to establish. Largely because of devoted, lifelong missionaries like these, there are strong twenty-first-century Deaf Catholic communities in several countries in Southeast Asia and Africa. With their visible language of signs and their ability to lift up the lives and spirits of deaf people who might otherwise be isolated and lacking in opportunities, these Catholic communities will certainly be an inspiration to the broader church as it continues its ongoing mission in Asia. Asian Deaf Catholic associations are particularly active in the Philippines, Singapore, and South Korea, where Catholicism is accepted, and Deaf Catholic leadership has been especially strong. Members of several national associations of Asian Deaf Catholics meet for fellowship, liturgy, and discussion of the challenges to integrating deaf people in church life. Father Harry Stocks first organized these conferences in the 1970s, but the number of participants in recent deaf-led events is much larger. In 2015, Thailand hosted the International Asian Deaf Conference in Bangkok, where over one hundred participants gathered from Thailand, Cambodia, India, Indonesia, Japan, South Korea, Laos, Macau, Hong Kong, the Philippines, Malaysia, Singapore, and Sri Lanka, as well as the United Kingdom and United States In 2018, the Philippines hosted the International Asian Deaf Catholic Conference in Tagaytay City with similar participants and themes, and Singapore will play host in 2020. From pioneering apostles to large deaf-run

31. Axelrod, *And the Journey Begins*, 195.

international associations, the pattern of deaf evangelization in Asia is remarkably similar to the missionary history of Deaf Catholics in Europe and the United States. While there will be cultural and financial challenges, the future looks bright and full of hope for both the larger deaf communities and the growing Catholic populations in these countries.

As in the history of mission activity in the West, one sign of spiritual health for recently evangelized people is participation in the full range of the church's sacraments—including priestly vocations from the group itself. True to this pattern, communities of Deaf Catholic Asians have benefitted greatly from the leadership of recently ordained deaf priests. On July 6, 2007, Cardinal Cheong Jin-Suk of Seoul, South Korea, ordained the first culturally deaf priest in Asia, Father Benedict Min-Seo Park. Born in 1965, Father Min-Seo Park lost his hearing at the age of two. At his school for the deaf he met Father Michael Cheong-Soon-o, to whom he expressed his long-held desire to become a priest. Because there were no accommodations for deaf students at South Korean seminaries, Park studied at Gallaudet University and St. Joseph's Seminary in New York. While in the United States, he met Father Thomas Coughlin, the first deaf priest in the United States, who became his spiritual director.[32] Since 2006, he has been pastor of the growing Catholic Church for the Deaf in Seoul, where he celebrates Mass in Korean Sign Language. The Catholic Church for the Deaf occupied a building owned by the Missionary Benedictine sisters of Tutzing, but the growing number of Mass attendees after Father Min-Seo Park's appointment forced the church to seek a larger space. In 2020, the community dedicated a new church building in Seoul, a sacred space especially designed for Deaf Catholic worship.

In 2015, a second deaf Asian priest, Friar Rowland Yeo, became the first Deaf Franciscan and the first Deaf Catholic priest in Singapore. Born deaf in 1957, Friar Rowland attended mainstream schools until secondary school, when he transferred to the Vocational Institute for the Handicapped. There, he learned sign language and felt "a new world opening to him." Born into a Buddhist family, he encountered the Catholic faith at age eleven, when he attended Mass with an aunt who was a Catholic. Later, in 1976, Australian Redemptorist Father Gasper catechized him by writing lessons back and forth, baptizing Rowland two years later at the age of twenty-one. While in the United States attending

32. "First Deaf-Mute Priest Ordained in Asia," *Catholic News Agency*, July 20, 2007.

a Catholic retreat, he met Father Thomas Coughlin, who told him there was a need for priests fluent in sign language. Coughlin found sponsorship for his studies at Gallaudet University, and in 1997, Yeo joined the Franciscan friars. He attended St. Joseph's Seminary in Yonkers, New York, before working with the deaf community at St. Elizabeth's Church in Manhattan and doing mission work with deaf children in Peru. Since 2005, he has been assigned to the Church of St. Mary of the Angels in Singapore, where he celebrates Mass in Singaporean Sign Language on Sundays.[33] A third vocation in Asia is Dong Jun Kim, a culturally deaf Jesuit who hopes to become a priest after completing his theology studies in South Korea.

Admittedly, this chapter says little about Deaf Catholics in Africa, except for the ministry of Father Cyril Axelrod (a white South African). There is still immense work to be done in Africa, beginning with gathering deaf children and adults for education, social services, and evangelization. Before they can become a people of God, those who are deaf must first be recognized as a people at all, as part of a human community in possession of the most basic attributes of self-awareness, language, and culture. As we look to the future of Deaf Catholics in Africa, one person who deserves special mention for helping to enculturate young deaf Africans in this way is Rhanna Evetts from Texas.

After an intense conversion and baptism into the Catholic faith at age eighteen, and with only high school ASL classes for training, Rhanna turned to missionary work at a school for the deaf in Kampala, Uganda. Her first day of school there was also the first day for a girl two years younger than Rhanna, who had never leaned a language. This lit a fire in Rhanna's heart. At the age of twenty-one, she travelled to a village in northern Uganda where hundreds of deaf children were receiving no services or education, and she simply asked the local bishop if she could teach them in an old religious education building. He told her to go ahead, and in February 2017, St. Francis de Sales School for the Deaf opened its doors. By 2018, there were fifty students ages three to thirteen, and that number was still growing; by 2019, many of the children had acquired sign language and had received their First Communion.[34] The

33. Interview by Audrey Seah, Notre Dame University, Franciscan Monastery, Singapore, January 18, 2017.
34. "God Did This: How a 22-Year-Old Texan Began a Catholic School for Uganda's Deaf Children," Archdiocese of San Antonio, accessed January 25, 2018, https://www.archsa.org/blog/god-did-this-how-a-22-year-old-texan-began-a-catholic-school-for-ugandas-de.

challenges to Rhanna's ministry are profound, not least because of cultural differences in a place where she is the only white—and female—Westerner, but the astounding and transformative gains are nothing short of grace.

Jesus' own saving ministry, reaching out to disabled and impoverished individuals and including them in the fabric of society is, after all, the gospel message. Following his example, the church can only continue to lift up those who are impoverished and isolated, in this case deaf people in nations where sign language—and evangelization—are still waiting to unfold in history.

CHAPTER 14

The Deaf-World Apostolate

From Jesus' biblical encounter with the deaf man to the development of sign languages across the globe, Deaf Christians have proven themselves a long-suffering group to whom the church might say, along with the First Epistle of Peter, "Once you were no people but now you are God's people" (1 Pt 2:10). In the twenty-first century, the church continues to discern the meaning of her ongoing mission of evangelization, including her relationship to culturally deaf people as individuals and as a collective group. A common idiom in many sign languages across the globe enables people who are meeting for the first time to share that they are both deaf. "Deaf-same," translated into English, means that no matter what nationality or larger cultural group a deaf person was born into, deafness itself transcends those differences with similarity of experiences and a common way of perceiving the world through sight and touch. When deaf culture combines with Catholicism, Deaf Catholics have more in common with other Deaf Catholics around the world than they do with people in their local communities who are Catholic but hearing or deaf but non-Christian.

International organizations and changing communication technologies are strengthening ties between geographically dispersed Christians, and Deaf Catholics are no exception to this trend. The church is now able to witness the confident vitality, strong heritage, and persistent mission activity of Deaf Catholics among people whose native or only fluent language is a signed language. In the West, many (but certainly not all) communities of Deaf Catholics have reached the last stages of a "missionary transformation" and are now giving back through evangelization to other communities and to the broader church. By sharing the history and heritage described in this book, Deaf Catholics have successfully cultivated spiritual vocations among deaf and hearing people who are part of their language community—the pastoral workers, interpreters, friends, and family members who learn sign language. Today in the West, culturally deaf individuals often lead centers of deaf ministry and serve as role models for this population. With their strong Catholic identity and native sign language, these leaders set high standards for other Christians, both deaf and hearing, who continue to serve deaf people by bringing them out of the margins of society and into the light of the church. As in the rest of the modern world, secularization and cultural fragmentation encroaches on Christian values in deaf culture today. Unfortunately, as preceding chapters illustrate, a history of social isolation and cultural prejudice has frequently contributed to deaf people's sense of alienation from the church. Many deaf people continue to see the church as a hearing institution, either one that does not understand deafness or one that is not compatible with deaf culture.

Yet the Deaf Catholic community itself is working to overcome these challenges with hope, faith, and solidarity. New efforts to evangelize deaf people and deaf culture are bearing fruit, both in areas where people have fallen away from the church and in countries where Christian teachings are not widely known. Based on the concept of "Deaf-same," established Deaf Catholic communities have developed international mission programs of their own. In the Eastern hemisphere, Asian missions thrive, such as the Deaf Development Center in Cambodia (described in chapter 13); in the Western hemisphere, groups such as the Deaf Catholic Youth Initiative for the Americas (described later in this chapter) regularly engage in foreign missions to underserved deaf populations. Locally and internationally, the larger Deaf Catholic community is becoming more visible as an essential part of the Body of Christ. In many new ways, Deaf Catholics engage in evangelization that makes them role models for the rest of the church. However, there is still much to be done, both in established deaf ministries and in underdeveloped regions of the world. The church has only begun to recognize that deaf people are "a people" needing and engaged in evangelization and that the church should, therefore, protect their history and religious practices—not only as social justice for people at the margins but as preservation of an important embodiment of Catholic heritage and culture. This chapter suggests several ways to ensure that the church never again forgets the needs and unique gifts of deaf people.

Catholicism and the Deaf World

The first notable historical use of the term "Deaf-World" to describe all deaf people was in the proceedings of the World Congress of the Deaf in Chicago as part of the 1893 World's Columbian Exposition. Approximately one thousand deaf people attended—not only from Canada and the United States but also from France, England, Ireland, Germany, Spain, Sweden, and Norway. In addition to reports from various national associations of deaf people, there were eight presentations on deaf missions, most of them Protestant. "Who would have dreamed one hundred years ago that this could be possible?" one participant mused, "Then the deaf were uneducated and widely scattered, unknown to each other; their influence, of course, was *nil*."[1]

Over one hundred years later, today's World Federation of the Deaf is still using the signed term "Deaf-World" to describe the seventy million people it claims to represent worldwide, 80 percent of whom live in developing countries. One hundred and thirty national deaf organizations are members. As the Deaf-World began to organize in an international body of people identifying with each other as "Deaf-same," the Catholic Church, too, began to recognize the Deaf-World as a network of related minority groups facing similar problems in every nation. For the church, this recognition was a major step towards greater understanding of deaf people as a language minority to serve through cultural acceptance and celebration of their languages and way of life. In 1955, His Holiness Pope Pius XII sent a message to the Third World Congress of the Deaf in Wiesbaden, Germany, expressing his devotion to deaf persons of the whole world and sending his best wishes. In 1966, Pope Paul VI gave an address to participants of the World Federation of the Deaf in Rome. He extended his prayerful greeting, saying, "We are happy to welcome you who have come from almost all the countries of the world.... We can only applaud your beautiful initiative, whose ultimate goal is the in-

1. *Proceedings of the World Congress of the Deaf and the Fourth Convention of the American Association of the Deaf* (Chicago: 1893), 10.

dividual and collective promotion of a class of men and women who ...
were often doomed to an existence that was marginal to the bosom of the
great human family."[2]

A third and especially vehement papal address took place during a
papal audience at the 1987 World Federation of the Deaf conference, entitled "One World—One Responsibility." Pope John Paul II said of deaf
ministry, "In this field it can certainly never be claimed that enough has
been done ... it must in fact be considered one of the important aspects
of that 'preferential option for the poor' which is so characteristic of the
gospel mission." Because of the specificity of the pope's exhortations on
deaf ministry, it is worth quoting this address at length:

Fraternal charity towards the non-hearing has given rise to an interesting collaboration, in Christ's name, among Christians of different confessions. This is
undoubtedly an ecumenical activity of great value. Still, in the Christian world
it is necessary to do more.... This endeavor, as well as the efforts expended in
assisting other human disabilities, is indissolubly linked to the witness on behalf
of man's salvation and redemption.... May those who feel this interest as a true
divine vocation, an urgent call of the will of God, be ever more numerous. In this
way, the human network of mediation between the world of the non-hearing
and the vaster body of society would be strengthened. Society, then, which has
so often been indifferent and alienating, could instead, in its structures and its
laws, open itself to and welcome the presence and contribution of these persons
to realize fully their specific human, social, cultural, and spiritual qualities.[3]

The needs and hopes of Deaf Christians today still ring true in this appeal for full inclusion and preferential treatment of deaf people in the
church. In these words, the Holy Father holds up the meaningfulness
of serving deaf individuals and communities in the context of Christ's
mission for the human family. Even thirty years later, the Holy Father's
appeal to reach out to deaf people—to recognize their often-ignored
gifts in society and in the church—reads as a call to action. That he understood deaf ministry as a special kind of vocation is also instructive for
the church's continued evangelization.

In some interesting ways, the international character of cultural deaf-

2. Pope Paul VI, "Address to the World Federation of the Deaf," Vatican City, September 24,
1966; Translated from French and issued by the National Catholic Welfare Conference, October 13,
1966; Deaf Catholic Archives, College of the Holy Cross, Worcester, Mass.
3. Pope John Paul II, "Address to the World Federation of the Deaf," February 21, 1987, translation in *L'Osservatore Romano*, no. 9 (March 2, 1987), Deaf Catholic Archives, College of the Holy
Cross, Worcester, Mass.

ness today resembles the international character of the Catholic Church in the modern world. Like cultural deafness, Catholicism is an identity that transcends the confines of nationality; and like Catholicism, the Deaf World is *in* the world but not *of* the world (at least, not the mainstream hearing world). With both deafness and Catholicism in common, Deaf Catholics from every nation have a doubly strong shared identity. For the Catholic Church and her hierarchy of leadership, this convergence of Deaf and Catholic cultures has led to the development of international associations of Deaf Catholics and those who work with deaf communities as minority language groups.

The Church's Global Mission and International Deaf Ministry

The International Catholic Deaf Association (ICDA), whose 1949 founding is described in chapter 8, was the first international association for the Deaf Catholics community. By the 1970s and 1980s, professional associations and organizations for pastoral work with deaf people had formed in most Western nations. Clergy and pastoral workers organized associations such as the National Catholic Office for the Deaf in the United States and the Catholic Deaf Association in England to facilitate professional development. Members of these associations began to attend each other's meetings, contributing to the international character of deaf ministry as an academic and professional interest (some would say vocation). Some of these professionals took part in a new kind of international organization—one that supported standards for ministry, religious education, and ecclesiastical attention to deaf people in the life of the church worldwide.

The International Catholic Foundation for the Service of Deaf Persons (ICF) first met in 1971 in Dublin, Ireland, under the direction of Mother Nicolas Giffey, OP. The purpose of the first conference was to discuss international trends in the religious education of deaf people. Two hundred delegates attended this conference, including bishops, priests, psychologists, social workers, and teachers of deaf children. Among the countries represented were South Africa, Australia, England, Germany, Ireland, the Netherlands, and the United States. These participants came together because they recognized an unmet need in the Catholic apostolate common to all these countries, as well as in nations with no organized representation for deaf people. The delegates expressed concern not only for the education of deaf children but also for the broader community of adult Deaf Catholics resulting from Catholic education with no follow-up for life as a practicing Catholic. Their founding documents laid out the purpose of the foundation—to make people aware of the difficult situation of the deaf person in the church and to provide publications and teaching aids for all those involved in the religious education of deaf people. It also sought to assist with deaf education training programs, especially in regions that have no resources.

The report of the 1971 Dublin Conference resulted in four resolutions concerning deaf people in the life of the Church:

1. To appeal to each nation's Catholic Conference of Bishops for more attention to deaf people and their spiritual needs.

2. That one bishop in each country should have responsibility for the spiritual welfare of deaf people.

3. That every diocese treats the spiritual needs of the deaf community as an ongoing missionary need.

4. That liturgical participation should involve special consideration for deaf people because of the complex and pervasive isolation caused by deafness.[4]

The ICF's intention to create a church-wide administrative and pastoral structure was evident from its inception, and the organization has had continuous episcopal representation from bishops. Archbishop Patrick Kelly of Liverpool was among the founding members, and Bishop Martin Holley of Memphis, Tennessee, further bolstered episcopal representation on the board of directors. As North American and European deaf culture continued to strengthen and develop in the 1990s, pastoral workers and church leaders who were deaf joined the foundation's board.

The ICF supports pastoral care, education, and religious formation for Deaf Catholics, particularly those who use sign languages—in other words, those who are culturally deaf. To do this, the foundation promotes international gatherings, collaborates with organizations sharing their mission, and serves as a resource for the spiritual formation of deaf people. The foundation aims to make the church more aware of the very presence of deaf people and to draw attention to their unique gifts and charisms that enrich the whole church. Since 1971, the foundation has hosted over fifteen international conferences in eleven different nations.

4. "Our History," International Catholic Foundation for the Service of Deaf Persons, https://icfdeafservice.org/our-history.

Conference topics have reflected the patterns of change and development that have taken place over the course of Deaf Catholic history, from the early stages of schools and missionary work to the encouragement of leadership from within the Deaf Catholic community. The theme of the first conference was the religious education of deaf people, and the second, in 1980, focused on sacramental life, particularly the Eucharist. Conferences in the 1980s and 1990s moved increasingly toward a clear vision of deaf communities as language groups, with chaplains and educators exploring working models of deaf culture and religious formation in a variety of pastoral settings. Early twentieth-first century conferences reflected the global nature of the Church's mission in the new century. While deaf ministries in the West continue to need support and expansion, now there is also urgent Deaf Catholic mission work in large parts of Asia and Africa.

Because the Deaf-World is globally dispersed and growing, yet often misunderstood and sorely neglected, the ICF has often struggled financially as its work expanded to meet global demands. The foundation does the work of an active advisory body to archdioceses worldwide and to the Vatican itself. However, it receives no financial support from Catholic Church authorities at any level. Its funding relies heavily on personal grants and donations and the dedication of lay pastoral workers, volunteers, and clergy who see the urgency of ministry with deaf people. In the early years, there was financial support from the Christian Brothers in Brussels, leading to some of the most focused cultural studies and advocacy work on behalf of Deaf Catholics since the organization's inception. Academic work on Deaf Catholic ministries thrived in the Netherlands during these years. Marcel Broesterhuizen, a sociologist with a specialty in the social-psychological development of deaf people, was named Chair for Pastoral Ministry with the Deaf in the Faculty of Theology and Religious Studies at the University of Leuven, a position created through a partnership between the University of Leuven and the ICF. The most visible activity of the ICF, however, has been its international conferences, which increasingly serve not only as professional development for Catholics in deaf ministry from all nations—but also as pilgrimages for Catholics in the Deaf-World.

Vatican Recommendations Left in Limbo

The 2008 ICF Conference, which took place in Rome, was the first ICF event promoted simultaneously as a professional gathering and a pilgrimage for Deaf Catholics. Father Joseph Mulcrone, an American priest who has served in deaf ministry in the Archdiocese of Chicago since 1977, and Archbishop Patrick Kelly of Liverpool, ICF board member and episcopal moderator for the British and Irish deaf community, planned and developed the program, entitled "Many Languages, One Faith: The Call to Discipleship in the Global Deaf Community." More than one thousand deaf people and pastoral workers made this pilgrimage to the Vatican and attended presentations on discipleship in the deaf communities of England, Ireland, Germany, Mexico, South Africa, South Korea, and the United States. During an outdoor audience with Pope Benedict XVI, the Vatican permitted sign language interpreters on the St. Peter's Square jumbo screens for the first time—a remarkable and memorable witness for all to see. A special guest of the conference, one who would prove instrumental in the Vatican's recognition of Deaf Catholics as a worldwide apostolate, was Bishop José Luis Redrado Marchite, secretary of the Pontifical Council for Pastoral Assistance to Healthcare Workers.

Bishop Redrado gave a keynote address on discipleship, but instead of leaving after his talk, he stayed to listen to the many deaf priests, deacons, and laypersons discussing their experience of being deaf in the church. Bishop Redrado and his soon-to-be successor as secretary of the Pontifical Council, Archbishop Zigmut Zimowski, came away from the 2008 ICF Conference with a sense that the Vatican needed to do something. Their eyes were opened to the suffering of deaf people caused by linguistic exclusion from church gatherings, and they saw how the invisibility (and inaudibility) of deafness perpetuated deaf people's exclusion in a hearing, speaking world. Soon after, Bishop Redrado determined that the 2009 Pontifical Conference on Health Care would be about "The Deaf Person in the Life of the Church." He invited the ICF to guide the event's development and to bring pastoral workers and Deaf Catholic lay people to present to the pontifical conference.

The 2009 event took place in the Vatican's New Synod Hall: over six hundred laypeople and clergy from all over the world crowded into a space meant to hold only five hundred. The conference started out much like other council gatherings geared toward scientific research and

THE APOSTOLATE   275

medical practices. Prominent audiologists and physicians talked about
hearing aid technology and the psychological impact of deafness and
"hearing loss."[5] Then, in a break from the detached and professional tone
of the conference, Archbishop Kelly and Archbishop Zimowski (by then
president of the council) had several Deaf Catholics witness about their
own lived experience in the life of the church. Young families from Italy
and lay professionals working with deaf people in Mexico, Ireland, and
the United States had an opportunity to tell their stories in person at the
Vatican. With the clarity of lived experience, presenters made their presence known as equals in importance and dignity in the body of Christ.

This had never happened at a meeting of the highly scientific and
decorous council. At all twenty-three preceding conferences, bishops
and archbishops sat in the front row, according to rank, but for the
twenty-fourth, they sat behind women and men serving as interpreters.
To accommodate deaf presenters and international deaf participants, interpreters were projected onto large screens as they translated into four
different national sign languages. Deaf conference goers sat in regional
groups with their own interpreters, listening or watching and simultaneously translating into their respective sign languages. In total, participants communicated in nineteen sign languages at the Vatican during the
three-day event, each as visual and meaningful as tongues of flame during
the multilingual miracle of Pentecost. For deaf people in attendance, it
was a time to demonstrate the visual-gestural nature of signed languages as true languages. For bishops, the experience was nothing short of
countercultural: it transcended the high decorum of Vatican events and
opened them to the traditional, person-centered ways of communicating
in deaf culture. They were deeply moved, and several members of the
Pontifical Council commented that it was the most inspiring conference
they had ever attended.[6]

The conference concluded as Pope Benedict XVI addressed participants in the Apostolic Palace's Clementine Hall surrounded by Renaissance frescoes of the virtues and the "Allegory of Art and Science." First,
the Holy Father recounted the iconic encounter in Mark 7, emphasizing
the direct, interpersonal communication between Jesus and the deaf

5. Pontifical Council for Health Care Workers, "Ephphatha! The Deaf Person in the Life of the
Church," Proceedings of the XXIV International Conference for the Pontifical Council of Health
Care Workers, Vatican City (November 19–21, 2009).

6. Mary O'Meara, executive director, Office of Special Needs Ministries, interview by Marlana
Portolano, Landover, Maryland, December 14, 2016.

man: "The Lord showed the deaf man his concrete concern, drew him aside from the confusion of the crowd, made him feel his closeness and understanding by several gestures full of meaning.... He then invited him to turn his interior gaze, that of his heart, together with him to the heavenly Father. Finally, he healed him and restored him to his family, to his people." In his comments on the passage, the pope chose not to discuss the medical repercussions of deafness and its treatment but, rather, the spiritual meaning of deafness for the individual and for the church:

Jesus does not only heal physical deafness but points out that there is another form of deafness of which humanity must be cured, indeed, from which it must be saved: it is deafness of the spirit, which raises ever higher barriers against the voice of God and that of one's neighbor, especially the cry for help of the lowliest and the suffering, and closes the human being in profound and ruinous selfishness.... we can see in this "sign" Jesus' ardent desire to overcome man's loneliness and incommunicability created by selfishness, in order to bring about a "new humanity."[7]

Reflecting on this enlightened address, members of the international Deaf Catholic community had great hopes that the 2009 Pontifical Council conference would usher in a time of deep listening and loving communication between the Vatican and deaf people, just as Jesus listened to and then restored the deaf man to the people of his community.

After these unusual presentations at the 2009 Pontifical Conference, with expert advice from veteran pastoral workers in the deaf community, the Pontifical Council for Health Care developed clear recommendations to promote and strengthen the church's ministry with deaf people, which they then published to every conference of Catholic bishops in the world. These recommendations sent a strong message about the deeply harmful (if inadvertent) exclusion of deaf people from the life of the church. The council advised that, because deaf people form language minorities in each nation, deafness is different from other physical disabilities in faith and religious practice. The council further emphasized the unique nature of deaf people in each nation as a social group with forms of communication that are natural to their range of human senses. To achieve full integration of deaf people into the life of the church, the Council proposed:

7. His Holiness Benedict XVI, Address, XXIV International Conference, Pontifical Council for Health Care Workers, November 20, 2009, https://w2.vatican.va/content/benedict-xvi/en/speeches/2009/november/documents/hf_ben-xvi_spe_20091120_operatori-sanitari.html.

1. That there should be a central office of the church at national levels which attends to and coordinates pastoral care for deaf people.

2. That every diocese should have at least one priest with the necessary skills and training for the sacraments (reconciliation in particular), the liturgy, and catechesis in the deaf community.

3. That there should be a course for seminarians on this special type of pastoral care and that seminarians interested in sign language should increase their knowledge of it.

4. That bishops pay greater attention to the needs of deaf people, ensuring there is space in their diocesan programs for catechesis and pastoral care for and with deaf people, and that some deaf people should also work in this pastoral care group.

5. That dioceses with large cities should identify a church or parish where the liturgy allows active participation of people with hearing problems.

6. That deaf people and their families should receive special attention in the planning of parish and diocesan pastoral care.

7. That there should be a website where deaf people can follow Mass and homilies in signed languages and learn about ethical questions of political relevance.

8. That deaf people should have opportunities to take courses on religion organized on the diocesan level.

9. That places of liturgy should use video screens [and printed text] to meet the needs of deaf people who do not know sign language.

10. That, at the national level, there should be structures for the promotion of vocations and formation of deaf candidates for religious and priestly life.

11. That dioceses should have a register of certified interpreters who work in churches.

12. That the church should advocate removal of every obstacle to full social integration of deaf people through the implementation of laws, conventions, and protocols designed to include deaf people in educational and work environments, so that they can contribute at all levels, according to each person's talents and capacities, to the good of society.[8]

The Holy See approved these recommendations and, as a matter of procedure, instructed the bishops in each country to follow up with a letter of instruction to all dioceses under their care.

However, not all recommendations from the Vatican reach their intended audience, and in some cases the audience is not yet prepared to listen. In many nations, including the United States, the Conference of

8. Pontifical Council for Health Care Workers, Final Recommendations, "Ephphatha! The Deaf Person in the Life of the Church." Items on this list were edited for clarity.

Bishops never sent a letter addressing the special needs of Deaf Catholics as a language minority to each local diocese. In 2017, the United States bishops approved new guidelines for the celebration of the sacraments with "persons with disabilities." These guidelines included some significant developments, including a statement that "Full accessibility should be the goal for every parish, and these adaptations are to be an ordinary part of the liturgical life of the parish."[9] While sacramental preparation, catechism, and the Eucharist in sign language are not mentioned, the guidelines do specifically indicate that Deaf Catholics should have an opportunity to attend the sacrament of reconciliation in sign language with a priest who signs or through an interpreter or, if these are unavailable, through writing or electronic communication (to be destroyed or returned to the penitent afterward). The 2017 guidelines also recognize that Deaf Catholics should have the opportunity to express matrimonial consent in sign language and that they may contract marriage with the assistance of a sign language interpreter. However, the language-based needs of culturally deaf individuals do not easily fit into the category of accommodations for persons with disabilities. Many of the services recommended by the 2009 Pontifical Council for Health Care are identical to services provided by ministries for any language group.

As we look to the future, full implementation of the 2009 Pontifical Council recommendations remains to be seen. Sadly, when Bishop Zimowski died in July of 2016, the Vatican lost one of its most visible advocates for a unified, worldwide deaf apostolate. Soon after his death, the Vatican announced that the Dicastery for Promoting Integral Human Development would assume the work of the Council on Health Care. Pope Francis gave this new administrative body responsibility for issues regarding people who are sick, excluded, marginalized, unemployed, or imprisoned, as well as migrants and victims of armed conflict, natural disasters, and all forms of slavery and torture. Broadening the focus from medical issues to the promotion of justice and peace as part of pastoral care seems promising and appropriate for the Deaf Catholic community as a language minority and cultural group. The church continues to deepen her commitment to people on the margins of society, but currently the ICF is the most active international Catholic organization

9. United States Conference of Catholic Bishops, "Guidelines for the Celebration of the Sacraments with Persons with Disabilities," rev. June 15, 2017, http://www.usccb.org/about/divine-worship/policies/guidelines-sacraments-persons-with-disabilities.cfm.

doing this work for deaf people—and the ICF struggles to stay visible to Vatican officials. Financial difficulties threaten the ICF's ongoing efforts to bring pastoral workers and Deaf Catholics together for more international conferences. After the 2008 ICF Conference and international pilgrimage to Rome, there was a concern that hosting sites might not be available for future conferences. The innovative solution to this problem was to incorporate the ICF into the World Eucharistic Congress as a Deaf Track of that major event. This combination event happened for the first time in Dublin in 2012. The second ICF Deaf Track of the World Eucharistic Conference took place in the Philippine city of Cebu in 2016.

As a result of ICF's conference in Mexico City in 2000, a new kind of international Deaf Catholic organization came forward to keep marginalized Deaf Catholics and their needs visible in the larger church. The Deaf Catholic Youth Initiative for the Americas (DCYIA) formed as a response to the needs of deaf young people in Mexico and Central and South America, especially those from impoverished areas. During the ICF's year 2000 conference in Mexico, a group of priests and pastoral workers in the international Deaf Catholic community focused their attention on the needs of deaf youth in Latin America. In these countries, the lives of Deaf Catholics are much more precarious than in most of North America and Europe. Sign language services are not widespread: few dioceses offer signed sacraments or religious education for deaf young people, and almost no one pays for interpreters for Mass. At their biannual, weeklong workshops, which have taken place since 2002 in different locations including Guatemala and the Mexican Deaf Catholic communities of Valle de Bravo, San Luis Potosi, Oaxaca, Mexico City, and (in 2020) in Chile, participants found time and again that, while sharing their lived experience, deaf young people disclose physical and sexual abuse. DCYIA offers a safe environment for marginalized young people to discuss this abuse in a wider community of understanding. Through their example, they offer the hope of spiritual healing in the church for deaf individuals and other vulnerable people who have suffered abuse.

During these encounters with deaf youth, DCYIA resolved to bring the deaf community face to face with the Holy Father and the Vatican, reminding the church once more of the largely unmet 2009 recommendations for the pastoral care of Deaf Catholics. Led by Father Joseph

Mulcrone in commemoration of the 2008 ICF pilgrimage to Rome, DCYIA completed a ten-year anniversary pilgrimage to Rome in 2018. A group of volunteers in Mexico worked full time for six months, putting together materials before the event. On June 25, 2018, in the chapel of the Congregation for the Doctrine of the Faith, Father Shawn Carey, a deaf priest from Boston, celebrated Mass in sign language with participants from Germany (including a deaf deacon and a deaf-blind deacon), Father Charlie Dittmeier of the Deaf Development Program in Cambodia, and deaf and hearing people from the United States, Mexico, Panama, Guatemala, Ukraine, and Italy. In many cases, it was a reunion of friends and colleagues who had not seen each other in years, as they had been working in support of Deaf Catholics in different parts of the world. The following day, Archbishop Paul Gallagher, secretary for relations with states for the Vatican, celebrated Mass in St. Peter's Basilica in Rome, accompanied by interpreters in five different sign languages—an eye-opening event and a visible inspiration to many present who had never attended a Mass incorporating sign language.

On June 27, 2018, the DCYIA pilgrims gathered together with members of the Special Olympics in Rome to celebrate the organization's fiftieth anniversary. Pope Francis arrived, greeting members of DCYIA and the Special Olympics and spending time with each of them individually. Young deaf people, many from poor backgrounds, were able to meet the pope with sign language interpreters on either side of him and to converse with him one on one. For many in the Deaf Catholic community, this was the very image of Jesus communicating with the deaf man in Mark 7. Images of Pope Francis joyfully using sign language with Deaf Catholic youth appeared in the media, proclaiming to the world that the Catholic Church stands with people who suffer at the margins of society.[10] At a conference presentation following the papal audience, Cardinal Peter K. A. Turkson, prefect of the Dicastery for Promoting Integral Human Development, referenced the 2009 recommendations of the Pontifical Council for Health Care. This new generation of the Deaf Catholic community, inheritors of a distinct visual language and Deaf Catholic cultural heritage, successfully accomplished their aim to *be seen* by the church on this anniversary pilgrimage. In this encounter between Pope Francis and the Deaf Catholic leaders of tomorrow, it be-

10. Father Joseph Mulcrone, "Deaf People, DCYIA, and the Vatican," Deaf Catholic Youth Initiative for the Americas, July 7, 2018, personal narrative provided by the author.

came clear that the Vatican's 2009 recommendations, although waylaid by administrative interruptions, are not forgotten.

Today, Pope Francis continues to look for opportunities to make Deaf Catholics visible and fully included in all levels of church life. In his papacy's ongoing effort to champion those on the periphery in society and in the church, he is reaching out from the Vatican to the deaf community, especially deaf people in Italy. Every Wednesday in Saint Peter's Square, thousands of pilgrims attend the pope's weekly audience and, after his warm greeting, listen as he delivers a teaching to people from all over the world. In April of 2019, he began to include a sign language interpreter at this weekly audience, so that anyone present or viewing from home would be able to *see* sign language in use at the Vatican. For Deaf Catholics worldwide, it was a communication breakthrough. By making sign language a regular feature of church life, Pope Francis and the Vatican are beginning to model what inclusive gatherings should look like for the entire church, ideally at all liturgies and in every parish and public service or celebration.

Soon after this development, in a private audience with members of the Italian Federation of the Deaf (FIAS), Pope Francis made clear his intent to lift up the deaf community and promote their full inclusion in church life. In his address, he spoke to the deaf community through a sign language interpreter, empathizing with their troubles and acknowledging their suffering in the world. "This is a part of life and can be accepted positively," he said. "What is not good, however, is that, like so many other people with different abilities and their families, deaf people often experience situations of prejudice, sometimes even in Christian communities." These moments, the pope told the deaf assembly, are precisely when deaf people become teachers and evangelizers of the world's leaders and all members of the ecclesial community: "You teach us that only by inhabiting our limits and fragility can we become builders of the culture of encounter in opposition to widespread indifference."[11]

The Holy Father's understanding of the important place of the deaf apostolate in the life of the church—and its great potential for evangelization—is apparent. Speaking to the Italian Federation of the Deaf, he took great care to evoke the role of every baptized Christian as an active missionary disciple, and to encourage the inclusion of deaf people among

11. Pope Francis, "Address to the Members of the Italian Federation Deaf Association (FIAS)," April 25, 2019, translated by the author.

pastoral workers. "I pray for you," he said, "so that you can make your unique contribution to society, being capable of a prophetic vision, capable of the interdependent processes of sharing and inclusion, capable of cooperation in the revolution of tenderness and closeness. Your presence is necessary in the Church to help build communities that are welcoming and open to all—the last being first."[12] Through Pope Francis's publicized addresses and pastoral initiatives with the deaf community, the worldwide Deaf Catholic apostolate dared to renew its hope that the church may finally meet the ecclesial needs of deaf people.

Ecclesial Needs in the Deaf Catholic World

In addition to papal audiences and addresses on the occasions of various conferences, the Holy See has recognized the Deaf World as a collective apostolate in other symbolic ways. In 2008, Pope Benedict XVI, impressed by the sign language ministry of Father Agustín Yanes Valer, called this Spanish deaf priest "the prelate of the Deaf World."[13] Although the title was an honorary one, the Deaf-World took notice. Deaf Catholics around the world were impressed by this recognition of a priest who was "one of their own" and who spent his life ministering to the deaf community in Spanish-speaking countries. Most Catholics who are part of the Deaf Catholic World would agree that an abundance of ongoing challenges justified Father Agustín Yanes Valer's honorary title and illustrated the wisdom of organizing ecclesiastical service to Deaf Catholics.

Would a permanent ecclesiastical office of deaf ministry, in either the Dicastery for Promoting Integral Human Development or another appropriate advisory body, be able to ensure the inclusion of deaf people in the church? While the answer to that question is beyond the scope of this book, it is not difficult to extrapolate possible duties for such an office from the history and cultural heritage presented here. Because deafness is indeed, on one level, a health-care issue, treatment and prevention of deafness as a medical condition must continue as an important part of health-care ministries. But on a cultural level and in the day-to-day lives

---

12. Pope Francis, "Address to the Members of the Italian Federation Deaf Association (FIAS)," April 25, 2019.

13. "Benedict XVI Names Deaf Priest 'Prelate of Honor,'" Catholic News Agency, March 27, 2008, https://www.catholicnewsagency.com/news/benedict_xvi_names_deaf_priest_prelate_of_honor.

of deaf people, the immediate and ongoing *pastoral* needs for deaf people are not disease prevention or speech therapy, but pastoral ministry, spiritual formation, the sacraments, and on a more rudimentary level, education and civic participation—in short, everything that provides dignity to the human person and places that person in an enriching community with his brothers and sisters in Christ.

Perhaps such an advisory body would begin where the 2009 Pontifical Conference on Health Care left off—by renewing the request for "a central office of the church at national levels which attends to and coordinates pastoral care for deaf people." Putting a bishop in charge of deaf ministry in each country would not conflict with canon law if the role were advisory and agreed upon by the bishops' conferences. A Vatican office could set guidelines and work to ensure that deaf people are not invisible, neglected, or ignored in each parish (as they often still are, even in wealthy Catholic dioceses in the West). In addition to drawing much-needed attention to deaf people in the life of the church, an authoritative church body could ensure that regional reports would recommend actions to each bishop.

Among the most important recommendations for deaf cultural ministries would be Eucharistic prayers and liturgy in signed languages. Some precedents already exist for the use of signed languages as religious languages, but Deaf Catholics need a more deeply informed approach as the science of linguistics and our understanding of deaf culture continue to develop. As described in chapter 7, the British bishop's conference approved the first official Eucharistic prayer for deaf people in 1977. However, the bishops approved this Eucharistic prayer not as a precise arrangement of signs and movements in a signed language but rather as an English text. According to the instructional note, it "must never be spoken in the Mass unless the celebrant signs at the same time, the spoken words must always accompany the signs, and liturgical gestures normally indicated in the rubrics are used flexibly or omitted as circumstances permit."[14] Moreover, the British bishops disseminated the English text "accompaniment" across Great Britain without recorded film footage of the signed Eucharistic prayer. Since it is impossible to speak

14. Catholic Bishops' Conference of England and Wales, *Eucharistic Prayer for the Deaf* (May 23, 1992). This document, an explanation to hearing priests on "Adapting the liturgy to the needs of the deaf," states, "This background note is drawn from the accompanying documentation submitted with the Eucharistic Prayer for the Deaf to the Congregation for Divine Worship in 1977. The Prayer was approved for use in England and Wales on 23 May 1992."

one language and sign a completely different language at the same time, the instructional note suggests a serious misunderstanding, widespread at the time, about the nature of true signed languages. One possible explanation is that the wording of the instructional note was a necessary compromise to get the prayer approved by the British bishops and recognized by the Vatican. In effect, the approval process simply avoided the issue of whether the Eucharistic prayer in a signed language could be a valid sacramental form.

With today's linguistic knowledge of signed languages, it is no longer possible to ignore the fact that Britain's *Eucharistic Prayer for the Deaf* is not a prayer in BSL at all but rather a gloss for the prayer in a mixed mode, meant to be spoken and signed at the same time. The text does not indicate the actual signs to use in this mixed-mode prayer, making its intelligibility for deaf people entirely dependent on the sign language fluency of the priest. Moreover, the document does not specifically name BSL, because BSL was not recognized as a language by the British government until 2003. In the 1970s, the field of linguistics had not yet developed a scientific understanding of BSL as a complete language. Based on the explanatory text of the prayer, a priest using this prayer could use Irish Sign Language (ISL), American Sign Language (ASL), or any other sign language, depending on the deaf assembly's needs.[15] Because the prayer was designed for hearing priests celebrating Masses with deaf people or a mixed assembly, a gloss made the most sense at the time. It provided some flexibility in the skill level required of the celebrant. A priest with fluent BSL could focus his efforts on clear, expressive BSL, while a priest new to deaf ministry could memorize signs to accompany his spoken prayer, thereby communicating with the deaf assembly as best he could while continuing to learn the actual language outside of Mass.

Although a mixed mode of communication is still useful for some Deaf Catholic assemblies, in many cases true BSL (or another true sign language) would be the best choice—or even the only language understood by a deaf assembly. Given the differences in spoken and signed grammar, speaking the English words of the text while signing correct BSL is prohibitively difficult or impossible. For a culturally deaf priest, speaking the words of the Eucharistic prayer while signing it can destroy a beautiful and accurate translation. For reasons explained by linguistic

15. English-speaking hearing people, on the other hand, always understand the spoken portion as a kind of verbal notation of the signs, even if it is slow and awkward.

science as well as by the basic conditions required for communication in any language, the sign language "text" of Britain's "Eucharistic Prayer for the Deaf" is still a work in progress, much like liturgies in ASL and other signed languages.

The need for an updated explanation of the British *Eucharistic Prayer for the Deaf* raises a new and challenging question: Should the church approve Eucharistic prayers in true signed languages? Again, this question is beyond the scope of this narrative, but the events of Deaf Catholic history, the accepted cultural heritage of Deaf Catholics themselves, and a modern understanding of linguistics should inform any deliberations toward an answer. To consider any signed languages for an established or "official" translation, a film or video "text" would need approval (rather than a printed text). The rapid development of internet communication has made this media of publishing and distribution quite possible. Video-recorded Mass prayers in BSL are easy for anyone to access online today—as are examples of Mass prayers in American, Australian, Brazilian, German, Korean, Philippine, Irish, Italian, Spanish, and Singaporean sign languages (and there are probably others). However, the quality of language in these videos varies greatly, depending on the state of development of that region's sign system as a true language, along with the skill level, dialect, and professional standards of the signer. In some countries, native signed languages still compete with missionary uses of ASL or BSL signs in the mixed mode, and the resulting forms of pidgin or creole are often unstable and in a state of rapid change.

However, in countries where the deaf community uses a standardized sign language, the question of an official translation of a Eucharistic prayer into this vernacular, both for celebrants and for interpreters, may bear serious investigation. Especially where there are culturally deaf communities served by a priest who is also culturally deaf, the priest may not use his voice—or if he does, his voice may be unintelligible to hearing people. Priests with the highest sign language competence, whether deaf or hearing, typically use voice-off, true signed language. As the events of Deaf Catholic history illustrate, Mass celebrated by a priest without an audible or intelligible voice may alarm church leaders who believe that, without spoken words of consecration, Mass is not valid.

Canon lawyer Edward Peters, in his article "The Ordination of Men Bereft of Speech and the Celebration of Sacraments in Sign Language," makes one of the best arguments to date for Mass in a true signed language. He notes that there is no question of the valid and licit nature of a sacrament celebrated in *both* speech and sign, as Pope Paul VI permitted the use of sign language in the Mass in 1965. The question is only whether a true signed language without speech fulfills the required form of sacraments. Peters argues that any sacrament must be communicated *in a language*. While the official textual form is written Latin, the proper form is fulfilled, through translation, in many spoken languages used around the world. Linguists now recognize several signed languages as complete human languages, capable of communicating any thought a spoken language can communicate. There is no doubt, for Peters, that a sacrament celebrated in a true signed language can be valid and licit.[16] An accurate, widespread understanding of signed languages as true languages is the first step. So long as the church does not explicitly validate the legitimacy of Mass and the sacraments in a true sign language, the issue will be contested again and again in Deaf Catholic communities around the world, wherever deaf or hearing priests regularly sign the Mass voice off with a deaf apostolate (even if a voice interpreter is present). Therefore, one of the most pressing and important tasks for any advisory body concerning Deaf Catholic ministry would be to address the theological legitimacy of sacraments celebrated in true signed languages.[17]

In addition to arguments based on the traditional acceptance of Masses in sign language, there is another way to argue in favor of sign language as a sacramental form. This route concerns the recognition of marriage vows in sign language—something that has been in practice since the medieval period. If the Church recognizes the validity of a sacramental marriage between a deaf man and a deaf woman who exchange their consent in true sign language (i.e., voice off)—and there is no doubt the church does so—then it must also be true of every other use of sign language to express the sacramental form, including both absolution and consecration at Mass.[18]

There remains the question of whether each sign language should go through a vetted process of translation from the Latin text, leading to an official signed "text" in video form. There are pros and cons for

16. Peters, "The Ordination of Men Bereft of Speech," 331–45.

17. Recent scholarship that may prove helpful in this vein is Matthew Hysell, "Five Arguments in Favor of Signed Words of Institution," *Worship* 91 (July 2017): 336–50; Father Thomas Margevičius, "A Model for Integrating Rubrical Gestures While Praying the Eucharistic Prayer in Sign Language" (PhD diss., The Catholic University of America, 2015).

18. I owe this argument to Father Anthony Schuerger.

creating such texts. ASL and BSL are the two most common sign languages throughout the world because of the spread of those languages in
nineteenth- and twentieth-century mission communities and (especially) schools for deaf children. In the United States, the U.S. Conference of
Catholic Bishops has already applied for approval of ASL as a liturgical
language for use in the Mass, but there has been no response from Rome.
If the Vatican approved ASL or BSL as liturgical language, local Catholic
communities, with appropriate expert assistance, could develop standard
translations of liturgical texts for their community, eventually preparing
them for approval by Episcopal Conferences and ultimately for Vatican
recognition. Over the course of several decades, Masses in BSL and ASL
have been tacitly accepted (through longstanding traditional use) as licit
in Britain and North America.[19] Accurate and usable Mass prayers in a
signed language require many hours of hands-on testing, practice, and
careful translation by groups of theologians and expert translators, deaf
and hearing, and this process is already underway in Deaf Catholic communities in the United States and Great Britain.[20] Fine translations of
the Mass in BSL, ASL, and German Sign Language (DSG) already exist
in electronic video recorded form.[21] However, none of these translations
are used exclusively in any nation, and translations vary significantly
from region to region. Once approved, a standardized translation into
ASL or BSL might serve as a "base language" for translations into other
signed languages.

One objection to "frozen texts" in signed languages is that they would
indeed be rigidly fixed. Sign languages are, as author Gerald Shea has recently called them, "languages of light" rather than languages of sound.[22]

19. Peters explains that they are accepted as *praxis Ecclesiae*, "The Ordination of Men Bereft of
Speech," 331–45.

20. The National Catholic Office of the Deaf in the United States has a Religious Sign Language
Committee currently composed of the following members: Dr. Susan Mather (deaf), Professor of
Linguistics at Gallaudet University; Deacon Patrick Graybill (deaf), Professor (retired) of Cultural
and Creative Studies, RIT-NTID; Maika Kovacs-Houlihan (deaf), University of Wisconsin; Father
Thomas Margevičius (hearing), Instructor, Liturgical Theology, St. Paul Seminary; Dr. Edward Pe-
ters, canon law (hearing); Arvilla Rank (deaf), Project Coordinator, NCOD, Landover Hills, MD;
Rev. Michael Depcik (deaf), OSFS, Chicago.

21. For the United States, see National Catholic Office for the Deaf (NCOD), "Liturgical
Prayers in American Sign Language: Basic Congregational Responses to the Mass," available for pur-
chase at www.ncod.org. For the U.K. and Ireland, see National Chaplaincy for Deaf People (NCDP),
"Liturgical Signs and Prayers," available for purchase at www.ncdp.ie. For Germany, see "DGS-
Wörterbuch für religiöse Begriffe," Taub und Katholisch, Katholische Seelsorge in Deutscher Geb-
ärdensprache, http://taub-und-katholisch.de/dgs-woerterbuch-fuer-religioese-begriffe/.

22. Gerald Shea, *The Language of Light: A History of Silent Voices* (New Haven, Conn.: Yale
University Press, 2017).

Through the ingenious invention of the written alphabet, speech sounds can be transcribed and recorded in a so-called frozen text. In literate societies, we hardly think of writing as an invented tool because it has become ingrained in our social and cultural histories as an essential part of human life. As a tool, the printed word has become an extension of our human selves in hearing, speaking societies. However, signed languages can only be recorded and published through media composed of both light and movement, and even then they are two-dimensional rather than three-dimensional as they are in real time, embodied communication. Approved sign language translations would not be frozen texts at all but rather moving-picture texts that would vary depending on the angle, distance, and context of the recorded communication. While the new media of film and video may be an aid for approving, preserving, and distributing standardized sign language texts, such an approval probably could not result in a single video "text" for all contexts and church environments. Frozen religious texts are, by nature, in the static format of print languages, but signed languages are both three-dimensional and always in motion. At the present time, signed languages have no established written or printed form. Developing one is probably impossible, because sign language requires the human body for expression, and signs can vary in meaning depending on the position of participants in any given instance of communication. Moreover, an approved ASL or BSL text would be an approval only of that one language. Once the church approved the signs, no deviation would be permitted, whether substituting a regional sign or a movement of the body.

The complexity of these issues is evident and addressing them fully will require ongoing work because of the dynamic nature of language change and use. Nevertheless, a valid and grace-filled solution is within the church's power as a people of God guided by the Holy Spirit in careful deliberations. Left unaddressed, the issues facing Deaf Catholics as a collective group could potentially lead to removal of religious sacraments and services from Catholics who require them in their own native language. Therefore, there is little doubt of the urgent need for the Catholic Church to address this issue in an authoritative and definitive way. A wise and workable solution would require the expertise of an advisory board consisting of sacramental theologians, canonists, liturgists, linguists, deaf culture specialists, and pastors, who together could advise the church in establishing a set of norms for the sacramental and pastoral care of deaf people in nations all over the world. Such recommendations could then receive appropriate papal approval, finally ensuring full inclusion for the Deaf Catholic apostolate.

The Role of Deaf Priests and Deacons

As several chapters in this narrative illustrate, the ordination of deaf men to the priesthood has been a providential development in Deaf Catholic history. In many countries around the world, one or more culturally deaf priests now serve the deaf community in their native sign language, and there are also several deaf permanent deacons. Whenever it comes about, Deaf Catholic communities celebrate the ordination of a culturally deaf priest because they are proud and inspired to have a shepherd who is one of their own. The larger Deaf-World also takes notice of this formidable achievement and the church's welcoming of deaf people into Catholic spiritual leadership.

In developed countries, the Deaf Catholic community is in transformation from "mission field" to established church community. The ordination of culturally deaf priests removes the historical classification of deaf ministry as "mission work," with all its colonialist connotations, and elevates deaf ministry to equality with other long-established Catholic communities. For this reason, it is especially important for culturally deaf priests to hold certain assignments in the heart of the Deaf-World. Cities where large deaf communities grew up around historical Deaf Catholic centers are good places for a deaf priest to serve but, most of all, the position of chaplain at Gallaudet University is glaringly in need of a culturally deaf priest.

As the first and largest institution of higher education for deaf people, Gallaudet University in Washington, D.C., educates or professionally influences most leaders of the Deaf-World today. With a faculty and student body empowered by the Deaf rights movement, Gallaudet's students, the future leaders of the Deaf-World, are not likely to look to a "missionary priest" from the hearing world for spiritual leadership, especially one who signs poorly. New evangelization among the one thousand six hundred students at Gallaudet should be an opportunity for Deaf Catholic ministry in the Archdiocese of Washington, because having strong future leaders of deaf ministry for the whole church may depend on it.

Historical and canonical precedents have established the permissibility of deaf candidates' ordination on a case-by-case basis, but in some counties, there is still a question of whether deaf men should be ordained at all.[23] Because of the shortage of priests in general, there is ample reason to encourage vocations from any part of the church. Still, some might argue that deaf, signing priests are only able to serve a small community of deaf people, an isolated group rather than a larger diocese or the church as a unity of people. This concern is understandable, given the significant cost and resources invested in preparing any candidate for priesthood—even more so a candidate requiring special services. Since its beginning, however, the church has sought ministers to serve newly evangelized or minority language groups. Selecting men to serve a specific population does not preclude their service in other communities. Typically, culturally deaf priests around the world travel frequently to lead retreats and celebrate special Masses for deaf communities in their own and other dioceses, including trips to deaf communities in other nations. Most deaf priests have, at one time or another, served hearing populations in much the same way non-signing priests have served the deaf community—with an interpreter. Some deaf priests, because they are bilingual or able to speak clearly while signing in a mixed mode, do not need an interpreter to serve hearing people. A deaf priest who is determined to be a spiritual servant-leader in both the deaf and hearing worlds often inspires hearing Catholics. Such a priest is not only an ambassador between the Deaf-World and the church but also a living illustration of Christ's kingship in every baptized person.

The Deaf Catholic community is in a time of transition. As the universal church faces new international and social challenges, Deaf Catholics experience their struggles surrounding worship in sign language as the birth-pangs preceding a new era of inclusion. Like Christian communities in Asia and Africa, the Deaf Catholic community is growing and bearing fruit in new ways. This growth challenges Deaf Catholics to deepen their understanding of what it means to be part of the universal church beyond the boundaries of the Deaf-World. Deaf Christians have often interpreted Jesus' call to "Be opened!" as a message especially for deaf people, but, in turn, deaf people bring the good news to their larger communities as integrated brothers and sisters made whole in the body of Christ.

23. Peters, "Canonical and Cultural Developments," 247–48.

Cherishing Deaf Catholic Heritage

Deaf Catholic history and heritage, including religious sign language, are among the many gifts that the deaf community brings to the church as a whole. As such, these gifts belong not only to Deaf Catholics and the Deaf-World but to all Catholics as traditions in the beautiful diversity of the human family. Although it is unfortunate for those who need it, sign language has become an endangered heritage in some places. Prevention, medical treatment, and social and educational integration are often (though certainly not always) positive experiences for deaf children and young adults today. However, an unintended side effect is the diminishment of deaf culture in the very countries where it once flourished most. Deaf culture is shrinking in much of the developed world, largely because of the widespread use of cochlear implants, mainstream schooling, and medical advances to prevent disease. In wealthy nations, most deaf children are born to hearing parents who aim to give their child the option of accessing the hearing world with greater ease. After a few years of weekly therapy, most individuals who receive cochlear implants as babies become auditory learners of spoken language. While many children in deaf families continue to learn ASL or BSL as their native or first language, deaf children with hearing parents generally learn to sign as a second language (if at all). In some cases, these individuals become bicultural, moving between the hearing world and the Deaf-World in a way that suits their mixed identity as they choose to express it.

Sometimes, however, the attempt to "turn a deaf child into a hearing one" causes children to suffer tragically unsuccessful schooling and the isolation of not fitting in to either the hearing world or the Deaf-World. Hard-of-hearing individuals suffer from similar isolation and academic delays. When an attempt to mainstream a deaf child is unsuccessful, parents typically put their now-much-older child into schools with instruction in sign language as a last resort. The result can be a poorly adjusted adult with severe delays in both signed and spoken/written languages—an especially sad outcome, which exposure to sign language at an early age could have prevented. Another reality resulting from advanced medical technology is the increased survival rates of children born with multiple disabilities—including deafness—who may not have survived decades ago. Such individuals have the challenge of living with multiple disabilities and often do not have high competence in sign language.

With cases like this on the rise, the culturally deaf community faces not only a dwindling population but also a larger proportion of deaf individuals who have low academic and social success. For those who identify with the Deaf World, this state of affairs is nothing less than an existential threat.

Even if medical technology and mainstream education shrink deaf populations in developed countries over time, the stories of Deaf Catholics' historic struggles against great odds will remain part of the deaf community's heritage. Bicultural deaf individuals are often proud to learn about deaf heritage and experiencing it can bolster their sense of belonging in a way that cochlear implants and mainstream education cannot. For this reason, today's bicultural deaf people often turn to deaf religious communities for social belonging. In much the same way, heritage-language Masses are important to many second- or third-generation immigrant populations, especially where Catholics struggle to retain their religious culture in secularized society.

Welcoming, preserving, and cherishing beautiful signed prayers for the purpose of communal Catholic worship can send a strong message of acceptance and inclusion for both deaf and hearing people. At the same time, Mass in a signed heritage language would continue to help immigrants who are deaf and who wish to be part of their new country's deaf community. Missionaries who are deaf usually try to learn the native sign language wherever they are living and working, but deaf people everywhere are curious about other deaf people and often eager to learn a second sign language, especially one as useful and widespread as ASL or BSL. For some, a Mass in ASL or BSL, whether in person or online, may be the closest they will come to worship in a language that is accessible to deaf people. Religious sign language opens the world to them in a host of ways.

Despite praiseworthy efforts on the part of deaf ministries, culturally deaf people and their languages remain on the margins of society. This is true where there is no established deaf community, but it also remains true for successful Deaf Catholic communities with long-standing heritage in the church. Just as the poor will always be with us, there will likely always be deaf people in the world. Pope Francis consistently describes the mission of the contemporary church as directed "to the peripheries." In his apostolic exhortation *The Joy of the Gospel* he writes, "In our day Jesus' command to 'go and make disciples' echoes in the changing scenarios and ever new challenges to the Church's mission of evangelization.... Each Christian and every community must discern the path that the Lord points out, but all of us are asked to obey his call to go forth from our own comfort zone in order to reach all the 'peripheries' in need of the light of the Gospel."[24] As a minority, deaf people are and will remain a minority "on the peripheries." However, with their language of signs and distinct visual culture, not only can Deaf Catholics become visible to the broader church and to society, they can also make their brothers and sisters "on the peripheries" visible as they continue to shine the light of Christ there.

Living in solidarity with one another is an essential part of being human, but in Christian faith, God is present in a special way with those who suffer. Human suffering is transformed when it becomes intimately connected to the cross and its astounding outcome of resurrection into transcendent life. Therefore, to be deaf and Catholic, accepted as part of the mission of evangelization, is a vital exemplar of the essential meaning of the Christian message. Deaf people are not a problem for the church to solve in pity but, rather, a source of abundant spiritual gifts and an opportunity to grow in understanding and togetherness. As healing and renewal continue to happen for the whole church in and through the Deaf Catholic community, there is great hope that the church will cherish and preserve liturgy and sacraments in sign language for the important part they play in the realization of God's kingdom.

24. *Evangelii Gaudium*, 20.

Recommended Reading
for Part II

The following works include introductions to Deaf Studies and histories of twentieth-century deaf culture. A selection of works focusing on deaf history before the twentieth century appears at the end of part I. Readers may view video resources in signed languages at the companion website, http://icfdeafservice.org/beopened.

Introductions to Deaf Studies

Gallaudet, Edward M. *History of the College for the Deaf, 1857–1907*. Washington, D.C.: Gallaudet College Press, 1983.

————. *Life of Thomas Hopkins Gallaudet—Founder of Deaf-Mute Instruction in America*. New York: Henry Holt and Co., 1888.

Neisser, Arden. *The Other Side of Silence: Sign Language and the Deaf Community in America*. Washington, D.C.: Gallaudet University Press, 1990.

Padden, Carol, and Tom Humphries. *Inside Deaf Culture*. Cambridge, Mass.: Harvard University Press, 2009.

Veditz, George. *The Preservation of the Sign Language*. USA, 1913.

Historical Overviews

Baynton, Douglas C. *Forbidden Signs: American Culture and the Campaign against Sign Language*. Chicago: University of Chicago Press, 1998.

Burch, Susan. *Signs of Resistance: American Deaf Cultural History, 1900 to World War II*. New York: New York University Press, 2004.

Fraser, Benjamin, ed. *Deaf History and Culture in Spain: A Reader of Primary Documents*. Washington, D.C.: Gallaudet University Press, 2009.

Gannon, Jack R. *Deaf Heritage: A Narrative History of Deaf America*. Washington, D.C.: Gallaudet University Press, 2012.

Nomeland, Melvia M., Ronald E. Nomeland, and Trudy Suggs. *The Deaf Community in America: History in the Making.* Jefferson, N.C.: McFarland Publishing, 2011.

Shea, Gerald. *The Language of Light: A History of Silent Voices.* New Haven, Conn.: Yale University Press, 2017.

Van Cleve, J. V. *Deaf History Unveiled: Interpretations from the New Scholarship.* Washington, D.C.: Gallaudet University Press, 1999.

———. *The Deaf History Reader.* Washington, D.C.: Gallaudet University Press, 2007.

BIBLIOGRAPHY

Archives

Assumptionist Archives, Rome, Italy.

The Catholic University of America Archives, Washington, D.C.

Deaf Catholic Archives, College of the Holy Cross, Worcester, Mass.

Gallaudet University Archives, Washington, D.C.

National Association of the Deaf, Silver Spring, Md.

National Catholic Office of the Deaf, Landover, Md.

Redemptorist Archives, Baltimore Province, Philadelphia, Pa.

Other Sources

Addison, W. H. "Historical Sketch." In *Deaf Mutism: A Clinical and Pathological Study* by James Kerr Love, 223–76. Glasgow: James MacLehose, 1896.

Agolia, Grace M. "Becoming 'Signs' of God: A Theological Aesthetics of Sign Language in the Liturgy." *Worship* 91 (September 2017): 415–34.

Allenstein Gondim, Lys Maria, Sheila Balen, Karla Zimmerman, Déborah Pagnossin, Indiara Fialho, and Simone Roggia. "Study of the Prevalence of Impaired Hearing and Its Determinants in the City of Itajaí, Santa Catarina State, Brazil." *Brazilian Journal of Otorhinolaryngology* 78, no. 2 (March/April 2012): 27–34.

Altschuler, Sari. "He That Hath an Ear to Hear: Deaf America and the Second Great Awakening." *Disabilities Studies Quarterly* 31, no. 1 (2011). https://dsq-sds.org/article/view/1368.

Anderson, Emma. *The Death and Afterlife of the North American Martyrs*. Cambridge, Mass: Harvard University Press, 2013.

Angoítia, A. Eguiluz, and Pedro Ponce de León. *Fr. Pedro Ponce de León, La Nueva Personalidad del Sordomudo*. Madrid: Instituto Profesional de Sordomudos "Ponce de León," 1987.

Aristotle. *History of Animals Books IV–VI*. Translated by A. L. Peck. Cambridge, Mass.: Harvard University Press, 1970.

Augustine. *Against Julian*. Translated by Matthew A. Schumacher. The Fathers of the Church: A New Translation 35. Washington, D.C.: The Catholic University of America Press, 1957.

—————. *The Greatness of the Soul; The Teacher*. Translated by Joseph M. Colleran. Ancient Christian Writers: The Works of the Fathers in Translation 9. Westminster, Md.: Newman Press, 1950.

Axelrod, Cyril. *And the Journey Begins*. London: Douglass MacLean, 2005.

Ayres, Bob. *Deaf Diaspora: The Third Wave of Deaf Ministry*. New York: iUniverse, 2004.

Bates, Laura McDill. "Ephphatha." *American Annals of the Deaf* 59, no. 2 (1914): 146–60.

Bauman, H-Dirksen L., and Joseph J. Murray, editors. *Deaf Gain: Raising the Stakes for Human Diversity*. St. Paul: University of Minnesota Press, 2014.

Bede. *Bede's Ecclesiastical History of England*. Translated by A. M. Sellar. London: George Bell and Sons, 1907. http://www.gutenberg.org/files/38326/38326-h/38326-h.html#Pg302.

Beere, Dolores. *History of the Catholic Deaf, Archdiocese of Detroit*. Detroit: Archdiocese of Detroit, 1984.

Bell, Alexander G. "Memoir upon the Formation of a Deaf Variety of the Human Race." Washington, D.C.: National Academy of Sciences, 1884.

Benedict XVI. Address. XXIV International Conference, Pontifical Council for Health Care Workers. November 20, 2009.

Berg, Otto B. *A Missionary Chronicle: Being a History of the Ministry to the Deaf in the Episcopal Church, 1850–1980*. Hollywood, Md.: St. Mary's Press, 1984.

Berthier, Ferdinand. *Forging Deaf Education in Nineteenth-Century France: Biographical Sketches of Bébian, Sicard, Massieu, and Clerc*. Edited and translated by Freeman G. Henry. Washington, D.C.: Gallaudet University Press, 2009.

Best, Ernest. "Two Modes of Encounter: An Exposition of the Relationship of the Eucharist and Preaching." *Interpretation* 17, no. 1 (1963): 25–38.

Bevans, Stephen B. *A Century of Catholic Mission: Roman Catholic Missiology 1910 to the Present*. Eugene, Ore.: Wipf and Stock, 2013.

Bevans, Stephan, and Roger Schroeder. *Constants in Context: A Theology of Mission for Today*. American Society of Missiology Series 30. Ossining, N.Y.: Orbis Books, 2004.

Blake, Joan. *Signing the Scriptures: A Starting Point for Interpreting the Sunday Readings for the Deaf, Year C*. Chicago: Liturgy Training, 2003.

—————. *Signing the Scriptures: A Starting Point for Interpreting the Sunday Readings for the Deaf, Year B*. Chicago: Liturgy Training, 2005.

Blanchard, Ray, Amy D. Lykins, Diane Wherrett, Michael E. Kuban, James M. Cantor, Thomas Blak, Robert Dickey, and Philip E. Klassen. "Pedophilia, Hebephilia, and the DSM-V." *Archives of Sexual Behavior* 38, no. 3 (2009): 335–50.

Boguslawski, Steven, and Ralph Martin, eds. *The New Evangelization: Overcoming the Obstacles*. Mahwah, N.J.: Paulist Press, 2008.

Brennan, Marcel. "Deafness, Disability and Inclusion: The Gap Between Rhetoric and Practice." *Policy Futures in Education* 1, no. 4 (2003): 668–85.

Brock, Brian. *Wondrously Wounded: Theology, Disability, and the Body of Christ.* Waco, Tex.: Baylor University Press, 2019.

Broesterhuizen, Marcel. "The Gospel Preached by the Deaf: Conversation as Complete Form of Language in Pastoral Ministry with the Deaf." *Louvain Studies* 27, no. 4 (2002): 369–75.

——. "Pastoral Ministry with the Deaf: From Care for the Hearing Impaired to Deaf Ministry." In *The Gospel Preached by the Deaf: Proceedings of a Conference on Deaf Liberation Theology, Held at the Faculty of Theology of the Catholic University of Leuven (Belgium), May 19th, 2003,* 1–12. Leuven: Peeters, 2007.

Bruce, Scott. *Silence and Sign Language in Medieval Monasticism: The Clunaic Tradition, c. 900–1200.* Cambridge Studies in Medieval Life and Thought: Fourth Series, Book 68. Cambridge: Cambridge University Press, 2007.

Brueggemann, Brenda J. *Lend Me Your Ear.* Washington, D.C.: Gallaudet University Press, 1999.

——. "'Writing Insight': Deafness and Autobiography." *American Quarterly* 52, no. 2 (2000): 316–20.

——. *Deaf Subjects: Between Identities and Places.* New York: New York University Press, 2009.

Burch, Susan. *Signs of Resistance: American Deaf Cultural History, 1900 to World War II.* New York: New York University Press, 2004.

Burnier, Vincente de Paulo Penido. "History of Sign Language in Brazil." In *The Sign Language of Brazil,* English Edition, by Harry Hoemann, Eugene Oates, and Shirley Hoemann, 21–23. Mill Neck, N.Y.: Mill Neck Foundation, 1981.

Carroll, Cathryn, and Harlan Lane. *Laurent Clerc: The Story of His Early Years.* Washington, D.C.: Gallaudet University Press, 1991.

Catholic Bishops' Conference for England and Wales. *Eucharistic Prayer for the Deaf.* May 23, 1992.

Catholic Church. *Catechism of the Catholic Church in accordance with the Official Latin Text Promulgated by Pope John Paul II.* Vatican City: Libreria Editrice Vaticana, 1997.

Center for Applied Research in the Apostolate. "Frequently Requested Church Statistics, U.S. Data Over Time." Washington, D.C.: Georgetown University. Accessed January 18, 2019. https://cara.georgetown.edu/frequently-requested -church-statistics/.

Clark, Andy. "Gesture as Thought?" In *The Hand, Organ of the Mind,* edited by Zdravko Radman, 255–68. Cambridge, Mass.: Massachusetts Institute of Technology Press, 2013.

Clarke, James. "Deaf People and Disability Issues." In *Ministry Issues for the Church of England: Mapping the Trends,* 101–20. London: Church House Publishing, 2001.

"The Claggett Statement." *Sojourners.* March 1985, 30–32.

The Cloud of Unknowing. Edited by James Walsh and Simon Tugwell. Mahwah, N.J.: Paulist Press, 1981.

Coburn, Carol, and Martha Smith. *Spirited Lives: How Nuns Shaped Catholic Culture and American Life, 1836–1920*. Chapel Hill: University of North Carolina Press, 2017.

Concilium for the Implementation of Constitution on the Liturgy. "Private Reply, December 10, 1965." In *Canon Law Digest VI: Officially Published Documents Affecting the Code of Canon Law 1963–1967*, by T. Lincoln Bouscaren and James I. O'Connor, 552–53. Milwaukee: Bruce Publishing, 1969.

Coughlin, Thomas, OP Miss. "God, Me, and the Van." *The Deaf Catholic* 28, no. 1 (1978): 4–5.

Council of Trent. "Concerning Defects Which May Occur at Mass." In *The Introductory Matters of the Roman Missal of 1962*. Edited by Christopher R. J. Ruder. Columbus, Ohio: 2009.

Currier, Charles Warren. "Our Indian Schools." *The Catholic Educational Association Bulletin* 4, no. 1 (1907): 54.

Daniels, Marilyn. *Benedictine Roots in the Development of Deaf Education: Listening with the Heart*. Westport, Conn.: Bergin & Garvey, 1997.

De l'Épée, Charles-Michel. *Le Véritable Manière d'Instruire les Sourds et Muets*. Première partie. Paris: Chez NYON l'aîné, 1776.

De Liguori, Alphonsus. "Petition to the Pope for Approbation of the Institute and Its Rules." *Spicilegium Historicum* 17 (1969): 220–23.

Desmarais, Camille L. "A Deaf Priest Examines the Deaf Church and the Community." *American Annals of the Deaf* 113, no. 4 (1968): 928–30.

Dolmage, Jay. "Disabled Upon Arrival: The Rhetorical Construction of Disability and Race at Ellis Island." *Cultural Critique* 77 (2011): 24–69.

Edwards, R. A. R. *Words Made Flesh: Nineteenth-Century Deaf Education and the Growth of Deaf Culture*. New York: New York University Press, 2012.

Fay, Edgar Allen. "What Did Augustine Say?" *American Annals of the Deaf* 57, no. 1 (1912): 108–20.

FitzGerald, William. *Spiritual Modalities: Prayer as Rhetoric and Performance*. University Park, Pa.: Pennsylvania State University Press, 2012.

Fox, Margalit. *Talking Hands: What Sign Language Reveals about the Mind*. New York: Simon & Schuster, 2008.

Francis, Pope. *Evangelii Gaudium*. Apostolic Exhortation. November 24, 2013.

————. "Address to the Members of the Italian Federation Deaf Association (FIAS)." April 25, 2019. Translated by Marlana Portolano.

Fraser, Benjamin, ed. *Deaf History and Culture in Spain: A Reader of Primary Documents* Washington, D.C.: Gallaudet University Press, 2009.

Gallitia, Peter Hyacinth. *The Life of St. Francis de Sales, Bishop and Prince of Geneva, from the Italian Book by Peter Hyacinth Gallitia*, vol. 2. Translated by Pier Giacinto Gallizia. London: Thomas Richardson, 1854.

Galvin, Thomas, CSsR. "A Call to Action: A Plea for Deaf-Mutes." In *Proceedings of the Catholic Educational Association*. Columbus, Ohio: Catholic Educational Association, 1910.

Gannon, Jack R. *Deaf Heritage: A Narrative History of Deaf America*. Washington, D.C.: Gallaudet University Press, 2012.

Gaurav, Mathur and Donna Jo Napoli, editors. *Deaf around the World: The Impact of Language*. Oxford: Oxford University Press, 2010.

Gerend, M. M. *In and About St. Francis, A Souvenir of St. John's Institute for Deaf-Mutes*. Milwaukee: St. Francis, 1891.

Gibney, Alex, dir. *Mea Maxima Culpa: Silence in the House of God*. New York: Jigsaw, 2012.

Hamon, André Jean-Marie. *The Spirit of St. Francis, by a Curé of Saint-Sulpice*. Translated by Cornelius J. Warren, CSsR. Boston: Mission Church Press, 1910.

Harrelson, Erin M. "SAME-SAME but Different: Tourism and the Deaf Global Circuit in Cambodia." In *It's a Small World: International Deaf Spaces and Encounters*, edited by Michele Friedner and Annelies Kusters, 199–211. Washington, D.C.: Gallaudet University Press, 2015

Herzog, Albert A. *Disability Advocacy among Religious Organizations: Histories and Reflections*. Abingdon: Routledge, 2012.

Hewes, G. W. "The Current Status of the Gestural Theory of Language Origin." *Annals of the New York Academy of Sciences* 280, no. 1 (1976): 482–504.

Hitchcock, Helen Hull and Susan Bendofy. "Translation Without Words: Should American Sign Language Become an Official Liturgical Language?" *Adoremus Bulletin* 3, no. 4 (June 1997). http://adoremus.org/2007/12/31/translation-without-words/.

Hitching, Roger. *The Church and Deaf People: A Study of Identity, Communication and Relationships with Special Reference to the Ecclesiology of Jürgen Moltmann*. Paternoster Theological Monographs. Milton Keynes: Paternoster Press, 2003.

Hodgson, K. W. *The Deaf and Their Problems*. New York: Philosophical Library, 1954.

Hoemann, Harry, Eugene Oates, and Shirley Hoemannn, *The Sign Language of Brazil*. English Edition. Mill Neck, N.Y.: Mill Neck Foundation, 1981.

Hollywood, Charles. "Visual Dimensions of (Prayer and) Liturgy." In *Seeing Is Believing: Proceedings from the Fourth International Catholic Conference on Religious Education of the Hearing Impaired*, 51–63. Manchester: Henesy House, 1991.

Hysell, Matthew. "Five Arguments in Favor of Signed Words of Institution." *Worship* 91 (July 2017): 336–50.

Iannone, Mercedes, and Mary A. Barth. "Seeking the God of Deaf People: A Deaf/Hearing Dialog." REA Presentation. St. Thomas University, November 2007. Miami Gardens, Fla.

Ignatius of Loyola. "Formula of the Institute of the Society of Jesus." In *The Constitutions of the Society of Jesus and Their Complementary Norms: A Complete English Translation of the Official Latin Texts*, 1:15. Saint Louis: Institute of Jesuit Sources, 1996.

International Commission on English in the Liturgy. *Documents on the Liturgy 1963–1979: Conciliar, Papal, and Curial Texts*. Edited and translated by Thomas C. O'Brien. Collegeville, Minn.: Liturgical Press, 1982.

——————. *Rite of Baptism for Children*. Totowa, N.J.: Catholic Book Publishing, 2004.

Jogues, Isaac. *Narrative of a Captivity among the Mohawk Indians, and a Description of New Netherland in 1642–3 with a Memoir of John Gilmary Shea (1856)*. New York: Press of the Historical Society of New York, 1856.

John Jay College of Criminal Justice. *The Nature and Scope of Sexual Abuse of Minors by Catholic Priests and Deacons in the United States, 1950–2002*. Washington, D.C.: United States Conference of Catholic Bishops, 2004.

John Paul II. *Dolentium Hominum*. Apostolic Letter. February 11, 1985.

——————. *Redemptoris Missio*. Encyclical Letter. December 7, 1990.

Key, William, Ann Albrecht, and T. Coughlin. *Eye Centered : A Study on the Spirituality of Deaf People with Implications for Pastoral Ministry*. Silver Spring, Md.: National Catholic Office for the Deaf, 1992.

Klopfer, Stephen. "The Confession of Deaf-Mutes." *American Ecclesiastical Review* 57, no. 1 (July 1917): 78.

Kroeger, James H. *Asia-Church in Mission*. Quezon City: Claretian Publications, 1999.

Labarta de Chaves, Teresa, and Jorge L. Soler, "Pedro Ponce de León, First Teacher of the Deaf." *Sign Language Studies* 5 (1974): 48–63.

Ladd, Paddy. *Understanding Deaf Culture: In Search of Deafhood*. Clevedon: Multilingual Matters, 2003.

Lane, Harlan. *When the Mind Hears: A History of the Deaf*. New York: Vintage, 1989.

——————. *The Mask of Benevolence: Disabling the Deaf Community*. New York: Alfred A. Knopf, 1992.

Lane, Harlan, Robert Hoffmeister, and Ben Bahan. *A Journey into the Deaf-World*. San Diego: DawnSign Press, 1996.

Lewis, Hannah. *Deaf Liberation Theology*. Farnham: Ashgate Publishing Company, 2007.

Lindgren, Kristin A., Doreen DeLuca, and Donna Jo Napoli. *Signs and Voices: Deaf Culture, Identity, Language, and Arts*. Washington, D.C.: Gallaudet University Press, 2008.

Luetke-Stahlman, Barbara. "Documenting Syntactically and Semantically Incomplete Bimodal Input to Hearing-Impaired Subjects." *American Annals of the Deaf* 133, no. 3 (July 1988): 230–34.

"Macau Sign Language," Endangered Language Archive, SOAS University of London, London. Accessed January 24, 2019. https://elar.soas.ac.uk/Collection/ MPI1029748.

Mangion, Carmen. M. "'The Business of Life': Educating Catholic Deaf Children in Late Nineteenth-Century England," 41, no. 5 (2012): 575–94.

Margevičius, Thomas. "A Model for Integrating Rubrical Gestures while Praying the Eucharistic Prayer in Sign Language." PhD diss. The Catholic University of America, 2015.

Massieu, Jean, and Laurent Clerc, Roch A. Sicard, Andrés D. Laffon de Ladebat, and Jean H. Sievrac. *A Collection of the Most Remarkable Definitions and Answers of Massieu and Clerc, Deaf and Dumb, to the Various Questions Put to Them at Public Lectures of the Abbé Sicard.* London: Cox and Baylis, 1815.

McCabe, Herbert. "The Eucharist as Language." In *Catholicism and Catholicity: Eucharistic Communities in Historical and Contemporary Perspectives,* edited by Sarah Beckwith, L. Gregory Jones, and James J. Buckley, 19–30. Oxford: Blackwell Publishers, 1999.

McCaffrey, Thomas F. "History of the Apostolate of the Catholic Church to the Deaf in the Archdiocese of New York." Master's thesis. Fordham University, 1943.

McCorkle, Ben. *Rhetorical Delivery as Technological Discourse: A Cross-Historical Study.* Carbondale: Southern Illinois University Press, 2012.

McDonough, Peter. *Deaf Resource Pack.* Manchester: Catholic Deaf Association, 2017.

McKee, Rachel, and Jemina Napier. "Interpreting in International Sign Pidgin: An Analysis." *Journal of Sign Language Linguistics* 5, no. 1 (2002): 27–54.

Miller, Donald. "Words or a Deed." *Interpretation* 6, no. 2 (1952): 131–46. DOI:10.1177/002096435200600201.

Mitchell, Ross E., and Michael A. Karchmer. "Chasing the Mythical Ten Percent: Parental Hearing Status of Deaf and Hard of Hearing Students in the United States." *Sign Language Studies* 4, no. 2 (2004): 138–63.

Moeller, Ferdinand. "Education of the Deaf and Dumb." In *The Catholic Encyclopedia: An International Reference on the Constitution, Doctrine, Discipline, and History of the Catholic Church,* vol. 5. Edited by Charles G. Herdermann et al. New York: Encyclopedia Press, 1913.

Morris, Wayne. *Theology without Words: Theology in the Deaf Community.* Routledge, 2016.

Morse, Tracy A. "Seeing Grace: Religious Rhetoric in the Deaf Community." PhD diss., University of Arizona, 2005.

Myklebust, Helmer R. *The Psychology of Deafness: Sensory Deprivation, Learning, and Adjustment.* Oxford: Grune & Stratton, (1960).

Naban-Warren, Kristy. "Embodied Research and Writing: A Case for Phenomenologically Oriented Religious Studies Ethnographies." *Journal of the American Academy of Religion* 72, no. 2 (2011): 378–407.

Neisser, A. *The Other Side of Silence: Sign Language and the Deaf Community in America.* Washington, D.C.: Gallaudet University Press, 1990.

Neuland, Paul A., SJ. *Learning the Signs: A Companion to Father Higgins's Dictionary "How to Talk to the Deaf."* New York: James Donnelly Publishing, 1933.

Nomeland, Melvia M., and Ronald E. Nomeland. *The Deaf Community in America: History in the Making.* Jefferson, N.C.: McFarland & Company, 2011.

O'Connell, Noel P. "A Tale of Two Schools: Educating Catholic Female Deaf Children in Ireland, 1846–1946," *History of Education* 45, no. 2 (2016): 188–205.

Ong, Walter. *The Presence of the Word: Some Prolegomena for Cultural and Religious History.* New Haven, Conn.: Yale University Press, 1967.

————. *Orality and Literacy: The Technologizing of the Word.* 2nd edition. New York: Routledge, 2002.

Padden, Carol, and Tom Humphries. *Inside Deaf Culture.* Cambridge, Mass.: Harvard University Press, 2009.

Park, Min Seo. "Deaf Culture and Deaf Church." *New Theology Review* 22, no. 4 (Nov 2009): 26–35.

Paul, Peter V. *Literacy and Deafness: The Development of Reading, Writing, and Literate Thought.* Needham Heights, Mass.: Allyn and Bacon, 1998.

Paul, Peter V., and Stephen Quigley. *Language and Deafness.* 2nd ed. San Diego: Singular Publishing Group, 1994.

Perreault, Stéphane-D. *One Community—A Sign of the Times: The Sisters of Our Lady of Seven Dolors.* Translated by Gloria Keylor. Montreal: Carte Blanche Editions, 2007.

————. "National Identities on Display: Québec's Deaf Schools at the World's Columbian Exposition 1893." *Études d'histoire religieuse* 75 (2009): 39–61.

Peters, Edward N. "Canonical and Cultural Developments Culminating in the Ordination of Deaf Men during the Twentieth Century." *Josephinum Journal of Theology* 15, no. 2 (2008): 427–43.

————. "The Ordination of Men Bereft of Speech and the Celebration of Sacraments in Sign Language." *Studia Canonica* 42 (2008): 331–45.

————. "Video Communication Technology and the Sacramental Confession of the Deaf." *The Jurist* 73, no. 2 (2013): 513–38.

Pierre, David, Jr. "Sex, Lies, and HBO Documentaries." *The Catholic World Report*, November 9, 2012. http://www.catholicworldreport.com/Item/1735/sex_lies_and_hbo_documentaries.aspx.

Plann, Susan. *A Silent Minority: Deaf Education in Spain, 1550–1835.* Berkeley: University of California Press, 1997.

Pontifical Council for Health Care Workers. "Ephphatha! The Deaf Person in the Life of the Church." Proceedings of the XXIX International Conference for the Pontifical Council of Health Care Workers. The Vatican, 2009.

Portolano, Marlana. "Shun Not the Struggle: The Language and Culture of Deaf Catholics in the U.S., 1949–1977." *U.S. Catholic Historian* 33, no. 3 (2015): 99–124.

Preston, Michael and Frances Preston. *The Journey of the ICDA from 1949 to 1989.* Silver Spring, Md.: International Catholic Deaf Association, 1989.

Proceedings of the World Congress of the Deaf and the Fourth Convention of the American Association of the Deaf. Chicago: American Association of the Deaf, 1893.

Qi, Sen, and Ross E. Mitchell. "Large-Scale Academic Achievement Testing of Deaf and Hard-of-Hearing Students: Past, Present, and Future." *Journal of Deaf Studies and Deaf Education* 17, no 1 (2012): 1–18.

Ramsey, Claire L. "Language Planning in the Deaf Community." In *The Sociolinguistics of the Deaf Community,* edited by Ceil Lucas, 123–46. New York: Harcourt Brace Jovanovich, 1989.

Ramsey, Claire L., and Jose Antonio Noriega. "Ninos Milagrizados: Language Attitudes, Deaf Education, and Miracle Cures in Mexico." *Sign Language Studies* 1,
no. 3 (2001): 254–80.

Reilly, L. W. "The Education of Catholic Deaf-Mutes in the United States," *Ecclesiastical Review* 14, no. 4 (April 1896): 289.

Ricoa, Antonia Gascón, and José Gabriel Storch de Gracia y Asensio. *Fray Pedro
Ponce de León, El Mito Mediático*. Madrid: Editorial Universitaria Ramón
Areces, 2006.

Roush, Daniel R. "Language between Bodies: A Cognitive Approach to Understanding Linguistic Politeness in American Sign Language." *Sign Language Studies* 11,
no. 3 (2011): 329–74.

Russo, Anthony. *In Silent Prayer: A History of Ministry with the Deaf Community in
the Archdiocese of Philadelphia*. Garden City Park, N.Y.: Square One Publishers,
2008.

Shea, Gerald. *Language of Light: A History of Silent Voices*. New Haven, Conn.: Yale
University Press, 2017.

Sordos Catolicos. "Murió Monseñor Vicente Burnier, primer sacerdote sordo de
América Latina." Testimonios y Trabajos de Catequesis para Personas Sordas.
Accessed May 2017, http://www.sordoscatolicos.org/Pagina%20de%20
Sacerdotes%20Sordos%20Vicente%20Burnier.htm.

St. John, Ambrose. *The Raccolta or Collection of Indulgenced Prayers & Good Works*.
London: Burns and Oates, 1910.

"St. Joseph's Institute for the Improved Instruction of Deaf Mutes," The Catholic Charities of New York, *The Catholic World* XLIII, no. 253 (September 1886): 815–16.

Stangio, Sebastian. *Hun Sen's Cambodia*. Bangkok: Silkworm Books, 2014.

Stokoe, William C. "Sign Language Structure: An Outline of the Visual Communication Systems of the American Deaf." *Journal of Deaf Studies and Deaf Education* 10, no. 1 (January 2005): 3–37.

Stokoe, William C., Dorothy Casterline, and Carl G. Croneberg. *Dictionary of
American Sign Language on Linguistic Principles*. Washington, D.C.: Gaulladet
University Press, 1965.

Stokoe, William C., W. J. Thomas Mitchell, H-Dirksen L. Bauman, Heidi M. Rose,
and Jennifer L. Nelson. *Signing the Body Poetic: Essays on American Sign Language Literature*. Berkeley: University of California Press, 2006.

Stone, Mary E., and Joseph P. Youngs. "Catholic Education of the Deaf in the United
States, 1837–1948." *American Annals of the Deaf* 93 (1948): 411–510.

Strangio, Sebastian. *Hun Sen's Cambodia*. Bangkok: Silkworm Books, 2014.

Supalla, Ted and Rebecca Webb. "The Grammar of International Sign: A New Look
at Pidgin Languages." In *Language, Gesture, and Space*, International Conference
on Theoretical Issues in Sign Language Research, edited by Karen Emmorey and
Judy S. Reilly, 333–52. Hillsdale, N.J.: Erlbaum, 1995.

Talbot, Francis Xavier. *Saint among Savages: The Life of Saint Isaac Jogues*. San Francisco: Ignatius Press, 2002.

Taylor, Joselyn. *Boston Spa: The Story of St. John's School for Deaf Children, 1875–1975*. Addlestone: British Deaf History Society, 2007.

United States Conference of Catholic Bishops. "Pastoral Statement of the U.S. Catholic Bishops on Persons with Disabilities." Washington, D.C., 1978.

———. "Guidelines for the Celebration of the Sacraments with Persons with Disabilities," rev. June 15, 2017.

U.S. Department of Health and Human Services. National Institutes of Health. *NICDC Fact Sheet: Cochlear Implants*. Updated 2011. https://www.nidcd.nih.gov/sites/default/files/ Documents/health/hearing/FactSheetCochlearImplant.pdf.

Taylor, Joselyn. *Boston Spa: The Story of St. John's School for Deaf Children, 1875–1975*. Addlestone: British Deaf History Society Publications, 2007.

Van Cleve, John V. *Deaf History Unveiled: Interpretations from the New Scholarship*. Washington, D.C.: Gallaudet University Press, 1999.

———. *The Deaf History Reader*. Washington, D.C.: Gallaudet University Press, 2007.

Van Cleve, John V., and Barry A. Crouch. *A Place of Their Own: Creating the Deaf Community in America*. Washington, D.C.: Gallaudet *University* Press, 1989.

Vatican Council II. *Sacrosanctum Concilium*. December 4, 1963. In *Vatican Council II: Constitutions, Decrees, Declarations*. Edited by Austin Flannery, OP. Northport, N.Y.: Costello Publishing, 1996.

———. *Presbyterorum Ordinis*. December 7, 1965. In *The Sixteen Documents of Vatican II: and the Instruction on the Liturgy, with Commentaries by the Council Fathers*. Translated by N.C.W.C. Boston: Daughters of St. Paul, 1967.

Veditz, George. *The Preservation of the Sign Language*. Washington, D.C.: Gallaudet University, 1913. Film.

Walls, Andrew F. *The Missionary Movement in Christian History: Studies in Transmission of the Faith*. Ossining, N.Y.: Orbis Books, 1996.

———. *The Cross-Cultural Process in Christian History*. Ossining, N.Y.: Orbis Books, 2002.

Woodward, James. *How You Gonna Get to Heaven if You Can't Talk to Jesus: On Depathologizing Deafness*. Silver Spring, Md.: T. J. Publishers, 1982.

Woodward, James, Anastasia Bradford, Chea Sokchea, and Heang Samath. "Cambodian Sign Language." In *Sign Languages of the World: A Comparative Handbook*, edited by Julie B. Jepsen, Goedele De Clerck, Sam Latalo-Kiingi, and William B. McGregor, 159–176. Berlin: Walter de Gruyter, 2015.

World Health Organization. *Global Costs of Unaddressed Hearing Loss and Cost-Effectiveness of Interventions*. Geneva: World Health Organization, 2017. https://apps.who.int/iris/ bitstream/ handle/ 10665/254659/9789241512046 -eng.pdf;sequence=1.

INDEX

Be Opened! The Catholic Church and Deaf Culture was designed in Garamond
with Hypatia Sans display type and composed by Kachergis Book Design of
Pittsboro, North Carolina. It was printed on 55-pound Natural Offset
and bound by Maple Press of York, Pennsylvania.